"This book brings a state-of-the-art approach in identifying and analyzing the complexities of building a democratic and functioning state after civil wars. Kosovo is an example of these challenges toward self-determination and recognition amid the intricacies of the international system. Dr Pereira Watts brings robust case analysis with a multidisciplinary perspective and up-to-date data that distinguishes it from the usual rhetoric on state-building. It is a must-read!"

Puhie Demaku,
Former Member of Parliament of the Republic of Kosovo, Foreign Affairs Committee

"It is a must-read volume for anyone interested in peacekeeping and civil wars. One of the biggest challenges confronting disrupted states is to move from interim stabilization toward sustainable democratic security promotion. With an insider perspective of UN peacekeeping and robust case analysis, the author contributes by creating awareness of the central dilemmas originating from the simultaneous efforts to build peace and democracy in civil wars. The book stands out in avoiding the pitfalls of vicious violence, including the complexities of DDR and SSR."

Luís Carrilho,
United Nations Police Adviser Department of Peace Operations. Former UN Police Commissioner in UN missions in Bosnia and Herzegovina, Timor-Leste, Haiti, Central African Republic and Mali

PEACE OR DEMOCRACY?

Contrary to the common belief that peace and democracy go hand in hand after a civil war, Pereira Watts argues they are, in fact, at a crossroads.

Offering an innovative framework based on Philosophical, Actors, and Tactical considerations, Pereira Watts identifies 14 dynamic dilemmas in democratic peacebuilding, with respective trade-offs. She focuses on explaining the contradictions in modern post-conflict recovery, the challenges facing interim governments, and the international community's role. Based on an analysis of more than 40 countries between 1989 and 2022 and more than 60 UN peace operations, she presents critical issues that commonly need to be addressed in such scenarios: Elections and Political Parties; the Constitution; Checks, Balances and Power-sharing; Transitional Justice; Human Rights, Amnesty, Truth Commissions and War Crimes Tribunals; Disarmament, Demobilization, and Reintegration; and Media Reform and Civil Society. Solving any of these dilemmas leads to others that shape a complex apparatus for restoring peace and installing a new political regime.

An essential resource for decision-takers, policymakers, international analysts and practitioners in the field of peacebuilding that will also be of great value to students of International Relations and Peace Studies as well as anyone interested in peacekeeping, democracy-building, and state-building.

Izabela Pereira Watts, PhD, is a Lecturer in International Studies and Political Sciences at the University of Wollongong in Australia. She is an expert in peacekeeping, democracy building with more than 15 years of experience in international development, including UN peacekeeping mission, UNDP and UN Woman in conflict zones, and several awards.

PEACE OR DEMOCRACY?

Peacebuilding Dilemmas to Transition from Civil Wars

Izabela Pereira Watts

Foreword by José Ramos-Horta

LONDON AND NEW YORK

Designed cover image: UN photo/martineperret. Civilians seeking refuge at UN Mission in South Sudan (UNMISS) following an outbreak of violence between rebel armed groups. June/2013.

First published 2023
by Routledge
4 Park Square, Milton Park, Abingdon, Oxon OX14 4RN

and by Routledge
605 Third Avenue, New York, NY 10158

Routledge is an imprint of the Taylor & Francis Group, an informa business

© 2023 Izabela Pereira Watts

The right of Izabela Pereira Watts to be identified as author of this work has been asserted in accordance with sections 77 and 78 of the Copyright, Designs and Patents Act 1988.

All rights reserved. No part of this book may be reprinted or reproduced or utilised in any form or by any electronic, mechanical, or other means, now known or hereafter invented, including photocopying and recording, or in any information storage or retrieval system, without permission in writing from the publishers.

Trademark notice: Product or corporate names may be trademarks or registered trademarks, and are used only for identification and explanation without intent to infringe.

British Library Cataloguing-in-Publication Data
A catalogue record for this book is available from the British Library

ISBN: 9781032247588 (hbk)
ISBN: 9781032247571 (pbk)
ISBN: 9781003279976 (ebk)

DOI: 10.4324/9781003279976

Typeset in Bembo
by Deanta Global Publishing Services, Chennai, India

CONTENTS

Preface xii
Acknowledgments xiv
Foreword xvi
List of peace operations xviii
List of illustrations xxi
Glossary of abbreviations and technical terms xxiii
About the author xxvii

Introduction 1

   I.1 *Concept foundations* 5
   I.2 *The objective* 9
   I.3 *Justification: why do peacebuilding, democratization, civil wars, and fragile states matter?* 12
   I.4 *A note on global peace data: is the world becoming more or less peaceful?* 16
   I.5 *A note on postwar democratization: democratic peace theory and sequential transition models* 19
   I.6 *Book structure* 24
   I.7 *Methodology: research design* 25
   I.8 *Definitions: what are we talking about?* 29
   I.9 *Overview of the chapters* 33
   Notes 37
   References 37

PART I
Transitional dilemmas, violent democracies, and the United Nations's statecraft   45

1 The transition *from civil war to hybrid peace:* 14 dilemmas of peace, democracy, and state-building in post-conflict societies   47

    1.1 Transition from hybrid war to hybrid liberal peace: background approach   48
    1.2 Theoretical foundation: transitional dilemmas   51
    1.3 Dilemmas and trade-offs between efforts to promote peace or democracy: an advanced approach   52
    1.4 Premises of the Philosophical–Actors–Tactical (P–A–T) framework of transitional post-conflict and peacebuilding dilemmas: its properties and limitations   60
    1.5 Summary of the chapter   63
    References   66

2 United Nations hybrid liberal peace dilemmas: Contingent sovereignty, responsibility to protect and moral selectiveness   68

    2.1 United Nations's statecraft: "benign" autocracy versus autonomy   69
    2.2 Westphalia versus post-Westphalia peace: legality, legitimacy, sovereignty, and R2P   72
    2.3 Who deserves to be free and safe? Selectiveness, efficiency, and other dilemmas   78
    2.4 Summary of the chapter   83
    Note   84
    References   84

3 From guns to votes to doves: Violent transition with ballots and bullets   89

    3.1 U curves and "violent democracy": anocracies, civil wars, and fragile states   91
    3.2 Dilemmas of violence in democratic civil peace transitions: causes and consequences of why violence breeds violence   95
        3.2.1 Dimension of actors   97
        3.2.2 Security dimension   98
        3.2.3 Institutional dimension   102
    3.3 Summary of the chapter   110
    Notes   110
    References   111

Contents **ix**

4 What role do UN operations play in bringing simultaneously peace and democracy to post-civil war countries? 114

    4.1 Methodology 116
    4.2 Analysis of promoting the state, democracy, and peace in post-conflict societies 121
        4.2.1 Postwar democratic civil peace through UN peacekeeping operations 121
        4.2.2 Autonomous postwar democratic civil peace: cases without UN intervention 124
    4.3 Addressing the role of UN peacekeeping operations in promoting the state, democracy, and peace with the P–A–T framework of dilemmas: why are there different results? 131
        4.3.1 The United Nations as savior: why do some missions triumph with the "positive but modest approach"? 131
        4.3.2 Relying on the United Nations: why do some missions fail? 132
        4.3.3 Not so peaceful nor so democratic: why are some countries stuck in the middle? 134
        4.3.4 Action for Peacekeeping: is the answer for more effective operations? 137
    4.4 Summary of the chapter 138
    Notes 139
    References 144

PART II
Transitions to political, legal, civil, and social orders **149**

5 From war to peace: When elections and political parties promote democracy? 151

    5.1 Elections: from the battlefield of war to the ballot box battlefield 152
    5.2 Elections in dangerous place: more dilemmas than solutions 155
    5.3 Demilitarization of politics and democratization of warlords: victorious guerrilla fighters turned democratic rulers 163
        5.3.1 Literature review: transforming warring armies into political parties 165
        5.3.2 Dilemmas of transforming warring armies into political parties 168
    5.4 Summary of the chapter 176
    Notes 177
    References 178

6 When the pen fails, the sword rules: Constitution building
and power-sharing for divided societies 182

    6.1 *Conceptualization of sharing power and constitutionalism:
division, competition, and institutional arrangements* 183
        6.1.1 *Constitutional reform and dual power-sharing: the
alternative of semi-presidentialism as cohabitation of power* 186
        6.1.2 *Risks of constitutional reform: balance and alternation of
power in democracy- building* 189
    6.2 *Consociational democracy and power-sharing: alternatives for
shared rule, self-rule, and the "tyranny of the majority"* 191
        6.2.1 *Power-sharing arrangements and five case studies: good
or bad for democracy and peacebuilding?* 193
        6.2.2 *Additional power-sharing arrangements: peaceful
alternatives but not so democratic* 197
        6.2.3 *Power-sharing in Kosovo: consensus, consociational
democracy, or no democracy at all?* 200
        6.2.4 *Summing up power-sharing dilemmas: positive peace and
negative democracy* 202
    Notes 204
    References 207

7 No Justice, (no) peace?: Democratic injustice or
undemocratic justice in the name of human rights and
reconciliation 210

    7.1 *Human rights: would amnesty ensure peace and democracy?* 211
    7.2 *Justice matters: Truth and reconciliation commission and ad hoc
tribunals* 215
    7.3 *Leges inter arma silent: in the limbo between traditional and
legal justice systems* 219
    7.4 *Summary of the chapter* 225
    Notes 226
    References 227

8 Silencing the guns through DDR and SSR: The
securitization of peace or governance of insecure democracy? 229

    8.1 *What do we know about DDR and SSR?* 230
    8.2 *Trusting the enemy: dilemmas of post-conflict securitization
and governance* 237
        8.2.1 *Good timing for DDR/SSR: cost, sequencing,
ownership, and other dilemmas* 242
        8.2.2 *A note on the privatization of peace: more problems than
solutions?* 244

8.3 *A case study on the security sector of Central African Republic: worse than a failure* 245
8.4 *A case study on the security sector of Timor-Leste: a partial or no reform?* 249
8.5 *Summary of the chapter* 249
Notes 255
References 255

9 **From war to peace: Voters but not yet citizens** — 258

9.1 *Civil society: the people's voice on human rights and the parallel state* 259
    9.1.1 *Dilemmas on how to go from civil strife to civil society in disrupted states: politicized and "uncivil" agents* 262
9.2 *Media reform and freedom of speech: (un)peaceful, (not) free and (un)fair* 267
9.3 *Summary of the chapter* 270
Note 271
References 271

PART III
Conclusion and recommendations — 275

From hybrid democratic peace toward an integrated transition: Conclusion, limitations, and recommendations — 277

Appendix — 283
Index — 309

PREFACE

When a civil war ends, what are the main dilemmas involved in seeking to mutually achieve "peace, democracy, and a functional state"? And what role do UN operations play in simultaneously bringing peace and democracy to post–civil war countries? Over three decades since the end of the Cold War, something seems wrong with the "democratic peacebuilding" agenda. The political transition to civil democratic peace is often conflict-ridden. Despite an unprecedented number of UN interventional operations "to enforce peace and build democracy," rarely can war-torn countries make a transition to both peace *and* democracy. Either they are trapped in an endless cycle of conflict or they achieve stability only through a nondemocratic rule.

The past decade has shown an exponential increase in the number of civil conflicts and authoritarian regimes as well as a decrease in the levels of democracy and of peace or security. Contrary to the common belief that peace and democracy go hand in hand after a civil war, this book explores how they are at a crossroads. It proposes an innovative set of 14 dynamic dilemmas with respective trade-offs called the **Philosophical–Actors–Tactical (P–A–T) platform of democratic peacebuilding dilemmas.** The focus is on understanding the contradictions in post-conflict recovery, the challenges facing interim governments, and the international community's role in transitioning from internal armed conflict toward political, legal, civil, and social orders from 1989 to 2022. The conceptual framework of transitional dilemmas is applied in analyzing a set of 12 issues commonly found during transition times: elections; political parties; the constitution; checks and balances; power-sharing; transitional justice; human rights and amnesty; truth commissions and ad hoc war crime tribunals; disarmament, demobilization, and reintegration (DDR and SSR); media reform; and civil society. Solving one dilemma leads to at least one or more other challenges that shape a complex apparatus for restoring peace while installing a new political regime. This book contributes by advancing the theoretical paradoxes already identified by the literature (temporal, systemic, horizontal, and vertical) with an additional ten dilemmas: central, existential, design, moral, operational, resource, security, sequencing, financial, and transparency. Understanding this systematic set of dilemmas may guide disrupted states through the convoluted transition process after conflict. This new procedural approach also helps explain why UN missions sometimes bring some peace but rarely a functional democracy to civil war–torn countries. The book claims that often a moderate level of each is achieved.

Civil wars represent contemporary challenges to a state's stability and legitimacy as well as to regional and international order and security. They often become "global civil wars." The transition is invested by hybrid forms of peace, along with hybrid forms of political structures and processes, imposed via a top-down approach by international actors. Beyond understanding the causes and consequences of civil wars, more research is necessary to foresee the challenges after civil war toward sustainable democratic peace, state-building, and perhaps even nation-building. Therefore, this book addresses the contemporary paradoxes interrelated to civil war, fragile states, peacebuilding, democratization, state-building, and the United Nations. It aims to avoid failed states and proposes a tool for better decision making through awareness of potential dilemmas faced in any post–civil war situation.

ACKNOWLEDGMENTS

The scope of this book is all about the paradoxes between civil wars, democracy, peacekeeping, and the United Nations. I dedicate this book to those who are the main characters: the past and future generations of modern civil wars. This topic involves political complexities and requires a robust emotional equilibrium to maintain research objectivity and a methodological structure for years without losing focus on what it is all about: humanity. Having been part of a UN peacekeeping mission myself and speaking different languages certainly added a layer of comprehension that was particularly effective for the case studies of Angola, Timor-Leste, Mozambique, Haiti, Côte d'Ivoire, and DRC. There is extensive literature on democratization, peacebuilding, and state-building. This book does not pretend to have discovered a miracle truth that somehow eluded all its predecessors. There is no magic formula for peacebuilding success. Nonetheless, by pulling together the strands of various theories, practices, and case analyses, the study discloses interesting insights into the contradictions of building peace, democracy, and a strong state as simultaneous goals in the aftermath of civil war.

I have never been alone. I owe a debt of gratitude to Professor Wayne Cristaudo, my principal "super-supervisor," who guided me throughout the journey with excellence. Not only has he provided academic insights, but he has also given me respect, support, and opportunities without ever doubting my capacities. In the same way, Dr. Joakim Kreutz provided substantive methodological review and support to be a visiting scholar at the prestigious Department of Peace and Conflict Research of Uppsala University (Sweden). I also thank Anna Jarstad, editor of the book *From War to Democracy: Dilemmas of Peacebuilding* (2008) whose work initially inspired this book. My thankfulness also goes to those who contributed with unique insights during field trips in Kosovo and Serbia and interviews in the United States, Ireland, and Northern Ireland (UK). In addition, special thanks go to all senior current and former UN officials of

DPKO, DPA, UNMIK, UNMIT, MINUSTAH, and MINUCA, and members of the Presidency and the Parliament of Kosovo. I am also grateful to the president of Timor-Leste and Nobel Peace laureate José Ramos-Horta, for his contributions. Furthermore, I also thank Charles Darwin University (CDU) and the Australian government for academic and financial support.

I owe everything to my family. I dedicate this work to my mother, Marli, who echoes perseverance, wisdom and moral principles without comparison. I also offer this *In Memoriam* to my sister Gleice and my father Jonas, who passed away during this book writing. To Rogerio; the best brother in the world. I especially dedicate this book to my husband, Anthony Watts, who deserves to co-share the title of Doctor of Philosophy due to his unquestionable financial and emotional support. *Meu amor, eu te amo mais e mais!* Importantly, I offer it to my children; Daniel, Julia, and Sofia. Far from any naivety, motherhood provided the space to widen my intellectual horizons and understanding of conflict from a perspective I never thought possible. My children have shown me the obvious: freedom and safety, also commonly known as "peace," should not be a privilege of the few. And that is precisely what keeps me passionate about continuing the study of the turbulent areas of humanitarian affairs, good governance and political affairs, international development cooperation, and peacebuilding.

FOREWORD

I have dedicated my life to the cause of peace. It is enthralling why so few fragile countries emerge as peaceful, healthy democracies on the path toward economic development after violent conflicts. This question has been at the epicenter of my journey when fighting for the independence of Timor-Leste, which led to my Nobel Peace Prize. The shift from war to democratic peace requires hard political choices. I witnessed those dichotomies being president (twice), prime minister, and minister of foreign affairs of Timor-Leste, as well as a Special Representative of the UN Secretary-General for the Integrated Peace-Building Office in Guinea-Bissau (UNIOGBIS).

Proudly, according to Freedom House, Timor-Leste has distinguished itself for several consecutive years as a nation with the highest score of political freedom and civil liberties in Southeast Asia. This achievement results from the Timorese people's resilience and the international community's support. Western-led interventions are designed to promote a liberal model of conflict transformation through multi-party democracy, market capitalism, and justice and security sector reform. Timor-Leste is a successful case of United Nations intervention. As the chair of the UN High-Level Independent Panel on Peace Operations (HIPPO), it is fundamental to keep improving those operations to safeguard fundamental rights.

When I was interviewed as part of Dr Pereira Watts's research in 2016, no one would have imagined that the world would face a global COVID-19 pandemic, coups from Myanmar to Mali, the takeover of the Taliban or the War in Ukraine. Yet, more than ever, this book comes in need and provides a comprehensive analysis of the nexus between violence, democratization, and fragile states through elections, constitutional power design, and the security sector reform.

The author's contributions include identifying and systematizing dilemmas that must be considered with an intersected analysis. Izabela provides a comprehensive study that will undoubtedly be at the forefront of anyone interested in conflict resolution and development, from decision-takers, advisors, or analysts. There is no one-size-fits-all recipe for transitioning from conflict to peace and how to effectively statecraft. Instead, Izabela shows robust evidence research and a multifaceted perspective that hopefully will promote awareness of the important choices that must be made to keep taking peacebuilding to the world.

I am proud to have contributed to this study and honored to be invited to write this foreword. Enjoy your reading!

Jose Ramos-Horta
President of the Democratic Republic of Timor-Leste
Nobel Peace Laureate

LIST OF PEACE OPERATIONS

TABLE 0.1 List of acronyms of active United Nations peace operations between 1989 and 2022

Acronym	Country	Mission name	Start date	End date
UNTSO	Israel	United Nations Truce Supervision Organisation	May 1948[a]	Ongoing★
UNMOGIP	India	United Nations Military Observer Group in India and Pakistan	Jan 1949	Ongoing★
UNFICYP	Cyprus	United Nations Peacekeeping Force in Cyprus	Mar 1964	Ongoing★
UNDOF	Israel (Golan)	United Nations Disengagement Observer Force	May 1974	Ongoing★
UNIFIL	Lebanon	United Nations Interim Forces in Lebanon	Mar 1978[b]	Ongoing★
UNAVEM I	Angola	United Nations Angola Verification Mission I	Jan 1989	Jun 1991
UNTAG	Namibia	United Nations Transition Assistance Group	Apr 1989	Mar 1990
ONUCA	Nicaragua	United Nations Observer Group in Central America	Nov 1989	Jan 1992
MINURSO	Western Sahara	United Nations Mission for the Referendum in Western Sahara	Apr 1991	Ongoing★

(*Continued*)

TABLE 0.1 (Continued)

Acronym	Country	Mission name	Start date	End date
UNAVEM II	Angola	United Nations Angola Verification Mission II	Jun 1991	Feb 1995
ONUSAL	El Salvador	United Nations Observer Mission in El Salvador	Jul 1991	Apr 1995
UNAMIC	Cambodia	United Nations Advance Mission in Cambodia	Oct 1991	Mar 1992
UNPROFOR	Croatia	United Nations Protection Force	Feb 1992	Mar 1995
UNTAC	Cambodia	United Nations Transitional Authority in Cambodia	Mar 1992	Sep 1993
UNOSOM I	Somalia	United Nations Operation in Somalia I	Apr 1992	Mar 1993
ONUMOZ	Mozambique	United Nations Operation in Mozambique	Dec 1992	Dec 1994
UNOSOM II	Somalia	United Nations Operation in Somalia II	Mar 1993	Mar 1995
UNOMIG	Georgia	United Nations Observer Mission in Georgia	Aug 1993	Jun 2009
UNOMIL	Liberia	United Nations Observer Mission in Liberia	Sep 1993	Sep 1997
UNMIH	Haiti	United Nations Mission in Haiti	Sep 1993	Jun 1996
UNAMIR	Rwanda	United Nations Assistance Mission for Rwanda	Oct 1993	Mar 1996
UNAVEM III	Angola	United Nations Angola Verification Mission III	Feb 1995	Jun 1997
UNCRO	Croatia	United Nations Confidence Restoration Operation in Croatia	May 1995	Jan 1996
UNPREDEP (FYROM)	Macedonia	United Nations Preventive Deployment Force	Mar 1995	Feb 1999
UNMIBH	Bosnia-Herzegovina	United Nations Mission in Bosnia and Herzegovina	Dec 1995	Dec 2002
UNTAES	Croatia	United Nations Transitional Administration for Eastern Slavonia, Baranja, and Western Sirmium	Jan 1996	Jan 1998
UNMOP	Croatia	United Nations Mission of Observers in Prevlaka	Jan 1996	Dec 2002
UNSMIH	Haiti	United Nations Support Mission in Haiti	Jul 1996	Jul 1997
MINUGUA	Guatemala	United Nations Verification Mission in Guatemala	Jan 1997	May 1997
MONUA	Angola	United Nations Observer Mission in Angola	Jun 1997	Feb 1999

(*Continued*)

TABLE 0.1 (Continued)

Acronym	Country	Mission name	Start date	End date
UNTMIH	Haiti	United Nations Transition Mission in Haiti	Aug 1997	Dec 1997
MIPONUH	Haiti	United Nations Civilian Police Mission in Haiti	Dec 1997	Mar 2000
UNCPSG	Croatia	UN Civilian Police Support Group	Jan 1998	Oct 1998
MINURCA	CAR	United Nations Mission in the Central African Republic	Apr 1998	Feb 2000
UNOMSIL	Sierra Leone	United Nations Observer Mission in Sierra Leone	Jul 1998	Oct 1999
UNMIK	Kosovo	United Nations Interim Administration Mission in Kosovo	Jun 1999	Ongoing★
UNAMSIL	Sierra Leone	United Nations Mission in Sierra Leone	Oct 1999	Dec 2005
UNTAET	Timor-Leste	United Nations Transitional Administration in Timor-Leste	Oct 1999	May 2002
MONUC	DRC	United Nations Organization Mission in the Democratic Republic of the Congo	Nov 1999	Jun 2010
UNMISET	Timor-Leste	United Nations Mission of Support in Timor-Leste	May 2002	May 2005
UNAMA[c]	Afghanistan	United Nations Assistance Mission in Afghanistan	Mar 2002	Ongoing★
UNMIL	Liberia	United Nations Mission in Liberia	Sep 2003	Mar 2018
UNOCI	Côte d'Ivoire	United Nations Operation in Côte d'Ivoire	Apr 2004	Jun 2017
MINUSTAH	Haiti	United Nations Stabilization Mission in Haiti	Jun 2004	Oct 2017
ONUB	Burundi	United Nations Operation in Burundi	Jun 2004	Dec 2006

[a]UNTSO was the first ever peacekeeping operation established by the United Nations and is still in operation until the date of this publication.
[b]Amended in 2002 due to new hostilities.
[c]Classified as a political mission.

ILLUSTRATIONS

Figures

I.1	Coexistence of hybrid system of peace and political regimes	6
I.2	Peace-Democracy-the State and the Security-Freedoms-Institutions nexus	8
I.3	Inter-sectorial scope of analysis	9
I.4	Transitional dilemmas from guns, votes to doves	11
I.5	Making war to peace transitions stronger	11
I.6	The state of democracy 1975–2020	22
I.7	Structure transition from civil war to democracy with five multifaceted axes	26
1.1	Forms of hybrid peace	50
1.2	Proposed set of peacebuilding dilemmas according to Jarstad and Sisk (2008)	53
1.3	Central dilemma: bad choices can undermine peacebuilding or democracy-building	54
1.4	P–A–T dilemmas at the intersection between war, peace, and democracy	60
1.5	Quadrants of peace and democracy	61
1.6	Security, economic, and moral aspects within the war–peace–democracy triad	62
1.7	Tridecagon_complex and dynamic set of dilemmas for democratization and peacebuilding after war	64
1.8	The P–A–T system of dilemmas and its corresponding trade-offs	65

2.1	Failed democracy and failed states: the inverted dynamic of war to peace transition and intervention cycle	72
2.2	UN intervention in civil wars: Westphalian versus post-Westphalian dilemma	76
3.1	Integrated approach to violence and democratization: conflict cycle and electoral cycle	91
4.1	Case study with UN intervention	121
4.2	Case study without UN intervention	124
5.1	Elections: hard choices between good for peacebuilding or bad for democratization	157
5.2	Elections at the center of peace and democracy-building dilemmas	163
6.1	Transitional dilemmas regarding power-sharing: a puzzle	204
7.1	Contradictory elements of justice	212
7.2	Dilemmas in transitional justice	225
8.1	Dilemmas for DDR/SSR: an integrated approach	246
9.1	Dilemmas facing social order	271
10.1	Tridecagonal structure of hybrid democratic peace transitional dilemmas	281

Tables

0.1	List of acronyms of active United Nations peace operations between 1989 and 2022	xviii
5.1	Post-conflict scenarios for former rebels	167
8.1	Definitions, common challenges, and typologies of DDR and SSR processes	234
8.2	Case study: SSR in Timor-Leste	250
A.1	The state of affairs of democracy and peace in the countries torn by civil wars with UN peace operations	284
A.2	Democracy and Peace in countries torn by civil wars without UN intervention	302

GLOSSARY OF ABBREVIATIONS AND TECHNICAL TERMS

3Rs	Reintegration, Reconciliation, and Rehabilitation
A4P	Action for Peacekeeping
AAK	Alliance for the Future of Kosovo (In Albanian: *Aleanca për Ardhmërinë e Kosovës*)
ARDE Democratic Revolutionary Alliance (In Spanish:	*Alianza Revolucionária Democrática*)
ARSA	Arakan Rohingya Salvation Army (Myanmar/formerly known as Burma)
BRIDGE	Building Resources in Democracy, Governance and Elections
CAR	Central African Republic
CDU	Charles Darwin University
CEP	Temporary Electoral Council (Haiti)
CNDD-FDD	National Council for the Defense of Democracy–Forces for the Defense of Democracy (French: *Conseil National Pour la Défense de la Démocratie–Forces pour la Défense de la Démocratie*) (Burundi)
CNRT	National Congress for Timorese Reconstruction (Portuguese: *Congresso Nacional de Reconstrução de Timor*)
COW	Correlates of War
CVR	Truth and Reconciliation Commission (Timor-Leste)
DDR	Disarmament, Demobilization and Reintegration
DFS	Department of Field Support
DPA	Department of Political Affairs
DPKO	Department of Peacekeeping Operations (former)
DPO	Department of Peace Operations (new)

DPPA	Department of Political and Peacebuilding Affairs
DRC	Democratic Republic of the Congo
ECOWAS	Economic Community of West African States
EDF	Eritrean Defence Forces
EISA	Electoral Institute for Sustainable Democracy in Africa
EMB	Electoral Management Bodies
ENDF	Ethiopian National Defense Force
EPRDF	Ethiopian People's Revolutionary Democratic Front
EU	European Union
EUTM	European Union Training Mission (in CAR).
EVER	Election Violence Education and Resolution
FACA	Forces Armees Centroafricaine (Central African Army)
FARCs	Revolutionary Armed Forces of Colombia – People's Army (In Spanish: *Fuerzas Armadas Revolucionarias de Colombia – Ejército del Pueblo*, FARC–EP and FARC) Transformed into political party *Fuerza Alternativa Revolucionária del Común* after the peace agreement in 2016
FDN	Nicaraguan Democratic Force (In Spanish: *Fuerza Democrática Nicaragüense*)
FFF	Feelings of Frustration and Futility
FMLN	Farabundo Martı́ National Liberation Front (El Salvador)
FRELIMO	Mozambican Liberation Front
FRETILIN	Revolutionary Front for an Independent East Timor (In Portuguese: *Frente Revolucionária de Timor-Leste Independente*)
FRUD	Front for a Restoration of Unity and Democracy (Djibouti)
FSI	Fragile State Index
FSLN	Sandinista National Liberation Front
GC	Greek Cypriots
GDI	Global Democracy Index
GPI	Global Peace Index
ICTY	International Criminal Tribunal for the former Yugoslavia
IDDRS	Integrated Disarmament, Demobilization and Reintegration Standards
IDP	Internally Displaced Persons
IEP	Institute of Economics and Peace
IEU	Intelligence Economic Unit
IFES	International Foundation for Electoral Systems
INEC	Nigerian Independent National Electoral Commission
INGO	International Non-Government Organization
IOs	International Organizations
IRA	Irish Republican Army
IRI	International Republican Institute
ISCI	International State Crime Initiative
ISIL	Islamic State in Iraq and the Levant (also ISIS, IS, Da'ish or Daesh)
KPC	Kosovo Protection Corps
LTTE	Liberation Tigers of Tamil Eelam (or Tamil Tigers)
LURD	Liberians United for Reconciliation and Democracy
MDGs	Millennium Development Goals
MILF	Moro Islamic Liberation Front (The Philippines/Mindanao)

Glossary of abbreviations and technical terms **xxv**

MPLA	Popular Movement for the Liberation of Angola (In Portuguese: *Movimento Popular de Libertação de Angola*)
NATO	*North Atlantic Treaty Organization*
NCP	National Congress Party
NDI	National Democratic Institute
NELDA	National Elections Across Democracy and Autocracy
NGO	Non-governmental organizations
NLD	National League for Democracy Party
NPFL	National Patriotic Front of Liberia
NPP	National Patriotic Party (Liberia)
NRA/NRM	National Resistance Army (NRA) and its political wing, the National Resistance Movement (NRM) (Uganda)
OAS	Organization of American States
OHCHR	UN Office of the High Commissioner for Human Rights
OLF/OLA	Oromo Liberation Front/Oromo Liberation Army
OSCE	Organization for Security and Cooperation in Europe
P5	Security Council Permanent Members
P–A–T	Philosophical–Actors–Tactical platform of post-conflict peacebuilding dilemmas
PBSO	Peace building Support Office
PDK	Democratic Party of Kosovo (originally Kosovo Liberation Army – UCK)
PEV	Prevention of Election Violence
PGA/EGP	People's Guerrilla Army (In Spanish: Ejército Guerrillero Popular), armed wing of the Communist Party of Peru ("Sendero Luminoso" or "PCP-SL")
PKK	Kurdistan Workers' Party (In Kurdish: *Partiya Karkerên Kurdistanê*)
PLP	People's Liberation Party (In Portuguese: *Partido de Libertação Popular*. Timor-Leste)
PMSCs	Private military and security companies
PR	Proportional representation systems
PRA	Popular Resistance Army (Uganda)
PSA	Power-sharing arrangements
PSI	Power-sharing institutions
R2P	Responsibility to protect
RENAMO	Mozambican National Resistance (In Portuguese: *Resistência Nacional Moçambicana*)
RPF	Rwandan Patriotic Front
RUF	Revolutionary United Front
RwP	Responsibility while protecting
SDGs	Sustainable Development Goals
SFI	State Fragility Index
SNTV	Single non-transferable vote
SSR	Security Sector Reform
SWAPO	South West Africa People's Organization (Namibia)
TARM	Tupac Amaru Revolutionary Movement (Peru)
TC	Turkish Cypriots
TDF	Tigray Defense Forces
TL	Timor-Leste
TPLF	Tigrayan People's Liberation Front

UCK/KLA	Kosovo Liberation Army
UFF	Uganda Freedom Fighters
UK	United Kingdom
UMD	United Council for Democracy (Djibouti)
UN	United Nations
UNDP	United Nations Development Programme
UNEAD	UN Electoral Assistance Division
UNOPS	United Nations Office of Project Services
UNTSO	UN Truce Supervision Organization
UNV	United Nations Volunteers
URNG	Guatemalan National Revolutionary Unity
USA	United States of America
VUCA	Military expression for a situation characterized by volatility-uncertainty-complexity-ambiguity

ABOUT THE AUTHOR

Dr Izabela Pereira Watts accumulates more than 15 years of experience in development cooperation projects with major international organizations, including with the United Nations and the Organization of American States, as well as with private and public sectors, including think tanks and the Brazilian Ministry of Foreign Affairs. As a pro-academic, her experience across Asia, Latin America, Africa, and Europe intersects with political advisory, public policy design, development project management, monitoring and evaluation, peacekeeping, elections, humanitarian affairs, strategic analysis, and gender in fragile states. She holds a doctorate in International Studies and Political Sciences and two master's degrees in Economics and Peace Studies, respectively. Her passion and energy led her to multiple awards, including "Top 99 Under 33 Most Influential International Leaders" by the global affairs magazine *Diplomatic Courier* (USA-2013), and she was nominated for the Outstanding Contribution for Teaching and Learning Award (OCTAL-University of Wollongong-2020). She is a senior international consultant and a lecturer at the University of Wollongong. She is also a research member of the Future of Rights Centre (FoRC) at the University of Wollongong and an adjunct fellow for the Humanitarian and Development Research Initiative (HADRI) at Western Sydney University. She is also a former visiting scholar at the prestigious Department of Peace and Conflict Research of Uppsala University (Sweden), former ambassador for the Global Peace Index of the Institute of Economics and Peace (IEP) and a former researcher coordinator of Armed Conflict Prevention and Resolution–(GapCON). She has many international relations publications and is fluent in English, French, Spanish, and Portuguese.

INTRODUCTION

> Civil war? What does that mean? Is there any foreign war?
> Isn't every war fought between men, between brothers?
> *Victor Hugo in* Les Misérables *(1862)*

International politics is as dynamic as a chessboard or billiard table. When this book project started in 2014, no one could have predicted that 2022 would witness Russia's invasion of Ukraine, a coup d'état in Burkina Faso, or evidence of human rights atrocities against the Uighurs by the Chinese government. Obituaries in 2022 include the death of José dos Santos, who ran Angola fiercely for almost four decades, and of Queen Elizabeth II, who is seen by some as an icon of imperial colonialization practices that had undeniable historical consequences in some cases of civil wars. In 2021, the number of coups, coup attempts, and violent demonstrations matched the highest point in the 21st century, accelerating cycles of violence in countries wracked by conflicts, such as Sudan. Similarly, the Taliban's taking power in Afghanistan was certainly not part of any expert prophecies. Beyond the COVID-19 pandemic, an "epidemic of coups" seems to have taken the stage in the international arena, as UN Secretary-General Antonio Guterres suggested. Despite the specificities of each conflict, it appears that a contagious coup phenomenon erupted in Myanmar, Guinea, Chad, Niger, and Mali. The year 2021 also witnessed several elections worldwide, including the fourth-term victory of President Bashar al-Assad in Syria and the 2021 Baghdad clashes that led to the consequent Iraqi political crisis.

On the one hand, despite efforts to revitalize global democracy with the "Summit for Democracy" (2021), for 16 consecutive years Freedom House's

DOI: 10.4324/9781003279976-1

annual report has documented a decline in the number of democracies worldwide. The year 2022 witnessed massive protests that upended the country's politics, such as in Kazakhstan and Sri Lanka. The COVID-19 pandemic has exacerbated these threats as democratic countries employed non-democratic tactics through the imposition of states of emergency, the spread of disinformation and fake news, as well as restrictions on freedom of expression to deal with the health crisis and restraints on judicial independence. As a result, data from 1975[1] to 2020 show that the number of countries moving toward authoritarianism is three times the number moving toward democracy (IDEA, 2021). Beyond counterforces over fragility or resilience, the Fragile States Index concludes that there has been "an erosion in public confidence in democratic institutions and an increase in social and political polarization in both rich and poor countries across the globe, which has contributed to a rise in authoritarianism" (FFP, 2022). On the other hand, there is a domino-effect intensification of armed civil conflicts, such as in Yemen, Ethiopia (Tigray), Nigeria, and the self-proclaimed Republic of Artsakh (2020-Nagorno-Karabakh). Despite the global democracy decline (Freedom House, 2022b), it is arguable that the absence of war between democratic states "comes as close as anything we have to an empirical law in international relations" (Levy, 2001, 1988).

It is intriguing why countries torn by civil war rarely emerge as robust democracies with sustainable peace. In the aftershocks of civil war, the political transition is usually turbulent and faces the conundrum of how to move mutually toward peace and democracy. And, more importantly, how to make state-building, or ultimately nation-building, succeed. Contrary to the common belief that peace and democracy reinforce each other, this book explores how efforts during times of transition create dilemmas in which choices for peace or democracy are at a crossroads with each other. To follow the path for one does not lead to the other. Thus, this book focuses on a central dilemma of transition from civil war: *peace versus democracy*.

The book tries to answer two main questions: What are the main dilemmas in seeking to mutually achieve peace, democracy, and a functional state? And, second, what role do UN operations play in bringing simultaneously peace and democracy to post–civil war countries? To assist in preventing failing states, the book proposes a tool for better decision making by identifying probable dilemmas between peace and democratization in any modern post–civil war context. Methodologically driven mainly by qualitative comparative analysis from civil war cases between 1989 and 2022, it proposes an innovative **Philosophical–Actors–Tactical (P–A–T) platform of democratic peacebuilding dilemmas**. The set of 14 dynamic dilemmas is composed of central, design, existential, financial, horizontal, moral, operational, resource, security, sequencing, systemic, transparency, temporal, and vertical paradoxes with respective trade-offs. It argues that comprehending the systematic platform of dilemmas may provide the key to guiding disrupted states through the complicated process of building political, legal, civil, and social orders after conflict. Moreover, it explores the contradictions during post-conflict recovery, the challenges facing interim governments, and the international community's role. This new approach might assist understanding why some war-torn countries can make the simultaneous transition to peace *and* democracy while others cannot.

The transition from the "rule of the gun" to the "rule of law" is not an obvious exercise but it is nevertheless critical. Researchers and policymakers have found that societal peace through non-violent politics, effective state institutions, and democracy are mutually reinforcing. Consequently, the peacebuilding agenda generally includes the divergent concepts of democracy-building and peacekeeping as parallel and reciprocally supporting processes. There is the assumption that creating the conditions for one or the other does so for both. By extension of the democratic peace theory, democratic civil peace supporters argue that there would be a decreased risk of civil war in countries under democratic regimes. This would be primarily due to the introduction of domestic conflict management tools to reduce arbitrary power and human rights violations, enforcement of the rule of law, and development of a culture of tolerance and respect among multiple disrupted segments of society. At the same time, fragile democracies or failed states are the major sources of civil wars. Extensive empirical studies suggest that intermediate regimes are the most conflict-prone (Hegre et al., 2001, p. 173). The transition from authoritarian states to democracy is the main source of peril: that is when it is more likely to involve armed violence than stable regimes; consequently, making semi-democracies more war-prone than autocracies or democracies (Henderson, 2002; Brock et al., 2012). Nevertheless, liberal democracy is not the miracle cure for internal conflict (Paris, 2004, p. ix).

In a globalized world, the "fight for democracy" cliché can also be lethal and a tool to legitimize the abuse of power or instigate potentially violent communities. The transition phase is inherently tumultuous. It can exacerbate social tensions, challenge an elite's powers, and undermine the prospects for stability in the politically fragile conditions typically existing in countries emerging from civil war. The inherent risks of democratic façades are a channel for recurrent animosities that promote an endless cycle of conflict instead of conversion toward a cycle of peace (Watts, 2008; IEP, 2014). Consequently, how can countries simultaneously move toward peace and democracy during the fallout of a civil war? In particular, how does UN intervention facilitate the peacekeeping, democracy-building, and statecraft processes? Promoting democracy in post-conflict or transition countries often does not prove to be successful. Not all good things go together. Trying to simultaneously achieve peace, security, prosperity, and other goals often leads to conflicting objectives, customarily referred as "challenges," that might hinder democratization processes (Leininger et al., 2012). This book argues that the democratic peacebuilding agenda of post-conflict reconciliation faces a contradiction in itself: choices for peace or for democracy can be mutually contradictory. Progress toward democratization might threaten peace; the concessions indispensable for amity may limit or defer democratization (Jarstad and Sisk, 2008, p. 1). Places like Afghanistan, Burkina Faso, and the Democratic

Republic of the Congo (DRC), to name only a few, reflect the evident dilemmas of war-to-democracy transitions, resulting in no peace.

Peace is here defined as the absence of violence. Therefore, peace is the ultimate goal of war as each warring party aims to win in order to gain power. Consequently, prioritizing peace prevails over the choice of democracy. The greatest paradox between democracy and peace is that using one lens, liberal democracy, as a political system is associated with peaceful conflict management, both within and between states. Ironically, in reverse, the path to democracy is often conflict-ridden (Mansfield and Snyder, 1995b). When civil war negotiations succeed, obstacles to democratization arise as state representatives or rebel forces face uncertainty about protecting their vital interests in the future through such democratic processes – particularly, though not exclusively, through elections. Peacebuilding may involve undemocratic restrictions, such as freedom of the press and mass demonstrations. In the long run, such constraints may cause turbulence, adversely influencing democratization but also turning into an obstacle to the implementation of the peace agreement. In that regard, an agreement for peace can be outweighed by previous undemocratic arrangements for strategic power-sharing. That might lead to further violence and, consequently, to a failure of the peace agreement. Importantly, free and fair elections may be democratic yet not lead to political stability, as in 2017 in Kenya and 2020 in Timor-Leste.

How can we bring political stability and democratization out of chaos? Throughout history, we have learned how to make war. But, as stated by Uri (2008, p. 2), "little in today's world is more progressive than modern warfare. Yet little is more archaic than today's peacemaking strategies." Democracy and peacebuilding, in both theory and practice, are the subject of a massive body of literature as the standard solution to successfully terminate civil wars. However, they are rarely explored as opposing forces. The paralysis in efforts to conclude the ongoing Syrian war is an example. Social, political, and economic elements of societies have evolved to encompass issues of globalization. Nevertheless, peacebuilding as a strategy has not evolved to the same extent despite several attempts to reform it (Guéhenno, 2018). A variety of studies have demonstrated that UN peace operations significantly facilitate, and might even be a prerequisite for, a lasting peace after civil wars (Fearon, 2017; Fortna, 2008a). Nonetheless, the dilemma inherent in peace interventions while promoting democratization in post-conflict countries requires further exploration to avoid the recurrence of the conflict and protect the vulnerability of fragile states. It is frequently assumed that the collapse of state structures, whether through defeat by external power or due to internal chaos, leads to a vacuum of political power. According to Chesterman et al. (2006, p. 1), "in the wealth of literature on state failure, curiously little attention has been paid to what constitutes state success and what enables a state to succeed" after a civil war. Despite proliferous literature on state-building in the last ten years (Levitsky and Ziblatt, 2018; Lockhart, 2018; Vincent Ashcroft, 2017, Kaspersen, 2017; Ghani and Lockhar, 2008), we still know less about how to build a democratic state that efficiently includes effective institutional capacities and a well-functioning government that assures stable security, power-sharing, checks and balances, respect for human rights, accountability, inclusive public policies, and socioeconomic development after years of deadly conflict and a traumatized society left on its own.

I.1 Concept foundations

War is not over when it is over. Instead, another transitional "war" starts, with conflicting old and new players, dynamics and rules headed toward an uncertain goal of "peace, democracy, and development." At the war's end, there is no democracy yet, nor a functioning state. Thus, peace is yet to begin. Consequently, the democratic peacebuilding agenda for post-conflict reconciliation faces a paradox that serves as the foundation of this book.

First, following the end of the Cold War, international actors increasingly intervened in interstate and intrastate armed conflicts. All UN peace operations since 1990 include elements of democratization and marketization (Paris, 2004, p. ix). In other words, the international community is not only expected to stop the violence, but it is also expected to engage in building democracy, free markets, and peace in the aftermath of conflict. Curiously, with the "third wave" of democratization (Huntington, 1996), the number of *official* democracies in the world more than doubled (Marshall and Gurr, 2015), and this political regime came to be seen as the most legitimate form of government despite its imperfections. However, although many armed conflicts ended in the 1990s, new and more complex civil wars have started. Since then, the number of UN peacekeeping efforts concomitantly in operation has been unprecedented, with a growing number of intrastate wars between 1993 and 2022 (UN-DPKO, 2022; UCDP, 2022). One of the possible reasons might be the ability of the UN Security Council (UNSC) to act compared to the time during the Cold War rivalry. Yet conflicts have increased recently when the UNSC has been politically paralyzed due to the use of veto powers, particularly by the United States, China, and Russia. Additionally, interventions involving the maintenance of peace, the UN's primary raison d'être, require multidimensional approaches to deal with such complex threats as regional spillover, internationalized civil wars, and terrorism. Conversely, the design of complex operations is often mismatched with existing institutional and operational capabilities as well as with the principles of international law. Those aspects will be further addressed in Chapter 2.

Second, in the fog of war, a hybrid system of peace—both positive and negative—and of political regimes—both democratic and authoritarian—coexists (Figure I.1). Because it is a transition, undemocratic elements are necessary to enforce a minimum state of peace and violence might erupt through democratic foundations (Brownlee, 2009; Diamond, 2002; Jarstad and Belloni, 2012; Richmond, 2015; Boege et al., 2009). Under this hybrid dynamic, if the post–civil war transition is not effective, it often results in anocracies. Yet, compared to

6 Introduction

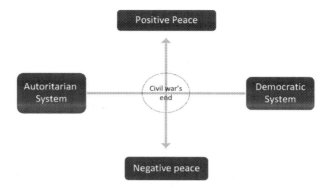

FIGURE I.1   Coexistence of hybrid system of peace and political regimes. Source: Author

consolidated democracies and non-democracies, fragile democracies have been proved to be more dangerous and turbulent, ultimately leading to a return to belligerence (Gleditsch et al., 2007). Thus, it is in the transition phase where most peril resides. For example, after the Arab Spring, Libya went from totalitarianism to anarchy, from a country with far too much government to a country without nearly enough. The Libyan state has become so weak that the government has to pay various warlords and militias to police whole swathes of the country (Totten, 2014). Under the concepts of a hybrid peace and hybrid forms of government, the so-called democratic risk transition requires a deep understanding of its contradictions to effectively set the foundations for sustainable peace, liberal democracy, and socioeconomic development after war (Issacharoff, 2015).

Therefore, the focus of this book is on the transition phase. When a civil war ends, what do we put in place? The standard prescription for fixing wartorn states includes a new constitution, elections, economic liberalization, and security reforms (Kaplan, 2008, p. 89). Nevertheless, democratization unleashes other conflicts that it tries to solve in the first place; thus, turning democratization into a problem of democracy (Kultgen and Lenzi, 2006). Despite best practice reports and theoretical "sequencing guides," something seems wrong with postwar democratization and peacebuilding operations. Despite a large number of official democracies and the enormous funding for democracy-building assistance provided by external aid, many post-conflict countries are caught up in a never-ending transition, resulting in perilous semi-democracies. Therefore, fragile states and anocracies deserve crucial attention from policymakers as the degree of democratization seems to be correlated with the likelihood of insurrection. Emerging democracies are hazardous, and the transition process is a delicate crossroad that can lead either to a vicious conflict cycle or to a race to stable development. Within this perspective, the transition from war to a consolidated democracy is fundamental for sustainable peace. Yet, as democracy is a process that takes time and is predicated upon specific social commitments, democratization often creates a weak governmental authority that fails to reconcile conflicting interests and may even invite new political conflicts (Mansfield and Snyder, 1995b).

It is essential to clarify a few issues. First, stopping the killing is urgent. There is extensive research on the causes and consequences of civil wars. However, more examination is needed to foresee the challenges when the war is over, whether by peace agreement negotiation or by victory. Second, there is no "recipe for a successful post–civil war transition." The consequences of different democratic architectures have crucial implications for peaceful outcomes as strategy and policy issues are most problematic where peace, prosperity, and democracy have all been lacking. The Gordian knot seems to be on what "kind of democracy" and "how to get there?" Transitologists defend technical sequencing and timing (Jarstad, 2015; Zaum et al., 2008; Savun and Tirone, 2011; Rustow, 1970b). Skeptics argue that democratization projects do not create democratic institutions as the design of projects to create organizations is not sufficient for achieving real democratic progress (Carothers, 2006; de Zeeuw, 2005; Swain et al., 2009). Therefore, this book aims to identify issues that merit reflection and consideration for better decision making and policymaking.

Third, there is no illusion: democratic systems of government are not a panacea for everything. As famously stated by Winston Churchill, it is the worst system except for all the others known. After an intrastate conflict, democracy ascends to an environment of failed state institutions, with a high level of distrust among political actors, the absence of a political culture of tolerance, and a non-existent or deficiently organized civil society. State failure remains either the reason for or the consequence of civil war. The government is mainly driven by years of one-party rule and a small ruling elite's exploitation of the country, widespread corruption and a lack of accountability, and the disempowerment and militarization of youth. Besides democracy's imperfections and limitations, it is promoted as the least bad option. Among all the possibilities, it seems understandable that promoting a "liberal and democratic state" would guarantee freedoms and rights instead of another dictatorship that would increase the political, social, ethnic-racial, or religious hiatus and possibly restart the conflict or support the status quo ante. Yet this alone is insufficient.

Fourth, there is no denial of the deficiencies of United Nations (UN) peacebuilding operations and the need for institutional reform. The adage that "the United Nations cannot keep peace where there is no peace to keep" (Boutros-Ghali, 1992, p. 7) remains valid. Despite its limitations as a burdensome bureaucracy, with geopolitical interests and limited financial resources, the United Nations is the organization that represents the international community's responsibility to provide protection and stability (R2P). Notably, as per article 1 of its Charter (UN, 1945), the purpose of the United Nations is to maintain international peace and security. It was not designed to deal with civil wars (Guéhenno, 2018, p. 185). Yet it is the organization with the most expertise in peacekeeping, accumulated over 75 years (William Maley et al., 2003; Banbury, 2016). In terms of measuring success or failure in the concluded missions from a security mandate perspective, Howard (2019) affirms that there is a two-thirds ratio of success since the end of the Cold War, as there are 11 successful cases out of the 16 mission completed and none have returned to civil war. It is worth noting that it is not the UN's purpose to promote a political system. Curiously, the term "democracy" is not mentioned in the UN Charter.

Fifth, state fragility has been mistaken as primarily a political problem, as if politics, policies, and processes were the same thing, particularly for post–civil war states worldwide. Policymakers have considered state-building an apolitical exercise of unrealistic technocratic reforms that are essentially politically driven decisions. Democracy-building in fragile states inevitably leads to local rivalries about the nature and basis of elections, the reintegration or de facto separation of ethnic communities, the consensus on school curricula and the national historical narrative, degrees of public ownership of companies, and gender equality and equity, to name a few (Mazarr, 2014). One of the main mistakes has also been implementing the same strategies for different conflicts as if they were remedies for the same disease (UN-DPKO, 2009; UNDP, 2009; UN-Brahimi, 2010). Although conflict scenarios share similar scenes of destruction, specific characteristics and national interests must be prioritized. More than just facilitating political change, post-conflict countries require a differentiated approach and case-by-case treatment to prevent them from spiraling into the cyclical conflict syndrome (Zeeuw, 2004; Carothers, 2006).

Importantly, as illustrated by Figure I.2, this book considers that peacebuilding, democracy-building, and state-building are respectively associated with security, freedoms, and institutions (Kultgen and Lenzi, 2006). If attempts of state-building fail, as in the cases of Liberia, Sudan, and Yemen, democracy-building and peacebuilding tend to become mere interludes between two wars. If democracy is considered a method for conflict resolution without force, then democracy and peace require similar institutions and norms. Consequently, they would be interdependent: peace would require a democratic state, and democracy would require peaceful norms and a legitimate state.

The peacebuilding literature often endorses a strong nexus between peace, democracy, and state-building, although they are not linear processes (Vincent Ashcroft, 2017; Richmond, 2013; Ottaway, 2002; Oliver and Jason, 2009; Paris and Sisk, 2009). By acknowledging that they are three distinct processes, this book

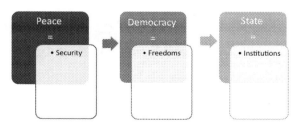

FIGURE I.2 Peace-Democracy-the State and the Security-Freedoms-Institutions nexus. Source: Author

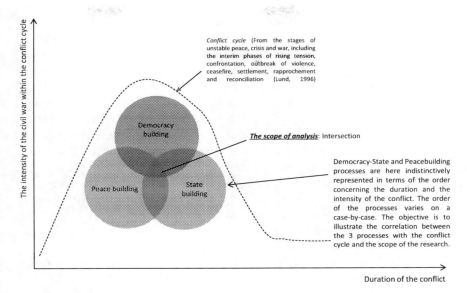

FIGURE I.3 Inter-sectorial scope of analysis. Source: Author

focuses on the intersections between areas that political science and security studies or peace and conflict resolution studies tend to view in isolation. It is important to remember that controversies are inherent to all human society (Galtung, 1998; Haavelsrud, 2005), and that non-violent conflict is a healthy feature of any democracy (Jarstad and Sisk, 2008, p. 19). Moreover, different types and levels of peace exist (Klare, 2002; Horowitz, 1985) as well as different types and levels of democracy. Both correlate with the conflict tension cycles of stability, instability, crisis, and war stages. Figure I.3 is an attempt to illustrate the correlation between the three processes, without particular order, with the cycles of conflict and to point out the scope of this book. Within this complex interplay, this book argues that a normative and systemic understanding of how common elements impede the three-cornered processes of peace, state, and democracy-building within a conflict cycle may be the key to guiding war-torn fragile states through the politically transitional process of reconciliation. Thus, with a new theory and practice approach, this study addresses the contemporaneous paradoxes related to civil war, fragile states, democratization, state-building, and UN peacebuilding operations.

I.2 The objective

By linking security, democracy, and peace, this study advances understandings about the synergy of making peace and building democracy through UN interventions since 1989. The focus is on war to peace transitions through democracy-building and state-building. The objective is to anticipate how to avoid failed states or anocracies by identifying a set of common transitional dilemmas that oppose peace and democracy. Democracy is not enough to deter social conflicts; rather, democratization brings uncertainty toward stability (Gottfried, 2013; Kultgen and Lenzi, 2006). While mature, stable democracies are safer, states usually go through a dangerous transition to democracy (Jarstad and Sisk, 2008). Contrary to the common belief that liberal democratization and peace would be mutually reinforcing, this book focuses on understanding the political tensions and contradictions in the transition from civil war toward liberal peace, the challenges facing interim governments, and the role of UN peace operations. This book seeks to fill that gap by examining the strategies and tactics of international actors, local political elites, and civil society groups to build or rebuild public institutions to make the state work.

A strategy for the postwar period is required to minimize what is known as "the hybrid peace dynamic," where liberal and illiberal features, as well as elements of violence and stability, coexist and compete (Boege et al., 2009). The much-vaunted "democratic peace dividend" might be successful only if prepared for in a systemic way and a multidisciplinary approach. The literature on peacebuilding and democratization in the aftermath of civil war already identifies a set of four structural and common dilemmas: temporal, systemic, horizontal, and vertical (Jarstad and Sisk, 2008). This book contributes to the body of knowledge by advancing theoretically the paradoxes faced by democratization and peacebuilding. It proposes an innovative set of 14 dynamic dilemmas described as Philosophical–Actors–Tactical (P–A–T) with ten additional impasses: central, existential, design, moral, operational, resource, security, sequencing, financial, and transparency dilemmas. Moreover, it analyzes those dilemmas with key elements for peace and democracy, such as power-sharing, elections, constitution, justice, human rights, and civil society as well as demobilization of militias, disarmament, and reintegration. Solving one dilemma leads to at least one or more other dilemmas that shape a complex dynamic apparatus for the restoration of peace and the establishment of a new political regime and an operational state. An awareness of those dilemmas may offer support to guide fragile states through the complex transition process.

The democratic peace theory implies that democracy is the path toward lasting peace. If so, it is fundamental to distinguish between the properties of stable democracies and the processes of democracy-building (Elman, 1999). Consequently, the book also aims to close the gaps in the theoretical framework of the process of conflict resolution. The book has a multi-layered perspective that aims to facilitate more effective and durable transitions from war to peace through democratic means by advancing theory and practice with policy-relevant results. Far from a "laboratory of solutions," the goal is to offer an instrument for the awareness and acknowledgment of potential dilemmas in any modern postwar situation. Awareness will help peacemakers take better and strategic decisions toward peace and democracy (Figure I.4). Consequently, the book contributes to making peacekeeping a more robust, more effective, and comparatively cost-efficient conflict resolution tool for conflicts nowadays as well as preventing failed transitions and fragile states. Finally, this book represents a response to the call for help to configure UN peacekeeping to better meet the challenges of contemporary and multidimensional conflicts (Figure I.5).

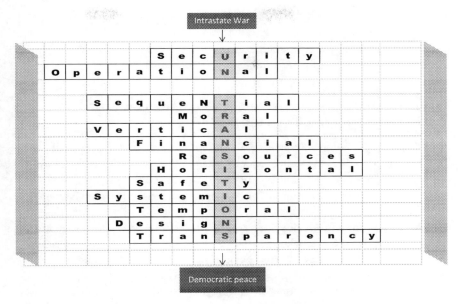

FIGURE I.4 Transitional dilemmas from guns, votes to doves. Source: Author

FIGURE I.5 Making war to peace transitions stronger. Source: Author

This book contributes to a better understanding of the synergy among peacemaking, democracy-building, and state-building. It assesses how UN peacebuilding operations have impacted when simultaneously building peace and democracy between 1989 and 2022. Therefore, the book:

- Focuses on the transition process of war to peace through democracy;
- Furthers the democratic peace theoretical premise;
- Advances the complex relationship between the theory and practice of democratic transition and state-building and its correlation with the theory and practice of war-making and peacebuilding;
- Anticipates how to avoid failed states or anocracies that can fuel the cycle of more conflict by proposing a systemic and normative set of common dilemmas that, if not managed correctly, can exacerbate a hybrid transitional dynamic that opposes peace and democracy;
- Contributes to the knowledge on peacebuilding by closing the gaps between the theory and practice of democratic governance and state-building in fragile states;
- Analyzes the effectiveness of the second generation of UN operations in jointly building peace and building democratic states;
- Explores how the processes of building peace are related to the processes of building more resilient, effective, and responsive states in war-torn societies;

- Contributes to the policy debates over peacebuilding and state-building and their effectiveness;
- Facilitates more effective and durable transitions from war to peace through democratic means by identifying complex dilemmas.

1.3 Justification: why do peacebuilding, democratization, civil wars, and fragile states matter?

Postwar reconciliation is invariably challenging, whatever the nature of the conflict. It is particularly challenging for countries that have experienced civil war to transition to democracy (Jarstad and Sisk, 2008, p. 243). Post–civil war democratization is particularly puzzling because it has to flourish within an environment with no political culture of tolerance, the state institutions have badly failed or even having collapsed, the civil society is weak, and political actors profoundly distrust each other (Wantchekon, 2004, p. 17). In recent years, major academic researchers and policymakers have been concerned with the danger of early democratization in fragile states. Conflict over territory, political ideology, or resources generates complex ongoing problems, regardless of whether civil war results in separation or reunification.

It is essential to contribute to the understanding of the complex nexus among civil war, democracy, and peace through UN operations for democracy-building and state-building in fragile states for several reasons. First, the relevance of the analysis is justified, predominantly because sustainable peace is the aim of all societies. Second, civil wars are not an obsolete matter. As in the case of Syria, Libya, and South Sudan, civil wars remain one of the most critical issues of our time. They often become "global civil wars," and, therefore, they are "everybody's business" (Ray, 2012). The modus operandi of conflicts has changed since the end of the Cold War. Originally, armed conflicts were mostly between states (interstate) ruled by classic world realpolitik. Interventions now occur more frequently within internal conflict scenarios (intrastate) or conflicts with a regional spillover (Brown, 2001; Fortna, 2008a; UNDP, 2009; Brock et al., 2012; Howard, 2019, 2008). More than two-thirds of all armed conflicts in the world since 1945 have taken the form of civil wars (Kim, 2007, p. 5). Importantly, civil wars are not a small version of interstate conflict (Kim, 2007, p. 34). They represent contemporary challenges to state stability and legitimacy and regional and international order and security. According to the Conflict Barometer 2021 (HIIK, 2022), 70 percent of armed conflicts nowadays is intrastate. According to Paul Collier (Menocal, 2010), 73 percent of the people living in such fragile settings have recently been through a civil war or are still in one; having experienced a civil war doubles the risk of experiencing another conflict. Put into perspective, this book concerns at least 1.5 billion people who live in countries at risk of instability and conflict (EU Commission, 2022).

Third, fragile states also matter. Limited statehood does not equal civil strife (Risse and Stollenwerk, 2018). Nevertheless, they are widely associated with civil wars, violent conflict cycles, and flawed democracies or hybrid regimes (Brock et al., 2012, p. 58; Mazarr, 2014; Menocal, 2010). Fragile states are 15 times more prone to civil war than developed countries and are the source of most of the world's refugees (Kaplan, 2008, p. 4; Patrick, 2006). Weak and failing states, where a government has no complete control, have arguably become the "single most important problem for international order" (Fukuyama, 2017). Particularly after the 9/11 attacks, the dominant national security narrative in the United States and the European Union stressed the dangers and menace posed by weak or failing states. Thus, fragile states have been considered to be "nests" of major threats and "factories" of volatilities. US agencies categorize these countries as breeding terrorism and creating regional chaos, crimes, demographic pressures, and environmental catastrophes (Brock et al., 2012; Menocal, 2010).

Moreover, on average, countries in conflict have 80 percent of their basic infrastructure destroyed (Crocker et al., 2001, Collier, 1999). Timor-Leste in 1999 is an example of this. As a result, the lack of state institutions is also a cause and a consequence of mass infrastructure destruction and the absence of capable human resources, as in Chad, Sudan, and Nicaragua.

As seen in the US campaigns in Afghanistan and Iraq, to help stabilize "anarchical countries" or quasi- or pseudo-states, interventions and engaging in state-building and enforcing democracy on a neo-imperial scale have been promoted as "just and necessary wars." Paradoxically, despite being devastated by poverty in fragile states, the fight for power and control of national resources is usually the cause of conflict. Territories with oil, ivory, or diamonds seem to increase their chances of having multiple UN interventions, such as Angola, Côte d'Ivoire and Sierra Leone, compared to those with no significant natural resources (Crocker et al., 2001; Collier and Hoeffler, 1998). Moreover, all UN interventions are in fragile states. The correlation among civil wars, fragile states, and UN intervention is even more evident when comparing the Fragile State Index (FFP, 2021) and the Global Peace Index (IEP, 2021). Countries in the category of "Very High Alert" or "Less peaceful," including Iraq, South Sudan, Somalia, DRC, and Sudan, have experienced UN intervention. Finally, natural disasters, such as earthquakes, cyclones, floods, or epidemics like Ebola or COVID-19, often accentuate current conflicts, as in Haiti (2010 and 2021), Liberia and Sierra Leone (2013–2016), and Myanmar (2020 and 2021). Recent natural calamities or outbreaks of disease have proven that states with more consolidated public institutions and effective governance, with efficient coordination, can better prevent or successfully recover from tragedies, as with Japan's tsunami and New Zealand's earthquakes or the COVID-19 pandemic (FFP, 2021; UN, 2020).

Fourth, democracy matters. The seventh Secretary-General of the United Nations, Koffi Annan, stated: "democracy matters as an international issue for conflict resolution" (Annan, 2002, p. 135). Thus, "liberal peacebuilding" or "democratic peacebuilding" considers that constructing democracy and building peace are inherently inseparable and usually appear within the same formula: a new constitution, parliamentary representation by political parties, the creation of an independent judiciary, and the revival of civil society based on human rights (Burnell, 2004; Elman, 1999; Evans, 2012; Ray, 1998; Baker, 2001). The vast majority of post-civil war agreements contain provisions for elections (Diehl, 2014, p. 15; Jarstad, 2009, p. 42). Half of all post-1945 democracies were achieved in a postwar context and a majority of these followed civil wars (Bermeo, 2003, pp. 159–61). Notwithstanding the paradox of warlord democracies, around 40 percent of civil wars ended up producing some form of democratic governments (Wantchekon, 2004. p. 17). It is argued that peacekeepers go not only where the job of keeping the peace is more complex, but also where building a new democratic state is less likely (Fortna, 2008b). Nevertheless, there has been a continuous decline since 2006 in the levels of democracy over authoritarian regimes (Marshall and Gurr, 2015; Fukuyama et al., 2015; FFP, 2021). Only 20 percent of the world's population lives in "free countries." That means that 8 in 10 people live in "not free" or "partly free" states (Freedom House, 2022a). IDEA claims that "more than a quarter of the world's population now live in democratically backsliding countries. Together with those living in outright non-democratic regimes, they make up more than two-thirds of the world's population" (2021).

Fifth, there have never been so many multidimensional UN operations "to enforce peace and build democracy." According to Fortna (2008a, p. 36), "the international community is indeed using peacekeeping to democratize war-torn countries." Active peacekeepers have more than doubled in 25 years, from roughly 50,000 in 1990 to nearly 130,000 deployed personnel in 2015 (UN-DPKO, 2015). Due to the 2019 reform of the UN Department of Peacekeeping Operations and Political Affairs and the closedown of some missions, nearly 88,000 military, civilian, and police personnel are involved as of February 2022[2] (UN-DPKO, 2022).

Combining "ballots and bullets" can legitimize dictatorial democracies and make international intervention a tool of harm (Henderson, 2002; Mansfield and Snyder, 2005b; Roeder and Rothchild, 2005; Burnell, 2006; Schlumberger, 2006a; Gowa, 2011). Beyond the political situation of Ethiopia or Mali (2022), Angola's case best exemplifies the controversy of international intervention during war and the efforts to build "peace and democracy." The intervention from 1991 to 1995 was considered a success by some experts because it allowed "transparent and free elections" on fragile levels due to the chaotic emergency context. Nevertheless, others also categorize it as a failure because it facilitated the legitimate revisiting of violent political groups to gain power. Consequently, the return to armed conflict undid all the previous efforts of 1989 (Diehl, 1996).

It is commonly believed that the state, democracy, and peace should be "built from within" (Woodward, 2017). Can democracy, as a political system that guarantees the self-determination of the people, freedom, and respect for human rights, be imposed? Is enforcing democracy with "guns and votes" (Watts, 2008; Collier, 2009) an illusion to end wars? (Henderson, 2002). When the international community intervenes to enforce peace, it represents another form of war-making (Doyle and Sambanis, 2006, p. 185). As suggested by Shaw (2006), organizing elections means organizing the exit of a UN peace operations in its effort to bring peace and democracy. Thus, the struggle for a democratic peace more and more frequently represents another form of armed conflict. On a parallelism with the notion of "war on terror," it becomes "war for democracy" as way to impose top down a system under the justification of settling "freedom."

Peacekeeping missions have rarely succeeded in creating successful states. Building stable state institutions is an arduous task, as evident in the cases of Sierra Leone, Rwanda, and Congo. The positive side is that they can shape the political process during the transition to peace so that neither side in the conflict can completely exclude the other. It also raises the probability that those keeping the peace have an incentive to play within the system, rather than going back to war. Peacekeeping missions cannot magically solve every controversy worldwide. However, it is worth analyzing the effectiveness of this tool for long-term peace. Thus, theoretical value and operational relevance justify the importance of this book for the effectiveness of UN peacebuilding operations regarding the promotion of democracy and governance in post-conflict societies.

Finally, the peacebuilding literature is significantly focused on humanitarian or military assessments of war interventions and various compilations on aid effectiveness. Despite a significant increase in the literature over the last decade, there is still room to explore the complex relationship between understanding the democratic transition and the theory and practice of state-building and its correlation with the theory and practice of war-making and peacebuilding. Without denying the importance of military intervention as part of the realistic theoretical perception of world realpolitiks, this book argues that international military deployment per se does not enforce a sustainable peace, as we can see in Iraq and Afghanistan. Military intervention is war-making. Democracy may be critical for peacekeeping, but it is not a sufficient cause or reason for intervention in itself. The Arab Spring movement is evidence of this. Vice versa, peacekeeping may be critical for consolidating democracy, but it is not a sufficient ingredient for lasting stability and peace. The democratic peace theory cannot be assumed as a simplistic inference. This premise merits a more profound analysis due to many empirical gaps and complex facets. Because of that, it is necessary to conduct research that focuses on the triangular relationship of war, democracy, and peace by including a more in-depth investigation of political regimes, governance, democratic transition, and statehood. Significantly, most of the literature is centered on binary correlations only, such as war-fragile states or democracy-peace, democracy and non-democracy, or peacebuilding-United Nations (Druckman and Diehl, 2013; UN-DPKO, 2022; Verrill, 2011; Zaum et al., 2008). The subjects falling under the scope of peace studies and conflict resolution and of democracy studies are topics of innumerable research. Nevertheless, they are usually analyzed in isolation and through predominately military or economic lenses or they are centered on case studies. Additionally, the relevant aspect of this book is its multifaceted perspective focused on strengthening democracy, governance, and institution-building best practices. With a world in transformation, there are new causes and complexities related to internal armed conflict. They require new strategies for peace operations. Therefore, studying these dynamics is necessary so as to be able to envisage new strategies to face such new threats from a more holistic perspective. The objective is not only to advance understanding war, democratic systems, or the UN missions. By deepening academic knowledge of political science and democratic studies as well as peace studies and conflict resolution, analysis in this book deals with possible dilemmas where peace and democracy oppose each other. Hopefully, this will contribute to strategic changes for more effective and efficient transitions from war to democratic peace.

With an unprecedented number of simultaneous international interventions, disillusion with the outcomes of the liberal democratic system as well as the propagation of failed states, something seems wrong with postwar democratization and peacebuilding operations, and therefore, requires further research. In sum, this book is justified by the strong nexus among intrastate conflict, disrupted states, and the UN democratic peacebuilding agenda. Fragile democracies remain dangerous and state-building has become a crucial matter of global security (Collier, 2009; Gillies, 2011; Fukuyama, 2017). Consequently, "building states to build peace" summarizes the contemporary literature, which proposes that states built on concrete democratic foundations have a higher probability of achieving sustainable security after war (Call and Cousens, 2008). In such circumstances, conflict resolution also means political reforms as a democratic experiment (Bratton, 1997).

I.4 A note on global peace data: is the world becoming more or less peaceful?

In the last decade, there has been a growing debate in the literature around whether and where there has been a trending decline or increase in armed violence and battles deaths since the early 1990s (UCDP, 2017; Goldstein, 2012; Pinker, 2011). This heightened interest is primarily due to methodological challenges in defining and codifying armed conflict and the timeframe (Newman, 2009).

According to the Global Peace Index (IEP, 2021), since 2010 the number of conflicts globally has increased by 88 percent. If the benchmark of post-conflict stability is ten years of peace, only 43 percent of all civil wars that have been terminated have achieved this goal. Victories are most likely to lead to a decade of peace (61 percent), followed by peace agreements (48 percent) and ceasefires (47 percent) (Kreutz, 2010). Some argue that, in a globalized world, there has been an increase in human insecurity, particularly since 2010 with the Arab Spring movement and the wars in Syria, Central African Republic (CAR), Yemen, and Ukraine (Crimea annexation–2014 and 2022). From this perspective, the world is not getting safer but, as unprecedented humanitarian and refugee crises show, far more dangerous (HIIK, 2017; IEP, 2017).

The 2022 Global Peace Index found that the global level of peace has deteriorated since 2008 in 84 countries out of 163 and highlights that countries tend to deteriorate much faster than they improve. Fifteen of the 23 GPI indicators worsened between 2008 and 2021, the largest deteriorations being in political instability, political terror scale, neighboring country relations, and refugees and IDPs. All these indicators strongly relate to civil conflict, reaching their worst levels since the inception of the GPI in 2008 (IEP, 2022). The intensity of internal conflict has reached its highest level; 42 countries have experienced a deterioration, such as Guinea, Burkina Faso, and Haiti, twice the number of countries that have improved (IEP, 2018, 2021). Since 2003, CrisisWatch, a global conflict tracker of the International Crisis Group, monitors war and conflict that can potentially escalate into war. Beyond the "eternal" wars in the Middle East or some African countries, war and potential escalation of armed conflict are more frequent and extensive than the usual news headlines. There are, on average, 70 situations of instability worldwide, 80 percent are intrastate conflict (International Crisis Group, 2022). In line with the Global Peace Index 2022, the number of countries experiencing deaths from internal conflict has increased from 29 in 2007 to 38 in 2022. Conflict deaths, either internal or external conflicts, rose around the middle of the 2010s to reach a peak of almost 238,000 in 2017 (IEP, 2017). The dramatic increase was concentrated in a few countries, with most deaths attributable to the war in Syria and a significant increase in South Sudan, Nigeria, and the Central African Republic at that time. The average intensity of internal conflict has also risen, despite the total number of deaths from internal conflict declining across the world since 2017. This has been driven by conflict becoming more widespread, even as the intensity of major conflicts such as Syria and Iraq continues to decrease. This is not because the conflict stopped, but mainly because there is "less to be killed" as a large part of the population was killed by Assad's regime or other rebels or fled the country.

Terrorism and civil unrest have been the biggest contributors to the global deterioration in peacefulness in 2020. A total of 90 countries recorded increased terrorist activity. The level of civil and political unrest has risen with violent demonstrations since 2008 in 61 countries (IEP, 2021). Over the last two decades, the humanitarian impact has been unprecedented: the number of refugees, IDPs, and others of concern to the UNHCR reached 100 million in June 2022 (UNHCR, 2022)[3]. At over 1 percent of the global population, the overall figure is equivalent to the 14th most populous country in the world. Beyond the conflict in Ukraine, the number of forcibly displaced people worldwide is propelled by new waves of violence or protracted conflict in Ethiopia, Yemen, Burkina Faso, Myanmar, Nigeria, Afghanistan, and the DRC. The economic impact of violence on the global economy reached US$16.5 trillion in 2021, in purchasing power parity (PPP) terms (IEP, 2021; IEP, 2022).

In contrast, what if civil wars were in decline? (Newman, 2009; Fazal, 2014). Proponents of what has become known as the "declinist book" argue that violence has declined worldwide, and they affirm that we have never lived in such "peaceful times in human history" (Goldstein, 2012; Pinker, 2011). Besides some new conflicts, they argue that more conflicts have ended either through peace agreements or through victories. Some possible reasons for this apparent shift in the conflict dynamic are political. First is the decline of potent ideologies since the end of the Cold War, which had hitherto ignited and exacerbated armed violence. Second is the growing number of consolidated democracies. Third is a shift in mentality so peace is considered more profitable than war. And fourth is the increasing investment in preventive war (Ray, 2012; Boutros-Ghali, 1992). Another hypothesis is tactical: from the Cold War to "cyber wars" a decline in the number of causalities in the field has occurred because soldiers have access to more medicine and protective equipment, and there is increased use of drones and robots (Fazal, 2014; Heintze and Thielbörger, 2015). Despite the mushrooming of terrorism groups, particularly in Syria, there has been a decline in deaths directly related to terrorism activity since 2016 (IEP, 2021). In this regard, Azar Gat claims that war has not become more lethal and destructive over the past two centuries, and thus this factor cannot be the cause of war's decline. Rather, peace has become more profitable (Gat, 2012). Finally, as the Global Peace Index argues, the world has not become more peaceful or conflictual. The problem is the wide gap between the countries ranked as very or less peaceful that has grown over the last decade (IEP, 2018).

Notably, the neorealist school fails to explain the causes and cures of civil wars. In intrastate conflicts, the state is not unitary but the opposite, with different actors and stimuli. Thus suggesting that domestic "anarchy" is a consequence of civil war and not its cause. As in the cases of Liberia and Sierra Leone, the governments continue to exercise some degree of control. Among the causes of civil wars and failed states are the imbalance in the distribution of political power and monopolies on the control of public goods (Collier and Hoeffler, 1998; Collier and Sambanis, 2002). As Doyle and Sambanis (2006, p. 40) clarify, the causes of civil wars are usually a mix of mass-level internal factors (serious domestic problems), mass-level external factors (bad neighborhoods); elite-level internal factors (poor leaders), and elite-level external factors (hostile neighbors). A large body of the literature on civil wars focuses on elites who dishonestly manipulate information and create mischievous phantasmagorias of a potential rival to obtain popular support and consolidate their own political and economic status (Mansfield and Snyder, 1995a). Similar cases can be observed in failed states such as Haiti and in the cases of civil war in Somalia and Sudan, where peaceful resolution is not in the self-interests of the leaders who first triggered the chain of violence (Zürcher et al., 2013; Kultgen and Lenzi, 2006).

Furthermore, there are the economic consequences of civil wars (Collier, 1999). They usually produce more devastating outcomes, such as massive casualties, displaced refugees, and mass starvation (Karl DeRouen, 2014; IEP, 2018). They also last longer than interstate wars because warring groups believe that it might bring political power or economic benefits. Consequently, they continue the conflict ad nauseam (Collier, 2004). Restoring a robust hierarchical power through military triumph is a problematic solution. As Zartman (1995) explains, there are cases where a government or rebel group realizes that the cost of staying in the conflict exceeds the benefits to be achieved. This "mutually painful stalemate" condition is an impediment to victory. Moreover, after achieving military victory, the new government is habitually inclined to be aggressive toward latent insurgent groups, such as in Niger and Mali, and, consequently, it ignites the security dilemma.

I.5 A note on postwar democratization: democratic peace theory and sequential transition models

Is the spread and consolidation of the democratic system the solution for ending armed conflict? It is a Churchillian cliché that democracy is not the best political regime but it is the least worst among the known possibilities. According to the democratic peace theory, democracy could be the answer for a lasting peace. The theory affirms that a democratic political regime prioritizes peace through peaceful solutions for problematic issues. Mature democratic states, it contends, are less prone to go to war against another democratic state and civil wars are unlikely to happen within states with a strong democratic tradition and institutions. By inference, the democratic peace theory would suggest that the larger the number of democratic states is, the fewer the number of armed conflicts between countries. Consequently, "liberal peacebuilding" conveys the idea that building democracy worldwide would not only contribute to the end of internal disruption, but would also lead to more stable interstate relations.

However, with an unprecedented number of official democratic states since the end of the Cold War, the relevant literature does not explain the unparalleled number of international interventions. The simple official preeminence of the "democratic political system" does not seem to be sufficient for analyzing the endogenous dynamic of conflict resolution, nor for identifying perspectives for the prevention of new disputes. The democratic peace premise has strong empirical support but shaky theoretical foundations (Russett, 1993). Skeptical authors such as Mansfield and Snyder (2005a), affirm that Western democracies are as war-prone as non-democracies and more likely to fuel interstate wars (Elman, 1999). Democracy does not suffice to deter social conflict. Therefore, its proliferation is considered by some authors as a "great illusion," although necessary in the absence of a better alternative (Henderson, 2002).

Contrary to the argument for an end of ideologies or democracy as a global phenomenon, and regardless of civil wars or UN interventions, there is a worldwide deterioration and frustration with democracy throughout the globe with significant setbacks in electoral process and pluralism, functioning of government, political participation, political culture, and civil liberties. Some analysts argue that the world has entered a "democratic recession" (Fukuyama, 1991,

2006; Fukuyama et al., 2015; FP, 2022). The 2021 Global State of Democracy report refers to it as "democracy erosion." Importantly, it argues that democracy is at risk by threats, both from within and from a rising tide of global authoritarianism. Despite the decline, "democracy is down, but not out" as some countries show great resilience, such as Liberia and Sierra Leone (IDEA, 2021). Some post-civil war countries have moved to authoritarianism, such as Angola, Rwanda, and Cambodia. Nevertheless, the concern is with the rise of hybrid regimes. Therefore, closer investigation suggests that many post-civil war countries get stuck in the anocratic dimension of the Polity spectrum. This gray zone fuels the vicious cycle of conflict.

Yearly reports since 2006 from the Economist Intelligence Unit, Freedom House, Institute of Economics and Peace and Fund for Peace (EIU, 2017, 2019, 2020, 2021) (FFP, 2016; FFP, 2017; FFP, 2018; FFP, 2022; Freedom House, 2017; IEP, 2015; IEP, 2018) state that democracy is in decline. Despite the end of several authoritarian regimes, many populations continue without access to their constitutional rights and suffer from a "democratic disillusionment" (Gauchet, 2004; Mouffe, 2003; Dominguez, 2003; Alsadi, 2007). The general dissatisfaction is one of the key elements that explain the rise in massive protest worldwide. Between 2011 and 2019, there was a 244 percent increase globally in riots, general strikes, anti-government demonstrations, and pro-democracy movements (IEP, 2021). Despite the coronavirus pandemic, 87 significant protests emerged worldwide in 2020, such as in Hong Kong as well as the #blacklivesmatter and the #metoo movements. Data from Carnegie's Global Protest Tracker[4] show that 76 new significant anti-government protests emerged in 2021, at a rate of roughly one new event every five days. Protests in Haiti, Iraq, Lebanon, and Yemen channeled public fury at dysfunctional political systems that have been unable to deliver basic governance. In 2021, the geographic breadth of protests encapsulated 58 countries, from Chad to Georgia and Myanmar to Tunisia with significant anti-government demonstrations. Approximately two-thirds of all countries have experienced at least one major anti-government protest since 2017 (Carnegie Endowment for International Peace, 2022). Despite this geographic diversity, many of the demonstrations in 2021 shared one of four cross-cutting drivers: (1) an increasingly authoritarian political landscape, (2) heightened political confrontation (elections and controversial judicial decisions), (3) rising economic insecurity, and (4) public discontent over how governments responded to the pandemic (Press and Carothers, 2022).

According to the Eurobarometer, 8 in 10 people surveyed are not satisfied with democracy in Europe. The 2022 Russian invasion of Ukraine comes at a time when liberal democracy in 29 countries covered in *Nations in Transit* in Central Europe to Central Asia marks its 18th consecutive year of decline, including Azerbaijan, Kyrgyzstan, and Belarus. Since 2021, for the first time in the 21st century, not only has democracy declined across the 29 countries covered in the *Nation in Transit* report in Eurasia, but it is of more concern that the dominant form of governance in this region is a hybrid regime with 11 cases, such as Kosovo, Armenia, Moldova, Hungary, Montenegro, North Macedonia, and Serbia (Freedom House, 2022b; EU Commission, 2021). In Poland, the introduction of a restrictive media ownership law and fears about the erosion of judicial independence drew at least 100,000 people into the streets in 2021 (Press and Carothers, 2022).

While declines in freedom were generally concentrated among autocracies and dictatorships transitioning from bad to worse, established democracies now dominate the list of countries suffering the highest decline in 2016, as in Europe (Denmark, France, Spain), the United States with the storming of the US Capitol on 6 January 2021, and policies to deal with COVID-19, such as South Korea (Freedom House, 2017, 2022b, 2021b). Populists and autocrats constitute a dual threat to global democracy with the danger they carry of a return to the iron fist (Freedom House, 2015, p. 1). For the 16th consecutive year, twice as many countries suffered declines as those that registered gains in 2020 (73 to 28). With populist and nationalist forces making significant gains in democratic states in 2017, the number of countries with improvements hit its lowest point and consolidated the wave of decline in global freedom over a decade (Freedom House, 2018, 2022a, 2021a, 2020, 2019). The global decline is translated into numbers, 83 rated free, 56 partly free, and 56 not free[5] (Freedom House, 2022a). Thus, combining partly free and not free outnumbers the number of countries rated free. By comparison, Global Democracy Index respectively identifies 53, 34, and 59 countries as flawed democracies, hybrid and authoritarian regimes while only identifying 21 countries as full democracies. According to the Economist Intelligence Unit, less than half (45.7 percent) of the world's population[6] now live in a democracy of some sort. Even fewer (6.4 percent) reside in a "full democracy"; this level is down from 8.4 percent in 2020, after two countries (Chile and Spain) were downgraded to "flawed democracies." Substantially more than a third of the world's population (37.1 percent) live under authoritarian rule, with a large share being in China (EIU, 2021). Put under another methodological scale, only 20.3 percent of the world's population lives in countries rated as free by Freedom House. Thus, 8 people in 10 live in non-democratic settings (Freedom House, 2022a). This is significant as studies have demonstrated that those are the cases with a higher probability of civil wars (Hegre et al., 2001; Gandhi and Vreeland, 2004), making this book significantly crucial for peace, security, and democratization studies. While some post-conflict countries seem to be on the right path, others have raised alarm, such as North Macedonia, Mozambique, Angola, and Nicaragua (Freedom House, 2018). The Middle East and North Africa region have had the worst ratings in the world since 2014, followed closely by Eurasia. Overall, not a single region improved its average score (EIU, 2017; IEP, 2022). There is a danger that some countries that have had the most remarkable transitions from dictatorship to democracy in the 1980s and 1990s are resorting to more authoritarian regimes through elected populist leaders. The very titles of the latest Intelligence Economic Unit reports are indicative of the deterioration identified: "Democracy and Its Discontents"

(EIU, 2015), "Democracy in an Age of Anxiety" (EIU, 2016), "Revenge of the 'Deplorables'" (EIU, 2017), "Free Speech under Attack" (EIU, 2018), and "A Year of Democratic Backsliding and Popular Protest" (EIU, 2019).

Others dispute that interpretation, emphasizing democracy's success in maintaining the massive gains it made during the last quarter of the 20th century (Diamond, 2016). Worldwide, there are constant and systematic calls for expanding and strengthening democracy. There is a global outcry for more, different, and "real" democracy, which comes at a time when the institutions that are supposed to represent the will of the people are disconnected from and are viewed as out of touch with the world and with life experienced by citizens on a day-to-day basis. Similarly, the respective titles of Freedom House reports also summarize it all: they include "democracy Is in Crisis" (2018), "Democracy in Retreat" (2019), "A Leaderless Struggle for Democracy" (2020), "Democracy under Siege" (2021a), and "The Global Expansion of Authoritarian Rule" (2022a). Considering the intensity and persistence of the global authoritarian trend, the economic recession, and the pandemic's perseverance, the forecast for the near future is obvious: a continued multiplication and intensification of violent protests globally and a popular disillusionment as democracy deteriorates (Press and Carothers, 2022; Figure I.6).

Moreover, some organized groups, such as Boko Haram, Al-Qaeda, and ISIS, show that democracy is not a worldwide aspiration, particularly in disrupted settings where the international community might want to promote it. By trying to block elections and other political processes, such groups argue that people should not be ruled by themselves but by God in an anti-secular approach to state governance (Aljazeera, 2015). New times create new challenges to the structures of politics, bringing further questions about the forms of representation and demanding innovative solutions for the opportunity of legitimate governance. As some would argue, all this might indicate that, despite strong statistical evidence, the core of democratic peace theory is not iron law but maybe just a causal assumption (Gärtner et al., 2015; Russett, 1993).

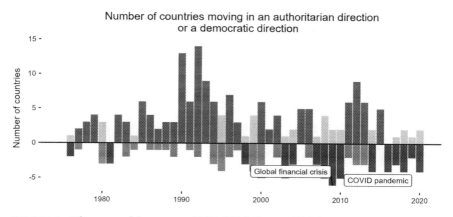

FIGURE I.6 The state of democracy 1975–2020. Source: IDEA

Another critical issue regarding democratization is "how" it should be implemented. Democratic transitions were initially considered evolving in certain predestined stages. Whenever possible, efforts to promote democracy should try to follow a sequence of building institutions before encouraging mass competitive elections. Thus, the dominant view of democracy aid is centered on the concept of "sequentialism." This carries the meaning that certain preconditions are necessary for democratization and that there is a preferred order of introducing reforms, with a specific emphasis on an institutional "checklist," "step-by-step" approach, or "timing" (Carothers, 2002; Jarstad, 2015). Policymakers on "transitology" disagree on which sequence is the most effective (Jarstad, 2015; Carothers, 2007; Mazzuca, 2014; Rustow, 1970b). Controversy revolves around the timing of elections and how this influences subsequent democratization and future internal armed conflict.

One of the core weaknesses of transitology is that democratization cannot be delineated by a step-by-step institutional checklist nor enabled by a diffuse set of efforts. Beyond possible common goals or needs, each case is unique; there is no single pathway to democratization after civil war (Geddes, 1999; Bermeo, 2003; Chesterman et al., 2006). The magic formula that "democracy can be cultivated anywhere under an institutional checklist approach" has failed and has been replaced by a "good enough, realistic attitude" (Grindle, 2007; Börzel and Grimm, 2018). The concept of the "globalization of democracy" or the "democratization of globalization" has proved so diverse and multidirectional that all attempts to formulate generalizations of the procedural steps leading to successful democratization have been challenged. And therefore, they have been claimed as a "sequential fallacy" (Carothers, 2007).

This book refutes the need for identifying standard solutions to standard problems. Instead, it aims to identify the common elements whereby building peace and a liberal democratic state act against each other during transitional times through a multidimensional perspective. In doing so, this book argues that gradualism should predominate over the sequentialist (or so called prioritization) approach (Carothers, 2007). The transition theory offers no clear answers on how components of democracy evolve in a given context, or how they are interrelated (Di Palma, 1990; Schlumberger, 2006b). Nevertheless, one of the few things that most scholars agree on is that no emerging democracy is likely to follow in the footsteps of its predecessor. Therefore, beyond gradualism or sequentialisn, the true choice should be to prioritize a country-specific approach (Rustow, 1970a; Parry and Moran, 1994; Geddes, 1999; Mross, 2018). This book supports this vision.

Notably, another debate within democratization studies and peace and conflict resolution studies is largely about what kind of democracy best suits post–civil war societies. Here there is a gap between theory and practice. Choices have to be made between the requisites for peace and the conditions for democracy; among the different implications for peace of *competing designs for democracy*; and about the kind of "democracy" and its relationship to other essential developments like state-building (Held, 1996; Burnell, 2006). There are several "kinds of democracy". Some are defined as "democracy with adjectives," such as "electoral democracy," "partial democracy," "managed democracy," "representative democracy," "participatory democracy," "constitutional democracy," and even "delegative democracy." The different institutional designs for democracy and the different time horizons required for democratization, may impact peacebuilding differently (O' Donnel, 1992). Among the concept of "models of democracy," delegative, representative, or participatory democracies would be ideal options, but they are not yet possible in the ashes of war (Held, 1996). As evidence of the importance of a political narrative to forge power legitimation, Vladimir Putin and Viktor Orbán, respectively, introduced new concepts in Russia and Hungary: "sovereign" and "illiberal" democracy. The game of adjectives is not accidental and has profound implications for regional security (Kazharski and Macalova, 2020).

Inclusiveness and stability are mutually supportive. The level or the lack of inclusiveness of the political system results in stability. Highly inclusive systems, such as the proportional representation (PR) system, are more stable than low inclusive systems that facilitate political exclusion, such as the majoritarian system (Reynal-Querol, 2005, p. 445). With a case by-case approach, the "best" model should be established according to the political will and at some infrastructural level. It is also argued that the so-called Schumpeterian democracy; defined as an "elite-centered game" with emphasis on elites holding a competition for power through elections, could fit nascent democratic institutions to the specific conditions of a traumatized society and contain political, ethical, and ideological tensions within peaceful bounds (Burlamaqui, 2019). Even if democracy does not appropriately respond to citizens' preferences or adequately control politicians or help reduce economic inequalities, the very fact that it might help change governments without bloodshed can help generate a peaceful resolution of conflicts (Jarstad and Sisk, 2008). This might suggest that the model of democracy that might prevail in the immediate aftermath of a civil war is a procedural and minimalist version of democracy where the warring parties and elites can best accommodate their interests. Arguably, if the ideal is not reachable, it is better just to have a "good enough" arrangement than to maintain the status quo of belligerence and lawlessness.

Finally, "governance-building" is a new concept engendering debate on how to overcome the challenges of the transition from civil wars beyond state-building, democracy-building, and peacebuilding (Börzel and Grimm, 2018, p. 116). As part of UN frameworks, such as *Agenda for Development* and *A new era of conflict and violence*, good democratic governance has led to development. In reverse, the lack of good democratic governance is the cause of non-development and armed conflict (Boutros-Ghali, 1994; UN, 2020).

I.6 Book structure

This book is divided into three main sections and nine chapters. The first section reviews the literature on already identified democracy-building and peacebuilding dilemmas and advances the field of knowledge by classifying additional quandaries. More importantly, it significantly contributes to peace and democratization studies by developing a theoretical set of 14 dilemmas concerning peacebuilding and democracy building in post–civil war transitions. It also explores the nexus among state-building, democracy-building, and peacebuilding after civil war by analyzing the problems related to democratization and their relationship to violence rather than peace. It further contributes to the literature by examining the role of UN peacekeeping missions in building a "peaceful, democratic and strong state." Peacekeeping seems good for peacebuilding, democracy-building, and state-building, and simultaneously bad for these three processes altogether. The analysis concludes that a more accurate result reflects the fact that UN intervention produces meso success, such as a "moderate level of peace and moderate level of democracy."

The transition from internal armed conflict requires movement toward political, legal, civil, and social order. Thus, the second section analyzes the proposed theoretical framework of dilemmas and respective trade-offs. It tests how they mutually interact with a set of 12 issues commonly identified during transition times: elections and political parties; the constitution, checks and balances, and power-sharing; transitional justice; human rights and amnesty; truth commissions and ad hoc war crime tribunals; disarmament, demobilization, and reintegration (DDR and SSR); media reform; civil society.

Finally, the third section presents its findings and recommendations. The gender perspective is a cross-cutting issue and not an opposing force to peace and democracy, and, therefore, it is included throughout an analysis and not as a specific section. Due to length restrictions, this book will not be able to cover the elements related to economic recovery and environmental issues (Figure I.7).

I.7 Methodology: research design

The book analyzes post–civil war state-building and democratization from 1989 to 2022. This period encompasses a significant shift in world politics and the spread of liberal democratic governments. This timeframe is essential for three reasons. First, the framework of dilemmas is related to UN peacekeeping efforts and civil wars. The current UN missions have distinct periods and characteristics, as some date from 1948 and the latest from 2014 (Central African Republic). Some missions have closed down in this period, and some have been replaced by minor operations, such as MINUJUSTH (2017–2019 Haiti).

Second, it is fundamental to consider the significant changes in the international world system and its impact on the evolution of early peace operations. These changes suggest an effect on the modus operandi of the missions and their results. As the Cold War ended, and democratization and globalization became more dominant, peace operations underwent a triple transformation: quantitative, qualitative, and normative (Bellamy et al., 2010). The "new world dis-order" has created a domino effect of civil wars. It allowed ethnic rivalries and mischievous behavior to flourish where superpowers states used to have control, particularly

26 Introduction

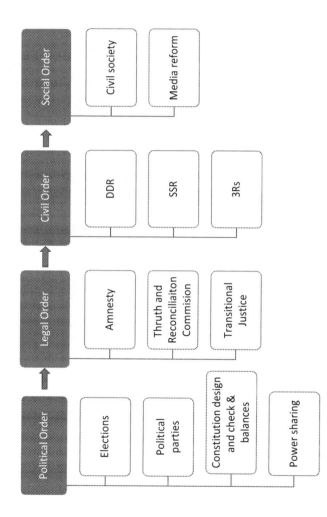

FIGURE I.7 Structure transition from civil war to democracy with five multifaceted axes. Source: Author

between 1990 and 1995. Consequently, it created a shift in the supply–demand chain to deploy peacekeepers in these newly "volatile regions." Nevertheless, despite constant appeals, the UN has historically struggled financially and operationally to face the humanitarian demand for intervention (OCHA, 2022).

Third, the "new wars" (Kaldor, 1999), the independence and anti-colonization movements, and the collapse of the Soviet Union have created a wave of official democracies that often serve as façades for warlord rule (Themnér, 2017). Post–Cold War insurgents (and states) have financed wars by looting, smuggling, and drug and human trafficking. They constitute international criminal activities and – arguably – make them more abusive to civilians. This behavior also extends to corruption, which results in the undermining of these "official" new democracies.

Moreover, peacekeeping required new approaches after some catastrophic interventions, such as in Somalia and Rwanda. From an "Agenda for Peace" (Boutros-Ghali, 1992) to the "Brahimi report" (UN-Brahimi, 2010) to the Report of the High-Level Independent Panel on Peace Operations (HIPPO-United Nations, 2015) to the Action for Peace (A4P/A4P+ 2018/2021), peacekeeping, state-building, and democracy-building have had to be re-conceptualized and adapted to the dynamic international order. Some argue that the COVID-19 pandemic and 2022 Russia's invasion of Ukraine have initiated a new world order. To keep methodological consistency, only time will tell whether this is indeed a new historical chapter in peace and stability in the 21st century. Moving away from the traditional two-sides parties, armed conflicts are more complex with the mushrooming of war factions, such as in Syria and Libya. Consequently, UN peace operations have become more complex and multidimensional as well. Nevertheless, they have not necessarily become more effective.

As for the methodology, due to the variables to be identified and tested, a mixed-methods approach was used, involving text analysis and literature review (Chapter 1–3), a cross-sectional qualitative examination of comparative policies (Chapter 5–9) and comparative quantitative analysis of different indexes available (Chapter 4). This takes into consideration 51 UN missions in operation in the period between 1989 and 2022, 31 countries with UN intervention, and 11 (approximately one-third) other countries without UN operations. Similarly, the book included field observations (Kosovo, Ireland) and open interviews with specialists.[7]

This book is not a case study of a specific post–civil war country. Instead, it analyzes several elements and tests them drawing on different intrastate conflict: Afghanistan, Bosnia-Herzegovina, Côte d'Ivoire, El Salvador, Georgia, Guinea-Bissau, Iraq, North Macedonia,[8] Mali, Mozambique, Namibia, Nepal, Nicaragua, Rwanda, South Sudan, and Western Sahara. In addition, special consideration is given to 13 countries with more than one mission: Angola, Burundi, Cambodia, Central African Republic (CAR), Croatia, Democratic Republic of the Congo (DRC), Haiti, Liberia, Sierra Leone, Somalia, Sudan, Timor-Leste, and Kosovo. The last two cases are relevant as they are sui generis operations of transitional state administration where the international organization takes responsibility for state administration and sovereignty.

To better address the dilemmas that arise in pursuing peace after civil war through processes of democratization and the impact of UN operations, text analysis was conducted under the following criteria: (1) the objectivity of the peace operations mandate, (2) financial, operational, and human costs, (3) the durability of the mission versus the durability of the peace agreement, (4) the political components of the conflict, (5) the predominance of particular countries as the major intervenors (donors' national interest versus the peacekeeping needs), (6) the concern by the international community regarding the conflict and the expectation of the UN mission, (7) the role of the international media, and (8) gender mainstreaming.

As this book considers the complex dynamic of war, democracy, and peace through international intervention, it is fundamental to analyze the *level of democratization* when investigating the *conflict cycle* and the *mandates and execution process of UN missions*. For this, a detailed qualitative design was selected to describe this phenomenon, rather than presenting numerical data. That is particularly pertinent in developing theories about people's experiences (Kumar, 2005). To best gather in-depth data, a qualitative method of inquiry provided the most effective means of addressing the research question and aims of this book. In addition, field visits to Kosovo, Ireland, and UN headquarters in New York complemented the textual analytical findings. Unstructured interviews with UN officials with experience in different missions, such as Cyprus, Sudan, Congo, Haiti, and Somalia, as well as politicians and high government officials from Kosovo, Timor-Leste, and the Philippines equally contributed to the study outcomes.[9]

Acknowledging that quantitative data are also necessary for robust findings, the use of different indexes are also employed in this book with findings presented since 2012 (ten years). These comprise the following: Democracy Index, Fragile States Index, Polity III Project, Global Peace Index, and additional data from the International Crisis Group, Intelligence Unit of The Economist, International Institute for Democracy and Electoral Assistance (IDEA), and Uppsala University. On a case-by-case basis, the book deepens the theoretical concepts of "peacebuilding," "peace enforcement," and "peacekeeping" as well as of "democracy building," "democratic reinforcement," "strengthening democracy," "state-building," and "nation-building." Depending on their methodologies, reports are published at different times throughout the year. Consequently, some findings only encompassed events and statistics until December 2021.

In addition, the book distinguishes the success of the implementation of a mission's mandate from its procedures and process (Doyle and Sambanis, 2006; Druckman and Diehl, 2013; Druckman and Diehl, 2012; Maley, 2012). Consequently, the book is guided by multi-level elements, including *micro, meso, and macro levels*. A functional cooperation with authoritarian regimes requires a multi-level perspective of objectives between political stability and democratic change (Freyburg, 2012). Furthermore, the book considers that state-building is not simply about "top-down" approaches of institution strengthening focusing on state actors and/or national elites. It also contemplates "bottom-up" approaches linking state and society by highlighting perspectives of the peace-kept and not only of the peacekeeper. When necessary, Chapter 4 provides additional methodological details.

I.8 Definitions: what are we talking about?

Some definitions are needed for a better understanding of the argument. A dilemma is considered a situation in which a choice must be made between alternatives that are both undesirable (Oxford, 2018). Contrary to policy recommendations based on what is more efficient or effective, decisions are made between what is merely possible or less unscrupulous in postwar situations. A differentiation must be made with what the literature often calls "challenges" when referring to the common difficulties that are faced in the postwar period, such as lack of infrastructure, the spread of diseases, and the absence of state governance. Challenges precede dilemmas and do not necessary mutually oppose the choice of peace or democracy. The first dilemma is the foundation of this book:

$$[\textit{transition from civil wars} : \textit{peace versus democracy}].$$

Unfortunately, the word "democracy" has been misappropriated and used as a synonym or justification for almost everything, from left and right, from same-sex marriage to pro-abortion, and even in the name of the "Democratic People's Republic of North Korea" and the "Democratic Republic of Congo." In this book, "democracy" refers to the general concept of "liberal democracy." This is to say, a political ideology and a form of government characterized by a constitution that enshrines the rule of law, an independent judiciary, a system of checks and balances between branches of government, with fair, free, periodic, and competitive universal suffrage and a distinct multiparty system, and with equal protection of human rights, civil rights, civil liberties, and political freedoms for all its people (Held, 1996; Reynolds, 2002; Dahl, 2001; Dahl, 2003). This book is based on the premise that democracy is a political arrangement that processes but never definitely resolves social conflicts (Przeworski, 1999). Very importantly, "democratic" does not mean a complete absence of social and political discord nor the mere existence of elections. Instead, "a functioning democracy serves as a *system of conflict management*, with potential conflicts channeled into constitutional arenas, such as non-violent competition between political parties, rather than armed conflict on the streets" (Reilly, 2008, p. 168). These principles are reinforced by empirical studies that emphasize the success of consolidated democracies in accommodating social cleavages and tensions through peaceful means. In the theoretical arena, the same principle of democratic peace or liberal peace is also translated at the intrastate level to the concept of "democratic civil peace" (Gleditsch et al., 2007; Doyle and Sambanis, 2006; Hegre, 2014). To better understand it, a standardization of concepts is necessary to be able to compare and analyze all the different indexes chosen for this book. The definitions below are provided by EIU (2017), EIU (2016), EIU (2015), FFP (2015), Freedom House (2017), and Freedom House (2022a).

- Full democracies: Countries in which not only fundamental political freedoms and civil liberties are respected, but these will also tend to be underpinned by a political culture conducive to the flourishing of democracy. The functioning of government is satisfactory. Media are independent and diverse. There is an effective system of state checks and balances. The judiciary is independent and judicial decisions are enforced. There are only limited problems in the functioning day-to-day democracies.
- Moderate democracies/flawed democracies/anocracies/weak democracies/partly free democracies: These countries also have free and fair elections and basic civil liberties are respected even if there are problems, such as infringements on media freedom. However, there are significant weaknesses in other aspects of democracy, including problems in governance, limited judiciary, an underdeveloped political culture, and low levels of political participation.
- Hybrid regimes: Elections have substantial irregularities that often prevent them from being both free and fair. Government pressure on opposition parties and candidates may be common. Serious weaknesses in the political culture, functioning of government, and political participation are more prevalent than in flawed democracies. Corruption tends to be widespread. The rule of law and the civil society are weak. Typically, there is harassment of journalists and the judiciary is not independent. Very often, state-building initiatives generate façade institutions where much governance and power continue to be concentrated in and implemented through informal structures, ranging from systems of patronage to regional or ethnic bonds to old political and military ties. The concept of hybrid governance (Diamond, 2002; MacGinty, 2011) can also be found under other concepts, such as neopatrimonial regimes (Zürcher et al., 2013), illiberal democracies (Zakaria, 1997), rentier states (Kahler, 2009), and Big Man politics (Utas, 2012).
- Autocracies: In these states, political pluralism is absent or heavily circumscribed. Many countries in this category are outright dictatorships. Some formal institutions of democracy may exist, but these have little substance. Elections, if they do occur, are not free and fair. There is a disregard for abuses and infringements of civil liberties. The media are typically state-owned or controlled by groups connected to the ruling regime. There is repression of criticism of the government and pervasive censorship. There is no independent judiciary.
- Failed/fragile states: The state is unable to perform its core functions and displays vulnerability in the social, political, and economic domains. Some of the most common attributes of state fragility may include the loss of physical control of its territory or a monopoly on the legitimate use of force, the erosion of legitimate authority to make collective decisions, an inability to provide reasonable public services, and the inability to interact with other states as a full member of the international community (Brock et al., 2012). As defined by the OECD a failed/ fragile state is characterized by dysfunctional political, economic, and socio- climates, with inefficient and corrupt

administrative and institutional structures, lack of rule of law and national economy, strong dependency on external actors, and limited nationhood or citizenship rights provided. Although acknowledging the theoretical differences, this book will use interchangeably the following concepts: failed, failing, collapsed, quasi, underdeveloped, disrupted, and undeveloped states (Kaplan, 2008; Menocal, 2010; Brock et al., 2012; William Maley et al., 2003). During a transition period from civil war, states are usually on a fragile situation, such as Angola, Mozambique, Cambodia, and Nicaragua.

Unless otherwise specified, the terminology "conflict" is used in this book to refer to "civil war." The term "civil war" is acutely political as it can bring legitimacy to forms of violence that would otherwise be suppressed or decried. Importantly, what makes a war "civil" often depends on whether one is a ruler or a rebel, victor or vanquished, sufferer or outsider. Calling a conflict a civil war can shape its outcome by determining whether outside powers choose to get involved or stand aside. In addition, it can convey recognition from the international community and enable various types of external support, such as economic, legal, and even military (Armitage, 2017). The peace studies body of literature usually applies the typology of the correlates of war (COW) project suggested by David Singer and Mel Small as an armed internal conflict that meets the following criteria: (a) the war has caused more than 1,000 battle deaths per year of conflict,[10] (b) the war represented a challenge to the sovereignty of an internationally recognized state, (c) the war occurred within the recognized boundary of that state, (d) the war involved the state as one of the principal combatants, and (e) the rebels were able to mount an organized military opposition to the state and to inflict significant casualties on the state (Fortna, 2008a; Stein, 1994; Collier and Sambanis, 2002; Sambanis, 2004). Notably, this includes state-based violence, non-state violence, and one-sided violence. Internal state-based violence is a conflict between two armed groups within a country, neither of which is a state, while one-sided violence is the organized use of armed force by the state against civilians, excluding extra-judicial killings (IEP, 2022).

"UN peace operations" refers to the deployment of international personnel, military and civilian, under the coordination of the UN Department of Peacekeeping Operations (DPKO)[11] to help maintain peace and security in war-torn societies. Very importantly, "peacebuilding" can be defined as "actions undertaken by international or national actors to institutionalize peace, understood as the absence of armed conflict (component of negative peace) and a modicum of participatory politics (component of positive peace) that can be sustained in the absence of an international peace operation" (Bellamy et al., 2010; Call and Cousens, 2008). The literature distinguishes peacemaking from peacekeeping and peacebuilding. It generally describes peacemaking as the political actions at the highest level, also known as "ceasefire making" and usually with the participation of war-makers. Peacekeeping is related to the military deployment on the field to enforce and "keep the peace," and peacebuilding refers to the recovery, reconstruction, and reconciliation process after the war. Not all missions are the same. Following Fortna (2008a), and besides acknowledging the different types of UN interventions, in this book, the terminology "UN peace operations" is used indistinguishably for "peacekeeping," "peacemaking," "peace missions," "traditional mission," "consent-based missions," or "peace enforcement missions" to avoid repetition. Whenever required, specifications and in-depth minutiae will be provided. Since 1 January 2019, a reform of the United Nations peace and security infrastructure created the Department of Political and Peacebuilding Affairs (DPPA) with the mandate to prevent deadly conflict and build sustainable peace around the world. DPPA monitors and assesses global political developments with an eye to detecting potential crises and devising effective responses. The Department provides support to the Secretary-General and his envoys in their peace initiatives, as well as to UN political missions around the world. As a result, it merged the former Department of Political Affairs (DPA), the United Nations Peacebuilding Support Office, and the former Department of Peacekeeping Operations (now the Department of Peace Operations, or DPO). Therefore, in this book, depending on the time of the publication, DPKO or DPO will be used interchangeably.

According to its mandate under Chapters VI or VII of UN charter, usually "six-and-half," the literature also differentiates a peacekeeping mission into categories such as preventive deployment, observation/traditional peacekeeping, wider peacekeeping, peace enforcement, assisting transitions/ multidimensional, transitional administrations, and peace support operations (Bellamy et al., 2010; Fortna, 2008a). This book will focus on operations active between 1989 and 2022 under the United Nations umbrella, regardless of whether it is consent-based or enforcement, instead of an individual country (USA) or alliance interventions or operations *only* led by regional organizations (AU, OEA, NATO).

In parallel, "state-building" refers to the set of actions undertaken by external actors, in conjunction with national counterparts, attempting to build, or rebuild, the institutions of a weaker, post-conflict, or failing state. The literature and political speeches often mention the need for a process to be nationally driven. It must include the domestic political will of the elites and the involvement of the disrupted segments of society. Nevertheless, state-building in itself is related to an area for development assistance and usually follows some form of intervention, such as a UN peacekeeping operation or bilateral cooperation projects. Although acknowledging the different nuances between state-building and peacebuilding, the literature often recognizes the nexus between them and their mutual reinforcement. Besides, both are two diverging perspectives on the same matter: an unstable social peace and a breakdown of political order. While there is no consensus definition of state-building, Paris and Sisk (2009) define it as a "subcomponent of peacebuilding" that is concerned with "the strengthening or construction of legitimate governmental institutions in countries that are emerging from conflicts." Therefore, over the past two decades, state-building has developed into becoming an integral part (and even a specific approach

– sometimes used as synonymous) to peacebuilding by the international community. The state-building approach has come to be seen as the preferred strategy for peacebuilding in a number of high-profile conflicts.

Importantly, state-building is based on threefold dimensions: security, political, and economic. Of these three, security is almost always considered the first priority for other state-building activities to succeed. Despite the central dilemma being related to democracy versus peace, there is a need to include the notion of state-building as illustrated by Figures I.2, I.3, and I.5 on the scope and objectives of the book. Thus, under the motto of "building states to build peace," the inclusion of the notion of state-building safeguards that essential aspects of the analysis will not be underestimated, nor the book results to be undervalued.

Additionally, there has been a significant shift within the international development community that state-society relations are central to state-building processes. This moves from a narrow preoccupation with building and strengthening formal institutions and state capacity toward recognizing that the state cannot be treated in isolation. As such, the core of state-building, especially "responsive" state-building, has come to be understood in terms of an effective political process through which citizens and the state can negotiate mutual demands, obligations, and expectations (Menocal, 2010). When rebuilding a collapsed state apparatus, most literature considers good governance as the element that most defines an effective state. Due to postwar challenges, most aid policies endorse a "good enough" approach to evaluate state effectiveness (SØRensen, 2001; Ottaway, 2002; Ignatieff, 2003).

I.9 Overview of the chapters

Chapter 1 is the main conceptual section of this book and fills the gaps between theory and practice on fragile states, civil wars, democratic governance, and state institution-building. It explains that hybrid forms of peace and hybrid forms of politics emerge in post-conflict places and reviews the literature regarding commonly cited dilemmas that confront peace and democracy. The chapter identifies and proposes an original structure of dilemmas that advance the field of knowledge. Due to the significant number of dilemmas, they are categorized under the clusters of Philosophical–Actors–Tactical (P–A–T) for a more practical use as an analytical tool. Finally, the chapter also presents its properties and limitations.

Chapter 2 examines the main dilemmas that the United Nations faces when enforcing peace and democracy in intrastate disputes. During transitional times, the UN frequently exacerbates the liberal peace hybridity and becomes part of the problem that it initially wanted to solve or prevent. Besides the lack of a legal basis, often caught in a limbo between Chapter VI and VII of the UN Charter, the first dilemma regarding building peace and democracy after civil war through UN operations is the intervention in itself: [intervention versus autonomy]. Based on a revision of the main theoretical pillars of international relations, a discussion follows outlining that transversal principles, such as

Westphalian sovereignty, post-Westphalian responsibility to protect (R2P) and while protecting (RwP), and contingent sovereignty are often challenges to UN operations. A revision of recent literature on UN interventions within states is given, which elucidates other dilemmas, such as legality versus legitimacy as well as the paradox of promoting democracy through a benevolent autocracy. Moreover, the "Holy Trinity" principle of neutrality, impartiality, and no use of force is juxtaposed against just, selective and preventive collective intervention. By applying the proposed P–A–T framework of transitional peacebuilding dilemmas, additional UN operations quandaries are identified in this chapter (design, moral, operational, resource, sequencing, systemic, and vertical).

Are elections worth dying for? Chapter 3 explores the democratization-violence-peace nexus that creates two main paradoxes in a post-conflict context: first, the peace and democratization processes develop new incentives for violence, particularly from elites taking advantage of the fragility of the institutions. Second, measures to fight violence can undermine democracy by violating human rights and rights to freedom. Through the analysis of elections, the media and security sector reform, it addresses why crucial driving forces such as elites, the lack of functioning state institutions and the hate media are tools for violence during transitional phases in conflict and in fragile states. Moreover, dilemmas of the causes and consequences of disruption in post-conflict scenarios are identified. Additionally, it presents the monitoring impasse. Finally, this chapter sheds light on the need to analyze transitional violence beyond the political and electoral spectrum through an integrated approach to the cycle of conflict. By including violence as a consequence and not a cause of the peace struggle, this book provides an in-depth understanding of the major quandaries in the transition from civil war to peace through democratization. As a metaphor from Collier's research on building democracy in dangerous places, it claims that from guns to doves, votes may generate more bullets than they intend to stop.

Notably, instead of focusing on why missions fail, the focus should be on understanding what makes them successful. Chapter 4 offers a cross-cutting analysis regarding whether UN peace operations help build "the state, democracy, and peace" in countries torn by civil wars. The book argues that post–civil war absence of statistical data on the positive effect of UN peace operations and successful democratization does not mean that there is no relation between the two processes. Instead, this might be evidence that they act against each other by echoing inherent dilemmas in the attempt to mutually foster stable peace and democracy in the aftermath of civil war. Away from picturing the UN as a savior or as evil, this chapter contributes to the literature with a systematic overview of UN multidisciplinary missions. It offers a study with an updated statistical analysis, a longer timeframe, and inclusion of more comparative indexes and provides a broader selection of mission cases with and without intervention. The vast majority of cases analyzed fall in the moderate category at the juncture of the double-axis of peace/war and democratic/undemocratic. Considering the elements of hybridity, and contrary to the binary arguments of success or failure, this chapter proposes five moderate perspectives: (1) "moderate level of peace, moderate level of democracy," (2) "high level of peace, moderate level of democracy," (3) "moderate level of peace, low level of democracy," (4) "low level of peace, moderate level of democracy," and (5) "low level of peace and hybrid regime." The moderate cases allow a more in-depth understanding of the different vectors of promoting conflict resolution and democratization. Being "stuck" in a meso level might mean success and not a failure despite a high probability of returning to violence or to authoritarianism. A "good enough" quality level to prepare a mission exit strategy and avoid being trapped in a systemic dilemma and becoming part of the conflict.

The remaining chapters are devoted to investigating various clusters of dilemmas that form the substance of this book's findings. Chapter 5 explores the dilemmas related to elections and the transformation of rebel groups into legitimate political parties. Although democratization is obviously not all about the ballot vote, elections are a condition sine qua non of democracy. Importantly, elections are widely seen as an integral part of war termination, international (dis)engagement, and nation-building processes. Postwar elections also permeate horizontal, vertical, systemic, temporal, existential, design, financial, moral, operational, resource, security, sequencing, and transparency dilemmas. Moreover, the conversion of ex-armed groups into political parties has been recognized as crucial for the success of various peace processes. However, their inclusion and participation also have, in several instances, proven problematic for the democratization process; they also face the same set of transitional dilemmas. It seems a contradiction in terms if victorious guerrilla fighters become democratic rulers.

Chapter 6 discusses how to move from the "rule of the gun" toward the "rule of power" through constitution-building and power-sharing. Politics is frequently about interests and power. When the pen fails, the sword historically rules. Besides extensive literature on democratization and checks and balances, power-sharing specific to post-conflict situations remains limited by political science and related disciplines such as conflict resolution and peace studies. Under the concept of consociational democracy, constitutional architecture must foresee an arrangement for power division, the separation of power, the competition for power, and, most of all, the balance of power and the alternation of power. Power-sharing institutions and power-sharing arrangements present alternatives to "shared rule" and "self-rule" in postwar societies, including economic resources, military, and cultural power-sharing mechanisms. This chapter focuses on state-building and explores in-depth how those political arrangements can be good for peacebuilding in the short term but can limit democracy in the long term and vice versa. It shows that the process of constitutional and power-sharing design is a mixture of obstructionism and opportunism. Consequently, P–A–T dilemmas must be managed for a successful transition.

Chapter 7 analyzes the dilemmas regarding transitional justice in terms of various cross-cutting issues: amnesty, human rights, a truth and reconciliation commission, and ad hoc tribunals as well as transitional law and justice sector reform. Although much has been said about transitional justice, the literature is limited regarding a proper systematization of the main controversies of the process that go beyond political, legal, or philosophical perspectives. That is to say, the literature often overstates the problems of morality, financial costs, time extensiveness, the inefficiency of international courts, unstable institutions, and the fragility of domestic legal apparatuses. Legal challenges that are usually undermined or ignored are identified in this chapter. Second, it points out that transitional justice is not limited to the "will for justice" as a moral social need. Instead, it claims that it is essential to avoid the conflict cycle and moving toward sustainable peace and liberal democracy. Amnesty, as a tool for stability, places peace and conflict resolution before justice and human rights. Consequently, it presents the amnesty process as a necessary evil for peace without justice. In contrast, truth and reconciliation commissions and ad hoc war crime tribunals might be pseudo-democratic variables for peace with limited justice. As for the legal limbo in the postwar context, evidence shows that traditional law might be the antithesis of the new democratic rule of law and may place human rights subject to different arguments for the same verdict. The chapter concludes that post-conflict transitional justice is a hybrid dynamic process: it can be peaceful and undemocratic as much as democratic and violent.

Chapter 8 highlights security as an opposing variable between peace and democracy. DDR and SSR are critical factors in state-building to bring back "order, law, and security" and move away from the myth of "once a soldier, always a soldier." Nevertheless, the process of silencing guns faces important dilemmas between a just enough approach to securing peace by disarming the conflict or democratically governing insecurity. A case study on CAR shows failure. A case study on Timor-Leste's experience shed light on the security sector's "non-reform" through the common practice of transforming guerrilla resistance groups into the national army. The key to success is to rethink integrated provisions that enable the movement from "interim stabilization" toward "democratic security promotion." Importantly, replacing a combatant-centric approach with a perspective that addresses the intermediary level is proposed: the inescapable relationships among elites, commanders, and the local community. Finally, it concludes that security matters and effectiveness depend more and more on cooperation and coordination among state and non-state actors.

Chapter 9 focuses on the "demos"; the people. Under the hybrid reality of postwar settings, the inclusion of civil society might be both an obstacle and an instrument to the transition to an enduring social order. The concept of "good governance" as a joint obligation of citizens and the state as well as the bottom-up approach of peacebuilding (instead of the usual top-down perspective) are explored. An analysis is given of the role of the media, the importance of media reform in building a peace-sustaining media platform, as well as the modern concept of mediocracy. It elucidates that a vibrant civil society and peace-promoting media are the effect of a well-functioning democratic state and not its cause. Without civic ownership and media reform, the reconstitution of social order in disrupted settings is unlikely to be self-reinforcing and sustainable. Therefore, it argues that active citizenship must be placed at the center of conflict resolution, not at its receiving end.

Notes

1 1975 marks the start of a decolonization era with several countries in Africa and Southeast Asia becoming independent and officially adopting a democratic regime.
2 According to the United Nations Peacekeeping website (28/04/2022), the data are filtered on mission, which keeps 12 peacekeeping operations of 24 active missions.
3 Data published on 13 May 2022.
4 The tracker focuses on anti-government protests. It excludes rallies in support of a political cause, party, or political figure CARNEGIE ENDOWERMENT FOR INTERNATIONAL PEACE 2022. Global Protest Tracker. *weakly*. 02/05/2022 ed. Washington, DC: Carnegie Endowement for International Peace.
5 *Freedom in the World 2022* assessed 210 countries and territories around the globe (195 countries and 15 territories).
6 "World" population refers to the total population of the 167 countries covered by the Index EIU 2021. Democracy Index: The China challenge. Economic Intelligence Unit.
7 Interviews with key academic experts on civil war transitions from Department of Peace and Conflict Research of the Uppsala University in Sweden, including Anna Jarstad whose work inspired this research *(From War to Democracy: Dilemmas of Peacebuilding _2008)*. I express my deepest thanks also to all those who contributed with special insights during field trips in Kosovo and Serbia and interviews in the United States (Institute of Economics and Peace and UN HQ), Ireland, and Northern Ireland. Special thanks go to all senior current and former UN officials of DPKO, DPA, UNMIK, UNMIT, MINUSTAH, and MINUCA, and members of the Presidency and the Parliament of Kosovo and the Presidency of the Philippines, whose name are preserved for ethical and security reasons. Very importantly, former president of Timor-Leste and Nobel Peace laureate José Ramos-Horta provided key contributions.
8 Updated. The Prespa agreement, also known as the Treaty of Prespa, the Prespa agreement or the Prespa accord, signed in 2018, entry into force on 12 February 2019, establishes constitutional name change to the Republic of North Macedonia *erga omnes*. Thus, for the purpose of UN operations analysis, the name Macedonia or North Macedonia will be used interchangeably in this book depending on the year.
9 For security purposes and ethical clearance, their identities are kept confidential unless specified in the book.
10 The Uppsala Conflict Data Program (UCDP) offers a number of data sets on organized violence and peacemaking. It defines armed conflict if it results in at least 25 battle-related deaths in one calendar year. www.pcr.uu.se/research/ucdp/definitions/.
11 It is important to understand the evolution of UN peace operations. The Department of Peace Keeping Operations was created in 1992. Since 1947, most of the operations were under the Department of Political Affairs. Thus, some missions that were established before DPKO but still in execution during the period 1989–2022 will also be analyzed for methodological consistency.

References

Aljazeera. 2015. Boko Haram threatens to disrupt Nigeria poll. *Aljazeera*, 18 Feb 2015 05:55 GMT.
Alsadi, W. 2007. *La democracia en America Latina, un barco a la deriva*. Fondo de Cultura Economica.
Annan, K. 2002. Democracy as an International Issue. *Global Governance*, 8, 135–142.
Armitage, D. 2017. *Civil Wars: A History in Ideas*. Penguin Canada.
Baker, P. 2001. Conflict Resolution versus Democratic Governance: Divergent Paths to Peace? *In*: Hampson, F. O., Crocker, C. A. & Aall, P. (eds.) *Turbulent Peace: The Challenges of Managing International Conflict*. United States Institute of Peace Press.

Banbury, A. 2016. I Love the U.N., but It Is Failing. *New York Times*.
Bellamy, A. J., Williams, P. D. & Griffin, S. 2010. *Understanding Peacekeeping*. Polity Press.
Bermeo, N. 2003. What the Democratization Literature Says-or Doesn't Say-About Postwar Democratization. *Global Governance*, 9, 159–77.
Boege, V., Brown, A., Clements, K. & Nolan, A. 2009. Building Peace and Political Community in Hybrid Political Orders. *International Peacekeeping*, 16, 599–615.
Börzel, T. A. & Grimm, S. 2018. Building Good (Enough) Governance in Postconflict Societies & Areas of Limited Statehood: The European Union & the Western Balkans. *Daedalus*, 147 Ending Civil Wars: Constraints & Possibilities, 116–127.
Boutros-Ghali. 1992. An Agenda for Peace. *Preventive Diplomacy, Peacemaking, and Peace-Keeping*. United Nations.
Boutros-Ghali. 1994. *An Agenda for Development*. United Nations.
Bratton, M. & Van De Walle, N. 1997. *Democratic Experiments in Africa: Regime Transitions in Comparative Perspective*. Cambridge University Press.
Brock, L., Holm, H.-H., Sorensen, G. & ET Stohl, M. 2012. *Fragile States: War and Conflict in the Modern World*.
Brown, M. 2001. *Ethnic and Internal Conflicts. Causes and Implications*. United States Institute of Peace.
Brownlee, J. 2009. Potents of Pluralism: How Hybrid Regimes Affect Democratic Transition. *American Journal of Political Science*, 53, 515–532.
Burlamaqui, L., & Kattel, R. 2019. *Schumpeter's Capitalism, Socialism and Democracy: A Twenty-First-Century Agenda*. Routledge.
Burnell, P. 2004. Democracy Promotion: The Elusive Quest for Grand Strategies. *Internationale Politik und Gesellschaft*, 100–116.
Burnell, P. 2006. *Promoting Democracy Backwards*. Fundación para las Relaciones Internacionales y el Diálogo Exterior (FRIDE). Nov 2006.
Call, C. & Cousens, E. M. 2008. Ending Wars and Building Peace: International Responses to War-Torn Societies. *International Studies Perspectives*, 9, 1–21.
Carnegie Endowment For International Peace. 2022. Global Protest Tracker. *Weakly*. 02/05/2022 ed. Carnegie Endowment for International Peace.
Carothers, T. 2002. The End of the Transition Paradigm. *Journal of Democracy*, 13, 5–21.
Carothers, T. 2006. Does Democracy Promotion Have a Future? In the Backlash Against Democracy Promotion. *Foreign Affairs*, march/april 2006, 55–68.
Carothers, T. 2007. The "Sequencing" Fallacy. *Journal of Democracy*, 18, 12–27.
Chester A. Crocker, F. O. H. & Aall, P. R. 2001. *Turbulent Peace: The Challenges of Managing International Conflict*. United States Institute of Peace Press.
Chesterman, S., Ignatieff, M. & Thakur, R. 2006. *Making States Work : State Failure and the Crisis of Governance*. United Nations University Press.
Collier, P. 1999. On the Economic Consequences of Civil War. *Oxford Economic Papers*, 51, 168–183.
Collier, P. 2009. War, Guns and Votes: Democracy in Dangerous Places. *Economic Affairs*, 29, 104.
Collier, P. & Hoeffler, A. 1998. On Economic Causes of Civil War. *Oxford Economic Papers*, 50, 563–573.
Collier, P. & Sambanis, N. 2002. Understanding Civil War: A New Agenda. *The Journal of Conflict Resolution*, 46, 3–12.
Collier, P., Hoeffler, A. & Söderbom, M. 2004. On the Duration of Civil War. *Journal of Peace Research*, 41, 253–73.
Crocker, H. & AALL 2001. *Turbulent Peace*.
Dahl, R. A. 2001. *Sobre a Democracia*.

Dahl, R. A. 2003. *Democracy Sourcebook*. MIT Press.
De Zeeuw, J. 2005. Projects Do Not Create Institutions: The Record of Democracy Assistance in Post-Conflict Societies. *Democratization*, 12, 481–504.
Di Palma, G. 1990. *To Craft Democracies: An Essay on Democratic Transitions*. University of California Press.
Diamond, L. J. 2016. Democracy in Decline. *Foreign Affairs,* July/August 2016.
Diamond, L. J. 2002. Thinking about Hybrid Regimes'. *Journal of Democracy*, 13, 21–35.
Diehl, P. 2014. Breaking the Conflict Trap: The Impact on Peacekeeping on Violence and Democratization in Post-conflict Context. Workshop "What Do We Know About Civil Wars?". University of Iowa.
Diehl, P. F., Jennifer, R. & Hensel, P. R. 1996. United Nations Intervention and Recurring Conflict. *In: International Organization 50*(4), 683–700.
Dominguez, J. E. 2003. *Conflictos territoriales y democracia en América Latina*. Siglo Veintiuno Editores Argentina.
Doyle, M. W. & Sambanis, N. 2006. *Making War and Building Peace: United Nations Peace Operations*. Princeton University Press.
Druckman, D. & Diehl, P. F. 2012. Peace Operation Success: The Evaluation Framework. *Journal of International Peacekeeping*, 16, 209–225.
Druckman, D. & Diehl, P. F. 2013. *Peace Operation Success: A Comparative Analysis*. Martinus Nijhoff Publishers.
EIU. 2015. *Democracy Index 2014: Democracy and Its Discontents*. The Economist Intelligence Unit.
EIU. 2016. *Democracy Index 2015: Democracy in an Age of Anxiety*. The Economist Intelligence Unit.
EIU. 2017. *Democracy Index 2016:Revenge of the "Deplorables"*. 9th ed. The Economist Intelligence Unit.
EIU. 2018. *Democracy Index 2017: Free Speech Under Attack*. The Economist. Intelligence Unit.
EIU. 2019. *Democracy Index 2019: A Year of Democratic Backsliding and Popular Protest*. Economist Intelligence Unit.
EIU. 2020. *Democracy Index: In sikness and in Health?* Economist Intelligence Unit.
EIU. 2021. *Democracy Index: The China Challenge*. Economic Intelligence Unit.
Elman, M. F. 1999. *Path to Peace: Is democracy the Answer?* CSIA Studies in International Security. MIT Press.
EU COMMISSION. 2021. *Eurobarometer 96.2*. European Parliament.
EU COMMISSION. 2022. *EU Aid in Fragile and Conflict-Affected Countries*. European Commission.
Evans, M. 2012. Just War, Democracy, Democratic Peace. *European Journal of Political Theory*, 11, 191–208.
Fazal, T. M. 2014. *Is War in Decline? Global Observatory*. International Peace Institute.
Fearon, J. D. 2017. Civil War & the Current International System. *Dædalus*, 146.
FFP. 2015. *Fragile State Index*. Fund for Peace.
FFP. 2016. *Fragile State Index*. Washington-DC: Fund for Peace.
FFP. 2018. *Fragile State Index*. Washington-DC: Fund for Peace.
FFP. 2021. *Fragile State Index*. Washington-DC: Fund for Peace.
FFP. 2022. *Fragile State Index*. Fund for Peace.
Fortna, V. P. 2008a. *Does Peacekeeping Work? Shaping Belligerents' Choices After Civil War*. Princeton University Press.
Fortna, V. P. 2008b. Peacebuilding and Democratization. *In:* Jarstad, A. K. A. T. D. S. (ed.) *From War to Democracy: Dilemmas of Peacebuilding*. Cambridge University Press.
FP 2022. 10 Ideas to Fix Democracy. *Foreign Policy*. Washington-DC.

Freedom House. 2015. *Freedom in the World 2015: Discarding Democracy: Return to the Iron Fist*. 9th ed. Freedom House.
Freedom House. 2016. *Freedom in the World 2016. Anxious Dictators, Wavering Democracies: Global Freedom under Pressure*. Freedom House.
Freedom House. 2017. *Freedom in the World 2017: Populists and Autocrats:The Dual Threat to Global Democracy*. Freedom House.
Freedom House. 2018. *Freedom in the World 2018: Democracy in Crisis*. Freedom House.
Freedom House. 2019. *Freedom in the World 2019: Democracy in Retreat*. Freedom House.
Freedom House. 2020. *Freedom in the World: A Leaderless Struggle for Democracy*. Freedom House.
Freedom House. 2021a. *Freedom World 2021: Democracy under Siege*. Freedom House.
Freedom House. 2021b. *Nation in Transit: The Anti-democratic Turn*.
Freedom House. 2022a. *Freedom of the World 2022: The Global Expansion of Authoritarian Rule*. Freedom House.
Freedom House. 2022b. *Nation in transit 2022: From Democratic Decline to Authoritarian Aggression*. Freedom House.
Freyburg, T. 2012. The Two Sides of Functional Cooperation with Authoritarian Regimes: A Multi-level Perspective on the Conflict of Objectives Between Political Stability and Democratic Change. *In*: Leininger, J., Grimm, S & Freyburg, T (ed.) *Do all Good Things Go Together? Conflicting Objectives in Democracy Promotion*. Routledge.
Fukuyama, F. 1991. Liberal Democracy as a Global Phenomenon. *Political Science and Politics*, 24, 659.
Fukuyama, F. 2006. *The End of History and the Last Man*. Free Press.
Fukuyama, F. 2017. *State Building: Governance and World Order in the 21st Century*. Profile Books.
Fukuyama, F., Kagan, R., Diamond, L., Carothers, T., Plattner, M. F., Schmitter, P. C., Levitsky, S., Way, L. & Rice, C. 2015. *Democracy in Decline?* Johns Hopkins University Press.
Galtung, J. 1998. *La transformación de conflictos por medios pacíficos. El método trascendente*. Asociación Nacional Presencia Gitana.
Gandhi, J. & Vreeland, J. 2004. Political Institutions and Civil War: Unpacking Anocracy. *Journal of Conflict Resolution*, 52(3), 401–425.
Gärtner, H., Honig, J. W. & Akbulut, H. 2015. *Democracy, Peace, and Security*. Lexington Books.
Gat, A. 2012. Is War Declining – And Why? *Journal of Peace Research*, 50, 149–157.
Gauchet, M. 2004. *La democracia contra si misma*. HomoSapiens Ediciones.
Geddes, B. 1999. What Do We Know about Democratization after Twenty Years? *Annual Review of Political Science*, 2, 115–144.
Ghani, A. & Lockhar, C. 2008. *Fixing Failed States: A Framework for Rebuilding a Fractured World*. Oxford University Press.
Gillies, D. 2011. *Elections in Dangerous Places: Democracy and the Paradoxes of Peacebuilding*. McGill-Queen's University Press.
Gleditsch, N. P., Hegre, H. & Strand, H. 2007. *Democracy and Civil War*. University of Michigan Press.
Goldstein, J. S. 2012. *Winning the War on War: The Decline of Armed Conflict Worldwide*. Plume.
Gottfried, P. 2013. *War and Democracy*. Arktos Media.
Gowa, J. 2011. *Ballots and Bullets: The Elusive Democratic Peace*. Princeton University Press.
Grindle, M. S. 2007. Good Enough Governance Revisited. *Development Policy Review*, 25, 553–574.

Guéhenno, J.-M. 2018. The United Nations & Civil Wars. *Daedalus*, 147, 185–196.
Haavelsrud, M. 2005. Resolución de conflictos pacífica: Perspectivas educativas. *Congreso Mundial de Cultura de Paz*.
Hegre, H. 2014. Democracy and Armed Conflict. *Journal of Peace Research*, 51, 159–172.
Hegre, H., Ellingsen, T., Gates, S. & Gleditsch, N. P. 2001. Toward a Democratic Civil Peace? Democracy, Political Change, and Civil War, 1816–1992. *American Political Science Review*, 95.
Heintze, H. J. & Thielbörger, P. 2015. *From Cold War to Cyber War: The Evolution of the International Law of Peace and Armed Conflict over the last 25 Years*. Springer International Publishing.
Held, D. 1996. *Models of Democracy*. Stanford University Press.
Henderson, E. A. 2002. *Democracy and War: The End of an Illusion?* Lynne Rienner Publishers.
HIIK. 2017. *Conflict Barometer 2016*. Heidelberg Institute for International Conflict Research, 25.
HIIK 2022. *Conflict Barometer 2021*. March 2022 ed. Heidelberg Institute for International Conflict Research.
Hippo-United Nations. 2015. *Report of the High-level Independent Panel on Peace Operations on Uniting Our Strengths for Peace: Politics, Partnership and People-HIPPO*. In: Nations, U. (ed.) A/70/95-S/2015/446. United Nations.
Horowitz, D. 1985. *Ethnic Groups in Conflict-Group Comparison and the Sources of Conflict*. Berkeley, US. University of California Press.
Howard, L. M. 2008. *UN Peacekeeping in Civil Wars*. Cambridge University Press.
Howard, L. M. 2019. Peacekeeping is Not Counterinsurgency. *International Peacekeeping*, 26, 545–548.
Huntington, S. 1996. The Clash of Civilizations? Simon & Schuster, US.
IDEA. 2021. *The Global State of Democracy 2021: Building Resilience in a Pandemic Era*.
IEP. 2014. *Global Peace Index*. Institute for Economics and Peace. Sydney, Australia.
IEP. 2017. *Global Peace Index*. 11th ed. Institute of Economics and Peace. Simon & Schuster.
IEP. 2018. *Global Peace Index*. Institute of Economics and Peace. Sydney, Australia.
IEP. 2021. *Global Peace Index*. Institute of Economics and Peace. Sydney, Australia.
IEP. 2022. *Global Peace Index 2022*. Institute of Economics and Peace. Sydney, Australia.
Ignatieff, M. 2003. *State Failure and Nation-Building*.
International Crisis Group. 2022. *Crisis Watch: Tracking Conflict Worldwide*. April 2022 ed. International Crisis Group.
Issacharoff, S. 2015. The Democratic Risk to Democratic Transitions. *Constitutional Court Review*, Vol. V, p.1–31 by Juta and Company.
Jarstad, A. 2015. *Democratization after Civil War: Timing and Sequencing of Peacebuilding Reforms*. Centre for Research on Peace and Development (CRPD).
Jarstad, A. & Belloni, R. 2012. Introducing Hybrid Peace Governance: Impact and Prospects of Liberal Peacebuilding. *Global Governance*, 18.
Jarstad, A. K. 2009. The Prevalence of Power Sharing: Exploring the Patterns of Post-Election Peace. *African Spectrum*, 46, 41–62.
Jarstad, A. K. & Sisk, T. D. 2008. *From War to Democracy: Dilemmas of Peacebuilding*, Cambridge University Press.
Kahler, M. 2009. Statebuilding after Afghanistan and Iraq. In: Sisk, R. P. A. T. (ed.) *The Dilemmas of Statebuilding: Confronting the Contradictions of Postwar Peace Operations*. Routledge.
Kaldor, M. 1999. *New and Old Wars: Organized Violence in a Global Era Paperback*. Polity Press.
Kaplan, S. D. 2008. *Fixing Fragile States: A New Paradigm for Development*. Greenwood Publishing group. US.
Karl Derouen, J. 2014. *An Introduction to Civil Wars*. University of Alabama.

Kaspersen, L., & Strandsbjerg, J. 2017. *Does War Make States? Investigations of Charles Tilly's Historical Sociology*. Cambridge University Press.

Kazharski, A. & Macalova, S. 2020. Democracies: "Sovereign" and "Illiberal". The Russian-Hungarian Game of Adjectives and Its Implications for Regional Security. *Journal of Regional Security*, 15, 235–262.

Kim, D. H. 2007. *Nurturing Peace: United Nations Peacebuilding Operations in the Aftermath of Intrastate Conflicts, 1945–2002*. 3269685 Ph.D., University of Missouri - Saint Louis.

Klare, M. 2002. Resource Wars: The New Landscape of Global Conflict. 1–50, 213–226.

Kreutz, J. 2010. How and when armed conflicts end: Introducing the UCDP Conflict Termination dataset. *Journal of Peace Research*, New York: Henry Holg Publishers, 47, 243–250.

Kultgen, J. H. & Lenzi, M. 2006. *Problems for Democracy*. VIBS, Value of Inquiry Book Series, v. 181, Rodopi, Netherlands.

Kumar, R. 2005. *Research Methodology: A Step-by-Step Guide for Beginners*. Pearson Longman, UK.

Leininger, J., Grimm, S. & Freyburg, T. 2012. *Do all Good Things Go Together? Conflicting Objectives in Democracy Promotion*. Routledge.

Levitsky, S. & Ziblatt, D. 2018. *How Democracies Die*. Crown.

Levy, J. S. 1988. Domestic Politics and War. *The Journal of Interdisciplinary History*, 18, 661–62.

Levy, J. S. 2001. *Theories of Interstate and Intrastate War. A Level of Analysis Approach*. In: Turbulent Peace, edited by Crocker, Hampson and Aall. Washington DC: United States Institute of Peace. 3–27.

Lockhart, C. 2018. Sovereignty Strategies: Enhancing Core Governance Functions as a Postconflict & Conflict-Prevention Measure. *Daedalus*, 147 Ending Civil Wars: Constraints & Possibilities, 90–103.

MAC Ginty, R. 2011. *International Peacebuilding and Local Resistance: Hybrid Forms of Peace*. Palgrave Macmillan.

Maley, W. 2012. Introduction: Peace Operations and their Evaluation. *Journal of International Peacekeeping*, 16, p. 199–207.

Mansfield, E. D. & Snyder, J. 1995a. Democratization and War. Foreign Affairs Vol. 74, ed 3, p. 79–97 US.

Mansfield, E. D. & Snyder, J. 1995b. Democratization and the Danger of War. *International Security*, 20, 5–38. Cambridge, MIT press.

Mansfield, E.D. & Snyder, J. 2005a. *Prone to Violence: The Paradox of the Democratic Peace*. National Interest, Inc.

Mansfield, E. D. & Snyder, J. 2005b. When Ballots Bring on Bullets Democratic Deceptions II. 3rd ed. *International Herald Tribune*, p.Newspaper Article.

Marshall, M. G. & Gurr, T. R. 2015. *Polity IV: Center for Systemic Peace and Integrated Network for Social Conflict Research*. https://www.systemicpeace.org/polityproject. Online database

Mazarr, M. J. 2014. The Rise and Fall of the Failed-State Paradigm. Requiem for a Decade of Distraction. *Foreign Affairs*.

Mazzuca, S. L. & Munck, G.L. 2014. State or Democracy First? Alternative Perspectives on the State-Democracy Nexus. *Democratization*, 21, 1221–1243.

Menocal, A. R. 2010. *State-building for Peace: A New Paradigm for International Engagement in Post-Conflict Fragile States?* Robert Schuman Centre for Advances Studies.

Mouffe, C. 2003. *La paradoja democrática*. Gedisa, Spain.

Mross, K. 2018. First Peace, then Democracy? Evaluating Strategies of International Support at Critical Junctures after Civil War. *International Peacekeeping*, 26, 190–215.

Newman, E. 2009. Conflict Research and the 'Decline' of Civil War. *Civil Wars*, 11, 255–278.

O' Donnel, G. 1992. *Delegative Democracy*. No.192.
OCHA. 2022. *Global Humanitarian Overview*. 2022 ed. OCHA.
Oliver, P. R. & Jason, F. 2009. *Liberal Peace Transitions: Between Statebuilding and Peacebuilding*. Oxford University Press.
Ottaway, M. 2002. Rebuilding State Institutions in Collapsed States. *Development and Change*, 1001–1023.
Oxford, D. 2018. *Oxford Dictionaries*.
Paris, R. 2004. *At War's End: Building Peace after Civil Conflict*. Cambridge University Press.
Paris, R. & Sisk, T. 2009. *The Dilemmas of Statebuilding: Confronting the Contradictions of Postwar Peace Operations*. Routledge.
Parry, G. & Moran, M. 1994. *Democracy and Democratization*. Routledge.
Patrick, S. 2006. Weak States and Global Threats: Fact or Fiction? *Washington Quarterly*, 29, 27–53.
Pinker, S. 2011. *The Better Angels of Our Nature: The Decline of Violence In History And Its Causes*, Penguin Books Limited.
Press, B. & Carothers, T. 2022. The Four Dynamics That Drove Protests in 2021. *Carnegie Endowment for International Peace*, January 13, 2022.
Przeworski, A. 1999. Minimalist Conception of Democracy: A Defense. *In*: Hacker-Cordon, I. S. A. C. (ed.) *In Democracy's Value*. Cambridge University Press.
Ray, A. 2012. *Peace Is Everybody's Business: A Strategy for Conflict Prevention*. SAGE India.
Ray, J. L. 1998. Does Democracy Cause Peace? *Annual Review of Political Sciences*.
Reilly, B. 2008. Post-war Elections: Uncertain Turning Points of Transition. *In*: Jarstad, A. K. A. T. D. S. (ed.) *From War to Democracy: Dilemmas of Peacebuilding*. Cambridge University Press.
Reynal-Querol, M. 2005. Does Democracy Preempt Civil Wars? *European Journal of Political Economy*, 21, 445–465.
Reynolds, A. 2002. *The Architecture of Democracy: Constitutional Design, Conflict Management, and Democracy*. Oxford University Press - Special.
Richmond, O. P. 2013. Failed Statebuilding Versus Peace Formation. *Cooperation and Conflict*, 48, 378–400.
Richmond, O. P. 2015. The Dilemmas of a Hybrid Peace: Negative or Positive? *Cooperation and Conflict*, 50, 50–68.
Risse, T. & Stollenwerk, E. 2018. Limited Statehood Does Not Equal Civil War. *Daedalus*, 147 Ending Civil Wars: Constraints & Possibilities, 104–115.
Roeder, P. G. & Rothchild, D. 2005. *Sustainable Peace: Power and Democracy after Civil Wars*. Cornell University Press.
Russett, B. 1993. *Grasping the Democratic Peace: Principles for a Post-Cold War World*. Princeton: Princeton University Press, US.
Rustow, A. D. 1970a. Transitions to Democracy: Toward a Dynamic Model. *Comparative Politics*, 2, 337–363.
Sambanis, N. 2004. What Is Civil War? Conceptual and Empirical Complexities of an Operational Definition. *The Journal of Conflict Resolution*, 48, 814–858.
Savun, B. & Tirone, D. C. 2011. Foreign Aid, Democratization, and Civil Conflict: How Does Democracy Aid Affect Civil Conflict? *American Journal of Political Science*, 55, 233–246.
Schlumberger, O. 2006. Dancing with Wolves: Dilemmas of Democracy Promotion in Authoritarian Contexts. *In*: Jung, D. (ed.) *Democratization and Development: New Political Strategies for the Middle East*. Palgrave Macmillan.
Shaw, S. E. 2006. *Building Peace and Democracy or Organizing Exit: Elections and United Nations Peace Operations*. Dalhousie University (Canada).

Sørensen, G. 2001. War and State-Making: Why Doesn't it Work in the Third World? *Security Dialogue*, 32, 341–354.
Stein, C. M. 1994. Stopping the Killing: How Civil Wars End (Book). *Contemporary Sociology*, 23, 387–388.
Swain, A., Amer, R., Öjendal, J., Humanistisk-Samhällsvetenskapliga, V., Samhällsvetenskapliga, F., Uppsala, U. & Institutionen För Freds- Och, K. 2009. *The Democratization Project: Opportunities and Challenges*. Anthem Press.
Themnér, A. E. 2017. *Warlord Democrats in Africa: Ex-Military Leaders and Electoral Politics*.
Totten, M. J. 2014. Year Four: The Arab Spring Proved Everyone Wrong. *World Affairs*, July/August 2014.
UCDP. 2017. *Uppsala Conflict Data Program. Yearly*. Uppsala.
UCDP. 2022. *Uppsala Conflict Data Program. Yearly*. Uppsala.
UN-BRAHIMI. 2010. *Brahimi Report- Comprehensive Review of the Whole Question of Peacekeeping Operations in All Their Aspects*. UN General Assembly Security Council Fifty-fifth Session A/55/305–S/2000/809.
UN-DPKO. 2009. *A New Partnership Agenda. Charting a New Horizon for UN Peacekeeping*.
UN-DPKO. 2015. United Nations Peacekeeping [Online]. Available: http://www.un.org/en/peacekeeping/about/dpko/ [Accessed 06 Feb 2015].
UN-DPKO. 2022. *List of Peacekeeping Operations*. UN.
UN. 1945. *Charter of the United Nations* [Online]. Available: http://www.un.org/en/documents/charter/ [Accessed 28.02.2015].
UN. 2020. *A New Era of Conflict and Violence*. United Nations.
UNDP. 2009. *Governance in Conflict Prevention and Recovery: A Guidance Note*. United Nations Development Program.
UNHCR. 2022. Operational Data Portal_ Ukraine Crisis. *Daily*. UNHCR.
Uri, S. 2008. *Peace First: A New Model to End War*. Berrett-Koehler Publishers.
Utas, M. 2012. *African Conflicts and Informal Power: Big Men and Networks*. Zed Books.
Verrill, D. L. 2011. *United Nations Peacekeeping Missions: The Effect of Peacekeepers on Mission Effectiveness*. 3464848 Ph.D., The University of Texas at Dallas.
Vincent Ashcroft, A. L. & Lockhart, C. 2017. *State Building in Conflict-Affected & Fragile States: A Comparative Study*. Institute of State Effectiveness.
Wantchekon, L. 2004. The Paradox of Warlord Democracy: A Theoretical Investigation. *American Political Science Review*, 80(98), 17–33.
Watts, S. 2008. *Enforcing Democracy? Assessing the Relationship between Peace Operations and Post- Conflict Democratization*. Amherst Paper prepared for the annual meeting of the International Studies Association, Chicago, February 28 – March 3, 2007. University of Massachussets.
William, M., Sampford, C. & Thakur, R. 2003. *From Civil Strife to Civil Society: Civil and Military Responsibilities in Disrupted States*. United Nations University Press.
Woodward, S. 2017. *The Ideology of Failed States: Why Intervention Fails*. Cambridge University Press.
Zakaria, F. 1997. The Rise of Illiberal Democracy. *Foreign Affairs*, 76, 22–43.
Zartman, W. 1995. *The Elusive Peace*.
Zaum, D., Lowe, V., Roberts, A. & Welsh, J. 2008. *The United Nations Security Council and War: The Evolution of Thought and Practice Since 1945*. Oxford University Press.
Zeeuw, J. D. 2004. *How to Make Democracy Assistance More Effective? Recommendations for Doing It Differently*. European Conference 'Enhancing the European Profile in Democracy Assistance'.
Zürcher, C., Manning, C., Evenson, K., Hayman, R., Riese, S. & Roehner, N. 2013. *Costly Democracy: Peacebuilding and Democratization After War*. Stanford University Press.

PART I
Transitional dilemmas, violent democracies, and the United Nations's statecraft

1

THE TRANSITION *FROM CIVIL WAR TO HYBRID PEACE*

14 dilemmas of peace, democracy, and state-building in post-conflict societies

> Peace cannot be kept by force.
> It can only be achieved through understanding.
> *Albert Einstein Einstein (1931, p. 3)*

Why do civil war-torn countries so rarely emerge as resilient democracies with sustainable peace? At the best of times, political transitions are typically periods with a heightened risk of instability. The path toward a liberal peace is built on post-conflict reconciliation conditions very different from those that predominate in a stable state. As illustrated by Figure I.2 (Introduction), institutions, freedoms, and security are associated with, respectively, the concepts of state, democracy, and peace. At a war's end, they all must be "built." Nevertheless, the pathway to post-conflict reconciliation toward a liberal peace requires hard choices: prioritizing peace in the aftermath of conflict might undermine the foundations of democracy and, conversely, prioritizing democracy can precipitate a return to war (Jarstad and Sisk, 2008). Ideally, political speeches exhaustively and rhetorically reiterate the wish for peace and democracy after the war as if it was the "only" form of government possible. Despite a large body of literature dealing with post-conflict peacebuilding, there is no one-size-fits-all consensus about how to minimize the turbulent effects of the transition to peace and, hence, also how to build an effective democratic state after conflict.

In the aftermath of armed conflict, there is a coexistence of hybrid forms of peace, with violent and non-violent aspects, along with hybrid forms of politics, with democratic and authoritarian elements. Hybrid peace commonly occurs where the distinction between armed conflict and peace, as well as what constitutes the political regime, is blurred. Although hybridity already exists before the deployment of an international peacebuilding mission, UN operations are at the center of hybrid forms of peace along with hybrid forms of politics.

DOI: 10.4324/9781003279976-3

When international actors impose such hybrid forms of peace and politics via a top-down approach, international norms and values might compete with local interests and identities. As a result, they often end up exacerbating this hybrid transitional milieu. Beyond the dilemmas relating to intervention versus autonomy, hybrid democratic peace also creates dilemmas related to local frameworks for politics and identity versus reforms and pluralism.

This chapter introduces a theoretical framework of dilemmas and corresponding trade-offs identified in the transitions from civil wars since the end of the Cold War. The framework focuses on understanding the tensions and contradictions in post-conflict reconciliation, the challenges facing interim governments, and the international community's role. The first section explains the concept of hybrid liberal peace during transition times. The second section explores the four transitional dilemmas already identified by the literature (Jarstad and Sisk, 2008). The third section introduces the additional ten dilemmas that advance this field of knowledge and its theoretical development. Finally, the fourth section presents the theoretical Philosophical–Actors–Tactical (P–A–T) platform of post-conflict peacebuilding dilemmas and its features and constraints. Consequently, this chapter seeks to move beyond the fallacy of sequentialism (Carothers, 2007) by identifying elements that impede effective peacekeeping after a civil war. It contributes to the literature in two ways. First, it proposes a platform of analysis based on what tends to be studied in isolation by the literature. Second, it combines understandings from peace and conflict resolution studies with those related to the political sciences, good governance, and democratization.

1.1 Transition from hybrid war to hybrid liberal peace: background approach

Peacebuilding and democratization are dynamic processes. Therefore, it is necessary to elucidate the challenges confronting international and local actors when establishing or re-establishing good governance as this process yields unsatisfactory results. Postwar situations should be better understood through two conceptual approaches. First, the volatility-uncertainty-complexity-ambiguity (VUCA) military framework related to identifying elements of VUCA is relevant. Respectively, it means that post-civil war conditions are at the intersection of the dynamics of change, the lack of predictability, the multiplicity of forces, the confounding of issues, no cause-and-effect chain and confusion, the haziness of reality, and the mixed meanings of conditions (Redeker, 2017; Heidbreder, 2016).

Second, as in the cases of Bosnia and Herzegovina, Lebanon, or the Democratic Republic of the Congo (DRC), politics may create a micro-dynamic of cooperation and competition, where violence, actual or potential, continues to play an important role. In this respect, it is fundamental to take into consideration that in the aftermath of domestic armed conflict, a condition of hybrid peace governance takes predominance in which conflicting elements still coexist. The concept of hybrid war combines conventional and unconventional military strategies, as used by Islamic State of Iraq and the Levant (ISIL) in 2014 in Syria and Iraq and by Hezbollah in 2006, 2008, and 2021 in Lebanon (COAR, 2021). Hybrid peace refers to a condition where liberal and illiberal norms, institutions, and actors coexist, cooperate, and compete in parallel with elements of violence and non-violence. By extension, the peacebuilding governance terminology refers to the activity of governing this hybridity (Jarstad and Belloni, 2012).

Therefore, hybrid peace contrasts markedly with liberal peace. The latter is based on accountable democratic institutions and formal practices, such as elections that provide shifting majorities, a market economy, and institution legitimacy. By contrast, hybrid peace governance invariably combines informal institutions, such as ethnic, hereditary, or traditional rule, with formal practices. On the one hand, liberal peace is based on values such as meritocracy, the rule of law, transparency, and human rights. It includes actors such as civil servants, politicians, police, judges, civil society, and a free press. On the other hand, hybrid peace encapsulates illiberal values such as patrimonialism, religious orders, authoritarian rule, and a state monopoly on violence based on sovereignty. It also empowers clientelism, neo-patrimonialism, and non-state authorities as actors, such as rebel and mafia groups, warlords, local chiefs, and religious institutions. Paradoxically, while liberal peacebuilding seeks to advance liberal norms, it often reinforces illiberal values and actors (Diamond, 2002; Mac Ginty, 2011; Willems, 2015).

Notably, there are positive and negative forms of hybrid peace. The first is related to the promotion of some social justice and a contextual form of progressive politics. It represents a contextually rooted process through which broader political and social injustices are addressed across local and international scales and implies significant legitimacy from the local scale. The latter is related to hybrid politics that maintain structural violence, fail to resolve the contradictions between local and international norms, and reflect the outsourcing of a colonial-style rule (Richmond, 2015).

Combining the dual dimensions of illiberal and liberal factors with war and peace makes it possible to identify an array of shapes of hybrid peace governance, as illustrated by Figure 1.1. First, the liberal democratic form, often promoted by the international peace agenda and rarely found in postwar contexts, combines stability, liberal norms, and democratic institutions. Second, the authoritarian and repressive state combines stability with the necessary formal inclusion of warlords into state institutions, which is usually found with peace by a victory. Although formal liberal and democratic institutions may be in place, undemocratic features play a decisive role in political and socioeconomic dimensions. Although elections are held, the opposition has been defeated usually by force and not necessarily because it accepts the majority's legitimacy to rule. Third, frequently characterized by a divided state, some democratic institutions coexist with various degrees of violence. Finally, anarchy exists where undemocratic and

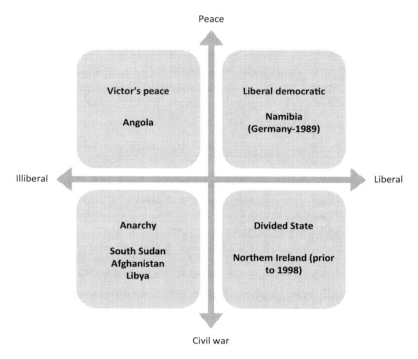

FIGURE 1.1 Forms of hybrid peace. Source: Author. Adapted from Jarstad and Belloni (2012, p. 3)

democratic norms, institutions, and actors coexist in a warlike setting (Jarstad and Belloni, 2012). When analyzing the efficiency of UN interventions in this kind of case, it is usually considered a failure. Chapter 4 demonstrates how most cases are positioned into five sub-categories toward the center of the double axes' hybridity: moderate levels.

Hybrid forms of peace and hybrid forms of politics are intertwined, but they are not synonymous (Brownlee, 2009; Richmond, 2015; Willems, 2015). Kosovo, Nepal, and Liberia are examples of clashes between the modern liberal state and customary praxis, law, or institutions. While international actors have provided a democratic model for peace and state reform, there has been a tendency to ignore historical practices, customary law, religion, or ethnicity when providing the foundation for stability and order. However, this formula has transmuted into a hybrid form of peace and politics that is exacerbated by the volatility-uncertainty-complexity-ambiguity (VUCA) elements. The next section identifies the common dilemmas that face peace-building and democracy-building due to such hybrid forms of peace and politics.

1.2 Theoretical foundation: transitional dilemmas

According to Jarstad and Sisk (2008), it is possible to identify four main dilemmas that may arise when the processes of democratization and peacebuilding oppose each other. First, the "horizontal" dilemma concerns the *inclusion versus exclusion* trade-off. Difficult choices about who participates in the processes must be addressed. A broad inclusion is in line with the democratic theory on power-sharing, which suggests that the more groups represented in the process, the more democratic it is (Jarstad and Sisk, 2008, p. 22). This dilemma is basically related to who is to be included in the transition phase among the elites of warring parties and democratic political parties. It is about including or excluding "spoilers" at the decision-making level. The critical question revolves around the relationships among the parties in civil war: the roles of states (political elites and military forces), rebel forces, and militias. Although including a broad spectrum of society in the peace agreement is likely to improve the legitimacy of the peace process, including warring groups remains an obstacle to democratization. Examples of horizontal dilemmas can be found when deciding who can participate in the electoral processes, or if amnesty should be granted to all former combatants, particularly those who have committed gross human rights violations. Where there are several rebel militias, it would also have to be decided which will be part of the transformation process into political parties as well as how to involve them in the demilitarizing plan. Political, ideological, religious, cultural, ethical, and military factors play a role and spoilers, political parties, and elites are usually the main elements involved with the horizontal impasse.

Second, the "vertical" dilemma countenances the *efficacy versus legitimacy* trade-off. Difficult choices on the legitimacy of actors and the efficacy of achieving peace and democracy must be addressed. Democracy and peace are "for, from and by the people." However, besides being the main interested party in the process, the people are rarely part of the substantive decision-making processes. Peacebuilding is an interactive process that involves collaboration between peacebuilders and the victorious elites of a postwar society. The peacebuilding literature often wrongly interprets two essential factors. It underestimates the role of the elites in peace and democracy-building processes by presupposing that the interests of domestic elites and peacebuilders coincide when in fact, they rarely do (Zürcher et al., 2013, p. 1). Domestic elites in postwar societies may desire the resources that peacebuilders can bring, but they are often less eager to adopt democratic reforms as it may endanger their substantive interests. Moreover, understanding peacebuilding and postwar democratization as a simultaneous task contingent upon the elites' direct influence might help explain why peacebuilding missions often bring some peace – but rarely democracy – to war-torn countries. Examples of vertical dilemmas can be found when formulating and accepting the rules of elections. Peace agreements might be supported by elites for their effectiveness, but if the legitimacy of the process is questioned, they will be considered undemocratic, and it is highly probable that the population may be motivated to return to war. Alternatively, the security sector reform might appear to comply with all legitimate procedures and actors and yet be inefficient. The elites, the mass population, and security contractors such as mercenaries are among the main actors within the vertical dilemma.

Third, the "systemic" dilemma confronts the *local versus international ownership* trade-off. This dilemma is related to the question of who the leadership is. Democratization and peacebuilding need to be driven by local motives and actors, not imposed or led by outsiders. After the war, a vacuum of expertise invariably remains. Usually, peace operations with the mandate of state-building are carried out by professionals who do not know the history of the conflict or the language. As "donors," they end up taking the process toward different agendas than those desired by national authorities and peoples, such as in Timor-Leste or Kosovo. This dilemma balances the relationship between national and international expertise and resources. Examples of systematic dilemmas: who should be the judge, prosecutors, and public defenders, who should draft the national budget to be approved by the Parliament, who should be the president of the Supreme Court, or who should lead the electoral process design and execution? The main players are national leaders and/or spoilers and the international community, mainly represented by a country-cluster of donors, international organizations, or INGOs.

Finally, the "temporal" dilemma is about the *short-term* versus *long-term* trade-off. The urgent need for an end to war contrasts with the never-ending process of peacebuilding, democracy-building, and state-building. Therefore, a key dilemma common to nearly all postwar contexts is the trade-off between the short-term and long-term goals of peacebuilding and democratization. It relates to the question of the best time for specific actions. Efforts to support democratization may, in the short term, increase the risk of violence, and, thereby, in the long term, undermine the chances for democracy to take root. Timing also raises questions about when the United Nations should intervene, when an intervention should cease, when elections or public consultation should be held and when the right time is to sign a peace agreement. A large spectrum of players is involved as spoilers, political parties, elites, the population at large, and international actors. Although Jarstad and Sisk (2008) did not visually represent their dilemmas, these could be translated as Figure 1.2.

1.3 Dilemmas and trade-offs between efforts to promote peace or democracy: an advanced approach

This book proposes 14 interconnected transitional dilemmas focused on the contradictory forces of mutually forging democracy or enforcing peace. The additional ten trade-offs to those addressed by Jarstad and Sisk (2008) are detailed in this section. Those dilemmas have multifaceted characteristics with cultural, economic, ethical, ideological, military, political, religious, and socio-humanitarian aspects and include spoilers, political parties, elites, the mass population,

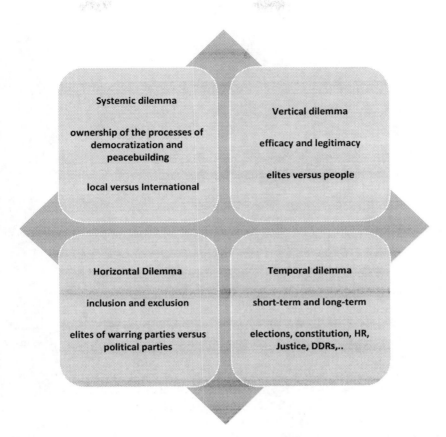

FIGURE 1.2 Proposed set of peacebuilding dilemmas according to Jarstad and Sisk (2008). Source: Author

and the international community. Due to the fact that this set of dilemmas frames competing elements and tendencies, the order of importance is highly dependent on the issue to which the model of analysis is applied. The following section of this chapter elucidates the impact on the analysis depending on the order of dilemmas.

The central dilemma of the book is to define what prevails after civil war: peace or democracy? This is directly linked to the other 13 dilemmas: horizontal, vertical, systemic, temporal, existential, design, moral, operational, resource, security, sequencing, financial, and transparency (Figure 1.3).

The "existential" dilemma is concerned with the *opportunity versus uncertainty* trade-off. This dilemma balances the relationship between lost certainties versus winning uncertainties. It answers the question: whether to struggle for power or to negotiate for freedom? In war, there is a constant dilemma between retaining the *status quo* and possibly losing or trying for an uncertain peace negotiation by being part of the democratic game and maybe winning power (i.e., war

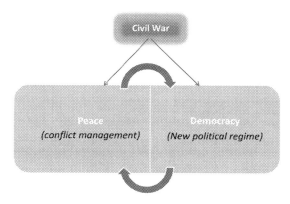

FIGURE 1.3 Central dilemma: bad choices can undermine peacebuilding or democracy-building. Source: Author

with some power versus peace with uncertain power). Conversely, it might be better to have a lesser but certain advantage in a war situation than a potentially greater advantage that may come to nothing. This existential quandary is also the case for perceived or feared losses of existence, property, prestige, position, and security.

Examples of existential dilemmas can be found among freedom fighters, where the resumption of struggle is an instrument to achieve a tentative statehood. Still, ceasing hostilities might lead to an uncertain shared alternative. Inherently, enemies cannot trust the other side to uphold an agreement in democratic governance after a winner takes all elections, making the losing side vulnerable. Understandably, some groups may not be willing to compromise on a peace agreement or a democratic order. A ceasefire can be a step toward peace, but it may well make rebels easy targets for slaughter, as in the case of the Tamil Tigers in Sri Lanka and massive killings in a no-fire zone (Ganguly, 2018). Moreover, in the case of a mass overseas exodus of victims or rebels, the fighting can expand to a regional or international spillover and, as in the Syrian war, provoke global security concerns.

In contrast to the security dilemma and its concern with the individual's safety, the existential dilemma has an institutional or ideological association. There is a realistic fear that a rival will become stronger after an election and monopolize state power and weaken or target those who have lost the elections. All fair elections involve elements of uncertainty; if the results were certain, elections would be unnecessary (Reilly, 2008, p. 166). The element of uncertainty might contribute to adversaries being willing to play by the rules of the democratic game. As in a lottery, to win one must play. But it is precisely this uncertainty that leads to violence. If competitors become convinced that an opposition's victory will ruin them, the uncertainties of democracy will become intolerable, and they will try to overturn the electoral process (Bermeo, 2003, p. 165). To overcome this dilemma, power-sharing increases the likelihood that adversaries will remain committed to peace in a win–win situation instead of a winner takes all system (Jarstad, 2008, p. 106).

The design dilemma relates to the *technical versus political choices* trade-off. The architecture of democracy is increasingly seen as the key to crafting stability in the fragile states of the developing world (Reynolds, 2002). Following the structural question of who, when, and what, the design is related to the methodological probe regarding "how" to address issues regarding configuration/model or strategic choices. Technical expertise can be undermined by the political choice of either a dominant warlord or intervention. Favoring a political system or policy may facilitate a political wing and, therefore, may jeopardize the process's credibility, efficiency, legality, viability, and legitimacy (e.g., elections, justice, or demilitarization). Encouraging ethnic, religious, or political polarization is undemocratic and can endanger the peace process through a return to violence. Examples of this quandary can be found in many situations. The choice of the electoral system, such as majoritarian, semi-proportional, or proportional, is one of the most important political decisions of a new country. Choices between presidential, semi-presidential, or parliamentarian systems will also be on the negotiation table. Additionally, the overall constitutional design of the new state is crucial for its stability and, in the shadow of the civil war, different constitutional choices must be examined for divided societies (Falk et al., 1993; Lipjhart, 2004; Pospieszna and Schneider, 2013; Moreno and O'Neill, 2013). For instance, will the legislative house be unicameral or bicameral? How will representation be set up? Thus, the design dilemma plays a significant role in making democracy and peace prevail after a war as constitutional engineering encompasses theories of democratic conflict management and socio-ethnic polarization.

Similarly, design involves the balance of checks and balances through institutional mechanisms. For example, how will the electoral commission be structured to organize elections: through an independent responsible authority or a political commission? How will parliamentarian commissions be distributed (e.g., agriculture, economy, defense, industry) or combined (e.g., education and culture)? The design dictates the political strategy and, therefore, the processes for prioritizing or neglecting certain portfolios. How should institutions such as the Supreme Court, Parliament, General Prosecutor's Office, or the Commission of Truth and Justice be institutionally designed to operate under the mechanisms of checks and balances? Similarly, the design of UN intervention, after approval, should be driven by technical choices (multidimensional, a mission, a monitoring mission, in partnership with a regional organization, with a military or a police component, etc.). Nevertheless, the "selective intervention," which means the debate *before* approval, is inevitably driven by political choices.

The financial dilemma is tax-related and deals with the *present needs versus future survival* trade-offs. Democracy-building and economic recovery have different timeframes. In the aftermath of war, a country is invariably devastated.

Generally, no state financial or fiscal institution is in place to manage its natural resources or to collect taxes from the survivors of the war. International funds to implement peacekeeping missions are restricted in size and limited in terms of the period in which they can be used. The dilemma is how to implement a state fiscal and financial structure without, or with very scarce, initial financial resources. Without a functioning legal tax system, the state collapses, as in Haiti, Afghanistan, and South Sudan. Thus, no wonder there is a high demand for "tax or public finance specialists" in the development industry. It is also essential to differentiate this financial dilemma from systemic and resource dilemmas. The financial dilemma is functional and related to the actual production or management of state revenue. The other two are related to ownership and to human and logistical resources.

As an example, Timor-Leste has resources of gas and oil that are responsible for 90 percent of the state's annual revenue, but only 3 percent of it can be withdrawn annually from the Petroleum Fund (Min of Finance of Timor-Leste, 2017; Timor-Leste, 2005). Although it might be essential to guarantee sustainable national resources for future generations, the population needs resources now. Roads, schools, and hospitals need to be built now for the population to have a better tomorrow. The usual solution is to borrow and, consequently, to create public debt and donor dependency. Another choice is to use exceptional executive powers and withdraw more than is constitutionally allowed. A further alternative is to do only what is manageable (usually very little, if anything) with the nation's own resources until the creation of a proper tax collection system, which may take time or never fully exist. The same dilemma applies to the United Nations. Peace operations are costly. Without funds, intervention is not operational, although it is justified for moral or security issues.

The moral dilemma should be weighed against the trade-offs of *cause versus effect* and is related to anything that is ethically associated with right versus wrong. Morality is at the epicenter of state-building conflict management and democracy-building. A decision can be morally right yet lead to devastating consequences. Philosophically, the problem may be expressed as of deontological versus consequential encumbrances; the nature of duty and obligation (deontology) is balanced against prioritizing the outcomes of the decision (consequentialist). Hazards of legalism and moralism have often inflamed discussions of governance, and their analysis is rooted directly within contemporary human struggles for peace and justice. With concerns related to what happens before, during, and after interventions, moral dilemmas include predicaments of *jus in bellum, jus ad bellum*, and, most of all, with the problems of *jus post bellum*. The dilemma can also be viewed as an alternative between following the rules versus maximizing the good or minimizing the bad. One might also see this dilemma as a conflict or trade-off between legalism versus moralism.

Ethical dilemmas relating to humanitarian intervention are hard choices because they are both unavoidable and complex. Very often, the genuine moral dilemmas confronted are as diverse as gender versus peace, religion in competition with conflict, culture contrasted to the rule of law, etc. Such questions can also illustrate examples of this dilemma in post-conflict transitional situations as to whether to intervene and aggravate war versus not to intervene and allow genocide, or to respect sovereignty or obey the principle of responsibility to protect. Can a peace intervention prevent war as in Haiti (MINUSTAH)? Whether to conduct a "preventive war mission" versus the usual "reactive intervention" also translates into a moral trade-off. Another example is the morality found in the dilemmas related to selective intervention (Somalia) versus non-intervention at all (West Papua). Such choices involve many questions: To approve economic sanctions to enforce international law or to minimize people's suffering in conflict? To use illegitimate and trained mercenaries (privatization of war) or legitimate and unskillful UN peacekeepers? To prioritize personal interests or humanitarian assistance? Once a selective intervention takes place, to be impartial and inefficient or to take sides and resolve the issue? To prioritize the institutional image or to investigate the facts and care about the consequences of non-reaction? To build a strategic logistical humanitarian alliance with military perpetrators at the expense of a loss of credibility with their victims? To promote effective personal humanitarian work or to keep the salary contract for a longer term? To establish an intervention to save friends or strangers? (Moore, 2013).

Alternatively, the operational dilemma concerns the *flexibility versus robustness* trade-off. This dilemma balances the relationship between hard and soft politics. It is mainly related to whether the rules are followed. When making war or building peace, there is a "fantastic gap" between the UN resolution and the operations in the field (Doyle and Sambanis, 2006, p. 185). There is a troubling divorce between the policy and the means. A successful peace intervention must offer both sides of a conflict rewards and coercion parameters to endorse the agreement. To analyze UN peace operations and democracy-building, it is fundamental to distinguish the success of the implementation of a mission's mandate from its procedures and process, including the micro, meso, and macro levels. Furthermore, successful peacekeeping is a shared responsibility and must engage three levels: those who mandate peacekeeping operations, those who contribute, and those who manage activities on the ground. For those in the field, reality changes constantly, and, most probably, things will not work according to the plan. The tempo, sequencing, methods, or rules are subject to unexpected contingencies on the ground to those who mandate and those who finance.

To "act following the script" may lead to disaster. However, being too flexible in the early stages may undermine the foundation of respect for the rule of law and the procedures that the operators are trying to facilitate as state builders. A balance between carrots and sticks is fundamental in the transition from civil war termination to the establishment of the political space for enduring peace. In the field, peacekeepers face daily operational dilemmas between being flexible and, hence, adjusting to the situation or cultural differences or implacably sticking to the rules or procedures. Justice sector reform represents the tensions between the traditional and the legalized justice systems during transitions. Whereas strict laws and their application may be considered necessary for protecting individual rights, indifference to social custom and a lack of flexibility to adapt to the reality on the ground may undermine the peace process by creating communal resentment.

The resource dilemma deals with the *efficiency versus viability* trade-off. This dilemma is mainly related to the question of: is it efficient and viable? This dilemma is mainly related to human resources, which international "experts may take over." This dilemma has a logistical aspect that differs from financial and operational issues. For example, countries with very low state capacity (poor educational levels, a lack of capable human resources, and high levels of poverty) and oil-based economies have a strong tendency to revert to authoritarian rule or fragile democracies (Ross, 2001, p. 1).

Very often, the use of resources is marred by corrupt schemes due to the lack of transparency about the mechanisms of decision-making and execution. Additionally, the lack of basic infrastructure leads to a logistical dilemma that impedes the democratization process. For instance, electronic elections might seem an efficient way to minimize corruption and attain faster results, but without reliable electricity, this is not viable. An example of a resource dilemma is when the country might have the financial capability and good infrastructure (new hospitals, new schools, etc.), but lack the necessary professionals, such as doctors, nurses, or teachers. Alternatively, talented human resources might be available, and there may even be a high level of employment, yet this may exist alongside the lack of basic infrastructures, such as water and toilets. The United Nations itself can have the necessary funds. And yet it may be very inefficient with slow deployment (e.g., Congo), inexperienced human resources to tackle terrorism (e.g., Mali, CAR), or inadequate logistical and operational facilities (water, fuel, communications systems, e.g., South Sudan), or insufficient human resources to achieve the mandate (e.g., Rwanda).

Safety is an inevitable concern regarding an armed conflict. The security dilemma involves the trade-offs between *exercising rights versus fulfilling duties,* and it is basically correlated to the protection of civilians. In contrast to the existential dilemma, institutions do not decide whom to destroy or kill or whether to make peace or war. At the end of the day, those decisions are the responsibility of individuals. It is an essential aspect of conflict resolution to understand parties' interests and motivations behind institutional façades. The available literature often does not distinguish between security and safety and overstates them as one single dilemma. This book differentiates institutional (the existential dilemma) and individual (the security dilemma) lenses. Examples of the latter are many. To get involved versus not to get involved as an individual? If rebels receive amnesty for the abduction of children for child-soldier recruitment, would it be safe to go to school? To go or not to go to the polls? Elections (pre-election, during elections, and post-elections phases) can be very violent, and the population may be threatened or intimidated to participate or to boycott the polls. They may or even be pressured to overthrow the election results.

The sequencing dilemma correlates the *bottom-up versus top-down approaches* trade-off. It mainly responds to the question of what the plan is. What is the priority when everything is crucial and changes all the time? Sequencing is related to "how" to address issues in terms of structure. Should the democratization process start from the national level (with national elections) or the local or district level (with local elections)? Another alternative holds that democratization is a hybrid process where bottom-up and top-down dynamics should operate simultaneously. Should the handover of the UN police to the new national police be gradual, a step-by-step approach commencing with the provincial level until reaching the capital, or vice versa? Should a new educational curriculum be implemented in the entire country or should there be a prototype so that gradual efforts spread out from nearby, more capable, and major provinces toward the less developed and neediest ones? Should capacity-building be done first for the soldiers or their appointed commanders? Once again, despite their obvious interconnectivity, the quandaries of sequencing, design, and operations must be differentiated, which can be done by referring to their respective trade-offs. It is important to distinguish the sequencing dilemma from the "sequencing narrative" of peacebuilding and democracy-building. The latter is related to a guiding recipe for a successful transition. As explained in the introduction, this book opposes the idea of peacebuilding "toolkits."

Last but not least, the transparency dilemma confronts the *impartiality versus accountability* trade-off. A choice must be made between untruth and stability versus truth and conflict. Transparency is also related to peace agreement negotiations, usually made behind closed doors by a *petit comité*. Too much transparency can ruin the peace process, but too little can undermine democracy. Therefore, impartiality and neutrality are crucial. However, accountability is also fundamental. The media can play two roles. It can be democratic or a tool of warlords. It may be a "media coup d'état" when influencing voters through misinformation, fake news, brainwashing, intimidation, and fear, or even paying for their support. As part of the transition, "media reform" is usually part of the agenda for post-conflict democratization. Still, laws on freedom of expression, human rights advocacy, the formation of independent media, and training are often against the interests of the warlords. Truth and reconciliation or war crime tribunals must also be set up for impartiality and accountability.

Thus, to sum up, in a postwar phase dominated by VUCA elements, a number of dilemmas may arise when the processes of democratization and peacebuilding oppose each other. Jarstad and Sisk (2008) suggest a set of four transitional dilemmas: horizontal, vertical, systemic, and temporal. Figure 1.4 contemplates the additional ten transitional post-conflict dilemmas of peace and democracy-building introduced in this chapter: central, existential, design, horizontal, moral, operational, resource, security, sequencing, systemic, temporal, financial, and transparency. With multifaceted characteristics of cultural, economic, ethical, ideological, military, political, religious, and socio-humanitarian aspects, each dilemma's order of importance depends on the issue analyzed. At the intersection

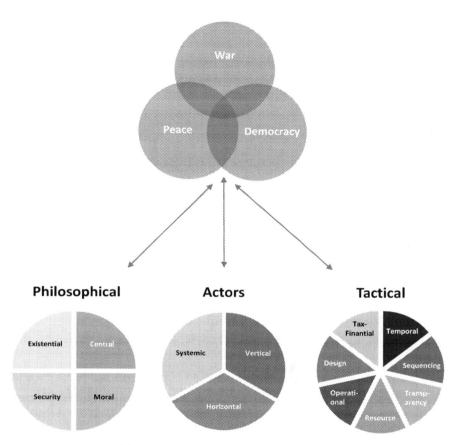

FIGURE 1.4 P–A–T dilemmas at the intersection between war, peace, and democracy. Source: Author

of war, peace, and democracy, it is possible to group the 14 dilemmas into three main clusters as Figure 1.4. The only purpose of assembling it into different clusters is to help manage the great number of dilemmas identified.

1.4 Premises of the Philosophical–Actors–Tactical (P–A–T) framework of transitional post-conflict and peacebuilding dilemmas: its properties and limitations

To better comprehend the proposed P–A–T model of dilemmas originating from the transitional efforts of building peace and democracy in fragile states in the fog of civil war, it is crucial to understand the following clarifications:

No examples were found where only one dilemma is in place at a time. Therefore, the analysis and understanding entail an interacting helical cogwheel perspective:

one dilemma leads to one or more additional quandaries of an even more critical and complex conundrum (see Figure 1.4). For example, institution-building simultaneously involves temporal, vertical, and systemic dilemmas, which makes the clear distinction blurred precisely because it is a transition and the interrelation of dilemmas. The shift from war to democratic peace requires hard choices. Some are related to "when, where, who, and why" (dilemmas *for* intervention), others to "what, how, which, how many, and how much" (dilemmas arising *from* intervention). For example, too little military intervention or intervention that comes too late are both very problematic, as the cases of Bosnia-Herzegovina and Rwanda illustrate. A promise of intervention that is not acted upon is worse than in the African Great Lakes. Yet there is also such a thing as over-intervention; the heavy-handedness of the UN intervention in Haiti hampered efforts to gain acceptance from the population and may have been ineffective (Badescu, 2007; Katz, 2013). Haiti's overall state of fragility is not that different in 2022 from 2004.

Thus, as explained in more detail in the methodology section of the introduction, this book focuses on the timeframe from 1989 to 2022 and on the following quadrants (Figure 1.5). The platform of dilemmas is subject to time and space. For example, analyzing postwar elections in Côte d'Ivoire in 2010 and 2015 will have different results in a quadrant scheme of "more peace, less democracy," "less peace, more democracy," "more peace, more democracy," and "less peace and less democracy." This is also the case if the analysis concerns the effectiveness of the UN mission in Timor-Leste as if it was the United Nations Mission in East Timor (UNAMET), the United Nations Transitional Administration in East Timor (UNTAET), the United Nations Office in Timor Leste (UNOTIL), or the United Nations Integrated Mission in Timor-Leste (UNMIT) as the conflict evolved in time and places differently.

The first and foremost dilemma is the central one in which the trade-offs are between peace and democracy themselves. Therefore, the other 13 dilemmas could be understood as sub-dilemmas derived from the central predicament. Figure 1.7 summarizes the central and the other 13 dilemmas with their corresponding trade-offs. Each dilemma can be analyzed separately, generating a different set of other impasses according to the issue and perspective under analysis.

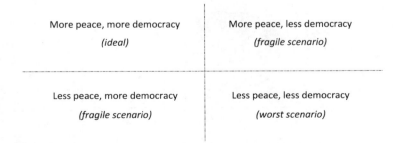

FIGURE 1.5 Quadrants of peace and democracy. Source: Author

Every binary set of dilemmas has its cause and consequences that vary according to the environment, leading to different results. For example, when analyzing elections starting with the security aspect, this might lead to a sequence of *security → moral → transparency → vertical → and et cetera dilemmas*. Further, if the analysis of the process of demobilization, disarmament, and reintegration starts with security issues, this might lead to a different series of dilemmas such as *horizontal → operational → systemic → moral etc*. This interrelation among the dilemmas is further explored in the following chapters, which deal with 12 issues common in post-conflict state-building and democracy-building.

Furthermore, as one trade-off choice leads to additional quandaries, dependency on resolving these dilemmas spirals. For instance, the temporal dilemma of elections can be successfully resolved and will lead to some requirements for democracy. However, democracy-building or peacebuilding depends on other trade-offs beyond holding elections at the right time. Similarly, an inclusive constitution is positive for a more democratic country, but stability, a social contract, and the rule of law depend on other factors contributing toward democracy *and* peace. Therefore, no dilemma is, by its nature, more important than another. Instead, its importance is dependent upon which primary dilemma generates other trade-offs.

In addition, a specific issue can lead to an overlay of different dilemmas. For example, the impasse of whether to intervene internationally or not is usually presented by international relations and political affairs scholars at the intersection of security, economic, and moral dilemmas. Figure 1.6 illustrates this triad interconnectedness within war–peace–democracy quandaries. The literature on international relations often analyzes conflict through the realist lens of security, the liberal-globalist lens of economic costs, or a pluralist vision that prioritizes humanitarian moralism. Therefore, analyses of the transition to democracy and

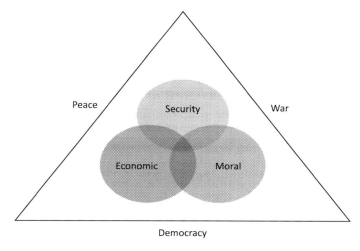

FIGURE 1.6 Security, economic, and moral aspects within the war–peace–democracy triad. Source: Author

peace have different designs, operational plans, strategies, and entry and exit timeframe tactics, if emphasizing political, economic, or social development (Crocker et al., 2001; Diehl, 1996; Doyle and Sambanis, 2006; Druckman and Diehl, 2013; Fiedler, 2000; Verrill, 2011).

The dilemmas represent common quandaries from theoretical and practical points of view; from real politics to the decisions in the field. Therefore, the dilemmas embrace the macro to micro levels of the policymaking and decision-making spectrum in the field. By moving from a micro- to a macro-level in-depth analysis, the nature and effectiveness of bottom-up peacebuilding are shown (Autesserre, 2014). This book aims to promote the perspective often ignored or undermined by the literature: peace from the middle. Beyond the critical role of elites and the need to empower the grassroots, the middle layer might be the key interface between less conflicting interests, as will be further elucidated in the book.

Remarkably, the issues of corruption, gender, and cultural sensitiveness permeate all the dilemmas in the transitional process of regime change. Therefore, those elements are not analyzed in separate chapters but incorporated within the issues analyzed. Moreover, the set of 14 dilemmas considers all the different actors, such as the so-called spoilers, political parties, elites, populace, and international organizations.

In line with the concepts of Galtung (1996), the P–A–T system includes the normative vision of a conflict triangle to incorporate the attitudes, behavior, and issues at stake. Beyond violence, peace also includes speech acts, social patterns, and discrimination actions. This aligns with the concept of the triangulation of peace proposed by Doyle and Sambanis (2006) composed of local capacities for peace, the available international assistance, and the depth of conflict-related hostility. Thus, the P–A–T system not only considers the causes of the conflict. It also highlights the complexity of a constellation of intertwined factors (economic, ethical, ideological, military, political, religious, and socio-humanitarian) and emphasizes their dynamism as solving one dilemma leads to another one (Figure 1.7). As proposed in the introduction to this book, a set of 12 issues will be analyzed according to the proposed 14 interlinked dilemmas, and these issues are grouped as follows:

- Elections and political parties (Chapters 3 and 5)
- Constitution, checks and balances, and power-sharing (Chapter 6)
- Transitional justice: human rights and amnesty, truth commissions and ad hoc war crime tribunals (Chapter 7)
- Disarmament, demobilization, and reintegration (DDR) and security sector reform (SSR) (Chapter 8)
- Media reform, civil society, refugees, and gender (Chapter 9)

1.5 Summary of the chapter

This chapter sets the foundation of the book's delineation. In the aftermath of civil war, choices for peace and democracy can be reciprocally opposing.

64 Transitional dilemmas, violent democracies, and the UN's statecraft

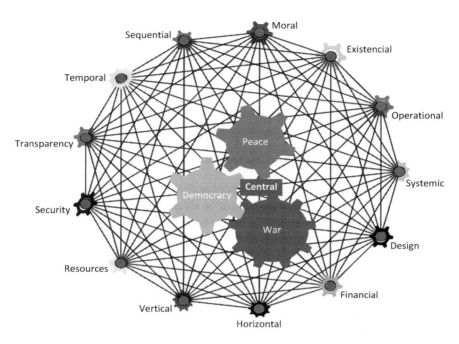

FIGURE 1.7 Tridecagon_complex and dynamic set of dilemmas for democratization and peacebuilding after war. Source: Author

Those civil war-torn countries so rarely emerge as resilient democracies with sustainable peace is closely related to the hybrid forms of peace and politics that appear in post-conflict locations and the elements of volatility, uncertainty, complexity, and ambiguity (VUCA). The conundrum resides in the transition to state-building or nation-building in the shadow of war. This chapter is key to moving beyond the ideas of sequentialism or providing a recipe for peacebuilding and democracy-building. It proposes a theoretical and normative framework of dilemmas that contrast the choices between peace and democracy after a civil war. The first section explained the concept of hybrid peace. In the second section, the four transitional dilemmas identified in the literature are reviewed, followed by a proposal of an additional ten dilemmas that advance this field of knowledge. Finally, the P–A–T framework of post-conflict peacebuilding dilemmas, its properties, and limitations has been presented. With a multi-layered perspective, an attempt has been made to fill the gaps between the theory and practice for fragile states, civil wars, democratic governance, and state institution-building. Awareness of those dynamics and challenges is a step toward a better approach to conflict resolution. The next chapter will explore the dilemmas related to the intervention by the United Nations to enforce "peace and democracy" (Figure 1.8).

The transition *from civil war to hybrid peace* 65

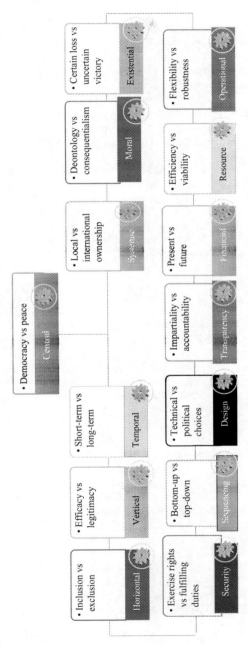

FIGURE 1.8 The P–A–T system of dilemmas and its corresponding trade-offs. Source: Author

References

Autesserre, S. 2014. *Peaceland: Conflict Resolution and the Everyday Politics of International Intervention*. Cambridge University Press.

Badescu, C. G. 2007. Authorizing Humanitarian Intervention: Hard Choices in Saving Strangers. *Canadian Journal of Political Science/Revue canadienne de science politique*, 40, 51–78.

Bermeo, N. 2003. What the Democratization Literature Says-or Doesn't Say-About Postwar Democratization. *Global Governance*, 9, 159–77.

Brownlee, J. 2009. Potents of Pluralism: How Hybrid Regimes Affect Democratic Transition. *American Journal of Political Science*, 53, 515–532.

Carothers, T. 2007. The "Sequencing" Fallacy. *Journal of Democracy*, 18, 12–27.

COAR. 2021. *Conflict Analysis. Lebanon. National Level*. Online: Centre for Operational Analysis and Research.

Crocker, C. A. Hampson, F. O., & Aall, P. R. 2001. *Turbulent Peace: The Challenges of Managing International Conflict*. United States Institute of Peace Press.

Diamond, L. J. 2002. Thinking about Hybrid Regimes'. *Journal of Democracy*, 13, 21–35.

Diehl, P. F., & Reifschneider Jennifer et Hensel, P. R. 1996. United Nations intervention and recurring conflict. *International Organization* 50, 4, 683–700.

Doyle, M. W., & Sambanis, N. 2006. *Making War and Building Peace: United Nations Peace Operations*. Princeton University Press.

Druckman, D., & Diehl, P. F. 2013. *Peace Operation Success: A Comparative Analysis*. Martinus Nijhoff Publishers.

Einstein, A. 1931. *Cosmic Religion: With Other Opinions and Aphorisms*. Covici-Friede.

Falk, R. A., Johansen, R. C. & Kim, S. S. 1993. *The Constitutional Foundations of World Peace: Logic and Tinkering*. State University of New York Press.

Fiedler, M. R. 2000. *United Nations Peace Operations: Conditions for Success*. Ph.D., University of Idaho.

Galtung, J. 1996. *Democracy: Dictatorship = Peace: War?* SAGE Publications Ltd.

Ganguly, S. 2018. Ending the Sri Lankan Civil War. *Daedalus*, 147, 78–89.

Heidbreder, C. E. A. 2016. *Volatility, Uncertainty, Complexity, and Ambiguity: The Evolution of Warfare Through the Process of Globalization*. Faculty of the Graduate School of the University of Colorado.

Jarstad, A. 2008. Power sharing: Former enemies in joint government. In: Jarstad, A. K. & D., S. T. (eds.) *From War to Democracy: Dilemmas of Peacebuilding*. Cambridge University Press.

Jarstad, A. & Belloni, R. 2012. Introducing Hybrid Peace Governance: Impact and Prospects of Liberal Peacebuilding. *Global Governance*, 18, p. 1–6.

Jarstad, A. K. & Sisk, T. D. 2008. *From War to Democracy: Dilemmas of Peacebuilding*. Cambridge University Press.

Katz, J. M. 2013. *The Big Truck That Went By: How the World Came to Save Haiti and Left Behind a Disaster*, St. Martin's Press.

Lipjhart, A. 2004. Constitutional Design for Divided Societies. *Journal of Democracy*, 15(2), p.96–109.

Mac Ginty, R. 2011. Hybrid peace: How does hybrid peace come about? In: S. Campbell, and D. Chandler & M. Sabaratnam (eds.) *A Liberal Peace? The Problems and Practices of Peacebuilding*. Zed Books.

Min of Finance of Timor Leste 2017. Annual State Budget. *In*: FINANCES, M. O. (ed.) Goverment of Timor-Leste.

Moore, T. 2013. Saving friends or saving strangers? Critical humanitarianism and the geopolitics of international law. *Review of International Studies*, 39, 925–947.

Moreno, P. D. & O'neill, J. 2013. *Constitutionalism in the Approach and Aftermath of the Civil War.* Fordham University Press.

Pospieszna, P. & Schneider, G. 2013. The Illusion of 'Peace Through Power-Sharing': Constitutional Choice in the Shadow of Civil War. *Civil Wars*, 15, 44–70.

Redeker, S. T. 2017. Understanding Victory: Adapting Operational Design to Address Resource Management Challenges. *Armed Forces Comptroller*, 62, 9–13.

Reilly, B. 2008. Post-war elections: Uncertain turining points of transition. *In:* A. K. Jarstad & T. D. Sisk (eds.) *From War to Democracy: Dilemmas of Peacebuilding.* Cambridge University Press.

Reynolds, A. 2002. *The Architecture of Democracy: Constitutional Design, Conflict Management, and Democracy.* Oxford University Press.

Richmond, O. P. 2015. The dilemmas of a hybrid peace: Negative or positive? *Cooperation and Conflict*, 50, 50–68.

Ross, M. L. 2001. Does Oil Hinder Democracy? *World Politics*, 53, 325–361.

Timor-Leste 2005. *Petroleum Fund Law. 9.* Timor-Leste.

Verrill, D. L. 2011. *United Nations Peacekeeping Missions: The Effect of Peacekeepers on Mission Effectiveness.* Ph.D., The University of Texas at Dallas.

Willems, R. C. 2015. *Security and Hybridity after Armed Conflict: The Dynamics of Security Provision in Post-Civil War States.* Taylor & Francis.

Zürcher, C., Manning, C., Evenson, K., Hayman, R., Riese, S. & Roehner, N. 2013. *Costly Democracy : Peacebuilding and Democratization After War.* Stanford University Press.

2
UNITED NATIONS HYBRID LIBERAL PEACE DILEMMAS

Contingent sovereignty, responsibility to protect and moral selectiveness

> At the centre of virtually every civil conflict is the issue of the state and its power – who controls it, and how it is used. No conflict can be resolved without answering those questions, and nowadays the answers almost always have to be democratic ones, at least in form.
>
> *Annan, 2002, p. 137*

To intervene or not to intervene (Morgenthau, 1967)? If so, what are the transitional dilemmas faced by UN operations in promoting liberal peace in post-civil war contexts? Between a "just war" and "just peace," the first dilemma regarding building peace and democracy after civil war through UN operations concerns the intervention itself: intervention versus autonomy (Chesterman, 2001, p. 1; Bellamy, 2006, p. 1; Evans, 2012, p. 191). Humanitarian intervention (HI) is one of the most contested issues in contemporary world politics (Bellamy, 2002; Hehir, 2008; Bellamy, 2006). A humanitarian military intervention to (re)install democracy and the rule of law holds an inherent contradiction: it means using force to end violence and protect civilians' freedom (Bueno de Mesquita and Downs, 2006; Watts, 2008; Castellano, 2014). In practice, bombing for peace and democracy is unpeaceful and undemocratic (Henderson, 2002; Sandholtz, 2002). In theory, peace and democracy should not be enforced but built from within to be sustainable (Watts, 2008; Boutros-Ghali, 1996). However, if there were room for a political resolution, there would not be a civil war in the first place and, therefore, no need for international intervention. By juxtaposing international norms and the interests of member states, UN operations are at the center of hybrid forms of peace along with hybrid forms of politics. This hybridity arrangement is related to the condition where liberal and illiberal norms, institutions, and actors coexist, cooperate, and compete. It undermines the paramount principle of state sovereignty in international affairs in that what takes

DOI: 10.4324/9781003279976-4

place within states does not concern any foreigner. Often in limbo between Chapters VI and VII of the UN Charter, HI lacks a legal basis and struggles between choices for legality versus legitimacy (Mac Ginty, 2011; Jarstad and Belloni, 2012; Richmond, 2015).

In this chapter, several aims are achieved. First, it provides an analysis of the UN and its democratic peacebuilding agenda through a statecraft exercise of benevolent autocracy. Second, based on a revision of the main theoretical pillars of international relations (IR), it examines the transversal principles that challenge UN operations, such as Westphalian sovereignty, post-Westphalian responsibility to protect (R2P) and responsibility while protecting (RwP), and contingent sovereignty. Third, it assesses other dilemmas that arise during interventions that foster this liberal peace hybridity.

2.1 United Nations's statecraft: "benign" autocracy versus autonomy

Should the United Nations be in the business of ensuring democracy at the barrel of a gun (Jarstad and Sisk, 2008 p. 6)? Exporting democracy faces a paradox between rhetoric and reality (Schraeder, 2002). There is an extensive debate in the literature about whether the UN can (or should) be involved in democratization. Its principal mandate is to safeguard international peace and security (UN, 1945). It is not the organization's mandate to promote any specific political system despite the efforts of all its agencies, funds, and programs to defend human rights, freedoms, electoral assistance, and governance. In addition, there is no explicit agreement on how to assist (or impose) the birth and consolidation of liberal and democratic states after conflict. Peacebuilding has become both an increasingly significant activity for the international community in the decades since the end of the Cold War and a fundamental dimension of responding to violent conflict. These operations combine a hybrid mix of realism and idealism. The first is ultimately military occupation. The latter is the belief that people can be "saved" from themselves through "help" from outsiders.

An assortment of theoretical understandings explicates why states pragmatically go to war with another state. However, it seems more complex to elucidate why states "fight for peace" by intervening in foreign civil wars for the supposed "promotion or restoration of democracy" through the auspices of international organizations rather than independently or via alliances. On the one hand, they embody a humanitarian response to the pressing needs of societies and states struggling with violent conflict. On the other hand, they often represent extensive interventions into political and social relations by trying to implement models of idealized social, political, and economic ties that might bear little relation to the values and practices of the populations where they are introduced. Skeptics of international intervention affirm that the path from state weakness must be made by the states themselves, gradually and, at times, intermittently.

The last decade has offered an extensive reminder that forcible state-building cannot be accomplished by outsiders in any sustainable or authentic way. Western governments are frequently criticized for having an imperialist endeavor that has brought disaster to some nations while liberties at home are gradually curtailed (Freedom House, 2017; EIU, 2021; Damboeck, 2012). The notion that all countries must be brought – by will or by force – into the democratic fold is itself a potential invitation for belligerence. Some also argue that pursuing peace based on world democratic conversion is a camouflaged response to the communist goal of bringing about world harmony through a worldwide socialist revolution. In this regard, the belief that only Western democracies are good can be interpreted as the equivalent of endorsing what Edmund Burke calls an "armed doctrine" (Gottfried, 2013). When governing institutions are weak, personalized, or kleptocratic, corruption is rampant, and the rule of law is noticeable by its absence. There are simply no proven methods for generating major social, political, economic, or cultural changes relatively quickly. Although freedom may be encouraged and even modestly shaped by outside contributions and pressure, it cannot be imposed (Mazarr, 2014). Thus, democracy, peace, and security can only be assisted (IDEA, 2010; Boutros-Ghali, 1996, art. 11).

Despite broad and extensive experience in assisting democracy, it is important to note that the word "democracy" does not appear in the UN Charter. Democracy is not a precondition for UN membership, and the organization is silent on other features of domestic political organization. It is as impartial to republics and monarchies as to presidential or parliamentary systems. Similarly, it is ambivalent on the issue of bicameral as opposed to unicameral parliaments. All these are domestic political concerns and are protected by the principle of sovereignty. The established system of the UN itself has far to go before fulfilling, to the extent possible, the democratic potential of its present design, and transforming those structures that are insufficiently democratic (Ghali, 2000). Yet, the organization propagates electoral democracy as the primary governance template for all nations to move along the paths of "development, peace and security" (Newman and Rich, 2004, p. 5).

First, the peace dividend of democratization is based on domestic checks and balances. The rational choice that might make democracies less war-prone than other democracies is that heads of states and governments are accountable to their electorate and require the approval of the legislative branch. Moreover, going to war might impact subsequent elections if taxpayers are not satisfied (Henderson, 2002). Second, democracy, development, and respect for human rights and fundamental freedoms are interdependent and mutually reinforcing. Therefore, the UN's justification for intervention is also based on the "principle of equal rights and self-determination of peoples." However, several member states do not respect human rights and they put UN body's credibility at stake. An example is Saudi Arabia (2016–2019), China (2020–2023), and Russia (2020–2023) sitting in the UN Humans Rights Council (UN OHCHR) despite criticisms for human rights abuses carried out both domestically and as part of military intervention in

Yemen, Hong Kong, Tibet and against the Uiguirs ethnical group, and Ukraine, respectively (Human Rights Watch, 2021; Al-Hajji, 2020). Third, it is believed that democracy and good governance promote development, social progress, and better standards of life in line with the Sustainable Development Goals (SDGs).

If peace operations aim to build states and societies capable of fulfilling their responsibilities, and if liberal and democratic societies are most effective, then it stands to reason that peace operations need to be in the business of aiding the spread of liberal democracy. Consequently, building peace out of "new wars" requires from outsiders the transformation of governing systems into those along liberal lines, and this also explains the expansion of the roles and responsibilities of the missions (Bellamy et al., 2010). The paradox of intervention versus autonomy is related to the possibility of establishing conditions for legitimate and sustainable national governance through a period of "benevolent foreign autocracy" (Chesterman, 2004, p. 126).

This contradiction between ends and means has plagued transitional efforts to govern post-conflict territories in Bosnia, Eastern Slavonia, Kosovo, and Timor-Leste, with mixed success (Doyle and Sambanis, 2006; Fiedler, 2000; Mosquera, 2011; Richmond and Franks, 2009). Some skeptics have even described transitional administration as the "UN's kingdom," the "United Feud," "benign colonialism," or "coerced transitions" (Chopra, 2000, 2002; Cotton, 2004; Lemay-Hébert, 2012). The challenges to consultation and accountability are evident as it seems contradictory to what extent the transitional administration should itself be bound by the principles that it seeks to encourage. In the case of Kosovo, the United Nations Interim Administration Mission in Kosovo (UNMIK) was not structured according to democratic principles, it has not functioned in accordance with the rule of law, and it has not respected important international human rights norms. The people of Kosovo were "deprived of the protection of their basic rights and freedoms three years after the end of the conflict by the very entity set up to guarantee them" (Chesterman, 2004). Similar arguments are found for Timor-Leste (Myrttinen, 2008; Chopra, 2002; Richmond, 2011). The accountability of international actors through local consent will inherently be limited during the inaugural phases of an operation. Therefore, this exacerbates the conditions for hybrid peace and hybrid democracy (Richmond, 2015; Willems, 2015; Jarstad and Belloni, 2012; Mac Ginty, 2011; Brownlee, 2009).

The dilemma of whether to intervene or not in failed democracies, or failed states, is critical. As shown in Figure 2.1, it alters the logical cycle of war to democracy to peace toward failed democracy to war by intervention and then to peace. Thus, it modifies the dynamic of peacekeeping as it is precisely the fragility of the state and/or the instability of the democratic regime that justifies a collective intervention. The democratic peace theory is not strictly about being democratic or non-democratic in transitioning from war to peace. But, as an extension of this theory, it is because of the fragility of the democratic regime or the instability of the state in safeguarding its sovereignty that international intervention is required.

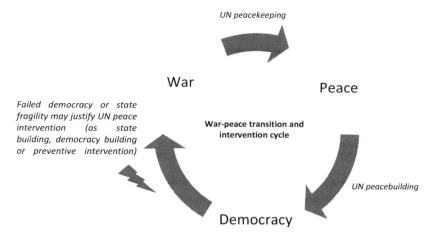

FIGURE 2.1 Failed democracy and failed states: the inverted dynamic of war to peace transition and intervention cycle. Source: Author

This, therefore, alters the peace-war dynamic. Libya, Iraq, and Guinea-Bissau are representatives of this scenario. By this rationale, failed states would be "failing or failed" because no international assistance helped with operations of state-building or nation-building. Accordingly, this logic leads to the proposition that a vulnerable or failing state should invite international assistance precisely to protect its state sovereignty and show its determination to achieve good governance (Deng, 2010).

2.2 Westphalia versus post-Westphalia peace: legality, legitimacy, sovereignty, and R2P

The other significant dilemma regarding the UN's intervention in civil wars is legality versus legitimacy. The principle of non-interference is clear in Article 2 §7 of the Charter (UN, 1945): "nothing contained in the present Charter shall authorize the United Nations to intervene in matters which are essentially within the domestic jurisdiction of any state." After World War II, the Westphalian order became predominant worldwide, particularly with the decolonization process rearranging the world order. With this proliferation of sovereignty, the international order also became more complex: in 1947, there were few sovereign states compared to nearly 200 states in 2017, including 193 UN member states. In line with this article, the UN Declaration on the Granting of Independence to Colonial Countries and Peoples (1960) also guarantees essential rights, such as (1) self-determination to freely determine their political status and form of government and to freely pursue their economic, social, and cultural development, and (2) prohibition of the use of force in internal and external affairs of other states (Bellamy et al., 2010; Taylor, 2001).

Sovereignty, territory, and borders cannot be dissociated from international law (Howland and White, 2008; Diener and Hagen, 2012). The perception of borders, as passive lines on a map serves as a constructivist means of national identity by defining "us" and "them." Determining who the actors are is crucial to conflict resolution. The nation-state system of borders was primarily built on the territorial notion of utis possedetis juris: as you possess, you may possess (Diener and Hagen, 2012). However, it should not be unfamiliar to human rights issues that problems in determining international boundaries of disrupted states are complicated. Those processes are closely connected to the principle of territorial integrity, sovereignty, and self-determination, which most probably ignited the internal armed conflict.

In this context, the uti possidetis juris principle and the right to self-determination contradict each other. They are crucial elements of failed states: the misuse of the territory provides bases for terrorists and human and drug trafficking. Cross-border institutions, border crossing refugees, intra-border conflict, and frontiers outside borders are blurred concepts in the new global modern state system. They are powerful counterpoints to the idea of a "borderless world" bought by globalization. Not only is state sovereignty about territories, laws, and populations, but also terror and territory can define the spatial extent of sovereignty (Howland and White, 2008; Elden, 2009). Global threats such as terrorism, drugs, human trafficking, money laundering, and weapon trafficking might justify internationalized intervention in failed states. Yet these threats exist precisely because they do not comply with the spatial borders of sovereignty (Elden, 2009). In this regard, Somalia and Kosovo are usually cited in international debates about the legality of the territory and the legitimacy of the UN mission (Jankov and Ćorić, 2008). This divergence on territorial sovereignty is also strategic to conflicts without UN intervention, such as Abkhazia, South Ossetia, Nagorno-Karabakh, and Transnistria. Notably, a failed state is "failed" precisely because there is no control over its territory. Therefore, if no sovereignty exists, international intervention is invariably justified, as politics "abhors a vacuum." Under this rationale, "intervention" is the "occupation of misused or (un)used space." In an era of weakened sovereignty, ungoverned spaces open alternatives to state authorities (Trinkunas, 2010). According to this logic, intervention in failed states would be legal and legitimate.

However, the question raised by T. Franck (1970, p. 809) remains highly relevant: "who killed Article 2 §7 of the UN Charter"? Changing norms governing the use of force require examining the idea of Westphalian sovereignty and its practice, particularly in times of military interventions, as in former Yugoslavia, Afghanistan, Iraq, Libya, and Crimea. Much of the debate can be simplistically reduced to the clash between the ideas of internationalism and globalization and the end of Westphalian sovereignty (Simonen, 2011; Camilleri and Falk, 1992). Some argue that state sovereignty is at risk because it has been redefined by globalization and international cooperation in a way that now seems anachronistic or obsolete (Jacobsen et al., 2008; Chayes and Chayes, 1995). Based on the relationship between the state and the individual, the Hobbesian idea of "social contract" is inverted: as mentioned by Kofi Annan, "the state is now widely understood to be a servant of its people, and not vice versa" (1999; Bellamy et al., 2010, p. 283).

Globalization not only provokes integration, intensification, and interdependence (Held et al., 1999). But it also results in de-territorialization and re-territorialization of political, economic, technological, and sociocultural spaces and the reconceptualization of sovereign political boundaries. Additionally, it also encompasses the revival of non-state sources of power and authority, along with the establishment of complex webs and networks among communities, states, international institutions, NGOs, and transnational corporations (Bellamy et al., 2010). Consequently, these parallel developments demand new ideas about how the UN should respond to political, human rights, and humanitarian crises worldwide.

Moreover, as new concepts emerge to accommodate new needs, such as the European Union's notion of "shared sovereignty," external agents are formed to interfere in the internal affairs of nations to preserve a "united security." For non-interventionists, interference in the affairs of a sovereign state in the name of humanitarianism can lead to abuse as these may be perceived to be interveners in defense of their own national interests. One could argue that the United States was not interested in the domestic anarchy of Haiti. MINUSTAH was carried out in a country that is not a global security threat and has no exploitable natural resources. The real purpose was to mitigate a massive refugee exodus to the United States. Furthermore, many post-colonial states also fear that the erosion of sovereignty means a new form of colonization by eliminating the right to self-determination and self-governing. Paradoxically, this is precisely what collective intervention wants to promote under the umbrella of liberal peace (Damboeck, 2012; Bellamy, 2002).

Let's further examine this rationale. If the humanitarian intervention is just, under what circumstances should it be justifiable (Guraziu, 2008)? When governments massacre their own citizens, sovereignty can be seen as organized hypocrisy and a pretext for governments to have a "license to kill" (Krasner, 1999; Wheeler and Bellamy, 2005, p. 556). The argument is that international society has the moral responsibility to protect (R2P) individuals when states are unwilling to, or incapable of, doing so. Consequently, the new concept of "contingent sovereignty" was introduced, which is not related to state unitary inherence but to government performance. Expanding the democratic peace theory, neoconservatism advocates that a lack of democracy may presage future humanitarian calamities. Or, if democracy itself constitutes a "human right," nation-states not respecting democratic principles open themselves up to a "just war" by other countries. Contingent sovereignty diminishes sovereignty itself at the expense of a political system of governance. During the democratic crisis in Uganda 2005, Yoweri Musevini made it clear that "aid is arrogantly mixed up with an effort to interfere with our sovereignty" (Wallensteen, 2008, p. 233).

With the need for revision of the role of the UN peace operations, post-Westphalians defend the move from "humanitarian intervention" (HI) or "sovereignty as responsibility" (S1R) to the "responsibility to protect" (R2P) (Deng, 2010; Gierycz, 2010). In this regard, R2P divides the responsibility for protecting populations from genocide, war crimes, crimes against humanity, and ethnic cleansing (mass atrocity crimes) into three pillars. First, it is a state's primary responsibility to protect its population against such crimes. Second, it is the international community's responsibility to assist the state in doing so. And third, it is the responsibility of the international community to use appropriate diplomatic, humanitarian, and other peaceful means to help protect the population if the state fails to do so or if the state itself perpetrates the atrocity. As a last resort, the collective use of force under the UN Security Council mandate should be used. Thus, the core of R2P is the notion that a state's sovereignty is conditional on its behavior toward its population (SIPRI, 2012). From this perspective, the people constitute the epicenter of the international order. In this regard, the UN Charter was issued in the name of "the Peoples," and, therefore, it protects the UN's sovereignty, not the governments of its member states. Intervention does assault sovereignty. However, the principle of respect for sovereignty cannot be a license for governments to trample on human rights and human dignity (Annan, 1999). Consequently, by this rationale, the defense of democracy, human rights, and freedom characterize the circumstances in which intervention is justifiable in contravention of Article 2§7.

Furthermore, the reports of UN peacekeepers perpetrating sexual abuses and/or other misconduct in Bosnia, the Democratic Republic of Congo (DRC), and recently the Central African Republic (CAR) have highlighted the fact that the UN's responsibility is not just to protect those who need help, but also it must do no harm while intervening (Gibbs, 2009). Thus, the concept of "responsibility while protecting" (RwP) marks a new stage in the development of a global norm to prevent and respond to mass atrocities by proposing a set of criteria for military intervention and a monitoring and review mechanism to assess the implementation of Security Council mandates as well as placing a renewed emphasis on capacity-building to avert crises before they happen (Almeida, 2013). With a need to rethink the concept of the law of armed force within the parameters of jus ad bellum, jus in bello, and jus post bellum, RwP stands in the intermediate spectrum between strict state sovereignty and modern humanitarian principles and forms part of the permanent debate around the costs and benefits of intrastate conflict interventions (Foley, 2012; SIPRI, 201; Stahn, 2006). Moreover, the quandaries of military intervention are usually centered on tactical, economic, and political considerations. Nevertheless, the culture of the intervening forces might be very different from that of the locals (Larsdotter, 2006). In that regard, the RwP allows the insertion of the cultural aspect, which might be key to the outcome of the intervention.

Finally, the dilemma of legality versus legitimacy ultimately defines a "just war." As previously discussed, collective intervention represents a form of war. If

76 Transitional dilemmas, violent democracies, and the UN's statecraft

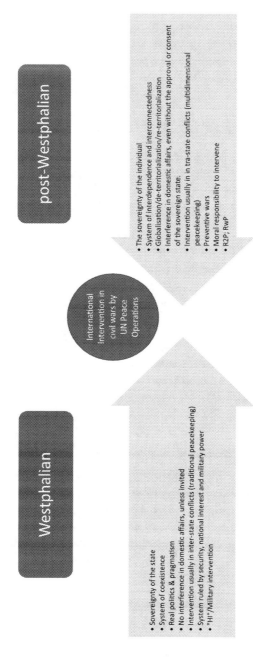

FIGURE 2.2 UN intervention in civil wars: Westphalian versus post-Westphalian dilemma. Source: Author. Inspired from Bellamy, A. J., Williams, P. D. & Griffin, S. 2010. Understanding Peacekeeping

so, can peace operations be war preventive? On the one hand, it might be justifiable to intervene because democracy is "failing" to secure freedoms or because a state "is failing" in controlling sovereignty of its territory, and incapable of protecting its population before it collapses. On the other hand, the precise nature and scope of the conflict are not often a certainty but merely a probability. The UN Stabilization Mission in Haiti (MINUSTAH-2004) is a frequently cited example of collective preventive intervention in a failed democracy and collapsed state (Brock et al., 2012). In addition, when the intervention is "preventive," it is often difficult to evaluate its success or plan an exit strategy. It may also exacerbate the conflict that it was supposed to prevent (Katz, 2013; Leininger, 2006; Peck, 2001; Call, 2012, Ray, 2012). Even though "preventive wars" are another contradiction of terms, they are also considered one of the major reasons why UN peace operations fail. In other words, it is uncertain if such military intervention contributes to building peace or creates an even more fragile future (Eudaily and Smith, 2008; Ozoukou, 2014; Touval, 1994; Jett, 1999; Call, 2012).

One of the main criticisms found in the literature is that the proponents of contingent sovereignty are concerned about democracy, human rights, and humanitarian crises only in countries that challenge Western global dominance. There is little or no consistency regarding the rules. There are also different approaches to undemocratic countries allied with the United States and, therefore, a state with veto power at the Security Council. Interestingly, brutal dictatorships in Latin America were tolerated and even sponsored during their civil conflicts with UN intervention in Central America (ONUCA), Nicaragua (ONUVEN), El Salvador (ONUSAL and MINUSAL), and Guatemala (MINUGUA). It is well known that the United States professed a commitment to democracy. But when faced with a choice between a communist or even left-leaning democracy and an autocrat who aligns with the West, "the United States chose the latter" (Krasner and Eikenberry, 2018, p. 197). The support and sponsorship to all dictatorships in Latin America during the 60′ until late 80′ is an example of it.

Nevertheless, the notion of "contingent sovereignty" illustrates the evolving nature of the realist nation-state system (Diener and Hagen, 2012). The problematic nature of contingent sovereignty was exposed by the international response to the so-called Arab Spring with various appeals to the ideals of justice and human dignity over state sovereignty. This can also be seen in emerging border constructions relating to minorities and indigenous peoples. In failed states or failed democracies, territorial sovereignty is no longer an inviolable authority of the state if it is challenged by the idea that threats such as human rights violations, genocide, or the proliferation of mass destruction weapons compel international action.

States with severe violations of global norms call into question the right to their own sovereignty in the international order, thereby empowering the international community to interfere in their domestic affairs to "enforce" peace and democracy. Moreover, after an intervention, a period of "monitoring and capacity-building" will follow to guarantee that the state does not "fail" again.

Therefore, besides governmental agreement, most post-civil war states, with limited or substituted national sovereignty, were formed under highly undemocratic conditions through international autocratic intervention, such as Timor-Leste between 1999 and 2002 (Howland and White, 2008).

As the above examples demonstrate, the legality and legitimatization of HI are based on questionable foundations in international law (Hurd, 2011; Heinze, 2011). For some authors, UN peace operations remain largely Westphalian because they are concerned principally with regulating a state-based international system and balancing the relations between states (Jacobsen et al., 2008; MacQueen, 2011). For others, individual and human rights take precedence, and there is no such thing as sovereignty in domestic affairs for some state abuses (Sandholtz, 2002). This implies that what happens in one place might impact regionally or even globally under the cliché argument that "we are all humans and in the same boat."

Consequently, for post-Westphalian supporters, international society has a responsibility to assist and, if need be, force states to fulfil their responsibilities. The logic is that because liberal democratic policies and institutions tend to be better at protecting their citizens from genocide and mass killing and settling disputes with other democracies without resorting to war, peace operations should be in the business of rebuilding war-shattered societies along liberal democratic lines. Yet, as the Westphalian notion does nothing to tackle the underlying causes of war, such as injustice, human rights abuse, and poverty, only with post-Westphalianism can stable peace be assured. Although the Westphalian concept dominates the "international order," it remains controversial, with the result that the place of UN peace operations in world politics and their future trajectory remain contested, inconsistent, unpredictable, and uncertain (Bellamy et al., 2010, p. 41)

2.3 Who deserves to be free and safe? Selectiveness, efficiency, and other dilemmas

Based on the explanations above, what are the transitional dilemmas UN operations face in promoting liberal peace in civil war contexts? Firstly, the moral dilemma related to the so-called selectivity gap of international politics explains why some crises have led to interventions and others not (Binder, 2009). The moral dilemma refers to the fact that the UN, and therefore member states, has selectively responded to the violation of humanitarian standards and civil crises (Damrosch, 2000; Brown, 2003). Humanitarian aid is a political act (Pereira Watts, 2017). A moral dilemma faces the trade-off between deontology versus consequentialism. Operationally, it is impossible to be everywhere and protect everyone in need. As selectiveness is an inevitable procedure, a moral dilemma is unmistakable and inevitable. In the politics of protection and the limitations of humanitarian relief in the new and old wars, hard choices must be made when saving lives (Damrosch, 2000; Moore, 2013).

Consequently, double standards still predominate when the international community faces the choice of whether or not to intervene, or whether it can or should respond consistently to war crises (Brown, 2001; Brilmayer, 1995). Moreover, it is naïve to expect coherence where the geopolitics of international intervention in civil wars is ruled by diverse ideologies, regimes, and political actors (Kathman, 2007). Therefore, selectivity or the defense of inconsistency can be described as the unfulfilled expectation that conceptually alike cases will be treated alike (Brown, 2003).

The selectivity gap reflects a problem of good governance and is undemocratic as friends and strangers should be eligible to be "saved" under the same human rights rhetoric (Kim, 2007, p. 33; Badescu, 2007). Another moral dilemma, which is sometimes described as an existential one, is related to the scope and length of interventions and missions. An international organization projects a public image that it strives to uphold. The legitimacy and credibility of the UN Security Council hinge on its ability to act as a guarantor of civilian protection under R2P, and it is essential to the survival of the organization. Assessment reports are not necessarily a reflection of the reality on the ground, but a tool to justify to the member states the importance of the organization and possibly to validate the extension of its mandate (Verrill, 2011). Among other ethical dilemmas, it is debatable if the UN should provide relief assistance with discretion, neutrality, and impartiality or if it should publicly denounce human rights violations. The latter would risk its agencies being expelled from recipient countries and ceasing assistance, ultimately impacting the people in need.

Moreover, what is the UN for? This interrogation is usually associated with the vertical dilemma related to efficiency versus legitimacy. What exactly has been done by the United Nations to achieve common goals like "peace," "freedom," and "justice" seems abstract or frustrating (Banbury, 2016; Touval, 1994). The paralysis regarding the invasion and annexation of Ukrainian territory by Russia is evidence of it. It is difficult to disagree with the conclusion that the UN is remarkably maladroit when it comes to war-making and better at peacemaking (Doyle and Sambanis, 2006, p. 185; Fortna, 2008). One of the main lacunae is that many studies limit the analysis to quantitative data in a short period – between two to five years from the peace agreement signature to the conclusion of the UN peace operation (Kim, 2007; Fortna, 2008). Peacebuilding, democracy-building, state-building, and nation-building are extensive processes that take time. Some experts even argue that it never ends. Therefore, the efficacy of the procedure or the different agents involved cannot be assessed in terms of "snapshots" (Doyle and Sambanis, 2006).

The point has been made in Chapter 1 that a successful UN peace operation is a shared responsibility and must engage actors at three levels: those who mandate peacekeeping operations, those who contribute, and those who manage activities on the ground (UN-DPKO, 2009). Significantly, efficiency is usually related to continuity. Interventionist actions are easy to start, challenging to maintain, and even more complex to exit strategically. From the emergency to sustainable development, humanitarian action requires continuity. The multibillion-dollar international aid industry is under pressure to reform how aid is delivered as supply does not match the high demand. The unprecedented amount of concomitant disasters and emergencies has exposed serious fragilities in the current international humanitarian aid system: financing is insufficient and unsustainable, and coordination policies result in more bureaucracy instead of adequately matching the available resources to those most in need in a timely manner (UNOCHA, 2016).

Additionally, there is the dilemma of transparency that involves impartiality versus accountability. International interventions are grounded on the principles of the "Holy Trinity": neutrality, impartiality, and no use of force (Bellamy et al., 2010, p. 196). Neorealism explains that in order to terminate a war, an outside state will have to "take sides, tilt the local balance of power, and help one of the rivals to win" (Robert J. Art and Greenhill, 2015, p. 357). This is limited partiality. As a result, it is expected that the interveners would increase their relative power through a permanent occupation or the inclusion of territory in their sphere of influence (Bellamy et al., 2010; Doyle and Sambanis, 2006). For neorealists, then, the exercise of public authority within a foreign jurisdiction is a façade for expansionist policies. From this perspective, there is no such thing as "true independence."

A major concern regarding UN intervention is also related to accountability. Funding is necessary. Even though most international organizations (IOs) receive a significant amount of funds from state members, this does not necessarily result in governmental control of policy as they are autonomous bodies. However, regardless of whether the financial support comes from governments or private donors, IOs face the dilemma of tackling emergency crises and sustaining aid projects while maintaining independence from their funders' interests. Ultimately, this might also infringe on the principle of "do no harm." Moreover, temporal, resource, sequencing, and systemic dilemmas are also constantly discussed by researchers and policymakers. "International responses to democratization crises are often too late to be effective" (Wallensteen, 2008, p. 236). Generally, the UN is poorly suited to interventionist strategies involving the tactical employment of coercive force as such deployment generally takes a minimum of six months. Thus, the dilemma concerns short-term versus long-term solutions. Without its own financial resources and army, it relies on state members and their military resources. Comparatively, UN resources devoted to intervention represent less the 0.5 percent of global military expenditure. Although the 2022–2023 UN peacekeeping budget was US$6.45 billion it is nowhere near adequate for dealing with current interventions (DPKO, 2022).[1] Curiously, it faces a gradual reduction over the years, also due to global economic recession. It represents a reduction of 8 per cent of the 2016–2017 budget of US$7.78 billion (UN-DPKO, 2016). The pressure for constant cuts is mainly pushed by the United States as the main contributor to the UN peacekeeping budget (average 25 percent) despite being the one who less contributes with troops. As noted by the Global Observatory of the International Peace Institute, those constant cuts in the peacekeeping budget leave fundamental questions unaddressed between different stakeholders' visions of peacekeeping that threaten to bring peacekeeping to a standstill. UN peacekeeping continues to be eight times cheaper for the United States than alternative approaches. Yet the US government continues to push for the total closure or cuts in the operations when, however, the reality is that very little can be safely cut, especially at smaller missions (Carver, 2018). Those financial strands also reflect the nature of budgetary negotiations, which are repeatedly disconnected from the many other constituencies peacekeeping must answer to. UN peacekeeping was not the consequence of a holistic design practice but rather arose as the by-product of a series of improvisations, compromises, and historical evolutions. As such, it has multiple stakeholders and centers of influence. If the UN peace operations need to be "robust to be efficient," it is not financially viable. Altogether, it raises the dilemma of efficiency versus viability trade-off. Yet, it might be cheaper to intervene compared to the political cost of indifference.

Regarding strategic planning, there is no universal consensus on the best approach. Most commonly, it is implemented on a top-down approach, but some of the literature suggests a bottom-up approach is essential for durable peace (Autesserre, 2014). Other analysts advocate for an approach from the middle with the elites operating as intermediaries between the rebels, the government, and the population (Zürcher et al., 2013; Chesterman et al., 2006). Alternatively, coordination might be the fundamental element of success (Zeeuw, 2004; Brock et al., 2012). Finally, some specialists suggest that the triumph of a peace operation in domestic conflicts requires "more money and time." However, as per the systemic dilemma between local versus international ownership, this may have negative impacts and lead to dependency. If so, the UN and its mission become part of the problem (Zeeuw, 2004), or even irrelevant toward a peace solution. This is often the criticism that is made of quasi-eternal interventions, such as in Cyprus and Kosovo. International aid creates a parallel market and helps to undermine governmental capacity instead of fostering cooperation and the pooling of resources. In the case of Cyprus, the UN might not be part of the problem, but just part of the landscape. As a metaphor to the International Criminal Court in the Netherlands, it is like the "Hague of the Mediterranean" and a geostrategic base in Europe. In the case of Kosovo, it is trapped on politics despite success. The mission has accomplished its mandate, but it cannot leave because that would mean that Serbia, through the vote of Russia and China in the UN Security Council (UNSC), would have to recognize the Republic of Kosovo. Thus, temporal, resource, sequencing, and systemic dilemmas are crucial when a UN peace mission is in place.

The design dilemma is related to political versus technical choices. The mandates are inherently vague and politicized while policies are technically driven and partially executed. Considering that in fragile states, democracy is intrinsically deficient and sovereignty is blurred, good planning is not enough to fix failed states. Thus, as technical perfection does not replace politics, international intervention might have the opposite effect, thereby contributing to a state's decline and disintegration (Zeeuw, 2004; Carothers, 2006). At the grand strategic or political command level, the UN suffers from a disconcerting divorce between its Security Council and UN operations on the ground. Peace operations depend on the approval of the UN Security Council, which is managed by high doses of political interest. Indeed, this suggests Clausewitz's maxim that war is the continuation of politics, and, by inference, peacekeeping is strongly associated with it (Doyle and Sambanis, 2006, p. 184; Henderson, 2002). At its worst, the Security Council appears, by issuing resolution after resolution, to be seeking rhetorical solutions to strategic problems and satisfying large media companies such as CNN and BBC and now also social media, such as Facebook. It also aims to please domestic audiences of its member countries, making these public relations priorities more critical than providing better-planned missions with sufficiently funded and equipped forces.

Consequently, if Clausewitz's dictum is applied to UN peace enforcement operations in foreign civil wars, peacekeeping interventions appear to be the continuation of Security Council politics. By passing a resolution, it seems to be doing something when, in fact, it is doing very little other than maintaining the status quo of state sovereignty and international (in)security and (im)balance. The UN is about politics and so is the Security Council. Wars are also political struggles. Conflict, intervention, and resolution are also inevitably entangled in the politics surrounding civil wars (Misra, 2013). To take this a step further, civil war intervention is inevitably caught up in geopolitics (Kathman, 2007). A good example of this was the backing-off of votes in the Security Council in the compromise between Russia's intervention in Georgia and the United States's proposal for a UN mission in Haiti (MINUSTAH). Both interventions were in these countries' respective "national political interests." The 2022 invasion of Ukraine also shows the systemic standstill as Russia was ironically in the Security Council Presidency an obviously will veto any intervention. The UN is, indeed, "not so united." Politics are inherent, funds are always in demand, and there are too many bureaucratic procedures that slow down urgent humanitarian assistance (Doyle and Sambanis, 2006, p. 163).

Finally, interventions face the operational dilemma as robustness might be required, although illegal. At the same time, some flexibility might jeopardize the legitimacy of the intervention, as has been the case in the former Yugoslavia and the DRC. This is particularly problematic considering the principle stipulating no use of force. Moreover, intervention requires negotiation with rebels for a humanitarian corridor. In some controlled areas, humanitarian assistance is only possible through help from insurgents because the government is the perpetrator of abuses against its own people. Beyond breaching the principle of impartiality over R2P, this situation creates room for moral dilemmas that encompass corruption and the deviation of aid to fuel the black market. When robustness is required, but flexibility is the condition of the government's survival, this also undermines both the government's capacity and fragile state institutions.

2.4 Summary of the chapter

Failed democracies and failed states are sources of civil wars and provide motives for collective intervention through the United Nations. However, it is debatable if the UN should be in the business of ensuring democracy at the barrel of a gun. Thus, humanitarian military intervention to (re)install democracy and the rule of law poses a severe contradiction. By exacerbating a hybrid mix of realism and idealism, this chapter identifies and analyzes the first dilemma regarding UN operations in building peace and democracy after civil war: the intervention itself. Much of the recent literature on UN interventions within states to implement its agendas for peace and democracy draws attention to other conundrums, such as those between legality and legitimacy, as well as the paradox of promoting democracy through benevolent autocracy. Importantly, transversal principles, such as sovereignty and its mutations (shared sovereignty and contingent sovereignty to accommodate the current outcome of new wars in a globalized order), lead to new justifications for intervention. Under the narrative of human rights, not only there is a moral responsibility to protect (R2P) but also the responsibility while protecting (RwP). Failed democracy in failed states opens controversial debates regarding justice, selectiveness, and preventive collective intervention that are juxtaposed against the triadic principles of neutrality, impartiality, and no use of force. Beyond Westphalian' and post-Westphalians' theoretical debates, UN operations also face additional vertical, transparency, temporal, resource, sequencing, systemic, design, and operational dilemmas. This chapter provides respective examples as those dilemmas are challenged to react to time, continuity, costs, and accountability. Frequently, the UN not only exacerbates the tension inherent in liberal peace hybridity during transitional times, but it also might become part of the problem that it wants to solve or prevent as an extra actor.

International law currently emphasizes that civilian populations should be protected from state violence to prevent the ignominy of a "second" Rwanda. However, international intervention in civil wars is situated within a continuum of domestic politics, geopolitics, the balance of power and the *mêlée* between imperialism and humanity, conflicting ideas, covert interests, a lack of accountability, and ineffective coordination. Despite a decade of criticism and budget cuts, the UN has far more expertise and hands-on experience in such interventions than any other organization in the world (Bellamy et al., 2010). Beyond the paradox of intervention for peace and democracy through more war, the enforcement of democracy might be a cause and consequence of violence instead of leading to peace and security. This is explored in detail in the next chapter.

Note

1 The UN Fifth Committee (Administrative and Budgetary) approved a peacekeeping budget for 1 July 2022 to 30 June 2023 of $6.45 billion (GA/AB/4388/ 29 June 2022). It covers 11 peacekeeping missions and includes nearly $66 million for the United Nations Logistics Base at Brindisi, Italy; $43.2 million for the Regional Service Centre in Entebbe, Uganda; and $371 million for the peacekeeping support account. The approved budget for UN Peacekeeping operations for the fiscal year 1 July 2021–30 June 2022 was $6.38 billion. (A/C.5/75/25<https://undocs.org/A/C.5/75/25>). This amount finances 10 of the 12 United Nations peacekeeping missions, including the liquidation budget for the United Nations – African Union Hybrid Operation in Darfur (UNAMID), supports logistics for the African Union Mission in Somalia (AMISOM), and provided support, technology and logistics to all peace operations through global service centres in Brindisi (Italy) and a regional service centre in Entebbe (Uganda). The remaining two peacekeeping missions, the UN Truce Supervision Organisation (UNTSO) and the UN Military Observer Group in India and Pakistan (UNMOGIP), are financed through the UN regular budget <https://undocs.org/A/72/6/Add.1>.

References

Al-Hajji, T. 2020. Saudi Arabia Shouldn't be Allowed to Join the UN Human Rights Council. *Foreign Policy.* 10/02 ed.

Almeida, P. W. 2013. From Non-indifference to Responsibility While Protecting: Brazil's Diplomacy and the Search for Global Norm. *South African Institute of International Affairs. African Perspectives. Global Insights.* Global Powers and Africa Programme.

Annan, K. 1999. Address of the Secretary General to the General Assembly. (GA/9596).

Annan, K. 2002. Democracy as an International Issue. *Global Governance,* 8, 135–142.

Autesserre, S. 2014. *Peaceland: Conflict Resolution and the Everyday Politics of International Intervention.* Cambridge University Press.

Badescu, C. G. 2007. Authorizing Humanitarian Intervention: Hard Choices in Saving Strangers. *Canadian Journal of Political Science/Revue canadienne de science politique,* 40, 51–78.

Banbury, A. 2016. I Love the U.N., but It Is Failing. *New York Times.*

Bellamy, A. 2006. *Just Wars: From Cicero to Iraq.* Polity Press.

Bellamy, A. J. 2002. Pragmatic Solidarism and the Dilemmas of Humanitarian Intervention. *Millennium - Journal of International Studies,* 31, 473–497.

Bellamy, A. J., Williams, P. D. & Griffin, S. 2010. *Understanding Peacekeeping.* Polity Press, UK.

Binder, M. 2009. Humanitarian Crises and the International Politics of Selectivity. *Human Rights Review,* 10, 327–348.

Boutros-Ghali 1996. *An Agenda for Democratization.* New York: United Nations.

Brilmayer, L. 1995. What's the Matter With Selective Intervention? *Arizona Law Review,* 37, 955–70.

Brock, L., Holm, H.-H., Sorensen, G. & ETM. Stohl, 2012. *Fragile States: War and Conflict in the Modern World.* Cambridge, UK, Polity Press.

Brown, C. 2003. Selective Humanitarianism: In Defense of Inconsistency. *In:* Chatterjee, D. K. & Scheid, D. E. (eds.) *Ethics and Foreign Intervention.* Cambridge University Press.

Brown, M. 2001. *Ethnic and Internal Conflicts. Causes and Implications.* United States Institute of Peace.

Brownlee, J. 2009. Potents of Pluralism: How Hybrid Regimes Affect Democratic Transition. *American Journal of Political Science*, 53, 515–532.
Bueno De Mesquita, B. & Downs, G. W. 2006. Intervention and Democracy. *International Organization*, 60, 627–49.
Call, C. T. 2012. *Why Peace Fails: The Causes and Prevention of Civil War Recurrence*. Georgetown University Press.
Camilleri, J. & Falk, J. 1992. *The End of Sovereignty? The Politics of a Shrinking and Fragmenting World*. Edward Elgar Publishing Ltd, UK.
Carothers, T. 2006. Does democracy promotion have a future? In The backlash against democracy promotion. *Foreign Affairs*, March/April 2006, pp 55–68.
Carver, F. 2018. *Peacekeeping Budget Approval and Cuts Leave Fundamental Questions Unaddressed*. Global Observatory. International Peace Institute.
Castellano, I. M. 2014. *Civil War Interventions and Their Benefits: Unequal Return*. Lexington Books.
Chayes, A. & Chayes, A. H. 1995. *The New Sovereignty. Compliance with International Regulatory Agreements*. Harvard University Press.
Chesterman, S. 2001. *Just War or Just Peace?: Humanitarian Intervention and International Law*. OUP.
Chesterman, S. 2004. *You, the People: The United Nations, Transitional Administration, and State-building*, GB. Oxford University Press.
Chesterman, S., Ignatieff, M. & Thakur, R. 2006. *Making States Work : State Failure and the Crisis of Governance*. United Nations University Press.
Chopra, J. 2000. The UN's Kingdom of East Timor. *Survival*, 42, 27–39.
Chopra, J. 2002. Building State Failure in East Timor. *Development and Change*, 33, 979–1000.
Cotton, J. 2004. *East Timor, Australia and Regional Order: Intervention and Its Aftermath in Southeast Asia*. Routledge Curzon.
Damboeck, J. 2012. Humanitarian Interventions: Western Imperialism or a Responsibility to Protect? *Multicultural Education & Technology Journal*, 6, 287–300.
Damrosch, L. F. 2000. The Inevitability of Selective Response? Principles to Guide Urgent International Action. *In*: C.Thakur, A. S. A. R. (ed.) *In Kosovo and the Challenge of Humanitarian Intervention: Selective Indignation, Collective Action, and International Citizenship*. United Nations University Press.
Deng, F. 2010. From 'Sovereignty as Responsibility' to the 'Responsibility to Protect'. *Global Responsibility to Protect*, 2, 353–370.
Diener, A. C. & Hagen, J. 2012. *Borders: A Very Short Introduction*. OUP.
Doyle, M. W. & Sambanis, N. 2006. *Making War and Building Peace : United Nations Peace Operations*. Princeton University Press.
Dpko, U. 2022. *Peacekeeping Fact Sheet*. United Nations.
EIU. 2021. *Democracy Index: The China Challenge*. Economic Intelligence Unit.
Elden, S. 2009. *Terror and Territory: The Spatial Extent of Sovereignty*. University of Minnesota Press.
Eudaily, S. P. & Smith, S. 2008. Sovereign Geopolitics? – Uncovering the "Sovereignty Paradox". *Geopolitics*, 13, 309–334.
Evans, M. 2012. Just war, democracy, democratic peace. *European Journal of Political Theory*, 11, 191–208.
Fiedler, M. R. 2000. *United Nations Peace Operations: Conditions for Success*. Ph.D., University of Idaho.
Foley, C. 2012. Welcome to Brazil's Version of 'Responsibility to Protect'. *The Guardian*, 11/04/2012.

Fortna, V. P. 2008. *Does Peacekeeping Work? Shaping Belligerents' Choices After Civil War.* Princeton University Press.

Franck, T. M. 1970. Who killed ARTICLE 2 (4)? Changing Norms Governing the Use of Force by States. *American Journal of International Law*, 64, 809–37.

Freedom House. 2017. *Freedom in the World 2017: Populists and Autocrats: The Dual Threat to Global Democracy.* Freedom House.

Ghali, B. 2000. An Agenda for Democratization: Democratization at the International Level. *In*: Holden, B. (ed.) *Global Democracy*. Routledge.

Gibbs, D. N. 2009. *First Do No Harm.* Vanderbilt University Press.

Gierycz, D. 2010. From Humanitarian Intervention (HI) to Responsibility to Protect (R2P). *Criminal Justice Ethics*, 29, 110–128.

Gottfried, P. 2013. *War and Democracy.* Arktos Media.

Guraziu, R. 2008. *Is Humanitarian Military Intervention in the Affairs of Another State Ever Justified?* Middlesex University, Global Security Political & International Studies.

Hehir, A. 2008. Humanitarian Intervention: Past, Present and Future. *Political Studies Review*, 6, 327–339.

Heinze, E. A. 2011. Humanitarian Intervention, the Responsibility to Protect, and Confused Legitimacy. *Human Rights & Human Welfare*, 11, 17.

Held, D., Macgrew, A., Goldblatt, D. & Perraton, J. 1999. *Global Transformations.* Polity.

Henderson, E. A. 2002. *Democracy and War: The End of an Illusion?* Colorado, US, Lynne Rienner Publishers.

Howland, D. & White, L. S. 2008. *The State of Sovereignty: Territories, Laws, Populations.* Indiana University Press.

Human Rights Watch. 2021. *Human Rights World Report.* Human Rights Watch.

Hurd, I. 2011. Is Humanitarian Intervention Legal? The Rule of Law in an Incoherent World. *Ethics and International Affairs*, 25, 293–313.

IDEA, U. U. 2010. Democracy, Peace and Security the Role of UN. *In*: Tommasoli, E. M. (ed.) *Report from the International Round Table on Democracy, Peace and Security: The Role of the UN Co-organized by International IDEA.* UN Development Programme, UN Department of Political Affairs and UN Department of Peacekeeping Operations.

Jacobsen, T., Thakur, R. P. & Sampford, C. P. 2008. *Re-envisioning Sovereignty: The End of Westphalia?*, GB. Ashgate Publishing Ltd.

Jankov, F. F. & Ćorić, V. 2008. *The Legality of Uti Possidetis in the Definition of Kovoso's Legal Status.* European Society of International Law.

Jarstad, A. & Belloni, R. 2012. Introducing Hybrid Peace Governance: Impact and Prospects of Liberal Peacebuilding. *Global Governance*, 18, p. 1–6.

Jarstad, A. K. & Sisk, T. D. 2008. *From War to Democracy: Dilemmas of Peacebuilding.* Cambridge University Press.

Jett, D. C. 1999. *Why Peacekeeping Fails.* St. Martin's Press.

Kathman, J. D. 2007. *The Geopolitics of Civil War Intervention.* The University of North Carolina at Chapel Hill.

Katz, J. M. 2013. *The Big Truck That Went by: How the World Came to Save Haiti and Left Behind a Disaster.* St. Martin's Press.

Kim, D. H. 2007. *Nurturing Peace: United Nations Peacebuilding Operations in the Aftermath of Intrastate Conflicts, 1945–2002.* Ph.D., University of Missouri - Saint Louis.

Krasner, S. D. 1999. *Sovereignty: Organized Hypocrisy.* Princeton University Press.

Krasner, S. D. & Eikenberry, K. 2018. Conclusion. *Daedalus*, 147 Ending Civil Wars: Constraints & Possibilities, 197–211.

Larsdotter, K. 2006. Culture and the Outcome of Military Intervention: Developing Some Hypothesis. *In*: Angstrom, J. & Duyvesteyn, I. (eds.) *Understanding Victory and Defeat in Contemporary War*. Routledge.

Leininger, J. 2006. Democracy and UN Peacekeeping: Conflict resolution through State-building and Democracy Promotion in Haiti. *In*: A. V. B. A. R. W. (ed.) *Mack Plank Yearbook of United Nations Law*. Volume 10, 465–530. Koninklijke Brill N.V. The Netherlands.

Lemay-Hébert, N. 2012. Coerced transitions in Timor-Leste and Kosovo: Managing competing objectives of institution-building and local empowerment. *In*: Leininger, J., Grimm, S & Freyburg, T (ed.) *Do All Good Things Go Together? Conflicting Objectives in Democracy Promotion*. Routledge.

Mac Ginty, R. 2011. *International Peacebuilding and Local Resistance: Hybrid Forms of Peace*. Palgrave Macmillan.

Macqueen, N. 2011. *Humanitarian Intervention and the United Nations, Edinburgh*. Oxford University Press.

Mazarr, M. J. 2014. The Rise and Fall of the Failed-State Paradigm. Requiem for a Decade of Distraction. *Foreign Affairs*.

Misra, A. 2013. *Politics of Civil Wars: Conflict, Intervention & Resolution*. Taylor & Francis.

Moore, T. 2013. Saving Friends or Saving Strangers? Critical Humanitarianism and the Geopolitics of International Law. *Review Of International Studies*, 39, 925–947.

Morgenthau, H. J. 1967. To Intervene or Not to Intervene. *Foreign Affairs*.

Mosquera, A. B. M. 2011. *Democratization through UN Peacekeeping Operations? Peacekeeping Regimes*. WLP.

Myrttinen, H. 2008. *External Democracy Promotion in Post-Conflict Zones: Evidence from Case Studies*. Freie Universität Berlin.

Newman, E. & Rich, R. 2004. *The UN Role in Promoting Democracy: Between Ideals and Reality*. United Nations University Press.

Ozoukou, D. 2014. Building peace or a fragile future? The legacy of conflict in the Cote d'Ivoire. *Insight on Conflict*, p.24/12/2014.

Peck, C. 2001. The Role of Regional Organizations in Preventing Conflict. In Turbulent Peace, edited by Crocker, Hampson and Aall (Washington DC: United States Institute of Peace) pp.561.

Pereira Watts, I. 2017. Is Humanitarian Aid Politicized? *E-International Relations*. Apr 13 2017 ed.

Ray, A. 2012. *Peace Is Everybody's Business: A Strategy for Conflict Prevention*. SAGE India.

Richmond, O. 2011. De-romanticising the Local, De-mystifying the International: Hybridity in Timor Leste and the Solomon Islands. *The Pacific Review*, 24, 115–136.

Richmond, O. & Franks, J. 2009. *Liberal Peace Transitions: Between Statebuilding and Peacebuilding*. Edinburgh University Press.

Richmond, O. P. 2015. The dilemmas of a hybrid peace: Negative or positive? *Cooperation and Conflict*, 50, 50–68.

Robert J. Art & Greenhill, K. M. 2015. *The Use of Force: Military Power and International Politics*. Rowman & Littlefield, 5.

Sandholtz, W. 2002. Humanitarian Intervention: Global Enforcement of Human Rights? *In*: Berkley, A. B. (ed.) *Globalization and Human Rights*. University of California Press.

Schraeder, P. J. 2002. *Exporting Democracy: Rhetoric vs. Reality*. Lynne Rienner Publishers.

Simonen, K. 2011. *The State versus the Individual: The Unresolved Dilemma of Humanitarian Intervention*. Martinus Nijhoff.

SIPRI. 2012. Responsibility While Protecting': Are We Asking the Wrong Questions? *In*: Avezov, X. (ed.). Stockholm International Peace Research Institute. Online Article. Available at https://www.sipri.org/node/409. Accessed on 02/08/2018

Stahn, C. 2006. 'Jus ad bellum', 'jus in bello' ... 'jus post bellum'? – Rethinking the Conception of the Law of Armed Force. *European Journal of International Law*, 17, 921–943.

Taylor, P. 2001. The United Nations and the International order: A brief history of the United Nations. *In*: Smith, J. B. S. (ed.) *The Globalization of World Politics: An Introduction to International Relations*. 2nd ed. ed. Oxford University Press.

Touval, S. 1994. Why the UN Fails. *Foreign Affairs*, 73.

Trinkunas, H. A. 2010. *Ungoverned Spaces: Alternatives to State Authority in an Era of Softened Sovereignty*. Stanford University Press.

UN-DPKO. 2009. *A New Partnership Agenda. Charting a New Horizon for UN Peacekeeping*. UN-DPKO.

UN-DPKO. 2016. *A Fact Sheet of Peacekeeping* [Online]. Available: http://www.un.org/en/peacekeeping/about/dpko/ [Accessed 5.12.2016].

UN. 1945. *Charter of the United Nations* [Online]. Available: http://www.un.org/en/documents/charter/ [Accessed 28.02.2015].

UNOCHA. 2016. *Global Humanitarian Overview 2016*. UNOCHA.

Verrill, D. L. 2011. *United Nations Peacekeeping Missions: The Effect of Peacekeepers on Mission Effectiveness*. Ph.D., The University of Texas at Dallas.

Wallensteen, P. 2008. International Responses to Crises of Democratization in War-torn Societies. *In*: Jarstad, A. K. & Sick, T. D. (eds.) *From War to Democracy: Dilemmas of Peacebuilding*. Cambridge University Press.

Watts, S. 2008. Enforcing Democracy? Assessing the Relationship between Peace Operations and Post-Conflict Democratization. University of Massachusetts. US. Amherst Paper prepared for the annual meeting of the International Studies Association, Chicago, February 28 – March 3, 2007.

Wheeler, N. J. & Bellamy, A. J. 2005. Humanitarian Intervention in World Politics. *In*: Smith, J. B. A. S. (ed.) *The Globalization of World Politics*. Oxford University Press.

Willems, R. C. 2015. *Security and Hybridity after Armed Conflict: The Dynamics of Security Provision in Post-Civil War States*. Taylor & Francis.

Zeeuw, J. D. 2004. How to Make Democracy Assistance More Effective? Recommendations for Doing It Differently. European Conference 'Enhancing the European Profile in Democracy Assistance'.

Zürcher, C., Manning, C., Evenson, K., Hayman, R., Riese, S. & Roehner, N. 2013. *Costly Democracy : Peacebuilding and Democratization After War*. Stanford University Press.

3
FROM GUNS TO VOTES TO DOVES
Violent transition with ballots and bullets

Election c pas gnaga.[1]
Expression in Nouchi, Ivorian street language

Are elections worth dying for? That is a beguiling question for post-conflict scenarios, as votes may generate more bullets than they are meant to stop (IFES, 2014; Gowa, 2011). Ironically, civil wars that end by a one-side victory are statistically more likely to experience a long-term period of non-violence through illiberal norms (Piccolino, 2015). Despite the association of democracy with peaceful means of conflict resolution through consensus building and respect for the rule of law, the democratization process might bring more violence instead of stability. In other words, in theory, democracy would promote internal security by institutionalizing political competition, effectively trading bullets for the ballot box. This trade-off would aid political elites by providing them with an incentive to avoid repressing their opponents and for the pretenders to prevent the use of force (Diamond, 2008; Jarstad and Sisk, 2008; Collier, 2009). However, while it is expected that, in a democracy, social actors should be able to pursue their demands and address legitimate grievances through non-violent political processes, in incomplete democratization sets, "voting and violence" or "fighting and voting" is perceived as synonymous (Linebarger and Salehyan, 2012; Dunning, 2011).

As Doyle and Sambanis (2006, p. 341) stated: "Premature democracy is dangerous and the transition process also carries new risks of renewed conflict." Statistically, embryonic democracies face turbulent transitions, and this rarely results in a "velvet revolution": they are 50 percent more prone to the recurrence of war. Additionally, during the transition phase of democratization, post-conflict countries are two-thirds (2/3) more likely to go to war with another state, including democratic ones (Mansfield and Snyder, 1995, p. 65; Crocker et al.,

DOI: 10.4324/9781003279976-5

2001; Kim, 2007). Paradoxically, elections in the aftermath of conflict can often trigger violence (Gillies, 2011; Mohan, 2015). Simply put, in rogue states, ballots might bring more bullets (Mansfield and Snyder, 2005b; Gowa, 2011). In that regard, democracy would be prone to violence, not to peace (Mansfield and Snyder, 2005a). This results in an "electing violence" epitome and makes the electoral process a political camouflage leading to a significant number of electoral autocracies (Claes, 2016). Electoral violence presents a major problem as it undermines the legitimacy of political leaders. It can destroy the entire purpose of the electoral process and its outcome as well as a country's concern for democratization.

The literature on democracy usually focuses on aspects of non-violence. However, it pays much less attention to addressing democratization as a cause and consequence of violence (Hoglund, 2008). The democratization, violence, and peace nexus engenders two main paradoxes: first, peace and democratization processes create new incentives for violence, particularly from elites taking advantage of the fragility of institutions to mobilize their supporters along ethnic and nationalist lines (IFES, 2014). Second, measures to "stop violence with more violence" are dangerous and might undermine democracy, peace, and state-building efforts. Even so, the use of coercive force that might violate human rights can often be the most effective violence deterrence policy against even worse violence. Besides the eruption of hostility on the actual days of elections, referendums, and peace agreement signing, election-related violence may also occur immediately before and after the polls. Although there is a substantive body of literature on electoral violence and monitoring, there is surprisingly little specifically focused on an integrated approach to the intersection between the conflict cycle, the democratization cycle, and the state institution-building cycle (Kammerud, 2012). Therefore, as illustrated in Figure 3.1, this suggests room for further analysis.

Consequently, although post-conflict transitions offer an essential window of opportunity for the (re-)construction and restoration of peace, they also entail a high risk of crisis that can rapidly degenerate into renewed warfare (Demetriou and Bosi, 2016). Thus, this chapter brings to light crucial correlating evidence concerning democratization, violence, conflict, and fragile states by formulating three guiding questions: (1) Why do democracy-building efforts create violence in fragile states? (2) What are the main peacebuilding dilemmas related to democratization and violence? (3) How to combat or prevent violence without undermining democracy, peace, and state-building processes? To address these questions, this section analyzes the relationship between democratization and violence instead of its usual association with peace. Second, it addresses the causes and consequences of violence during transition times, based on a set of dilemmas and their connection with state disruption. The inclusion of violence as a consequence – not only a cause of the peace struggle – enables a more inclusive and in-depth understanding of the transitional challenges from civil war to peace through democratization. Finally, it concludes that moving from civil war toward peace via democracy-building can be a turbulent transition. Methodologically, the nexus between violence, democratization, and fragile states will be analyzed through elections, media, and security sector reform. Notably, the dilemmas related to these indicators will be further elucidated in thefollowing chapters (5 to 9), without solely focusing on them as drivers of violence.

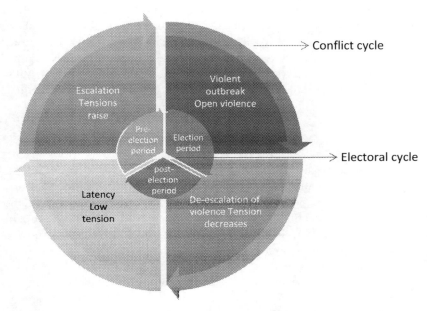

FIGURE 3.1 Integrated approach to violence and democratization: conflict cycle and electoral cycle. Source: Author. Inspired from Kammerud (2012 pp. 3 and 5)

3.1 U curves and "violent democracy": anocracies, civil wars, and fragile states

Political violence is frequently a response to too little democracy (Hoglund, 2008 pp. 101). A political system is not democratic because the majority rules but because the institutions are designed to prevent the rise of a totalitarian government that can, in principle, be dismissed through popular accountability instead of through violent revolution. In fragile democracies, particularly in war-shattered societies, politics is contentious, and elections too often feature intimidation or violent protest, such as in Somalia in 2021. Flawed democracies relate closely to civil war through an inverted U curve: semi-democracies are much more prone to violence than either consolidated democracies or autocracies because, in the latter, institutions can prevent or manage demonstrations that could turn violent (Gleditsch et al., 2007). Consequently, electoral violence has gained prominence over the years within the broader fields of peace and security studies. Much of the literature looks at the micro-level dynamics of drivers, triggers, perpetrators, and victims of violence surrounding general elections instead of the macro level. Part of the reason for this gap in the literature on violence related to the democratization process in war-torn societies is the lack of credible cross-national data (Linebarger and Salehyan, 2012).

As seen in the 2016 elections in the Philippines and the Democratic Republic of the Congo (DRC), high-stakes elections frequently trigger anxiety, tension, violence, or the threat of unrest (Claes, 2016). For example, in 2016, Gabon's presidential election resulted in violence with more than 1,000 arrested, some killed, and opposition party headquarters and the National Assembly bombed (CNN, 2016). In addition, the tensions and turmoil in Haiti (2015–2017/2018–2022), Uganda (2016) and Macedonia (2017) demonstrate the complex relationship between elections, democratic stability, and peace.

As democracy is in decline (Freedom House, 2021; Freedom House, 2019; IDEA, 2021), it is not surprising that there will be a rise in violent protests. Instead, it becomes evidence of the deterioration of people's satisfaction with their governments regarding a plethora of issues, such as cost of living, restrictions of freedoms, racism, justice, and response to the coronavirus pandemic. This upsurge of violent demonstrations can be seen in every corner of the globe, including in the United States after Trump's electoral defeat and Sudan in 2019 (EIU, 2019; Wright, 2019). In 2021 – the year that marked the thirtieth anniversary of the collapse of the Somali state – an electoral crisis tipped into violence over President Farmajo's mandate. The most significant risk is that continued clashes further fracture the Somali security sector along clan lines. Resolving the electoral crisis requires political reconciliation among Somali elites, reducing the gaping trust deficit between the opposition and the government, and reinforcing the need for external intervention (ICG, 2021). Additional to the existing conflict in Somaliland, between 60,000 and 100,000 people were forcibly displaced due to the electoral crisis (HRW, 2021). Due to migration, and globalization to a larger extent, electoral political violence can be perpetrated outside the country. The Turkish 2017 referendum that strengthened the power of the office of the president incited violent riots in Germany and in Brussels, Belgium. Coincidently or not, Erdogan's decision also impacted on the fight with Kurdistan Workers' Party (PKK) militants and escalated other international political tensions in the region, including the Syrian war and the refugee crisis. Beyond direct elections relation, Myanmar (2021), Thailand (2019), Hong Kong (2019–2020), and Tunisia (2021) are also examples of popular protests turning violent.

In Burundi, peace was sacrificed (UNHCR, 2015). Less than a decade after the Arusha Accords, a political crisis erupted in 2015 as President Pierre Nkurunziza attempted a third mandate after already being reelected in 2010 in violent battles. The "Halte au troisième mandat"[2] street movement escalated into violence during which at least 1,200 people were killed. More than 400,000 Burundians fled the violent outbreak into Rwanda, Tanzania, and the DRC, resulting in a spillover effect in the already politically and ethnically violent Great Lakes region. Nevertheless, Nkurunziza, a Hutu and a former rebel of the National Council for the Defense of Democracy – Forces for the Defense of Democracy (CNDD–FDD), held power for almost 15 years from 2005. The regime in Burundi became rapidly more authoritarian under President Pierre Nkurunziza's third and fourth mandate until his COVID-related death in 2020. Rhetoric and frictions that led to war and massacres in the past returned with a rapid escalation of violence, particularly during the 2018 referendum undertaken to alter the constitution. Thus, it is debatable if "the last ten years of peace in Burundi have not become a mere interlude between two wars" (ICC, 2015; UN News Centre, 2015).

Political violence is not only about elections per se. In South Africa, "black-on-black" violence, also known as "informal repression," killed 20,000 between 1985 and 1994, and it almost disrupted the transition to majority rule (Berkeley, 2001; Szablewska and Bachmann, 2014). In Timor-Leste, the 2006 crisis erupted due to embryonic and factionalized state institutions, political rivalries dating back to the independence struggle, extreme poverty, and a large and disempowered youth population. Sections of the army, known as "the petitioners," rose in response to alleged regional discrimination by officers originating from eastern areas of a small territory of approximately 300 km long. Violent clashes were widespread between groups of Easterners and Westerners within the army and police and youth gangs among the wider population. It ended up with almost 40 people killed, around 3,000 houses destroyed, over 2,000 severely damaged, and 150,000 people internally displaced among 65 camps (IOM, 2012; IDMC, 2009). While the causes of violence may stem from other grievances, the increased political mobilization during election times increases the risk that even minor provocations will spark violence.

Additionally, 2015 anti-government protests resulted in outbreaks of electoral violence in Ethiopia. A state of emergency was declared in October 2016 by the Ethiopian People's Revolutionary Democratic Front (EPRDF), mainly led by the Tigrayan People's Liberation Front (TPLF). An estimated 900 people were killed in clashes with security forces in Oromia alone throughout a year of violent anti-government protests. Demonstrators of the Oromo and Amhara ethnic groups, representing 60 percent of the population, demanded social and political reforms, including an end to human rights abuses (such as government killings of civilians, mass arrests, government land seizures, and political marginalization of opposition groups) and more access to power. The government responded by restricting access to the internet and the use of lethal force by the police, attacking and arresting 11,000 people in the first months of protests. The state of emergency was also used as a tool to crack down on political opponents and the media. The increased pressure in 2017 marked a continuation of a long-term worsening trend in state fragility (FFP, 2017). The electoral crisis fueled preexisting tensions and a civil war erupted in 2020 in the Tigray region between the local Tigray Defense Forces (TDF), Tigrayan People's Liberation Front (TPLF), Ethiopian National Defense Force (ENDF), and Oromo Liberation Army (OLA). The conflict spilled over to Sudan, Somalia, and Eritrea with the involvement of the Eritrean Defence Forces (EDF), the UN mission in Somalia, and the African Union. By March 2022, it is estimated that half a million people were displaced: between 50,000 and 100,000 from the fighting, 150,000 to 200,000 from starvation, and more than 100,000 from the lack of medical attention. Thus, some argue that the "world's deadliest war isn't in Ukraine, but in Ethiopia" and Prime Minister and Nobel Peace Prize winner Abiy Ahmed should be listed as a war criminal (Ghosh, 2022). In this regard, the query of de Waal (1992) remains contemporaneous. Ethiopia: transition to what?

Africa is the continent with the most peacekeeping missions as it is also the one with the highest number of civil wars and fragile states. Thus, it might provide some insights to better understand violence and democratization, peacebuilding, and state-building dynamics. Burchard (2015) shows that out of nearly 300 elections held from 1990 to 2014 in sub-Saharan Africa, between 50 and 60 percent experienced some form of violence. However, according to the African Electoral Violence Database, even in sub-Saharan Africa, 10 to 20 percent of elections involve the type of widespread killings as seen in Kenya in 2008 or Nigeria in 2011 (Claes, 2016). Research on elections in Africa from 1995 to 2014 shows that state actors have been the biggest perpetrators of electoral malfeasance and violence on the continent (Birch, 2016). Although most of the misconduct is in the forms of threats rather than actual assaults, this creates intimidation, violates rights, and, thus, undermines democracy. Nevertheless, non-state actors are likelier to commit violent acts, intending to boycott elections and any other democratization process (Mohan, 2015).

Thus, competitive elections, the sine qua non of a democratic government, often give rise to severe political violence attacks (Mary Beth Altier et al., 2016). Indeed, roughly one-fifth (1/5) of all elections worldwide are marred by electoral violence (Norris, 2012). These findings also reveal a U-shaped relationship between the state's concentration of power and the likelihood of electoral violence: disruption occurs at high levels in failed states and in authoritarian states where violence is concentrated in the hands of a few, and the "people" do not really participate in any legitimate decision making. Recent studies also suggest that socioeconomic conditions play an even more critical role in peace than the political regime (Hegre, 2014). In fact, there seems to be an inverse U-curve correlation between economic development and levels of electoral violence: the less economically industrialized, the more prone to violence. For instance, Bourne argues that "Zimbabwe's tragedy is not just about Mugabe, but a representation of failed democratization and state-building processes in a fragile state" (2012). Considering the nexus between violence, civil war, and disrupted settings, state fragility is mutually the cause and the consequence of a lack of democracy. Hence, violence related to democratization breaks out in some places and not others due to the state's fragility, which is exceptionally high during transition phases.

Additionally, there is a special relationship between terrorism and other forms of political violence mobilization (Vines, 1996). Terrorist organizations might use democratic elections to foment violence (Mary Beth Altier et al., 2016). Research has demonstrated that terrorist attacks increase in about 52 percent of cases as elections approach (Newman, 2016). One of the main challenges for effective democratization is holding elections when it is complicated to ensure a workable level of security (Newman and Rich, 2004). For example, the first indirect election since 1969 was held in Somalia in 2017. Nevertheless, the constant threat of attacks by Al-Shabaab put the process in jeopardy. The relationship between terrorism and political violence is particularly important in this book. It involves boycotting any democratization process, such as those perpetrated, respectively, by the Tuareg Rebellion, Al-Qaeda, and Boko Haran in Mali in 2013 and 2018 and Nigeria's 2015 political contests (Aljazeera, 2015). Similarly, terrorist groups also often paralyze the peace process if they can take more advantage of the status quo of belligerency instead of democratic stability and order.

3.2 Dilemmas of violence in democratic civil peace transitions: causes and consequences of why violence breeds violence

Many reasons are attributed to political violence during democratization. Before clarifying its causes and consequences, it is primordial to distinguish criminal violence from political and electoral violence. Political assassinations, violent riots, threats, voting sabotage, the destruction of public or private property, and coercion are common menaces to a new political dynamic. Armed insurgents commonly use criminal acts, such as extortion and kidnapping, for political purposes, such as financing the armed struggle. Electoral violence is defined as any harm or threat of harm to any person or property involved in the election process or to the process itself (IFES, 2014). Electoral violence is a subcategory of political violence (Fjelde and Hoglund, 2014). A rise in criminal violence due to poverty and changes in how rebel forces are funded can also stimulate anti-democratic political forces to be elected due to the promises of "going heavy-duty to combat crime and to restore peace and order," such as in the Philippines (Mindanao) under Duterte. The gangs in El Salvador and Honduras are examples of post-civil war countries with high levels of crime, abuse of human rights, as well as a lack of protection for civilians (Call, 2002). Importantly, as part of the peace negotiations, many belligerents transform themselves into political parties, including the Revolutionary Armed Forces of Colombia (FARC), see Chapter 5. Nevertheless, new creative forms of masqueraded political violence can be perpetrated by the spoilers as criminal violence without them being charged with breaking the ceasefire. As with the Irish Republican Army (IRA) in Northern Ireland, the same group uses fraud and robbery instead of kidnapping to finance its activities. If so, violence will reescalate. And perpetrators will be part of the formal political power structure holding key positions and guaranteeing financial support without a commitment to the peace agreement. Moreover, rising violence, even when politically masqueraded, might undermine the entire peace process cycle. Therefore, during political transition, legal enforcement and the differentiation between political, electoral, or criminal activity is particularly blurred, making it difficult to tackle them appropriately.

Second, it is also essential to distinguish between two types of elections, or democratization violence: strategic and incidental. Perpetrators often also intentionally disguise their motives, making those types of violence frequently indistinguishable. As typically seen in Ethiopia, Liberia, and Zimbabwe, strategic violence is unleashed in a pre-planned and systematic fashion, sometimes committed by youth groups or party-affiliated militias, to affect the outcome of an election and ensure a particular candidate or party wins office. Incidental violence, such as in 2020 in Belarus, requires no planning and is generally borne out of frustration and spontaneous circumstances. The 2012 elections in Senegal and the 2016 elections in Niger are also examples of incidental violence with clashes between protesters and overzealous security forces or between supporters of opposing candidates or parties (Burchard, 2015). Although the difference between strategic and incidental violence is based on motivation and planning, most cases involve a combination of these two. Both may occur before, during, and after the voting.

The 2021 Ugandan election assured President Yoweri Museveni would rule for his sixth term. He has used political violence to control power since 1986, including acts to prevent opposition candidates from participating in election-related activities and to harass, intimidate, and arrest opposition supporters from voting. In 2016, the opposition leader, Kizza Besigye, was detained by the police four times in eight days without charges and placed under house arrest for several days directly after the results were announced. Prior to the election, Red Berets, a senior military police force, stormed through the streets with AK-47s and armored police vehicles, killing and injuring civilians. Alleging "security concerns," the government blocked social media on election day as a calculated move to make it challenging to share timely information about the elections and potential incidents of fraud and human rights abuses (Meyerfeld, 2016; MacDougall, 2016). Previous elections in 2001, 2006, and 2011 have all followed a similar script of violence, detention, widespread fraud, voting irregularities, repeated arrest of opposition politicians, and a climate of voter intimidation leading to the victory of Museveni.

To address electoral violence, it is necessary to tackle "electoral security." Those policies intend to prevent, mitigate, or respond to electoral violence. The problem is that they will differ according to how violence is classified. Electoral security encompasses all aspects of protecting electoral stakeholders, such as voters, candidates, poll workers, the media and observers; electoral information such as voting results and registration data; electoral property, such as campaign materials, ballot papers, results sheets, and indelible ink; electoral facilities, such as polling stations and counting centers; and electoral events, such as campaign rallies and efforts to prevent disruption, damage, or death (IFES, 2007). Therefore, due to the blurred differentiation between political and criminal violence and strategic and incidental, electoral security is subject to constant improvement. This chapter will proceed with a double-integrated approach named "transitional violence" for a more robust concept-based analysis. It will consider all kinds of violent political incidents occurring during the entire electoral cycle (before, during, and after) and in-between elections as part of the democratization dynamic in parallel with peacebuilding and state-building efforts.

Importantly, in the transition period, there are five situations where violence is most likely to manifest and to undermine the democratization process: (1) in the opening of space for political competition that is required for elections, (2) in the freedom of expression required by the media, (3) in the military and police force, who are essential players in reforming the security sector, (4) by the inclusion of spoilers in politics, and (5) by the use of force to manage violence so that organized political conflicts generate new forms of violence that require new tactics. Furthermore, in postwar elections, violence will depend, to a large extent, on whether the insurgent group conquers the government and attains power by force or assumes the role of an opposition party (Soderberg Kovacs, 2008). Furthermore, four dynamic processes are especially relevant for radicalization and violence in contentious politics: the dynamics of oppositional movement groups and their interaction with the state, the dynamics of intra-movement competition, the dynamics of meaning formation and transformation, and the dynamics of transnational diffusion (Demetriou and Bosi, 2016).

3.2.1 Dimension of actors

How do violence, conflict, and fragile states, respectively, oppose democratization and peace and state-building processes based on the framework of transitional dilemmas? The vertical dilemma can explain why elites play a role in fomenting violence (Zürcher et al., 2013). For actors wishing to influence the system, instability equals opportunity. These elites can also be referred to as spoilers. As explained by Stedman (2000), leaders and parties might perceive that peace emerging from negotiations threatens their power. Consequently, they are tempted to use violence to spoil the democratic peacebuilding process. Local elites base their legitimacy on traditional authority and ethnic sectarianism. Civil wars, particularly when they are extensive, highly destructive, and fought amid identity groups, create highly divided societies and elites who deeply mistrust one another. Therefore, this situation decreases a society's capacity for a stable and democratic peace because "actors may lack the capacities to overcome the cooperation problem and be unable to engage in a meaningful peace process or to accept the bounded uncertainty that comes with democratic rules" (Zürcher et al., 2013, p. 3).

If so, violence erupts when the political system has not managed the inevitable manipulation from insiders, nor peacefully brokered the necessary alternation among power holders, and it cannot prevent attempts at usurpation by ambitious groups. When elites or spoilers are uncertain of the guarantees on their status quo of power, and when the domestic guiding rules are unclear, democratization results are a test of power. Elites, in this case, use political manipulation instead of democratic procedures. Additionally, politicians of all ideologies have incentives to play the nationalist card to recruit mass supporters so as to enable their survival in the new and more competitive political arena. This often results in xenophobic, ethnic separatist and religious racist speech instead of narratives to unify the "people" around public policies. Consequently, very often the electoral result represents an ethnic census instead of more general deliberations about public issues. Moreover, regional identities can be manipulated for political ends. Despite perceived differences in the roles played by each group in the independence struggle in Timor-Leste, there was no history of violence between Easterners and Westerners before 2006 (IOM, 2012). Easterners constituted the bulk of survivors of the resistance movement, and they also gained the best access from 2002 to institutions and resources, mainly through the FRETILIN party.

As per the temporal dilemma, early elections also might reinforce divisions in an already divided society. The party able to mobilize the quickest holds an advantage during elections. Still, it might be less effective in delivering good governance in comparison to a political party that places emphasis on forging sound policies and an institutional structure but requires more time to mobilize its supporters. At the embryonic stage of democratization and in the immediate aftermath of a democratic constitution, nationalistic parties often go to war, as happened in 1998 between Eritrea and Ethiopia. Additionally, short-term activities may help manage crises, while long-term investments in the state's capacity to provide adequate security present with a more evidence-based approach for addressing the risk of violence across and between election cycles (NDI, 2014; Donno, 2013). Thus, pushing countries too early when they are poorly prepared into competitive electoral politics risks stoking war, sectarianism, and terrorism and makes the future consolidation of democracy more difficult.

Furthermore, the horizontal dilemma is inevitable by including spoilers in political competition. It can, nevertheless, be a democratic tool for peace through power-sharing as much as it is for promoting violence. On the one hand, this is achieved by offering power patronage to the masses. But, on the other hand, by legitimating violence-makers and by the continuation of violence as a political tool. For example, the parliament that emerged following Afghanistan's 2005 and 2010 elections led to the empowerment of tribal leaders, warlords, and drug leaders alongside "marionettes" controlled by outside forces (Forsberg, 2010; Hoglund and Zartman, 2006; Stedman, 2000).

3.2.2 Security dimension

Democracy-building requires a certain level of security, raising the question of how violence is best deterred. Coercive measures normally require the use of force, which can be effective in minimizing and hopefully stopping violence, but this might create a cycle of "combatting violence with violence." This is the opposite of the democratization rhetoric of resolving conflict through non-forceful means, but through the rule of law and procedures. This controversy was present during Duterte's strong man political style in the Philippines (2016–2022). In many cases, successful violence deterrence is not achieved in accordance with human rights principles. However, to be successful, the "excessive" use of force is, in some instances, unavoidable.

Operational and design dilemmas arise when it is unclear when the use of force is "too much" or when deterrence has been "effective." Moreover, "reconciliation elections" are not always conducive to post-conflict democracy nor to peacebuilding. The organization of popular consultation in postwar societies is fundamentally different from how this operates under normal circumstances. Political competition requires freedom of movement. As per the security dilemma, this right often lacks genuine substance or is completely non-existent. It can be misused as an instrument for militant political organization through intimidation, sabotage, and violent demonstrations.

A strategy of violence is not only deployed to intimidate people from voting, as in Uganda in the 2011, 2016, and 2021 elections, but also to prevent political actors from participating in standing for election. High levels of intimidation may force a political party to leave the process. This was the case of the Oromo Liberation Front (OLF) in the 1992 elections, (Hoglund, 2008). What began, ostensibly at least, as a multiparty affair ended in, what appeared to be, the consolidation of one-party rule (Ethiopian People's Revolutionary Front–EPRDF) In fact, it generated more violence. After withdrawing from the elections, the OLF pulled its 15,000 troops out of the camps where they were vulnerable, and a short civil war ensued. The EPRDF quickly deployed a major military campaign and detained 19,000 Oromo, many allegedly rounded up as suspected sympathizers rather than combatants. This brief conflict demonstrated that behind the EPRDF's political strategy of ethnic affiliates and regional elections was an experienced and battle-hardened military that could act decisively when necessary (Lyons, 1996; de Waal, 1992). Since then, regional authorities in Oromia have cultivated a climate of fear and repression by using state power to punish political dissent in often brutal fashion. Regional and local authorities have consistently harassed and abused perceived critics of the government (HRW, 2005). After three decades of exclusive political dominance that made Ethiopia a classic electoral autocracy, the Ethiopian Peoples' Revolutionary Democratic Front (EPRDF) was dismissed by violent protest in 2018. A civil war in the Tigray region erupted in 2020. Despite COVID-19, problems with voter registration and a humanitarian crisis, many expected the 2021 election to be a litmus test of whether Ethiopia was departing from its authoritarian tradition and transitioning to democracy (IDEA, 2022). Many political parties withdrew because of the temporal dilemma between holding elections as per the constitution or postponing them for logistical and health reasons. Violence, political polarization, and a humanitarian crisis in Tigray are evidence that the fragile state of Ethiopia is not transitioning from armed civil conflict toward democracy or peace.

Similarly, the referendum on self-determination in Timor-Leste in August 1999 demonstrated the courage of the Timorese people despite militia harassment. It also showed the importance of UNAMET's presence, providing the population with some reassurance that a secure environment exited in which to vote. However, the majority pro-independence party unleached a severe outbreak of violence by militia groups supported by the Indonesian government. A new mission (UNTAET) was then established to provide an interim transitional civil administration and also to restore law and order – almost 10,000 military and 2,000 police personnel were deployed. The causes of the 2006 and 2008 political crises are clearly non-related to elections; nonetheless, it resulted in a high level of violence, deaths, and IDPs. Yet, the following legislative and presidential elections in 2012, 2017, and 2022 were held in a secure environment with peaceful results and a high turnout of between 71 and 85 percent (IFES, 2017).

As for the existential dilemma, it is important to note that during armed conflicts, security forces hold extreme powers for counter-insurgency and the repression of the opposition. During democratic times, security forces are expected to protect civilians. However, during transition times, new dilemmas arise due to the change of the security forces' raison d'être as well as the shift in power relations as new security threats increase and security forces themselves diminish. As for rebel forces, the economic activities and security plans used to fund the conflict are frequently transmuted into organized crime. Thus, the security vacuum resulting from this existential shift of security forces away from violent conflict may lead to an increase in criminal violence.

Exchanging political violence for criminal violence leaves the impression that it is like changing six of one for half a dozen of the other. And it is hardly a successful transition to peace and stability. Legislation that gives broad powers to the security forces, whether through the retention of powers accrued from war or through expansion, ostensibly for peace prevention, is also an invitation for the continuity of the abuses that were committed during the previous period of armed struggle. Normally, there are not enough peace contingents, either national or international. Even more often, they are not trained or well equipped. Under such circumstances, it is highly improbable that security forces will deter violence successfully, especially without abuses of human rights.

Additionally, in the aftermath of civil war, a vacuum of power rarely, if ever, exists. When state institutions fail to provide security, vigilante groups and private security companies fill the vacuum. The privatization of the security forces undermines democracy by eroding the legitimacy of state institutions. Historically, African police units such as in Uganda, Sierra Leone, and the DRC were tools of colonial repression. Thus, rather than being associated with safety, the uniform is often seen as a source of fear and oppression, abuse, and extortion. The increase of private securities, often better equipped and paid, motivates high officials to be involved in private security forces as a highly profitable source of additional income. Such activities create vast income differences within the police force, generate cutthroat competition for more profitable jobs, and erode overall morale. In countries such as Angola and Liberia, security forces are politicized. Thus, there are also questions of undue political influence, since some high-ranking government and military officials in some countries reportedly own security firms (Kimani, 2009). Therefore, the irregular nature of such activities, including corruption, debilitates the public security forces and reduces the legitimacy of already weak governments as a public protector in the eyes of their citizens. Police officers may lose the incentive to serve the public, and the population increasingly sees security as a commodity that only the rich can afford. Furthermore, it also polarizes the society between the elites and the "rest" who will have to deal with violence on their own (Hoglund, 2008). Although the terms "privatization of war (or peace)" are normally used for mercenaries (Bellamy et al., 2010), the privatization of domestic conflict/peace poses similar problems of polarization and factionalism. When such privatized security affects daily life, an escalated perception of crime and instability contributes to the cycle of violence and impedes the efforts to foster state, democracy, and peacebuilding (Figure 3.1). Vigilante groups and other militias are often the cheapest and most reliable form "to provide the protection services that the state is not able to provide" (Kimani, 2009). However, some vigilante groups, such as Kamjesh in Kenya or the Bakassi Boys in Nigeria, have themselves evolved into criminal organizations and extortion rings. The conundrum of privatization of peace has become even more complex as, in most of these countries, private security providers are allowed to carry arms. Without regulation, they can easily be misused for criminal purposes.

Furthermore, a temporal dilemma again emerges regarding the security dimension as it is particularly crucial regarding democratization and violence. Security institutions, such as the police and military, must also be democratized. Reform takes time and might leave society particularly vulnerable to violence. Inaction and a lack of reform for creation of a secure environment, including monitoring of human rights, are also motives for violence, as instability, fear, and the perception of impunity generates grievances, potentially resulting in outbreaks of violence.

Moreover, popular consultations, such as elections, referendums and plebiscites, are often set when the Disarmament, Demobilization, and Reintegration (DDR) process has not finished nor even begun, as in the Afghan (2004, 2009, and 2014) and Iraqi (2005, 2010, and 2014) elections. With a large number of weapons in social circulation and easy access to them, the result can be a population that "votes in fear" (Bekoe et al., 2012). Abuses of power and violence inevitably continue because the security forces are also the same people who have been the perpetrators of "institutionalized violence" during the war. In times of transition, as in the cases of Guatemala and Honduras, the perpetuation of the same operational mindset frequently leads to the continuation of abuses by security forces, thereby impeding the reconciliation necessary for democratization (Fischer, 2017b).

3.2.3 Institutional dimension

Democracy needs a functioning state in which to operate. A design dilemma is related to the method of democratic political competition and achieving peaceful results. Where large ethnopolitical groups are excluded from power, and significant economic inequalities exist, majoritarian institutions are particularly prone to provoking violence. Political violence remains a pervasive feature of electoral dynamics even where multiparty elections have become the dominant mode of regulating access to political power. Research with cross-national data drawn from polls on electoral violence in sub-Saharan Africa between 1990 and 2010 illustrates that electoral violence is more likely in countries that employ majoritarian voting rules and elect fewer legislators from each district. Majoritarian systems tend to reward larger parties disproportionately and impose high barriers to political representation (Linebarger and Salehyan, 2012; Fjelde and Hoglund, 2014).

Where democratic institutions are consolidated, the threat of a decisive electoral defeat is not sufficient to motivate the use of violence. However, in nonconsolidated democracies, these formal rules interact with powerful informal institutions, such as patron-client relationships, that bond political power to economic benefits for the individual politician and his relatives and ethnic group. These informal institutions heighten the stakes of the electoral contest in two critical ways. First, politicians are motivated to seek public offices for the privileges they entail, and voters are motivated to support politicians from their own ethnic group who will be able to allocate more state resources to that group. This creates a perception of exclusion of minorities.

Second, an electoral advantage is provided to those politicians who already have political power. In this context, the winner takes all dynamics introduced by majoritarian systems reinforce the perception of electoral competition as a zero-sum contest for the dominance of the state and its sources of patronage. The perceived costs of electoral loss and the fear of permanent exclusion under majoritarian rules induce incumbents to employ violence to influence the outcome of the elections. Hence, authors like Fjelde and Hoglund (2014, p. 298) argue that "not only electoral violence will be more likely in countries employing majoritarian electoral rules, but also, it will be particularly prone to violence when large ethnopolitical groups are excluded from political power." An opposition with a sizeable electoral constituency might represent a real threat to the incumbent party. Consequently, it motivates all incumbents to rely on violent strategies to win an election.

Additionally, majoritarian institutions are particularly prone to violence in countries with high levels of economic inequality. This is because the stakes of the elections and the costs of electoral defeat increase when both political power and economic capital are scarcely distributed and tightly intertwined. Thus, electoral violence is more likely in countries with majoritarian rules and small electoral districts than in proportional representation (PR) systems. As well, it is more probable where large ethnopolitical groups are excluded from formal political power and where land is controlled by a narrow sector of a divided society (Fjelde and Hoglund, 2014). Moreover, hand in hand with the design dilemma, the sequencing impasse is also activated as it is unclear if violence could break out more at local or national elections or even in the space between the two.

Strategic violence is generally related to electoral institutions that promote a winner takes all mentality and where judiciaries and the rule of law are weak. Peaceful transition requires moving away from patronage and repression as the basis of government rule and introducing economic reforms that enable the development of a more competent and impartial state administration (Chesterman et al., 2006; Zürcher et al., 2013; Themnér and Utas, 2016). There is a natural struggle when dealing with such a large number of cases, aggravated by the lack of funding and human resources, which is clearly an operational dilemma. Hence, for example, in November 2012, the Nigerian Independent National Electoral Commission (INEC) prosecuted only 200 of the 870,000 electoral offenders during the 2011 elections (IFES, 2014). The consequences of deliberately engaging in electoral violence are rarely enforced, usually leaving the perpetrators free. As there is unlikely to be a judicial trial of the perpetrators of violence, whether from the government or from non-government actors, perceptions of a lack of justice and a culture of impunity readily become an incentive for violence.

With a lack of appropriate legislation, the electoral management bodies (EMBs), local organizations, and other institutions also play a fundamental role regarding violence, democratization, peacebuilding, and state-building. The credibility, cooperation, planning, and training programs of political groups and public trust in the political process play an important role in ensuring a peaceful process and conflict prevention, even in the face of irregularities or crises. Skepticism toward the electoral process fuels anger among opposition supporters. Research demonstrates that countries suffering from electoral malpractice are more susceptible to electoral violence. The National Elections Across Democracy and Autocracy Database (NELDA, 2013) shows that elections became the scenes of fatal violence in places with the lowest electoral integrity scores. Kenya's 2007 presidential election is cited as a common example of an election in a dangerous place and the paradoxes of democracy and peacebuilding (Gillies, 2011). The failure of the Electoral Commission of Kenya to achieve transparent and accountable vote counting was identified as one of the most significant triggers of the violence that broke out during the presidential election. Ballot casting went well, but ensuing irregularities (both real and alleged), bad communication strategies, and underlying grievances combined to fuel violence as the EMB announced the results under pressure and without addressing the issues. Moreover, the lack of a clear statement of the problem and possible solutions (e.g., election contests, mediation, and results audit) left the situation vulnerable to escalating violence.

The benefits of trust and transparency are most evident when things go wrong, not when they go well (Kammerud, 2012; Mohan, 2015). This leads to a transparency dilemma. Institutional trust forms an integral role in all phases of the democratization and peacebuilding process. Hand in hand with the temporal trade-offs, the operational dilemma also shows that too often elections take place without judicial mechanisms to rule on election-related disputes. Institutions are not in place or human capital is not legitimized to solve such disputes, and violence is a ready alternative. Thus, the financial dilemma also is identified: it is a challenge to finance elections as the tax system is not yet in place or is very fragile in the aftermath of war.

Technical expertise is not enough for operational success. The promotion of democracy and the prevention of electoral violence (PEV) in countries at risk are better analyzed when elections are understood as a process (Kammerud, 2012). Mistakenly, elections are very often analyzed as a one-day event. Peaceful elections are no guarantee for democratic quality, while free and fair elections are no guarantee of election security. The paradox is well illustrated by the 2010 elections in Côte d'Ivoire: while the democratic quality of the polls had improved compared to past elections, the elections were among the most violent in the country's history (Claes, 2016; IFES, 2014). The 2011 elections in Nigeria were also an example of this contradiction.

Notably, the systemic dilemma also plays a role in the ownership of the democratization process after a civil war or military intervention. In recent decades, international non-governmental organizations, national development agencies, and international organizations have increasingly adopted a role in election support with their focus on political violence prevention (Gillies, 2011).[3] Usually, when external forces aim to impose democratization, they do so by dividing and ruling. This only creates more polarization, and, consequently, more violence, further prolonging the transition. In most cases, peacekeepers take the task of policing and even judiciary powers with a mandate for prosecution and trial. Consequently, peacekeepers might also violate human rights, particularly when torture means obtaining information and a coercive tool (Hoglund, 2008). Accordingly, this might also erode sovereignty and the legitimacy of state institutions, precisely when this legitimacy is most fragile and needed. Additionally, it also reduces the authority of the peacekeepers and the enforcement of international law.

International assistance can easily become a two-edged sword: it can reduce violence in some circumstances and increase it in others. A new specific sub-dilemma appears: the monitoring dilemma. International organizations can influence election violence by altering the incentives of domestic actors. The effect depends on the type of International Organisations' (IOs) assistance (technical assistance or monitoring) and the election phase (before or after election day). Technical assistance builds trust in election management bodies and contributes to reducing violence in the aftermath of elections, particularly through the use of consolidated methodologies such as Election Violence Education and Resolution (EVER) and Building Resources in Democracy, Governance, and Elections (BRIDGE) (Gillies, 2011; Kammerud, 2012). One of the most common practices is using monitoring and fraud alerts because they address impunity, secrecy, and rumors that often foster electoral conflict in transitional democracies.

Monitoring and watchdog mechanisms help limit the space and opportunity for fraud and corruption, reducing the potential for conflict. Such mechanisms include the transparency measures the EMB introduces, political finance regimes, conflict monitoring and early warning systems, election dispute resolution (EDR) case monitoring, and election observation, among many others. During the pre-election phase, governments can send a credible sign of good intentions by inviting IOs for assistance to generate a deterring force that reduces domestic actors' incentives for violence. Nevertheless, as monitoring makes violent and non-violent manipulation more costly and technical assistance makes it more difficult, some elites and warlords might oppose external aid based on a "costly democracy" calculus (Zürcher et al., 2013). They will claim that the international community should not interfere in domestic affairs. However, such governments' strategic appeals to intervention by the international community also sends a signal to opposition groups to trust the system and to avoid the use of violence precisely "because everyone will be watching." In contrast, during the post-election phase, violence often erupts when the election process or results are not perceived as credible. International condemnation of an election, in the form of a negative report by an international election monitoring organization, is associated with a 35 percent increase in the probability of post-election violence (Borzyskowski, 2016). Consequently, a "good" intention can have the opposite effect: IOs would end up influencing electoral losers' incentives to challenge results, based on IOs' own reports, with greater popular support. Thus, violence is perceived as the only possible resort due to the lack of trust in the fragile state institutions: either because the loser challenges violently or because the loser's challenge is violently crushed. This contradicts the common belief in international relations and comparative politics that monitoring is always beneficial. An alternative to avoid post-election violence or the misuse of an IOs report to back up violence is to release monitoring results in homeopathic doses instead of as one large report: interim statements over time before and after elections would lay the groundwork for a potentially critical assessment.

The systemic dilemma denotes that international intervention either reduces or promotes violence. Preventive diplomacy with political dialogue has proved to be an important tool, as in the cases of The Gambia, Côte d' Ivoire, and Haiti. More specifically, the monitoring sub-dilemma is evident as observers may increase the conflict risk through condemnation. Nonetheless, endorsing a fraudulent election is negative in the short term for democratization and peace-building, but it also reduces their credibility over the long run. In the 2016 Ugandan political crisis, international observers criticized the electoral process for its lack of transparency, alleging that the government hampered opposition campaigns with tactics such as constricting access to the media and using police to suppress campaign rallies. Opposition candidate Kizza Besigye subsequently refused to concede the electoral victory of Yoweri Museveni and was arrested. Although it is hard to identify a cause-and-effect relationship between the international observer statements and Besigye's decision, these actions and reactions fit the hypothesis (Borzyskowski, 2016). An alternative to not legitimizing what will be illegitimate elections is the withdrawal of international organizations from elections in anticipation of fraud, as the EU did in 2015 in Burundi (Claes, 2016). Nevertheless, international organizations might need to consider if there is a security force apparatus able to deter violent outbreaks caused by the instability perceived from its departure before withdrawing.

Coordination among EMBs is paramount to achieving an integrated approach against violence. But coordination is also essential to the international community in order to minimize this systemic dilemma as well as to avoid a culture of bad governance. Specifically, it is common for election management support to be separated from the management of political tensions and conflicts that commonly arise during the electoral period. That is, donors, organizations, and domestic apparatus compartmentalize their work: election management, on the one hand, and conflict and peacebuilding, on the other. For example, the UN has several bodies that may become involved directly or indirectly in the electoral cycle, such as the Department of Political Affairs (DPA), the Department of Peacekeeping Operations (DPKO), the United Nations Development Programme (UNDP), the Office of the High Commissioner for Human Rights (OHCHR), the United Nations Volunteers (UNV), the United Nations Office of Project Services (UNOPS), and the UN Electoral Assistance Division (UNEAD). Often, more than one body is present within a given country, and, within each, more than one program may focus on democracy or violence issues. To make matters more complicated, in most countries, each of these bodies would have its own offices, objectives, funding pools, and partnerships with local organizations and institutions (Kammerud, 2012).

Additionally, international intervention to enforce democracy and peace can create troubling precedents. The 2016 Gambian election resulted in the loss of Yahya Jammeh, who stayed 22 years in power. A violent crisis followed this. To enforce "democracy" and guarantee "peace and stability," troops from the Economic Community of West African States (ECOWAS), with the support of the African Union (AU) and the UN, were sent to the Gambian capital while the elected president was sworn in at the Gambian Embassy in Dakar, Senegal. To stop the violence, Jammeh accepted stepping down under the provision of amnesty for his crimes and the grant of asylum in Nigeria and Morocco. This episode marks a rare confluence of tactics and motives in electoral violence resolution. The threat of an ECOWAS military action to remove the president of a member state appeared to be a deciding factor, combined with high-level diplomatic negotiations in this resolution. Although the military engagement of

"Operation Restoring Democracy" was successful, the use of such intervention tactics to enforce democracy and peace should be exceptional as it involves risks and precedents that might jeopardize the long-term perceptions of the efficacy of electoral democracy (Fischer, 2017a). Peacekeepers should play the role of violence deterrents, acting as a buffer between belligerents without violating human rights and, at the same time, without being injured or killed. Notably, the follow-up to election observation missions needs to be more robust by seizing opportunities to work with new administrations to address much-needed reforms.

Moreover, on the one hand, the media can be a powerful tool to promote hatred and the rapid mobilization of hostility or intimidation, which involves the transparency dilemma. Successful transitions usually include the creation of laws that encompass the guarantees of freedom of expression and the creation of independent media. Curbing media freedom can be dangerous. For example, the media blackouts in 2011 in South Sudan, 2015 in Burundi, and 2016 in the Central African Republic (CAR) combusted fear and violence. However, in war-shattered societies, the media are commonly polarized and act as a tool for propaganda. Nevertheless, premature popular consultations do not wait for media reform to take place and become consolidated. Thus, media liberalization comes with the risk of creating media platforms for biased reports and nationalistic propaganda. Although it is expected to be a "peace media," inflammatory consequences played an essential role in the violent riots in Kosovo and the extreme case of the Rwandan genocide (Snyder, 2000; Mansfield and Snyder, 2005b). Importantly, the problem of "fake media" and the relationship among violence, democracy, and peace are not exclusive to fragile states as events in consolidated democratic states such as in the United States, the United Kingdom, and France since 2017 show. On the other hand, the media can play a positive role, as in the cases of the South Sudan referendum on self-determination in January 2011 accompanied by the slogan "Say no to violence" and the appeal that "Election is not about violence" in 2010 in Côte d Ivoire. Several measures may be taken to prevent hate media. The endorsement of codes of conduct, a licensing system or the interruption of transmission or dissemination, and passing and enforcing specific legislation related to political violence are options that promote a "peace media." A well-trained media should be independent, transparent, and objective. Beyond the transmission of messaging for peace in conjunction with civic education, responsible media and security forces should stop violence from occurring in the first place, more so than containing its spread.

Finally, a moral dilemma comes to the surface: when is violence "good" or "bad" for democratization and peace? Is democracy worth dying for? Some would say that one death is too many (IFES, 2014). Under the Charles Tilly's notion that "war makes states," others would argue that violence is the only path toward democratization and peace, as one cannot ignore the fact that modern European democracies invariably came into being through violent revolutionary processes (Sorensen, 2001; Kaspersen, 2017). In the case of a state failure like Haiti, it is argued that a violent democracy might be a "necessary evil" (USIP, 2013). This poses the difficult dilemma of distinguishing between a "good" use of violence to achieve a better and ultimately more peaceful political objective, compared with a "bad" use of violence for similar purposes (Fischer, 2017a). "Radical" or "righteous" violence is part of political contestation in disrupted states (Viterna, 2016).

Some authors suggest the legitimization of violence based on the hypothesis that warring societies legitimize its use beyond the sphere of armed conflict (Snyder, 2000; Hoglund, 2008; Collier et al., 2009). Despite social fatigue, transitions are usually violent because societies "used to" civil war generally have a higher tolerance for the use of violence. However, permissiveness of violence can also have a countereffect on democratization. Political violence affects the way citizens relate to their government. Those who fear political violence are much more likely to believe that their country is neither a democracy nor at peace, and they are much less likely to believe in their state institutions (Mohan, 2015; NDI, 2014). The 2017 and 2013 elections in Kenya did not reproduce the mass carnage of 2008. Some argue that this calm resulted from the fear and memory of past inter-ethnic clashes around the elections and was an effect of successful mitigation or the prevention of violence by national and international actors. As a consequence of having lost credibility with their political leaders and in the electoral process, many Kenyans expressed their unwillingness to fight the results and accepted the results rather than risking contesting them for fear of further outbreaks of violence (Claes, 2016). This reflects the fact that sometimes there is a preference for disillusionment in a "good" democracy compared to the stability of a "bad" authoritarian regime. Similarly, since 2015, the "Vetevendosje!" Albanian self-determination movement has justified using tear gas at the National Assembly of Kosovo on various occasions as the "only" strategic way to stop discussion and voting on various bills, such as the EU-brokered deal that would give more power to a Serb minority and the blocking of the 2016 budget, which included the creation of the national army and the military demarcation of a border with Montenegro. Although strategic violence is a contravention of the law, it was perceived as preferable from Vetevendosje!'s perspective to the further damage that such political decisions would possibly cause to the nation.

Rarely are matters so desperate that "there is no alternative to forced-pace democracy promotion at gunpoint" (Mansfield and Snyder, 2005a, p. 45). Although this book will not address in detail mechanisms to prevent violence due to size and scope restrictions, it is worthwhile mentioning a few recommendations. Specific policy measures that have proven helpful in mitigating violence in one fragile state might not be applicable or relevant in another. However, some tentative conclusions are still discernible. Above all, it seems crucial to have an integrated approach to democracy and peace, particularly in transitional post-civil war societies. Free and fair political competition and violence prevention through security and state institutions are mutually reinforcing. The technical quality of the electoral process is as important as security. Prevention, coordination, and capacity-building of all institutions and actors involved seem to pay off. Measures cannot be the same as those used in stable and democratic societies: transition requires fresh and case-by-case tactics (Fjelde and Hoglund, 2014).

Beyond "fighting violence with more violence," prevention of electoral political violence must be addressed. Preventing "violent democracy-building" requires institutional adjustments to reduce incentives to violence, including clauses about the non-use of violence as part of the peace process. The inclusion of the threat of exclusion from political participation in peace negotiations, elections, and transitional efforts as well as future power-sharing mechanisms is fundamental, although it might have the opposite effect: more violence from spoilers. Similarly, it should include counter-measures of economic coercion through ceasing financial support. Also, it requires strengthening state institutions, such as the security forces, legislative and electoral institutions, through specific legislation, training, and equipment. Ideally, a well-trained and disciplined security sector, coupled with an institutionalized, legitimate, and effective judiciary and EMBs, tend to create the largest reductions in politically related violence (Mohan, 2015; IFES, 2014; Kammerud, 2012; Gillies, 2011). Legislation should not give broad powers to the security forces to avoid the continuum of abuses committed during armed conflict, but these powers need to be sufficient to be able to "protect citizens and to enforce order." Security sector institutions must also be trained and must incorporate a specific intelligence unit that deals with transitional violence through an integrated approach: both criminal and political violence. Additionally, counter-terrorism measures should also be considered. As part of the Security Sector Reform (SSR) and DDR, training and equipment must be provided with a strong focus on human and civil rights. In addition, community-police relationships must be built up and fostered. Furthermore, empowering the courts or other dispute resolution mechanisms to prosecute offenders is another requirement that will not only contribute to reducing the perception of impunity, but also reduce the use of impunity as a motive for violence.

EMBs must also be empowered with capacity-building, in terms of human and operational resources, in order to be effective and build their credibility for preventing and managing violence and disputes. Moreover, key efforts must be made regarding civic education and media training. Likewise, coordination is paramount among all international agents and national actors. Finally, for a better understanding of violence, democratization and peace in war-shattered societies, more disintegrated data are needed that are not only limited to "electoral violence" or "electoral security," but that also adopts an integrated approach to the processes specific to transitional times. By the same token, it would also be important to have gender-based data as females can be particularly oppressed or manipulated in these contexts due to financial dependency (IFES, 2007).

3.3 Summary of the chapter

Paradoxically, democracy is built on principles of the non-use of violence. However, moving from civil war to peace via democracy-building can be a turbulent transition. The literature on democracy usually focuses on aspects of non-violence and often fails to include democratization as a cause and consequence of violence. This chapter explores the intersection between the cycles of conflict, democratization, and state institution-building and the relationships between these three processes and violence. Based on the framework of transitional dilemmas proposed in this book, this chapter contributes by explaining why crucial driving forces, such as elites, security forces, the lack of functioning state institutions, and the hate media, are tools for violence during transitional phases after civil war in fragile states.

The promotion of democracy and the PEV in countries at risk are better analyzed when elections are understood as a process and not as a day event. The democratization, violence, and peace nexus creates two central paradoxes: first, the peace and democratization processes create new incentives for violence, particularly by elites taking advantage of the fragility of the institutions. Second, measures to fight violence can undermine democracy through violation of human rights and rights to freedom. Beyond elections, violence is positively related to democratization, peacebuilding and state-building efforts and generates the following dilemmas: horizontal, vertical, systemic, temporal, existential, design, financial, moral, operational, security, sequencing, and transparency as well as the central one. These have been discussed in terms of the dimensions of actors, security, and institutions. Additionally, this chapter introduces a dilemma usually ignored in the literature on international organizations: the monitoring impasse. Overall, it should be neither radical nor righteous, neither should democracy nor peace be worth dying for. Based on these dilemmas, in the transition from guns to doves, votes may generate more bullets than they are meant to stop.

Notes

1 "Elections are not about violence", a message of peace in Nouchi, Ivorian street language, attributed to stopping the 2010 and 2015 violence outbreak.
2 English translation: Stop the Third Mandate.
3 Examples of institutions well known by their involvement in electoral assistance:

- NGOs: National Democratic Institute (NDI), the International Republican Institute (IRI), the International Foundation for Electoral Systems (IFES), and the Carter Center.
- National development agencies of the United States and the United Kingdom.
- International Organisations (IOs): UN, the Organization of American States (OAS), the European Union (EU), and
- Regional organizations: Organization for Security and Cooperation in Europe (OSCE), the Commonwealth of Nations, and the Electoral Institute for Sustainable Democracy in Africa (EISA).

References

Aljazeera. 2015. Boko Haram threatens to disrupt Nigeria poll. *Aljazeera*, 18 Feb 2015 05:55 GMT.
Bekoe, D. & All, E. 2012. *Voting in fear: Electoral Violence in Sub-Saharan Africa*. USIP Press Books.
Bellamy, A. J., Williams, P. D. & Griffin, S. 2010. *Understanding Peacekeeping*.
Berkeley, B. 2001. *The Graves Are Not Yet Full: Race, Tribe and Power in the Heart of America*. Basic Books.
Birch, S. 2016. *Project on Explaining and Mitigating Electoral Violence*. The University of Glasgow.
Borzyskowski, I. V. 2016. *A Double-edged Sword: International Influences on Election Violence*.
Bourne, R. 2012. *Catastrophe: What Went Wrong in Zimbabwe?*. Zed Books.
Burchard, S. M. 2015. *Electoral Violence in Sub-Saharan Africa: Causes and Consequences*. Lynne Rienner.
Call, C. T. 2002. Assessing El Salvador's Transition From Civil War to Peace. *In*: Stephen John Stedman, D. R. & Elisabeth Cousens (ed.) *Ending Civil Wars*. Lynne Rienner Press.
Chesterman, S., Ignatieff, M. & Thakur, R. 2006. *Making States Work : State Failure and the Crisis of Governance*. United Nations University Press.
Claes, J. 2016. *Electing Peace: Violence Prevention and Impact at the Polls*. United States Institute of Peace Press (USIP Press).
CNN. 2016. Gabon violence: More than 1,000 arrested after disputed election. *CNN*, 2 September 2016.
Collier, P., Hoeffler, A. & Rohner, D. 2009. Beyond Greed and Grievance: Feasibility and Civil War. *Oxford Economic Papers*, 61, 1–27.
Crocker, Hampson & AALL. 2001. *Turbulent Peace*.
De Waal, A. 1992. Ethiopia: Transition to What? *World Policy Journal*, 9, 719–737.
Demetriou, C. & Bosi, L. 2016. *Dynamics of Political Violence: A Process-Oriented Perspective on Radicalization and the Escalation of Political Conflict*. Taylor & Francis.
Diamond, L. 2008. The Democratic Rollback: The Resurgence of the Predatory State. *Foreign Affairs*. March/April 2008.
Donno, D. 2013. Elections and Democratization in Authoritarian Regimes. *American Journal of Political Science*, 57, 703–716.
Doyle, M. W. & Sambanis, N. 2006. *Making War and Building Peace : United Nations Peace Operations*. Princeton University Press.
Dunning, T. 2011. Fighting and voting: Violent conflict and electoral politics. *Journal of Conflict Resolution*, 55, 327–339.
EIU. 2019. *Democracy Index 2019: A Year of Democratic Backsliding and Popular Protest*. EIU.
FFP. 2017. *Fragile State Index*. The Fund for Peace.
Fischer, J. 2017a. *The Gambia: Enforcing Election Results through a Military Intervention*. January 23, 2017 ed.
Fischer, J. 2017b. The Prospects for Electoral Violence in Honduras 2017. *In*: Violence, P. O. E. A. M. E. (ed.). The University of Glasgow.
Fjelde, H. & Hoglund, K. 2014. Electoral Institutions and Electoral Violence in Sub-Saharan Africa. *B.J.Pol.S.*, 46, 297–320.
Forsberg, C. 2010. *Politics and Power in Kandahar*. Afghanistan Report 5. The institute for the study of war.
Freedom House. 2019. *Freedom in the World 2019: Democracy in Retreat*. Freedom House.

Freedom House. 2021. *Freedom World 2021: Democracy Under Siege.* Freedom House.
Ghosh, B. 2022. The World's Deadliest War Isn't in Ukraine, But in Ethiopia. *The Washington Post*, March 23, 2022 at 9:09 a.m. EDT.
Gillies, D. 2011. *Elections in Dangerous Places: Democracy and the Paradoxes of Peacebuilding.* McGill-Queen's University Press.
Gleditsch, N. P., Hegre, H. & Strand, H. 2007. *Democracy and Civil War.*
Gowa, J. 2011. *Ballots and Bullets: The Elusive Democratic Peace.* Princeton University Press.
Hegre, H. 2014. Democracy and armed conflict. *Journal of Peace Research*, 51, 159–172.
Hoglund, K. 2008. Violence in war-to-democracy transitions. *In*: Jarstad, A. K. A. T. D. S. (ed.) *From War to Democracy: Dilemmas of Peacebuilding.* Cambridge University Press.
Hoglund, K. & Zartman, I. W. 2006. Violence by the State: Official Spoilers and their Allies. *In*: Darby, J. (ed.) *In Violence and Reconstruction.* University of Notre Dame Press.
HRW. 2005. Suppressing the dissidents. *In*: Region, H. R. A. A. P. R. I. E. S. O. (ed.) 09 may 2005 ed. Human Rights Watch.
HRW. 2021. *World Report 2022: Somalia Event 2021.* Human Rights Watch.
ICC. 2015. International Criminal Court [Online]. Online. Available: https://www.icc-cpi.int/en_menus/icc/situations%20and%20cases/Pages/situations%20and%20cases.aspx [Accessed 04 Jan 2016].
ICG. 2021. *Why Somalia's Electoral Crisis Has Tipped into Violence.* By Omar Mahmood. International Crisis Group.
IDEA. 2021. *The global state of democracy 2021: Building Resilience in a Pandemic Era.* IDEA International, Washigton DC.
IDEA. 2022. *Covid-19 and Ethiopia Sixth General Elections. Case Study, 30 March 2022.* IDEA.
IDMC. 2009. *Timor-Leste: IDPs Have Returned Home, but the Challenge of Reintegration Is Just Beginning.* Internal Displacement Monitoring Centre (IDMC).
IFES. 2007. *Violence Against Women in Elections (VAWIE) Framework.* IFES.
IFES. 2014. Elections Worth Dying For? A Selection of Case Studies from Africa. *In*: Cyllah, A. (ed.). International Foundation for Electoral Systems.
IFES. 2017. *Election Guide* [Online]. Available: http://www.electionguide.org/countries/id/63/ [Accessed].
IOM. 2012. Ending the 2006 Internal Displacement Crisis in Timor-Leste: Between Humanitarian Aid and Transitional Justice. *In*: Auweraert, P. V. D. (ed.) *IOM migration Research Series.* International Organization for Migration (IOM).
Jarstad, A. K. & Sisk, T. D. 2008. *From War to Democracy: Dilemmas of Peacebuilding*, Cambridge University Press. UK.
Kammerud, L. 2012. *An Integrated Approach to Elections and Conflict. IFES White Paper.* IFES.
Kaspersen, L. & Strandsbjerg, J. 2017. *Does War Make States? Investigations of Charles Tilly's Historical Sociology.* Cambridge University Press.
Kim, D. H. 2007. *Nurturing Peace: United Nations Peacebuilding Operations in the Aftermath of Intrastate Conflicts, 1945–2002.* 3269685 Ph.D., University of Missouri - Saint Louis.
Kimani, M. 2009. Security for the highest bidder. *Africa Renewal*, 10.
Linebarger, C. & Salehyan, I. 2012. *Elections and Social Conflict in Africa, 1990–2009* [Online]. San Diego, CA. Available: https://ssrn.com/abstract=2182694 [Accessed].
Lyons, T. 1996. Closing the Transition: The May 1995 Elections in Ethiopia. *The Journal of Modern African Studies*, 34, 121–142.
Macdougall, C. 2016. One Killed as Tensions Rise Before Uganda's Election. *Newsweek.*
Mansfield, E. D. & Snyder, J. 2005a. *Prone to Violence: The Paradox of the Democratic Peace.* National Interest, Inc.

Mansfield, E. D. & Snyder, J. 1995. Democratization and the Danger of War. *International Security*, 20, 5–38.
Mansfield, E. D. & Snyder, J. 2005b. When Ballots Bring on Bullets Democratic Deceptions II: 3 Edition. *International Herald Tribune*, p.6. Newspaper Article. International New York Times. Paris, FR
Mary Beth Altier, S. M. & Weinberg, L. B. 2016. *Violence, Elections, and Party Politics*. Routledge.
Meyerfeld, B. 2016. Yoweri Museveni, roi d'Ouganda. *Le Monde*, 18.02.2016 at 17h39.
Mohan, V. 2015. Preventing Electoral Violence through Enhancing Security, Trust and Electoral Integrity. Available: http://www.ifes.org/news/preventing-electoral-violence-through-enhancing-security-trust-and-electoral-integrity.
NDI. 2014. *Monitoring and Mitigating Electoral Violence*. (NDI) National Democratic Institute for International Affairs.
NELDA. 2013. *The National Elections Across Democracy and Autocracy Database*. Yale University's Department of Political Science.
Newman, E. & Rich, R. 2004. *The UN Role in Promoting Democracy: Between Ideals and Reality*. United Nations University Press.
Newman, L. S. 2016. Do terrorrist attacks increase closer to elections? *In*: Mary Beth Altier, S. M., Leonard B. Weinberg (ed.) *Violence, Elections, and Party Politics*. Routledge.
Norris, P. 2012. Why Electoral Malpractices Heighten Risks of Electoral Violence. *In*: APSA 2012 Annual Meeting Paper, p. 14.
Piccolino, G. 2015. Winning wars, building (illiberal) peace? The rise (and possible fall) of a victor's peace in Rwanda and Sri Lanka. *Third World Quarterly*, 36, 1770–1785.
Snyder, J. 2000. *From Voting to Violence: Democratization and Nationalist Conflict*.
Soderberg Kovacs, M. 2008. When Rebels Change Their Stripes: Armed Insurgents. *In*: Jarstad, A. K. A. T. D. S. (ed.) *From War to Democracy: Dilemmas of Peacebuilding*. Cambridge University Press.
Sorensen, G. 2001. War and State-Making: Why Doesn't it Work in the Third World? *Security Dialogue PRIO*, 32, 341–354.
Stedman, S. 2000. Spoiler Problems in Peace Processes. *In*: Druckman, P. S. A. D. (ed.) *International Conflict Resolution After the ColdWar*. National Academy Press.
Szablewska, N. & Bachmann, S. D. 2014. *Current Issues in Transitional Justice: Towards a More Holistic Approach*. Springer International Publishing.
Themnér, A. & Utas, M. 2016. Governance Through Brokerage: Informal Governance in Post-civil War Societies. *Civil Wars*, 18, 255–280.
UN News Centre. 2015. *As Parties Meet in Uganda, UN Official Urges Consensual Solution to Burundian Crisis. 28 December 2015 ed.* Online: UN.
UNHCR. 2015. UNHCR says more than 105,000 refugees have fled violence in Burundi. *UNHCR News*, 15 May 2015.
USIP. 2013. Haiti's Election Conundrum: Fraught But Necessary? *In*: Gienger, V. (ed.).
Vines, A. 1996. *Renamo: From Terrorism to Democracy in Mozambique?* James Currey.
Viterna, J. 2016. Radical Our Righteous? Using Gender to Shape Public Perceptions of Political Violence. *In*: Demetriou, C. A. L. B. (ed.) *Dynamics of Political Violence: A Process-Oriented Perspective on Radicalization and the Escalation of Political Conflict*. Taylor & Francis.
Wright, R. 2019. The story of 2019: Protests in every corner of the globe. *The New Yorker*.
Zürcher, C., Manning, C., Evenson, K., Hayman, R., Riese, S. & Roehner, N. 2013. *Costly Democracy : Peacebuilding and Democratization After War*. Stanford University Press.

4
WHAT ROLE DO UN OPERATIONS PLAY IN BRINGING SIMULTANEOUSLY PEACE AND DEMOCRACY TO POST-CIVIL WAR COUNTRIES?

> The United Nations was created not to lead mankind to heaven, but to save humanity from hell.
> *UN Secretary-General Dag Hammarskjöld*
> *(1953 to 1961)*

Do UN peace operations help build "democracy, peace and a functioning state" in countries in the aftermath of civil wars? There are controversies when limiting the options of categorizing the UN as savior or evil. Howard (2019a) argues that peacekeeping is effective and does not incur a counterinsurgency toll. Regarding measuring success or failure in the concluded missions from a mandate perspective, Howard argues that, since the end of the Cold War, blue helmets have completed 16 missions, 11 successfully (five departed the countries before completing most components of their mandates). That is a two-thirds success rate, and none of those countries has returned to civil war. In opposition to the major focus of the literature on UN peace operations that stresses why it fails, it is fundamental to instead identify why they are efficient. In this regard, Howard (2019a) and Fortna (2008a) agree that (1) warring parties are more likely to reach negotiated settlements when there is a promise of peacekeepers to oversee the agreement; (2) peacekeepers can contain the geographic spread of war within a state and across borders; (3) peacekeepers save lives; and (4) civil wars often restart but are shorter and recur less often when peacekeepers are present.

Some researchers also support the belief that international intervention fosters democracy (Doyle and Sambanis, 2006; Heldt, 2007; Newman and Rich, 2004). In theory, promoting democracy along the lines of Western liberalism would create the conditions under which political violence is no longer an option: the rule of law and democratic processes will channel political disagreements to a peaceful means of conflict resolution. Taking this point further in analyzing violent democratization (Chapter 3), Pickering and Peceny (2006) argue that forging or enforcing democracy at gunpoint is a necessary means. As ironic as it sounds, it depicts a machiavellian view of the process without morality.

Against this way of thinking, some claim that "the UN ambition to promote democratization via peacebuilding operations in post-civil war cases has largely failed" (Jarstad, 2015). Peacebuilding missions may promote peace, but they seldom bring democracy (Zürcher et al., 2013, p. 1). This viewpoint is also supported by Pouligny (2000), Jett (1999), and Bueno de Mesquita and Downs (2006). Still, other authors argue that there is no relation between the two processes. For Fortna (2008a, p. 36), the international community is "indeed using peacekeeping in an attempt to democratize war-torn countries and peacekeeping, specifically by enforcement, is less likely to occur in more democratic countries than in more authoritarian ones." In this regard, she suggests that peacekeepers go where the job of keeping the peace is more difficult, as well as where building a new democratic state is less likely. But even though this promotes stability, there is no strong positive or negative relationship with democracy.

This book claims that after a civil war, the absence of a statistically confirmable effect of UN peace operations and democracy-building does not mean that there is no relationship between these two processes. Instead, it might be the case that they act against each other by virtue of the inherent dilemmas in fostering simultaneously a stable peace and a democracy in the aftermath of civil war. Therefore, this opens room for further research on the role that UN interventions play in democracy, peacebuilding, and state-building processes. Success in democratization cannot be analyzed in terms of a dichotomous "to be or not to be" democratic or "peaceful" (end of civil war). Instead, an investigation is needed into how democratic the regime is in terms of its qualities and trends on a spectrum of indicators of political freedoms and civil liberties that encompasses specific issues, such as the electoral process, political pluralism and participation, the functioning of government, freedom of expression and belief, associational and organizational rights, the enforcement of the rule of law, as well as respect for human rights, personal autonomy, and individual rights. This approach offers a better-informed position to explain why some countries develop a certain level of democracy and less peace, and why others demonstrate a higher level of peace and partial democracy. And it also explains why others show a kind of "good enough" level after a UN multidimensional peace intervention. The introduction of a moderate level of success might be the key to a more accurate approach. This is the subject of this chapter. Notably, instead of focusing on why missions fail, the focus should be on understanding what makes them successful (Howard, 2019b).

Problems related to democratization can be divided into three categories: morals and values, processes and procedures, and forms and substance (Kultgen and Lenzi, 2006). Differently from the normative Chapters 1–3, this book section focuses on quantitative and qualitative measurements of processes, procedures, and forms of political and civil rights, such as the implementation of elections and representation and the rule of law. In the face of mixed results stemming from the impact on democracy, there is scope for further investigation into how peacebuilding has affected post-civil war democratization after the end of the Cold War.

Based on mix methods, this chapter investigates what role UN peacekeeping operations play in the democratization of postwar societies. It explores this in two ways. First, by providing a study with an updated dataset, with a longer timeframe, the inclusion of more comparative indices, and a broader selection of multidimensional mission cases, with and without intervention. Second, it addresses the dilemmas that might clarify the paradoxical relationship between democracy, peace, and state-building in post-civil war societies. In view of the dilemma related to intervention versus autonomy, a cross-sectional analysis of five hypotheses usually found in previous research is given:

- **Hypothesis 1**: UN peace operations simultaneously bring peace and democracy to post-civil war countries.
- **Hypothesis 2:** Multidimensional operations are more likely to bring democratic civil peace.
- **Hypothesis 3:** Operations led by the Department of Peacekeeping Operations (DPKO)[1] are more successful than those led by the Department of Political Affairs (DPA) or "hybrid missions" (jointly with other organizations such as the Organization of American States [OAS] and African Union [AU]).[2]
- **Hypothesis 4:** Multiple interventions are more likely to be successful in building democracy and peace.
- **Hypothesis 5:** If peace and democracy should be built from within, the prospects for post-civil war democratization and peacebuilding are better without UN intervention.

4.1 Methodology

Since 1948, there has been a total of 71 UN peace operations (UN-DPKO, 2022). However, for methodological accuracy, this book will include analyses of cases that encompass only four criteria: (1) civil war, (2) interventions with deployment of more than 200 international personnel for a substantive multidimensional impact, (3) mandates that include state and democracy-building elements of reconciliation, equitable economic growth, and effective institutions, such as the development of a federal system and good governance, transitional justice, administration and the monitoring of elections, constitutional drafting, reform of the security sector, support of the reintegration of ex-combatants, and the establishment of the rule of law as well as freedom of the press and media, (4) cases that were in operation between 1989 and 2022.

This timeframe is justifiable for several reasons. First, the end of the Cold War triggered a new world dynamic and a wave of democratization (Marshall and Gurr, 2015; Freedom House, 2015; Huntington, 2007). Second, 84 percent of all UN peacekeeping operations have been deployed since 1989 (UN-DPKO, 2016). A total of 20 new operations were authorized between 1989 and 1994, raising the number of peacekeepers from 11,000 to 75,000 in just five years (UN-DPKO, 2015; UN-DPKO, 2009; Bellamy et al., 2010; Andersson, 2000). Peacekeeping is no longer only a post-conflict activity: approximately 53 percent of the current 110,000 personnel are deployed in countries with an active armed conflict, such as Sudan and the DRC (IEP, 2017). Third, the timeframe of almost 30 years permits a deeper analysis. Most of the literature concentrates only on "snapshots" of two, five, or ten years from the beginning of the mission.

Therefore, 64 cases[3] were identified affecting 31 countries[4] that are now independent: Afghanistan, Angola, Bosnia-Herzegovina, Burundi, Cambodia, Central African Republic (CAR), Côte d'Ivoire, Croatia, Cyprus, Democratic Republic of the Congo (DRC), El Salvador, Georgia, Guinea-Bissau, Haiti, Iraq, Kosovo, Liberia, North Macedonia, Mali, Mozambique, Namibia, Nepal, Nicaragua, Rwanda, Sierra Leone, Somalia, South Sudan, Sudan, Timor-Leste, and Western Sahara. Special consideration is given to 12 countries with more than one mission: Angola (4), Burundi (3) Cambodia (2), CAR (5), Croatia (5), DRC (2), Haiti (7),[5] Liberia (2), Sierra Leone (2), Somalia (3), Sudan (4),[6] and Timor-Leste (5). Additional attention is given to Timor-Leste and Kosovo due to their *sui generis* operation of transitional state administrations where the international organization takes comprehensive responsibility for state administration and sovereignty. Initially, Libya was not considered under the category of UN peace operations since, when the study started, the conflict had just began and only a special envoy was present. Under the UN SC mandate 2542 (2020), the United Nations Support Mission in Libya (UNSMIL) has substantive staff in political affairs, human rights, transitional justice, mine action, demobilization, development, women's empowerment, public information, and communication. Therefore, Libya was added to this study and its data were updated for 2022.

For methodological coherence, the data also include the mission in Cyprus as the interests of Greece and Turkey have directly limited Cypriot sovereignty and, therefore, also potentially jeopardized the state-building and consolidation processes. Moreover, besides the United Nations Peacekeeping Force in Cyprus (UNFICYP) having been initiated in 1964, it is still in operation today, which provides an opportunity for even longer-term analysis.[7] The data also include the UN presence in Afghanistan, although it is considered a "political mission" as well as in Darfur despite its joint operation with the African Union and in Haiti (MICIVI), in cooperation with the Organization of American States (OAS).

As the first preventive diplomacy and deployment operation of the UN, the UNPREDEP is usually recognized as a significant instrument for facilitating dialogue, preventing violence, and fostering compromise between different segments of society. The addition of these cases allows for comparing the relationship between democracy and peacebuilding through different types of missions as well as those under sole or joint responsibility. Hence, while peacekeeping operations usually pertain to Chapter "6.5," the methodology also encompasses other operations classified under Chapters 6–8 of the UN Charter (1945).

Finally, it is fundamental to understand the evolution and operational administrative structure of peace missions throughout history (Bellamy et al., 2010). Operations began in 1948 with the UN Truce Supervision Organization (UNTSO) and UN Military Observer Group in India and Pakistan (UNMOGIP). However, the Department of Peacekeeping Operations (DPKO) was only formally implemented in 1992 through Boutros-Ghali's Agenda for Peace. It was composed of five main bodies: the Office of Operations, the Office of the Rule of Law and Security Institutions, the Office of Military Affairs, the Policy Evaluation and Training Division, and the Head of Department. The Department of Political Affairs (DPA) of the UN Secretariat and its Electoral Assistance Division manages political missions engaged in conflict prevention, peacemaking, and post-conflict peacebuilding in Africa, Central Asia, and the Middle East. It also helps prevent and resolve conflict,[8] supporting complex political transitions in coordination with national actors and UN development and humanitarian entities on the ground (DPA, 2016).[9] Nevertheless, many missions are still under the DPA but do not meet all the four criteria in this book, which may cause some discrepancy among the many other research results as well as an overlapping of activities in the field. In response to the Brahimi (2010) and HIPPO (2015) recommendations, DPKO and the Department of Field Mission (DPS) were agglomerated to the newly created Department of Peace Operations (DPO) in 2019. Notably, the Department of Political Affairs (DPA) and the United Nations Peacebuilding Support Office (DPSO) became the Department of Political and Peacebuilding Affairs (DPPA). As for 2022, DPPA had 24 special political mission and other "Good Offices" operating.[10] Together, DPO, DPPA, and eight regional divisions that cover the Americas, Europe, Africa, Asia, and the Pacific compose the Department of Political and Peacebuilding Affairs and Peace Operations.[11] Therefore, despite the fact that this book's timeframe of analysis is from 1989 to 2022, most missions started and finished under DPKO structure. Thus, this book will keep mentioning "DPKO," unless specified as DPO if it is related to an issue post-2019. It will not include in the data set elements of A4P/A4P+ roadmap because those initiatives only officially started in 2018 and 2021; therefore, no substantive records are available yet.

Conflict prevention, peacemaking, peacekeeping, and peace enforcement rarely occur in a linear or sequential way. UN peace operations are rarely limited to one type of activity and the definitional boundaries have become increasingly indistinguishable and abstruse, particularly when facing new threats such as terrorism. These diverse mission operations categories should be mutually reinforcing, but when used in isolation it misses the momentum of providing the comprehensive approach required to address the root causes of conflict and to reduce the risk of its recurrence.

Significantly, as the operation in Afghanistan clearly illustrates, political missions are not smaller or less important than peacekeeping missions.[12] All peacekeeping operations are inherently "special" and "political" and mirror the international political dynamic that rules the Security Council. The UN officially acknowledges that "Peacekeeping is political and its ultimate success depends on active and sustainable political processes or the real prospect of a peace process."[13]

Political missions should not be underestimated as they are part of a continuum of UN peace operations working in different stages of the conflict cycle. In some instances, following the signing of peace agreements, political missions overseen by the DPA during the phase of peace negotiations have been replaced by DPKO missions. On the other hand, DPKO operations have also given way sometimes to special political missions overseeing longer-term peacebuilding activities. In Iraq, the UN Assistance Mission for Iraq (UNAMI) was administered by the DPA and supported by the DPKO as well as the Department of Field Support (DFS) (UN IRAQ, 2016).

Furthermore, following the efforts for a more realistic set of objectives for peacebuilding and state-building in fragile and conflict-affected countries, since 2005 the Peace Building Support Office (PBSO), jointly with the Peace Building Commission and its Peace Building Fund, has operated in six countries. Except for Guinea, which has no history of peacekeeping operations, this book will only focus on the five countries under the peacebuilding agenda: Burundi, Sierra Leone, Guinea-Bissau, Liberia, and the CAR. Therefore, in contrast with other research and for a more in-depth understanding, the data collected in this chapter will distinguish not only the mission type through its mandate, but also under whose responsibility it operates: the DPKO, DPA, or both (if after 2019), and if it is part of the PBSO.

On one side of the triangle of Democracy–State–Peacebuilding processes (Figure 1.6) the data are used to analyze democratization by comparing three different indices of democracy and governance. First, Freedom House (Freedom House, 2022a) is a traditional and well-used index on worldwide democracy. Second, Polity IV examines the concomitant qualities of democratic and autocratic authority in governing institutions rather than discrete and mutually exclusive forms of governance.[14] This perspective envisions a spectrum of governing authority that spans from fully institutionalized autocracies through anocracies to fully institutionalized democracies. Third, the Global Democracy Index of the Economist Intelligence Unit (EIU) provides a snapshot of the state of democracy worldwide based on five categories: the electoral process and pluralism; civil liberties; the functioning of government; political participation; and political culture.[15] Therefore, moving from minimalist forms of democracy measurements, it also allows a qualitative analysis that can provide substantive information on post-civil war democratization by classifying regimes according to whether they are: a "full democracy"; a "flawed/moderate democracy"; a "hybrid regime"; or an "authoritarian" regime types. The corresponding definitions of those conceptual categories have been provided in section 6 of the Introduction.

For the second aspect of the triangle on democracy, state, and peacebuilding processes, the data compare two state fragility indices. The first is the Fragile States Index.[16] This is based on the Fund for Peace's proprietary Conflict Assessment Software Tool (CAST) analytical platform that annually ranks 178 nations based on their levels of stability and the pressures faced according to 12 key political, social, and economic indicators and over 100 sub-indicators.[17] Second, the State Fragility Index (Marshall and Elzinga-Marshall, 2015) also examines the same number of countries, across 12 social, economic, and political indicators and 100 sub-indicators in order to assess state pressures such as uneven development, state legitimacy, group grievances, and human rights abuses that can lead to state failure, fragility, instability, and, as mentioned earlier, stability.[18] Finally, for the third aspect, the Global Peace Index (IEP, 2022) is considered. This is the world's leading measure of national peacefulness that includes 23 qualitative and quantitative indicators with data from the last 16 years.[19]

The combination of all six indices as well as the inclusion of the missions in the PBSO agenda, their typology, leadership, and duration contribute to the assessment of the extent to which UN peace operations build peace, democracy, and a functioning state in civil war-torn societies. This comparative set of indices contributes to the cross-cutting field of democratization and peace studies by providing up-to-date data, longer timeframes, more indices, and additional mission cases. Therefore, it leads to different conclusions from those drawn by researchers such as Doyle and Sambanis (2006), Fortna (2008a), Fortna (2008b), Watts (2008), Diehl (2014), and Jarstad (2015). Due to the complex nature of peace and democracy in the aftermath of civil war, it is essential to include meso-level categories on the larger spectrum of peace and democracy, such as "moderate level of peace, moderate level of democracy" or "high level of peace, moderate level of democracy," "moderate level of peace, low level of democracy," etc. By providing a detailed analysis of the different indicators drawn from different indices, this book gives a more accurate account of the problems posed in democracy and peacebuilding. This is particularly helpful when discrepancies are found among the indices due to their different methodological platforms.

When applicable, the data set compares the trending after 2, 5, 10, and 15 years from the commencement of the UN missions instead of from their official termination alone. This is important as it provides a better spectrum to assess whether democratization actually occurs during a peacekeeping mission. Except for the Global Democracy Index (GDI) report that refers to the year in which the report was written, all other publications present analyses from the previous year. In other worlds, the 2022 Global Peace Index (GPI) reports refer to data from 2021, and so on. The data also includes a trending arrow to allow easier visualization of the trending over the last 16 years based on the Freedom House index.[20] Importantly, success or failure is related to the capacity of the operation to jointly bring democracy and peace in civil war contexts between January 1989 and December 2021 (with the latest reports published in 2022). The compiled data can be found in the appendix of this book, Tables A.1 and A.2, with comparative data since 2012 (10 years). Notably, the timeframe also allows inferring some analysis of the effect of democratic movements, such as a decade after the Arab Spring.

4.2 Analysis of promoting the state, democracy, and peace in post-conflict societies

4.2.1 Postwar democratic civil peace through UN peacekeeping operations

Out of all 31 countries, when combining the outcomes from Freedom House, the Global Democracy Index, Polity IV, as well as the Fragile States Index, State Fragility Index, and Global Peace Index, a mix of results challenges what the literature recurrently claims, such as failure in Cyprus and success in El Salvador (Doyle and Sambanis, 2006). The main reason is the Introduction of new evaluation categories (Figure 4.1). It is important to recognize that there is no "full democracy," nor "full peace" in any of the cases. But those ideal types do not exist even in the most consolidated states. Yet, Namibia, Timor-Leste, and Croatia are consensual post–civil war cases of success in practice. It is important to note that in 2021, Namibia has shown some decline in the scores of democracy and peace. But considering that this decline is worldwide and that the country has been consistent on its date since 2012 (Freedom House, 2022a, EIU, 2021, IEP, 2022), it remains a successful case according to this methodology. Moreover, Namibia was also the UN's first effort in the scope of democracy-building.

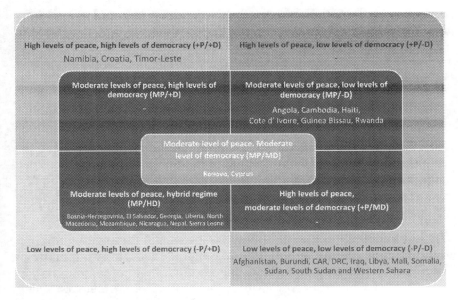

FIGURE 4.1 Case study with UN intervention. Source: Author

At the other end of the spectrum, Burundi, CAR, DRC, Mali, Somalia, Sudan, South Sudan and Western Sahara are unsuccessful cases: all are autocracies, with indices results showing a combination of "extreme high fragility" and "very low peace." The "Democratic" Republic of Congo is statistically not as democratic as its official name suggests. Significantly, six countries, Angola, Haiti, Cambodia, Côte d'Ivoire,[21] Guinea-Bissau, Mozambique, and Rwanda have moderate levels of peace but low levels of democracy, mostly classified with the highest rate of partly free (i.e., 5, 5, 5) or as consolidated autocracies or state failures. Thus, missions in similar contexts might be in jeopardy due to either high levels of state fragility, which might include the hybrid elements of autocracy and democracy, or anocracy. Ironically, Rwanda has been consistently cited by good governance reports for the unprecedented number of females elected to its Parliament, respectively 61.2 percent and 38.5 percent in its lower and upper houses, far more than any other country (Women, 2017; Hunt, 2014). Nevertheless, the legislative pillar generally lacks independence and merely endorses presidential initiatives as it uses the political nomination of females as puppets. Its 2003 constitution marked the end of a transition from the nation's post-genocide political period, yet the 2015 constitutional amendment granted broad powers to president Paul Kagame and is evidence of the Rwandan Patriotic Front's (RPF) (the main Tutsi party) complete domination of the political arena. Among other issues, political pluralism is being effectively limited by repressed media, forced disappearances, and the political emphasis on "national unity." Thus, in all indices analyzed, Rwanda is considered a consolidated autocracy with a very high rate of state fragility. Interestingly, out of 31 cases investigated with UN intervention, 16 percent are classified by Polity IV trend as failed states (i.e., Haiti, CAR, South Sudan, and Western Sahara), or susceptibility to collapse (i.e., Bosnia-Herzegovina).

Considering that some interventions are titled "special political missions" and yet with a multidimensional mandate under the United Nations Department of Political and Peacebuilding Affairs (DPPA), it seems methodologically relevant to analyze the cases of Afghanistan, Iraq, and Libya separately. Nevertheless, United Nations Assistance Mission in Afghanistan (UNAMA), the United Nations Assistance Mission for Iraq (UNAMI), and the United Nations Mission in Liberia (UNAMIL), respectively, falls under the category of failure with "low levels of peace, low levels of democracy (-P/-D)."

This book brings an innovative dimension to the categorization of UN missions in terms of their success or failure: the dimension of meso-success. Thus, although some interventions are considered successful, I argue that they show elements of moderate peace and moderate democracy, of which Kosovo and Timor-Leste are examples.[22] Cyprus show interesting results, as it continues to show signs of flawed democracy, particular after the Cyprus paper scandals. In terms of peace, it still suffer external influence from Greece and Turkey as well as a large change in its internal dynamic due to the massive influx of Middle Eastern refugees, particularly from Syria and Lebanon. Another innovative category proposed is the recognition of hybrid regimes that combine democratic and autocratic procedural forms of governance, instead of simply classifying them as moderate or partial democracies. In that, El Salvador indicates evidence of a hybrid regime and drug-related violence. Similarly, albeit for different reasons, Bosnia-Herzegovina, Georgia, Liberia, North Macedonia, Mozambique, Nicaragua, Nepal, and Sierra Leone show elements of moderate peace with a hybrid regime. Figure 4.1 illustrates that 60 percent are classified as having a "good enough approach," with moderate levels of peace or democracy or both. This result suggests that, although peacebuilding, democracy-building, and state-building are dynamic processes that can progress as well as regress, they can also get stuck in a vicious cycle that impedes the goal of mutual democratic peace consolidation. This is significant. For example, the Mozambique mission is usually considered successful in bringing peace (Doyle and Sambanis, 2006, p. 79). Nevertheless, Mozambique has reverted its peace and democratic status due to an estimate of over 744,000 people being internally displaced due to an ongoing Islamist insurgency in Cabo Delgado by December 20211 (UNHCR, 2022) and the power control of the Front for the Liberation of Mozambique (FRELIMO) marred by political violence. It confirms the correlation that "anti-democratic practices lead to civil war and humanitarian crisis. They facilitate the growth of terrorist movements, whose effects inevitably spread beyond national borders. Corruption and poor governance fuel economic instability" (Freedom House, 2015).

Interestingly, no cases were found in which there were "high levels of peace and low levels of democracy" or "low levels of peace and high levels of democracy." This supports the democratic peace principle that democracy and peace work hand in hand, although, rarely at equal levels and within the same time-frames. Consequently, this suggests that a bottleneck exists regarding timing and sequencing (Langer and Brown, 2016).

Moreover, there is no relationship between success and failure in cases of multiple interventions. Out of the 12 cases with more than one operation, only Croatia and Timor-Leste are successful according to the set of criteria established in the book. Five cases with multiple operations are identified as failures: Burundi, CAR, DRC, Somalia, and Sudan. The other remaining five cases present meso-levels of success: Angola and Haiti failing with the democratization process but with medium success in keeping the peace or in preventing a state collapse. Cambodia, Liberia, and Sierra Leone are not stable in delivering peace, though hybrid in their form of governance (with elements of both democratic and autocratic governance). Similarly, the five countries under the peacebuilding agenda analyzed here (Burundi, Sierra Leone, Guinea-Bissau, Liberia, and CAR) also present pole-apart results.

One could assume that if the conflict is more severe, subsequent interventions would be expected if the first fails. Nevertheless, determining how "severe" a case is subjective as all interventions are the last resources. Therefore, for countries with multiple operations, it is not enough to infer a relationship between the degree of intensity of a conflict and the success or failure outcome. In other words, it is not because a conflict had multiple interventions that there is any higher correlation with bringing peace and democracy simultaneously. After all, politics might play a more prominent role than the intensity of the conflict.

Finally, considering the "regionalization" of peacekeeping with hybrid category, there is no evidence that partnering with the African Union or the Organization of American States makes the case more or less successful in keeping the peace and building democracy.

4.2.2 Autonomous postwar democratic civil peace: cases without UN intervention

Based on the above-mixed results, why in some cases do UN peace operations successfully promote democratic civil peace while others not? Previous studies show that war is much more likely to resume if belligerents are left to their own devices (Fortna, 2004). A deeper understanding of the phenomenon requires analyzing cases of civil wars, without UN operations, during the same period. Another way of looking at the issue is to ask: is the UN indispensable to global democratization efforts? Based on the same set of criteria of the cases with UN participation, 11 cases, representing around one-third of the cases with UN interventions in this study, were identified: Algeria, Djibouti, Colombia, Ethiopia (Tigray war), Myanmar, Nigeria, Peru, the Philippines, Sri Lanka, Syria, and Yemen (Figure 4.2).

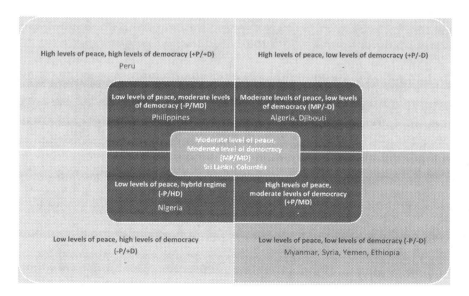

FIGURE 4.2 Case study without UN intervention. Source: Author

Colombia deserves special consideration as it was initially not part of the study. During the long-lasting period of the armed civil conflict, there has not been a direct operation to keep the peace. Nevertheless, considering the Peace Agreement with the FARC in November 2016, a special political UN Verification Mission under DPPA was established in 2017 to monitor the peace agreement and assist in the socioeconomic inclusion of ex-combatants. Therefore, under the methodological design of this study, it is still a case without UN intervention as it came after the conflict had ceased. Importantly, to avoid incorrect snapshots inferences, it is also important to acknowledge that the process of inclusion of former guerrilla member is still going alongside the political inclusion of the FARC as a political party (Comunes) within the state system through periodic elections (2017 and 2022). Thus, only with a longer timeframe it will be possible to evaluate if the peace agreement will indeed bring peace and democracy to Colombia and, consequently, assess the UN Good Offices. On the other hand, the fact that its democracy index has stayed constant instead of declining might be a good trend for the near future.

No successful cases[23] were found. Syria, Yemen, and Myanmar are ongoing conflict cases without UN direct operation, only Special Envoys under DPPA. Seven of these 11 countries still find themselves within the moderate spectrum. Algeria and Djibouti present moderate levels of peace and low levels of democracy. Nevertheless, a more extensive overview of peacekeeping appears to confirm the findings of Fortna (2008a) and other authors that UN peace operations in countries that border any of the five Security Council Permanent members (P5) are unlikely to occur, with the exception of Georgia.[24]

Peru stands out with results showing positive peace. It is worthwhile noting that, after Colombia, Peru was the second-longest internal conflict in Latin America. It has been estimated that nearly 60,000 people have died between 1982 and 1996 in the conflict between the government, the insurgent People's Guerrilla Army (Ejército Guerrillero Popular), the armed wing of the Communist Party of Peru (known as Shining Path, Sendero Luminoso or "PCP-SL") and the Tupac Amaru Revolutionary Movement. The 2003 final report of the Truth and Reconciliation Commission (CVR) to investigate the war was surrounded by controversy among almost all political parties, the military, and the Catholic Church. It estimates that the Shining Path guerrilla group killed about half the victims, roughly one-third died at the hands of government security forces, and some of the other assassinations by a smaller guerrilla group and local militias. Although the conflict had primarily diminished by 2000, violence again erupted in 2014 as the treats of Sendero Luminoso reemerged through regional warlords' followers (De La Pedraja, 2013, p. 211). Besides the 2009 political crisis, serious accusations of corruption and oppression of the media during Ollanta Humala's presidency, the fear of a return to the past during the 2011 and 2016 presidential elections with Keiko Fujimori's candidacy, as well as economic decline enabled a political shift in 2016 with the presidential victory of Pedro Pablo Kuczynski. Nevertheless, his government was short-lived as he resigned in 2018 to avoid impeachment. However, this enchained political instability and violent protest in a domino-effect style over the nomination of Vice President Martín Vizcarra, than later Manuel Merino from the center-right Acción Popular party until Francisco Sagasti, the president of the Congress. Finally, elections in 2021 shed some light into the political power structure with the narrow victory of Pedro Castillo of the leftist Peru Libre over the right-wing candidate Keiko Fujimori in a runoff with 50.13 percent of the vote. With the COVD-19 pandemic and the rise of economic struggles, Indigenous discrimination and inadequate political representation, and environmental impact over the mines, Peru has shown resilience and demonstrated working democratic political institutions. Thus, as the conflict officially ended in 1996, it is possible to evaluate a longer timeframe. Peru's status improved from partly free to fee by Freedom House (Freedom House, 2022a). This case merits attention in line with the narrative that peace-building and democracy-building are more likely to succeed if it comes from within, not from outsiders' intervention.

As for Sri Lanka, since 2021, the country is about to collapse financially partially due to the impact of the COVID-19 pandemic, the rise of fuel prices, and the government political economy inability. Sri Lanka experienced improvements in political rights and civil liberties after the 2015 election of President Maithripala Sirisena, which ended the more repressive rule of Mahinda Rajapaksa. However, the Sirisena administration was slow to implement transitional justice mechanisms needed to address the aftermath of a 26-year-long civil war between government forces and ethnic Tamil rebels, who were defeated in 2009. Gotabaya Rajapaksa's election as president in November 2019 and the Sri Lanka Podujana Peramuna's (SLPP) victory in the August 2020 parliamentary polls emboldened the Rajapaksa family, which has taken steps to empower the executive, roll back accountability mechanisms for civil war–era rights violations, and further militarize the island (Freedom House, 2021). Notably, the government continues to deny allegations of war crimes committed in 2009, during the final phase of the military's campaign against the Liberation Tigers of Tamil Eelam (LTTE or Tamil Tigers) rebel group. However, since 2011, although the Lessons Learned and Reconciliation Commission was government-backed, the implementation of its recommendations remains irregular. Moreover, in March 2014, the UN Human Rights Council mandated the UN Office of the High Commissioner for Human Rights (OHCHR) to investigate alleged wartime atrocities between 2002 and 2009. Moreover, controversial promises over the Prevention of Terrorism Act (PTA) to avoid international censure and "selective and arbitrary pardons" by Rajapaksa over political assassination have undermined the rule of law in the country. Importantly, despite the end of the armed conflict, few policy initiatives have been undertaken in its wake to address the underlying grievances of the Tamil citizenry that had contributed to the outbreak of the civil war in the first place. It is argued that in the absence of concerted efforts to address the human and material costs of the civil war and its antecedents, Sri Lanka is likely to remain a nation deeply fractured by ethnic cleavages. Without a shared sense of national identity to underpin a state's legitimacy, substantial parts of the Tamil community remain skeptical of the Sinhala-dominated Sri Lankan state (Ganguly, 2018). The financial struggle and violence might fuel fear of return to conflict.

The Philippines offers a different category compared to the cases with UN operations and is classified as a country with "low levels of peace and moderate levels of democracy." Rodrigo Duterte's style of governance, with his war on drugs and large numbers of extrajudicial killings, the 2017 attack in Manila and the battles in Mindanao against insurgents affiliated with Islamic State in Iraq and the Levant (ISIL), has created serious concerns about the rule of law, human rights, and the integrity of the country's fragile political institutions.[25] Although the Philippines transitioned from authoritarian rule in 1986, the rule of law and the application of justice are haphazard and heavily favor political and economic elites. Democratic institutions that provide oversight and accountability are either weak or undermined. Long-term violent insurgencies have continued for decades, though their threat to the state has diminished in recent years. Impunity remains the norm for violent crimes against activists and journalists (Freedom House, 2019). In fact, Polity IV shows that its authoritarian features have not been as high since 1988. From 2016 to 2022, Philippine democracy declined substantially due to Duterte's autocratic policies, from 65 to 55 in Freedom House's democracy rankings. Alongside the influence of entrenched political dynasticism and online misinformation, the 2022 presidential elections were an example of illiberal populism. Ferdinand "Bongbong" Marcos Jr., the son of the former dictator, won by historic margins along with his incoming vice president, Rodrigo Duterte's daughter, Sara Duterte. Those electoral results unveil the limitations of democracy serving to empower political dynasties.

Myanmar embodies the image of a roller coaster with peaks of democratization and of authoritarianism. A technically civilian government was installed in March 2011, which raised hopes for democratization and reconciliation, particularly with Aung San Suu Kyi's National League for Democracy Party's (NLD) victory in 2015. Among other reasons, the low level of democratization is because the military-drafted constitutions prevent the full transfer of power to elected politicians. Moreover, the worsening situation of Rohingans facing ethnic cleansing has been categorized as genocide in several reports issued by the UN as well as by the International State Crime Initiative (ISCI) and other human rights organizations based on the six stages of genocide: stigmatization (and dehumanization), harassment, violence and terror, isolation and segregation, systematic weakening, mass annihilation, and, finally, symbolic enactment involving the removal of the victim group from the nation's history (Green et al., 2015). In August 2017, mutual attacks between the Muslim insurgents of the Arakan Rohingya Salvation Army (ARSA) and Myanmar security forces resulted in 680,000 Rohingyan Muslims fleeing to Bangladesh and joining at least 100,000 who had already escaped persecution from the military Buddhist majority in Myanmar due to intensified mass killings since 2012 (UN News

Centre, 2017; UNHCR, 2018). Moreover, the conflict in Kachin has resulted in a humanitarian crisis and human rights violations from Myanmar's central government. Nevertheless, the already stalled democratic transition was derailed entirely in February 2021, when the military, known as the Tatmadaw, seized control of the government and detained dissenting voices, including Aung San Suu Kyi. Thus, in a dynamic world of politics, Myanmar at the initial stage of this study was a moderate case without UN intervention. But from 2017 to 2022, its democratic score eroded from 32 to 9 (Freedom House, 2022a). Despite the presence of a Special Envoy, the case falls in the category of "low level of peace, low levels of democracy" and confirms the global trend of expansion of authoritarian rule.

Since its transition to democratic rule in 1999, Nigeria has made significant improvements to the quality of its elections. Nevertheless, the 2019 presidential and National Assembly elections were marred by irregularities and resulted in the reelection of President Muhammadu Buhari and the All Progressives Caucus (APC) regaining its legislative majority. Security challenges, including insurgencies, kidnappings, and communal and sectarian violence in the Middle Belt region, threaten the human rights of millions of Nigerians. Corruption remains endemic in the key petroleum industry. In this hybrid regime,[26] the military and law enforcement agencies often engage in extrajudicial killings, torture, and other abuses. Civil liberties are undermined by religious and ethnic bias, while women and LGBT+ people face pervasive discrimination. The vibrant media landscape is impeded by criminal defamation laws, as well as the frequent harassment and arrests of journalists who cover politically sensitive topics. Abubakar Shekau, the leader of the Boko Haram militant group, died by suicide in 2021 after being captured by the Islamic State West Africa Province (ISWAP), a Boko Haram splinter group. Over 1,000 fighters and relatives reportedly surrendered in subsequent weeks. Nnamdi Kanu, the leader of the separatist Indigenous People of Biafra (IPOB), was arrested and returned to Nigeria. Armed attacks against electoral offices impacted the Anambra state gubernatorial election in November; only 10 percent of voters participated from fear of violence. It is important to mention that Boko Haram has been called the world's deadliest terrorist group, in terms of the number of people it has killed since 2009 (Sieff, 2017). With its affiliation with Al-Qaeda and ISIL, the insurgency has become a major regional conflict as it has spilled over to neighboring Cameroon, Chad, and Niger. Similarly to the cases with UN intervention, there have been no cases with "high levels of peace and low levels of democracy" or "low levels of peace and high levels of democracy" or "high levels of peace and moderate levels of democracy." This finding supports the conventional wisdom that democracy cannot be established without peace.

Ethiopia is an authoritarian state ruled by the Ethiopian People's Revolutionary Democratic Front (EPRDF), which has been in power since 1991 and currently holds every seat in Parliament. Multiple flawed elections showcased the government's willingness to brutally repress the opposition and its supporters, journalists, and activists. Muslims and members of the Oromo ethnic group have been specifically singled out. Perceived political opponents are regularly harassed, detained, and prosecuted—often under the guise of Ethiopia's deeply flawed Anti-Terrorism Proclamation. The appointment of Prime Minister Abiy Ahmed set off a transitional period after the resignation of Prime Minister Hailemariam Desalegn upon mass protests. Abiy pledged to reform Ethiopia's authoritarian state, and it has held elections and implemented some liberalization policies. However, Ethiopia remains beset by political factionalism and intercommunal violence, abuses by security forces and violations of due process are still common, and many restrictive laws remain in force. Since November 2020, fighting between the Federal Government and the Tigray Defense Force (TDF) has led to the displacement of hundreds of thousands and credible allegations of atrocity crimes, and violence has spilled over into neighboring regions. The Tigray War included allegations of massacres of Tigrayans by Eritrean Defense Forces aligned with the federal government, and sexual violence against civilians. In the regions of Benishangul Gumuz, Oromia, and Amhara, hundreds of civilians have been killed basis on their ethnicity. Moreover, the country faces famine due to drought, climate change impact, and conflict. Despite the concerns, the Tigray War had no UN intervention.

It is interesting to observe and compare the trending in political system and peace arrows. Out of 31 cases with UN operations, only four improved their political status (Croatia, Sierra Leone, Timor-Leste, and Côte d'Ivoire) within 10 years while the vast majority of 22 cases remains the same. But among the cases without UN operations, none improved their political status. As for Global Peace Index, five cases with UN operations improved their categories compared to only two when "left on their own." Therefore, despite its challenges, statistically the cases with UN operations perform better transitions toward peace and democracy than those without it.

Therefore, it is possible to make the following inferences concerning the hypotheses posed:

- **Hypothesis 1**: UN peace operations simultaneously bring peace and democracy in civil war cases.

Some evidence has been found to support UN peace operations for the promotion of peace and democracy. Yet no correlation has been found to support the hypothesis that these are brought about to the same extent. Most modern peacekeeping missions include democratization components, such as monitoring or running elections, civil rights monitoring and training, and democratic political institutions. But the two main goals of peacekeeping, maintaining peace and stability, on the one hand, and fostering democracy, on the other, may often be in direct conflict. UN peace operations can simultaneously bring peace and democracy in societies torn by civil war, but most of the cases result (within the timeframe under review) in a moderate level of either peace or democracy or both. As no cases were found with high levels of the one and low levels of the other, this suggests that peace and democracy do emerge simultaneously. However, they do not emerge to the same extent. The evidence supports the "good enough" approach that allows for managing, controlling, or freezing the conflict sufficiently to avoid returning to war.

- **Hypothesis 2:** If peace and democracy should be built from within, post-civil war democratization and peacebuilding are better without UN intervention.

No correlation has been found to support this hypothesis. However, each case is unique. Overall, without UN intervention, moderate levels of peace and/or democracy were identified. Although democracy cannot be imported or exported, it can be supported (IDEA, 2010).

- **Hypothesis 3:** Multidimensional operations are more likely to bring democratic civil peace.

No correlation has been found to support this hypothesis. Despite the expectation that more complex mandates would be more efficient, success or failure in building a peaceful and democratic consolidated state after a civil war is not primarily related to the type of operation but the conditions under which it takes place. This result corroborates previous findings from the literature (Fortna, 2008b) as well as the fact that the distinctions between mission types are becoming increasingly ambiguous.

- **Hypothesis 4:** Operations led by the DPKO are more successful than those led by the DPA or jointly with other organizations.

No correlation has been found to support this hypothesis. Success or failure does not seem to be defined by who leads the mission, but by other factors such as how the mission has been conducted in the context of the internal and external dynamics of the conflict and of international affairs.

- **Hypothesis 5:** Multiple interventions are more likely to be successful in building democracy and peace.

No correlation has been found to support this hypothesis. Success and failure in building democratic civil peace are not related to the number of interventions. Moreover, no missions of significant size have resulted in the establishment of strong state institutions, peace, and liberal democracy, including those in DRC, Kosovo, and Afghanistan.

Based on the findings above, we can infer that the role that UN peacekeeping plays in the democratization, state-building, and peacebuilding processes in postwar societies is polychromatic. If so, why do UN peace operations have different outcomes of success, failure, or a meso-level when promoting democratic civil peace? First, as explained in more detail in Sections 2 and 3 of the Introduction, regardless of civil wars or UN interventions, there is a global trend toward the deterioration and frustration of democracy with significant setbacks in political rights, civil liberties, or both (Freedom House, 2018; Fukuyama et al., 2015; EIU, 2016; Freedom House, 2022b). Moreover, as the Global Peace Index shows, the world has not become more or less peaceful. The problem is the wide gap between the countries ranked as very or less peaceful (IEP, 2016). Interestingly, if we analyze the trending of the results provided by the Global Peace Index over the last 10 years, there is not a significant change of the category (high, medium, low, or very low). But in terms of scores, almost as many countries with UN intervention have improved their GPI score (12, equivalent to 40 percent) as those that have deteriorated (11, equivalent to 36 percent). In contrast, over the last decade, 50 percent of the countries analyzed without UN intervention have deteriorated their GPI score, compared to only 30 percent that have improved. This trend might suggest that UN intervention contributes to peacebuilding, although not solely responsible.

Nevertheless, it is generally more accurate to infer that the UN's ambition to promote democratization via peacebuilding operations in post-civil war succeeds on a moderate level. This can be explained by the idea that full democracy or peace is a very protracted process. Of more importance is the clarification that democracy or peace is not to be considered in absolute "all or nothing" terms and that a "good enough" approach" indicates moderate success. This allows for minimalist mechanisms as starting points that are to be improved over time, allowing for new internal dynamics and external influences (Jarstad and Belloni, 2012). This is closely related to Schumpeter's understanding of procedural democracy and how a government is chosen (Jarstad, 2015). Finally, given the uniqueness of each conflict and controversy in the proliferating literature on culture, religion, peace, and democracy, it is nevertheless debatable whether a "democratic enough" political regime can or should emerge everywhere. Between the two alternatives of peace or democracy, peace should be prioritized over regime type: peace first.

4.3 Addressing the role of UN peacekeeping operations in promoting the state, democracy, and peace with the P–A–T framework of dilemmas: why are there different results?

4.3.1 The United Nations as savior: why do some missions triumph with the "positive but modest approach"?

Getting the right balance between principles and pragmatism is essential political art. Neither peacekeeping nor efforts for democratization are panaceas for the problems that plague post-conflict states. Yet under certain conditions, both can promote peace and stability (Diehl, 2014). In this book, more indices and more cases are analyzed and it also relies on more recent events. Thus, its results differ slightly from Jarstad (2015) and Fortna (2008b). Nevertheless, the results are in line with the interdependent logic of a "peacebuilding triangle" presented by Doyle and Sambanis (2006): the deeper the hostility, the more the destruction of local capacities, the more one needs international assistance to succeed in establishing a stable peace. Even so, the results are slightly different regarding Cambodia, Mozambique, and Bosnia-Herzegovina. However, they do show consistency in the possible causes for success suggested.

With technical expertise, UN peacekeeping missions can be effective in providing a road to democracy in many ways. For example, supporting new actors committed to peace, providing security during the tense periods of election campaigning and balloting, and during the reform of armies and police forces, providing human rights training, protecting political rights, and monitoring and policing the implementation of peace settlements. Additionally, the required preconditions for democracy are low levels of violence and low levels of mistrust. Peacekeeping helps reduce violence and increase trust between former belligerents and competing political forces. In these ways, peacekeepers can help foster the conditions for successful democratization, which supports the notion that state-building, peacebuilding, and democracy-building are intertwined by timing and sequencing dilemmas. Another option suggests that economic development is the best way to decrease the risk of new fighting in the long run. Therefore, peace and democracy will become consolidated in places where national institutions are working, and economic growth is in place by creating jobs and capacity building that might lead to socioeconomic development.

4.3.2 Relying on the United Nations: why do some missions fail?

Many reasons can be suggested for why democracies rarely emerge successfully from civil war (Call, 2012; Ukashi, 2008; Jett, 1999; Touval, 1994). First, societies recently affected by warfare lack functioning political institutions, an adequate economic infrastructure, and vibrant civil society. In such environments, state-building, in the sense of creating a Weberian monopoly of violence over a defined territory, is often in contradiction to the rule of law, which limits the central state's authority to legitimately execute its jurisdiction and, hence, to create the very conditions that are essential to a functioning democracy. In general, state-building is claimed to be accomplished under liberal and democratic rule, rather than permitting the sequencing of state-building prior to the promotion of the rule of law and democracy, which may simply freeze conflicts that will eventually emerge (Fukuyama, 2007, p. 12).

Second, by overseeing the transition from war to peace, UN peace operations have a herculean task to keep the peace in the aftermath of civil war. Adding another task of shepherding a country toward democracy is to set a goal likely to fail. The dilemmas of legitimacy and ownership reinforce the possibility that foreign intervention may impede the development of strong politically democratic and robust economic institutions. As per the systemic dilemma, postwar societies may be better off if left to their own devices in the process of "autonomous" or "self-ruling" recovery. In principle, the imposition of democracy is undemocratic in itself. Therefore, peacekeepers should limit their goals to providing stability only, instead of political transformation. The quandary is that without democratic political settings, it is unlikely that peace will be kept. Moreover, the temporal dilemma is identified as in the short term, democracy has no chance of taking root within the crossfire, and in the long term, peacekeeping can undermine conditions for a legitimate and sustainable national governance through a period of benevolent foreign autocracy and the direct limitation of national sovereignty (Chesterman, 2004).

Third, there is a wide operational gap between the field and headquarters. Missions are burdened by their own heavy bureaucratic apparatus and internal politics. Moreover, they are regularly underfunded, underequipped, and understaffed. Mandates, which themselves are often unrealistic and vague, are frequently designed at the last minute. Furthermore, they often possess short **timelines and unclear benchmarks (Banbury, 2016). In the near future, it will** be possible to assess if the A4P (2018) and A4P+ (2021) initiatives to enhancing the effectiveness and impact of the 12 peacekeeping operations in operation in 2022 were indeed successful. Fourth, some cases include the characteristics that invariably impede a democratic transition: a large, impoverished population deeply divided along ethnic and religious lines, no previous experience with democracy, and a track record of maintaining stability only under the grip of a strongly autocratic government (Newman and Rich, 2004). Iraq and DRC are some examples of this.

Fifth, some authors question if the UN can advance democratization only in relatively small societies (Newman and Rich, 2004). There seems to be a correlation between the size of the problem and the degree of UN achievement, as in the cases of Kosovo, North Macedonia, and Timor-Leste. However, just as civil war does not mean a small war (Kim, 2007), the problems in smaller societies are no less complex than in large populations (Newman, 2014; Fortna, 2008a; Collier, 1999).

Sixth, as the mission in Mali, the UN's deadliest ongoing peace operation, shows, the UN is remarkably unprepared for the threat of terrorism.[27] Beyond the legal, operational, and financial challenges, it is debatable if UN forces should be engaged in counterterrorism at all. Moreover, the UN is not good at intervening in ongoing wars. If the conflict is controlled by spoilers, or if the political groups involved are not ready to make peace, the UN cannot play an effective enforcement role, nor can it enforce a democratic regime (Doyle and Sambanis, 2006). Politics involves more than technical expertise, building peace, democracy, and even securing the authority of the state. Providing technical expertise may be helpful, but this is destined to fail if it is unable to deal with the main driving forces of the conflict.

4.3.3 Not so peaceful nor so democratic: why are some countries stuck in the middle?

To be stuck in the "not so peaceful nor so democratic" middle is explained not only by the effectiveness of UN missions, but also by the dilemmas and trade-off choices made by the belligerents. Three main points may explain the state's paralysis "in the middle" with its mitigated peace and mitigated democracy.

The first concerns the argument that war creates democracy. According to this contention, it is precisely the conflict that generates solid incentives for rulers to secure the consent of the governed and build representative institutions with remnants of the rebel army groups, such as Colombia. As the democratic warlord paradox shows, it is the cost of war that makes warlords democratize by creating legitimate mechanisms for extracting resources more efficiently from the people (Wantchekon, 2004). If this argument is correct, if peacekeeping is too successful in keeping the peace, there is no need for further efforts for democratization, as actors would no longer need to bargain to reap the benefits of peace that could be offered through democracy. Thus, peacekeeping and the stable peace it helps to produce can become a substitute for democracy rather than an aid to it, leaving room for moderate democracy or hybridity (Fortna, 2008b, p. 47). Importantly, if the peacekeeping mission conforms to the principle of neutrality to the point that it is too neutral, it is perceived as weak. In the case of Kosovo, the United Nations Interim Administration Mission in Kosovo (UNMIK) headquarters has been physically pushed away from the center of Pristina as a sign of today's irrelevance. "Far from the eye, far from people's eyes," a former UNMIK's national staff stated.[28] Ironically, it is also positive as it focuses more on the elected government representatives and allows for international exposure and de facto recognition. Importantly, peacekeeping operations are viewed as more legitimate when compared to having a sole external state as an enforcer. Either because of the timing of the conflict or the role of elites or external pressures, the attempts to advance democracy can provoke violent outbreaks and can limit democratic development through old political and military ties or systems of patronage.

The second deals with the argument that democracy creates peace. The rationale is that democratic states and their leaders are more responsive to citizens' demands and have a series of institutional mechanisms, checks, and balances that channel dissent and manage conflict without using weapons (Henderson, 2002; Elman, 1999). Under the notion of "disarmed democracy," the state conflict behavior is dependent on domestic institutional structure and intragovernmental bargaining (Auerswald, 2000). Nevertheless, there is the danger that civil war by other means takes over: to be either a hybrid regime or a flawed democracy with a controlled level of peace is a strategic choice to retain domestic power. As per the existential dilemma, the trade-offs between lost certainty versus win uncertainty are better managed by taking advantage of the options that are somewhere in between the two. This can also be seen as a variant of the economic concept of Pareto's optimum balance: politically, it is possible to retain supremacy through a strategic selection of those democratic criteria, which, though far from perfect, are sufficient for a democratic regime and stability. If so, it might mean that warlords and elites do not have to be responsive to domestic institutional mechanisms (e.g., courts) and popular ratification by maneuvering the system. As a façade, elections are held but are not truly free and fair. Additionally, where there are too many shared power elements in the constitution, political bribery, or politicization of judges, although these are democratic deficiencies, they are also ways to bargain and overcome the political impasses destabilizing peace. As in the case of Kosovo, these are the kind of elements that shift the equilibrium of power by moving it from the battlefield to the political field (Ozoukou, 2014, McEvoy and O'Leary, 2013, Mansfield and Snyder, 1995). As per the temporal dilemma, rapid democratization produces "illiberal democracies" including abuse of power by many newly elected leaders, lack of institutional control of checks and balances, and the same patronage power structures remaining in place after the war (Zakaria, 1997).

A third concern is that "oil and democracy don't mix"' (Ross, 2001; Collier and Hoeffler, 1998). The argument is mainly related to natural resources, such as oil, diamonds, and minerals, and to the idea that democracy is not suitable everywhere or for "every people." This could explain the causes and consequences of civil war and the failure of democratization in countries like Angola,[29] Iraq, and DRC. Their oil resources fuel the conflict and therefore obstruct peace and democracy. The conflict-incentivizing effect of such reserves are (a) rebels may want access to the resources for greed, (b) rebels may be able to use natural resource income to fund their mobilization, and (c) the absence of a strong state needed to implement taxation also makes rebellion more likely to succeed. In the cases of moderate success or failure, natural resources are used to limit democracy by: allowing governments to use low taxes and patronage to avoid pressures for reform; funding efforts to repress reformist movements; and/or producing economic growth that, unlike other forms of economic development, does not lead to social and cultural development, such as education and economic specialization, which would have tended to foster democracy. This could explain the moderate levels of peace with hybrid regimes or flawed democracies such as Côte d'Ivoire, Liberia, and Sierra Leone.

Hybrid regimes are primarily found in the aftermath of conflict. The state institutions are non-existent or weak. Moreover, governance and power continue to be concentrated in and implemented through informal structures that range from systems of patronage, either regional or ethnic bonds, to old political and military ties (Themnér and Utas, 2016). In other words, it is in the best interests of elites to further democratization if the benefits of moderate peace are sufficient to keep their status quo through a hybrid regime or an anocracy. This is related to the vertical dilemma: the incentives of the elites are not aligned with what peace and democracy might be able to offer, making democracy too costly compared to the benefits for elites and warlords (Zürcher et al., 2013). That was the case with the People's Movement for the Liberation of Angola (MPLA), after reaching an agreement with the National Union for the Total Independence of Angola (UNITA) and the National Liberation Front of Angola (FNLA). The hybridity quickly turned to authoritarianism.

Additionally, when missions exit, they usually leave behind at least nascent democratic institutions. On the one hand, precisely for democratic reasons, it is up to the "people" to run their national sovereignty and development in a peaceful, stable, and democratic way in the long term. On the other hand, this is a dangerous practice. The hybrid regime comes into place when an artificial political structure is created, leaving room for pseudo-authoritarianism. Thus, for all the reasons presented above, to break the conflict trap, it might be preferable to have robust and functional state institutions instead of weak democratic ones (Diehl, 2014). Besides the financial dilemma, an increase in funds does not create institutions (de Zeeuw, 2005). Moreover, the democratic façade creates room for regime legitimacy within the international community or, at least, garners support from major external power supporters or allies. As per the systemic dilemma, this kind of legitimacy might enable substantive international financial support based on conditional aid policy for peace or liberal democracy at the end of missions.

In any case, it seems that the UN can only facilitate progress when domestic and international conditions coalesce around a democratic future and broad acceptance of the democratic rules of the game (Newman and Rich, 2004). This is also related to the "positive but modest" impact of postwar democratization. That means, as in the example of Cambodia, the country would have remained undemocratic without UN intervention, although many achievements are attributed to the UN, such as the constitution, a multiparty electoral system, elections on a regular basis, and a decline of political violence, as political parties now seem willing to accept election outcomes. However, DDR, media transparency, law enforcement in relation to electoral laws, and political justice may still be deficient. At the time of the UN's arrival, Cambodia had no genuine democratic culture and the socioeconomic factors were not favorable. Today, despite the hybrid elements of democracy listed above, a return to war seems unlikely (Peou, 2004).

Last but not least and based on all the above, there is the question of whether being at a meso-level is good or bad for democratic civil peace. On the one hand, to be stuck in the "middle" might not mean that the peace operations were unsuccessful. It might mean that prioritization of one aspect at the expense of the other, depending on the momentum of the specific conflict, was necessary. Such a situation supports the argument that pursuing *both* peace and democracy in the aftermath of civil war may undermine each other. On the other hand, it may be a success if achieving a medium level of peace and of democracy is "good enough" to enable a mission exit strategy so that the intervention itself is not enmeshed in a systemic dilemma, thus the intervention avoids becoming part of the conflict. Moreover, some conflicts might not be able to be "resolved, but transformed" (Galtung, 1996). Under this alternative premise of transforming conflict rather than resolving it, the medium level should be sufficient for the states to move on as the inertia of armed conflict and autocracy has been transformed into a different dynamic.

4.3.4 Action for Peacekeeping: is the answer for more effective operations?

Under the constant pressure for UN reform and accusations of sexual misconduct (former Yugoslavia, Mali) or operational failure (Somalia, Rwanda), it is relevant to note efforts to improve UN interventions. "Peacekeeping has never been more relevant and its success more urgent" justified the Secretary-General Antonio Guterres when launched the Action for Peacekeeping (A4P – United Nations, 2018) and the Action for Peacekeeping Plus (A4P+ – United Nations, 2021) initiatives. The goal is to strengthen peacekeeping by urging collective action by all peacekeeping stakeholders, including all member states, the Security Council, the General Assembly, financial contributors, troop and police contributing countries, host countries, intergovernmental and regional organizations, and the UN Secretariat. The A4P declaration includes 45 commitments across eight areas are to be implemented solely by member states, some solely by the UN Secretariat, and some are shared and will be implemented by both the UN Secretariat and the member states. The endorsement by 154 member states is a significant political achievement in itself.

The A4P plant encompasses: (1) politics (advance political solutions to conflict and enhance the political impact of peacekeeping), (2) women, peace, and security (implement the women, peace, and security agenda), (3) protection (strengthen the protection provided by peacekeeping operations, (4) safety and security (improve the safety and security of peacekeepers), (5) performance and accountability (support effective performance and accountability by all peacekeeping components), (6) peacebuilding and sustaining peace (strengthen the impact of peacekeeping on sustaining peace), (7) partnerships (improve peacekeeping partnerships to enhance collaboration and planning), and (8) conduct of peacekeepers and peacekeeping operations (strengthen conduct of peacekeeping operations and personnel).

To accelerate those efforts, the 2021 A4P+ strategy consists of seven priorities and two cross-cutting themes: (1) collective coherence behind a political strategy, (2) strategic and operational integration, (3) capabilities and mindsets, (4) accountability to peacekeepers, (5) accountability of peacekeepers, (6) strategic communications, and (7) cooperation with host countries. The Women, Peace, and Security (WPS) agenda and innovative, data-driven, and technology-enabled peacekeeping (Strategy for the Digital Transformation of UN Peacekeeping) are cross-cutting issues to those priorities.

As analyzed in Chapter 2, all interventions carry an inherent political drive. Both initiatives are welcomed and urgent under the plea for more efficient intervention and UN reform. Thus, their endorsement and implementation are in itself an achievement, including the fact that A4P+ was negotiated under COVID-19 as well as a "coup-d'état pandemic." It presents a good structure design and mirrors what the literature has for long identified as gaps. The near future will show if it is the answer for a new "peacekeeping operation generation." In itself, they are signs for hope.

4.4 Summary of the chapter

Do UN operations bring democratic civil peace? This question cannot be answered with a simple yes or no. The UN is not the savior, not evil. Intervention versus autonomy is one of the main dilemmas of UN involvement in civil wars. The aim of the chapter is neither to praise nor to condemn the UN, but to assess how well the organization performs its democracy promotion agenda while enforcing peace. In spite of a large body of literature on the effectiveness of UN peace operations in keeping the peace or in promoting democracy, the question was posed whether it can *jointly* secure peace and liberal democracy with functioning and strong state institutions. Peacekeeping seems good for peace, democracy and state-building, and bad at the same time. The point has been made in this chapter that, despite UN missions' technical expertise, it is unrealistic to expect that peace, democracy, and a consolidated state will emerge from the ashes of war all at the same time and at the same levels. The lack of cases in the category of a high level of one and a low level of the other shows evidence that democratization after civil war only takes place when there are simultaneous processes of state-building and peacebuilding. The international community justifies its intervention in war-torn states to help maintain peace and to foster the growth of democracy. However, there are no illusions that peacekeeping is a cure-all. Such operations alone are unable to transform war-torn states into ideal democratic societies. It would be naïve to expect an outsider body enmeshed in the international politics of its members to get it right every time.

This chapter opposes the arguments of those who are in favor or against the proposal that the UN promotes peace *and* democracy. Instead, this chapter argues that in the post-civil war context, the absence of any identifiable statistical effect of peace operations on the stability of peace, democracy, and the state does not mean that there is no relationship between these three latter processes. As an alternative, this might indicate evidence that these outcomes might limit each other depending on their timing, momentum, and sequencing. In distancing from binary arguments, this chapter greatly contributes to the book's questions as it defends an innovative moderate perspective when classifying post-civil war cases into peace, state, and democracy-building levels after UN intervention, such as "moderate levels of peace, moderate levels of democracy" or "high levels of peace, moderate levels of democracy," "moderate levels of peace, low levels of democracy," etc. With the inherent dilemmas in the attempt to foster both stable peace and democracy in the aftermath of civil war, some countries get stuck in a meso-level of success or failure through a hybrid regime or a flawed democracy, while nevertheless achieving a high or moderate level of peace. The cases outlined in this chapter illustrate that promoting stability may advance democracy or undermine it. While a functioning state, democracy, and peace can be mutually reinforcing, the pathways to achieve these ideals are contradictory, nonlinear, and at risk of undermining each other. Therefore, the cases in the middle spectrum are valuable lessons learned for a more in-depth understanding of the different transitional vectors and that promoting conflict transformation might be more realistic than of conflict resolution.

Moreover, with a systematic overview of UN multidisciplinary missions, the data set offers the opportunity for an up-to-date statistical analysis, a longer timeframe, and the inclusion of more comparative indices as well as a broader selection of mission cases with and without intervention, when compared with other studies reviewed in the literature. Additionally, in its use of five common hypotheses, it has addressed the dilemmas of the paradoxical relationships among peacebuilding, democracy-building, and state-building, which can be seen as three intersecting processes. While countries tend to have better chances of success with UN intervention, multidimensional types of intervention are not necessarily more efficient. In spite of these conclusions, a better understanding of the meso-level cases of success requires further investigation to be able to analyze, case by case, both with and without UN intervention, other possible variables. These may include the level of democracy before the war starts, the GDP per capita, the level of illiteracy, how the war ended, the terrorist threat, natural resources, failed past agreements, and whether the country is a former colony or has borders with a Perm-5 country, the geography, the predominant religion, the predominant ethnicity or race, the length of the conflict, the number of rebel groups, the scale of destructiveness, and numerous other variables. Importantly, it is highly recommended to keep monitoring and evaluating the A4P and A4P+ initiatives and other UN reforms launched to make peace operations more efficient.

Notes

1 DPO created in 2019. No mission has been created since under new structure.
2 The last mission initiated in 2014 (Mali). Thus, the 2019 structural reform does not alter this hypothesis.
3 Therefore, although in operation in 1989, the following cases are excluded for not meeting one or more of the set criteria: UN Aouzou Strip Observer Group (Chad), UN Iraq–Kuwait Observation Mission, UN Military Observer Group in India and Pakistan, UN Iran–Iraq Military Observer Group, UN Good Offices Mission in Afghanistan and Pakistan, UN Mission in Ethiopia and Eritrea, UN Observer Mission Uganda–Rwanda, UN Verification Mission in Guatemala, UN Interim Force in Lebanon, UN Disengagement Observer Force (Golan. Israel–Syria), UN Mission of Observers in Tajikistan and UN Truce Supervision Organization (Middle East. HQ in Israel), UN mission in Georgia (UNMIG), and UN Supervision Mission in Syria (UNSMIS).
4 The case of Chad was excluded from this chapter on UN operations, but it will be included for case analysis on violence, elections, and security reform. Since 2003,

more than 240,000 Sudanese refugees have fled to eastern Chad from the conflict in Darfur, joined by approximately 45,000 refugees from the Central African Republic (CAR). With the around 180,000 Chadians displaced by the civil war in the east of the country, this has generated increased tensions among the region's communities. The United Nations Mission in Central African Republic and Chad (MINURCAT) was established by Security Council resolution 1778 (2007) on 25 September 2007 in order to contribute to "the protection of civilians; promote human rights and the rule of law; and promote regional peace," by facilitating the provision of humanitarian assistance in eastern Chad and the north-eastern Central African Republic (CAR). The Mission completed its mandate on 31 December 2010, in accordance with Security Council resolution 1923 (2010) and at the request of the Chadian government, which had pledged full responsibility for protecting civilians on its territory. Following MINURCAT's withdrawal, the UN country team and the UN Integrated Peacebuilding Office in the Central African Republic (BINUCA) remained in the country to continue to work for the benefit of the Chadian people. Reporting to the Security Council in December, the Secretary-General said: "MINURCAT has been an unusual and unique United Nations peacekeeping operation in that it was devoted solely to contributing to the protection of civilians, without an explicit political mandate. It has gone through the stages of planning, deployment and withdrawal in the short span of less than four years." Therefore, this short mission was focused on protection of civilians at the border in cooperation with European Union Military force (EUROFOR) and not to build democracy or peace (conflict resolution). See https://peacekeeping.un.org/sites/default/files/past/minurcat/background.shtml Accessed in 01/05/2021.

5 Including MICIVI, under the hybrid administration of the UN and the Organization of American States (OAS).
6 Including UNAMID in Darfur and the consequential mission in South Sudan after its partition (UNMISS).
7 UN Peacekeeping Force in Cyprus (UNFICYP) Security Council resolution 186 (1964) of 4 March 1964. Also, see *Security Council Resolution S/RES/2300* of 26 July 2016. UNFICYP's main mandate is to supervise a de facto ceasefire effective since 1974 and to maintain a buffer zone. The latest attempt to find a comprehensive settlement of the Cyprus problem was launched under UN auspices in September 2008 encompassing peace, democracy, and state-building elements: a bizonal, bi-communal federation, with political equality and a single international personality. In the interests of preserving international peace and security, the mandate has been periodically extended to use its best efforts to prevent a recurrence of fighting and, as necessary, to contribute to the maintenance and restoration of law and order and a return to normal conditions. It includes undertaking humanitarian activities, demining, supporting the Good Offices Mission of the Secretary-General, and the development and engagement of civil society with state institutions.
8 For methodological coherence, this research is only on peacekeeping missions with democracy and state building mandates. "Good Offices" as special envoys and advisers of the Secretary-General or Sanctions Panels and Monitoring Groups for the resolution of conflicts or the implementation of other UN mandates as in Yemen, Myanmar, Syria, and the FYROM-Greece are not included. Similarly, political missions in Libya and Colombia have been established in 2016.
9 Many activities are also jointly implemented with UNDP and other specialized agencies depending on the issues. For methodological purposes and viability, this research only focuses on missions, even though the actions are joint, overlapping and shape the "UN country voice."
10 Personal Envoy of the Secretary-General for Mozambique, Western Sahara, Cyprus, Myanmar, Syria, Great Lakes Region, Horn of Africa, Yemen, and Special Envoy of the Secretary-General for the Implementation of Resolution 1559: United Nations Representative to the Geneva International Discussions (UNRGID); BINUH: United

Nations Integrated Office in Haiti, Port-au-Prince; CNMC: United Nations Support for the Cameroon–Nigeria Mixed Commission, Dakar; UNAMA: United Nations Assistance Mission in Afghanistan, Kabul; UNAMI: United Nations Assistance Mission for Iraq, Baghdad; UNITAMS: United Nations Integrated Transition Assistance Mission in Sudan, Khartoum; UNMHA: United Nations Mission to Support the Hudaydah Agreement, Hudaydah; UNOAU: United Nations Office to the African Union, Addis Ababa; UNOCA: United Nations Regional Office for Central Africa, Libreville; UNOWAS: United Nations Office for West Africa and the Sahel, Dakar; UNRCCA: United Nations Regional Centre for Preventive Diplomacy for Central Asia, Ashgabat; UNSCO: Office of the United Nations Special Coordinator for the Middle East Peace Process, Jerusalem; UNSCOL: Office of the United Nations Special Coordinator for Lebanon, Beirut; UNSMIL: United Nations Support Mission in Libya, Tripoli; UNSOM: United Nations Assistance Mission in Somalia, Mogadishu United Nations Verification Mission in Colombia, Bogotá. DPPA also maintains liaison presence in Bangkok, Beijing, Brussels, Buka, Cairo, Gaborone, Jakarta, Kathmandu, Kyiv, Nairobi, and Vienna: https://dppa.un.org/sites/default/files/dpa_ousg_4561_r14_mar22.pdf. Accessed on 1 April 22.

11 Information available at https://peacekeeping.un.org/en/department-of-peace-operations. Accessed on 1 July 22.

12 "UNAMA is a political mission that provides political good offices in Afghanistan; works with and supports the government; supports the process of peace and reconciliation; monitors and promotes human rights and the protection of civilians in armed conflict; promotes good governance; and encourages regional cooperation. UNAMA was established by the UN Security Council Resolution 1401 in March 2002 at the request of the Government of the Islamic Republic of Afghanistan. Its mandate is reviewed annually with the latest mandate renewal being on 15 March 2016 when the Security Council unanimously adopted Resolution 2274 (2016)". Source: UNAMA official website: https://unama.unmissions.org/mandate. Accessed on 5 December 2016.

13 Information available at https://peacekeeping.un.org/en/department-of-peace-operations. Accessed on 1 July 22.

14 The "polity" score recorded in the Polity V data series provides a general indicator of the country's regime type on 31 December 2016. An upper case "AUT" indicates that a country is governed by an institutionalized autocratic regime (POLITY -6 to -10); a lower case "aut" indicates that the country is governed by an uninstitutionalized, or "weak," autocratic regime (POLITY -5 to 0). A lower case "dem" indicates an uninstitutionalized, or "weak," democratic regime (POLITY 1 to 5). An upper case "DEM" indicates an institutionalized democracy (POLITY 6 to 10) and countries listed with "SF" (state failure) are experiencing a "collapse of central authority" such that the regime has lost control of more than half of its territory through some combination of human and natural factors, usually due to serious armed challenges, poor performance, and a diminished administrative capacity (Central African Republic, Haiti, Libya, South Sudan, Syria, Yemen); a dash "—" indicates that the central government is propped up by the presence of foreign forces and authorities that provide crucial security support for the local regime, without which this central authority would be susceptible to collapse (Bosnia). Countries with transitional governments at the end of 2015 are classified as either weak democracies (dem) (Myanmar) or weak autocracies (aut) according to the transitional regime's authority characteristics. As the Polity V indicator of "polar factionalism" has proven to be a very potent indicator of political instability, regimes that are denoted as factional (i.e., PARCOMP=3) are shaded. In addition, transitional (POLITY score -88), failed (POLITY score -77), and occupied (POLITY score -66) are also considered unstable, and so they are shaded for emphasis on this referent indicator.

15 The Economist Intelligence Unit's index of democracy, on a 0 to 10 scale, is based on the ratings for 60 indicators grouped in these five categories: electoral process and

pluralism; civil liberties; the functioning of government; political participation; and political culture. Each category also has a rating on a 0 to 10 scale, and the overall index of democracy is the simple average of the five category indices. The category indices are based on the sum of the indicator scores in the category, converted to a 0 to 10 scale. Adjustments to the category scores are made if countries do not score a 1 in the following critical areas for democracy: (1) whether national elections are free and fair, (2) the security of voters, (3) the influence of foreign powers on government, and (4) the capability of the civil service to implement policies. If the scores for the first three questions are 0 (or 0.5), one point (0.5 point) is deducted from the index in the relevant category (either the electoral process and pluralism or the functioning of government). If the score for 4 is 0, one point is deducted from the functioning of government category index. The index values are used to place countries within one of four types of regimes: (1) full democracies: scores of 8–10, (2) flawed democracies: scores of 6–7.9, (3) hybrid regimes: scores of 4–5.9, and (4) authoritarian regimes: scores below 4. Threshold points for regime types depend on overall scores that are rounded to one decimal point.

16 For more information, see http://fsi.fundforpeace.org/. The Fund for Peace methodology triangulates data from three primary sources and subjects them to critical review to obtain final scores for the Fragile States Index. The main data collection methods are: content analysis (electronic scanning); quantitative data; and qualitative input. Taken together, the three methods serve as internal checks. Aggregated data are normalized and scaled from 0 to 10 to obtain final scores for 12 social, economic, and political/military indicators for 178 countries. These range from "very sustainable," "sustainable," "highly stable," "very stable," "stable," "low warning," "warning," "high warning," "alert," "high alert," "very high alert." These results are then critically reviewed by analysts different from those who conducted the original research. This multi-stage process has several layers of scrutiny to ensure the highest standards of methodological rigour, the broadest possible information base including both quantitative and qualitative expertise, and the greatest accuracy.

17 Fragile States Index covers a wide range of state failure risk elements such as extensive corruption and criminal behavior, inability to collect taxes or otherwise draw on citizen support, large-scale involuntary dislocation of the population, sharp economic decline, group-based inequality, institutionalized persecution or discrimination, severe demographic pressures, brain drain, and environmental decay.

18 The State Fragility Index and Matrix 2015 lists all independent countries in the world in which the total country population is greater than 500,000 in 2014 (167 countries). The Fragility Matrix scores each country on both effectiveness and legitimacy in four performance dimensions: security, political, economic, and social, at the end of each year. Each of the Matrix indicators is rated on a four-point fragility scale: 0 "no fragility," 1 "low fragility," 2 "medium fragility," and 3 "high fragility" with the exception of the economic effectiveness indicator, which is rated on a five-point fragility scale (including 4 "extreme fragility"). The State Fragility Index then combines scores on the eight indicators and ranges from 0 "no fragility" to 25 "extreme fragility." A country's fragility is closely associated with its state capacity to manage conflict; make and implement public policy; and deliver essential services and its systemic resilience in maintaining system coherence, cohesion, and quality of life; responding effectively to challenges and crises; and sustaining progressive development. Fragility Indexes: State Fragility Index = effectiveness score + legitimacy score (25 points possible); effectiveness score = security effectiveness + political effectiveness + economic effectiveness + social effectiveness (13 points possible) and legitimacy score = security legitimacy + political legitimacy + economic legitimacy + social legitimacy (12 points possible). Therefore, "no fragility" 0–3 points; "low fragility" 4–7 points; "medium fragility" 8–11 points; "high fragility" 12–15 points; "very high fragility" 16–19 points and "extreme fragility" 20–25 points.

19 The scores go from 1 to 5 over 163 countries, categorized as "very low," "low," "medium," "high," and "very high." The higher the score, the less the peace. More methodological details and a full definition of "peace" can be found at http://www.visionofhumanity.org/#/page/indices/global-peace-index. Accessed on 6 December 2017. Although the GPI arrow is for each country, it is not measured as if the country had improved or deteriorated in isolation. The rank takes into consideration an indexation of how other countries evolved, and therefore, it gives a more worldwide parameter.

20 Source: https://freedomhouse.org/report/freedom-world-2016/methodology. Accessed on 1 August 2016.
Trend arrows – although based on the data from Freedom House over 15 years, in this research, the trending arrow is different from the trending concept of Freedom House itself which assigns an upward or downward trend arrow to highlight developments of major significance or concern related to a notable change in a *single year* or an important event in a country that is particularly influential in its region or the world. In this research, a country or territory may be assigned an upward or downward trend arrow to highlight developments of major significance or concern over *multiple years* within the timeframe of analysis.

21 "Cote d'Ivoire crisis" is usually related to the First Ivorian Civil War (2002–2007) and to the consequentially Second Ivorian Civil War (2010–2011). As the second one is strictly related to the reminiscent unsolved issues of the Ouagadougou peace agreement and in-between violence, the statistical data encompasses both crises.

22 It is important to distinguish the cases of Timor-Leste and Kosovo, as the latter is still not fully independent. Therefore, some data are not available. There are generally free and fair [municipal] elections, yet security concerns and problems with freedom of movement and freedom of expression for ethnic minorities. Serbia, through Russia's veto at the Security Council, impedes any international legal recognition of Kosovo besides it being de facto an independent state recognized by 110 countries worldwide Kosovo, B. I. 2018. *Be in Kosovo* [Online]. Online. Available: www.beinkosovo.com/countries-that-have-recognized-kosovo-as-an-independent-state/. Accessed on 5 February 2018.

23 Although it is not possible to predict the future, a possible case could be Ireland. Besides some deep remaining concerns about reconciliation as well as the potential withdrawal of EU funding to Northern Ireland as a result of Brexit, there is a serious threat to the implementation of the Good Friday Agreement and the peace process. In most of the literature on democratization and peacekeeping in Northern Ireland, there is a lack of statistical data as all the indices show results at the national level, which means the United Kingdom as a whole, which is not representative of the reality on the ground for both sides of the island (participatory observation during field research and interviews with specialists in Dublin and Belfast in September 2016). Based on the ethical principles of social research, interviews were conducted with respect, integrity, consensus, social responsibility, and confidentiality.

24 It is worthwhile to remember that UNOMIG's mandate was to verify compliance with the ceasefire agreement between the Government of Georgia and the Abkhaz authorities in Georgia. UNOMIG came to an end on June 2009 due to a lack of consensus among Security Council members on mandate extension, not because of the performance of the operation. That fact corroborates the geopolitical veto of P5 to have a UN peacekeeping presence at its borders.

25 Rodrigo Duterte declared in September 2016 that he wanted to do to Filipino drug addicts what Hitler had done to Jews and had pushed to reduce the age of criminal responsibility from 15 to 9 and to reinstate capital punishment (formally) for drug trafficking. See *THE ECONOMIST* 2016. The Philippines under Rodrigo Duterte: Sceptred bile. *The Economist*. Manila: The Economist Newspaper Limited.Edition of 17 September 2016. www.economist.com/asia/2016/09/17/sceptred-bile.

26 See definitions in the Introduction and the difference from flawed/partial democracy.

27 Between 2012 and 2016, 118 peacekeepers were killed, making MINUSMA the world's most dangerous UN mission. Most of its troops from Africa and South Asia brought tanks and vehicles that were easy targets for explosives. The UN compounds are vulnerable to the massive car bombs used by al-Qaeda in the Islamic Maghreb (AQIM), and for a while, UN forces did not have a single attack helicopter. (Sieff, K. 2017. The world's most dangerous U.N. mission: The Al-Qaeda threat in Mali presents a new challenge to U.N. peacekeepers. *Washington Post*, 17 February 2017.

28 Interview conducted face to face in Pristina in September 2016 for the purpose of this research. Anonymity, integrity, and consensus are ethical principles respected in this social research.

29 José dos Santos, president of Angola from 1979 to 2017, died on 8 July 2022. Dos Santos was the leader of the People's Movement for the Liberation of Angola (MPLA), Angola's ruling party that fought against the National Union for the Total Independence of Angola (UNITA), and the National Liberation Front of Angola (FNLA). In 1991, a peace agreement was reached between the MPLA led by dos Santos and UNITA, headed by Jonas Savimbi. But the following year, Savimbi did not accept election results that showed the MPLA winning, so war erupted again. It was not until after Savimbi was killed in a clash with government troops in February 2002 that a second peace agreement was made. Note that MONUA verification mission left in fev 99. His legacy of "peace architect" or "corruption and dictator" continues to divide opinions inside and outside Angola.

References

Andersson, A. 2000. Democracies and UN Peacekeeping Operations, 1990–1996. *International Peacekeeping*, 1–22.

Auerswald, D. P. 2000. *Disarmed Democracies: Domestic Institutions and the Use of Force*. University of Michigan Press.

Banbury, A. 2016. I Love the U.N., but It Is Failing. *New York Times*.

Bellamy, A. J., Williams, P. D. & Griffin, S. 2010. *Understanding Peacekeeping*. Polity Press, UK.

Boutros-Ghali. 1992. An Agenda for Peace. In *Preventive Diplomacy, Peacemaking, and Peace-keeping*. United Nations.

Bueno De Mesquita, B. & Downs, G. W. 2006. Intervention and Democracy. *International Organization*, 60, 627–49.

Call, C. T. 2012. *Why Peace Fails: The Causes and Prevention of Civil War Recurrence*, Georgetown University Press.

Chesterman, S. 2004. *You, the People: The United Nations, Transitional Administration, and State-building, GB*. Oxford University Press.

Collier, P. 1999. On the Economic Consequences of Civil War. *Oxford Economic Papers*, 51, 168–183.

Collier, P. & Hoeffler, A. 1998. On Economic Causes of Civil War. *Oxford Economic Papers*, 50, 563–573.

De La Pedraja, R. 2013. *Wars of Latin America, 1982–2013: The Path to Peace*. McFarland, Incorporated, Publishers.

De Zeeuw, J. 2005. Projects Do Not Create Institutions: The Record of Democracy Assistance in Post-Conflict Societies. *Democratization*, 12, 481–504.

Diehl, P. 2014. Breaking the Conflict Trap: The Impact on Peacekeeping on Violence and Democratization in Post-Conflict Context. Workshop *"What Do We Know About Civil Wars?"*. University of Iowa.

Doyle, M. W. & Sambanis, N. 2006. *Making War and Building Peace : United Nations Peace Operations*. Princeton University Press.

Dpa, U. 2016. *Political Missions*. Online: UN.
EIU. 2016. *Democracy Index 2015: Democracy in an Age of Anxiety*. The Economist Intelligence Unit.
EIU 2021. *Democracy Index: The China Challenge*. Economic Intelligence Unit.
Elman, M. F. 1999. Path to Peace: Is Democracy the Answer?
Fortna, V. P. 2004. Does Peacekeeping Keep Peace? International Intervention and the Duration of Peace After Civil War. *International Studies Quarterly*, 48, 269–292.
Fortna, V. P. 2008a. *Does Peacekeeping Work? Shaping Belligerents' Choices after Civil War*. Princeton University Press.
Fortna, V. P. 2008b. Peacebuilding and Democratization. In: A. K. Jarstad & T. D. Sisk (eds.) *From War to Democracy: Dilemmas of Peacebuilding*. Cambridge University Press.
Freedom House. 2015. *Freedom in the World 2015: Discarding Democracy: Return to the Iron Fist*. 9th ed. Freedom House.
Freedom House. 2018. *Freedom in the World 2018: Democracy in Crisis*. Freedom House.
Freedom House. 2019. *Freedom in the World 2019: Democracy in Retreat*. Freedom House.
Freedom House. 2021. *Freedom World 2021: Democracy Under Siege*. Freedom House.
Freedom House. 2022a. *Freedom of the World 2022: The Global Expansion of Autoritarian Rule*. Freedom House.
Freedom House 2022b. *Nation in Transit 2022: From Democratic Decline to Authoritarian Aggression*. Freedom House.
Fukuyama, F. 2007. Liberalism versus State-building. *Journal of Democracy*, 18, 10–13.
Fukuyama, F., Kagan, R., Diamond, L., Carothers, T., Plattner, M. F., Schmitter, P. C., Levitsky, S., Way, L. & Rice, C. 2015. *Democracy in Decline?* Johns Hopkins University Press.
Galtung, J. 1996. *Democracy: Dictatorship = Peace : War?* SAGE Publications Ltd.
Ganguly, S. 2018. Ending the Sri Lankan Civil War. *Daedalus*, 147, 78–89.
Green, P., Macmanus, T. & De La Cour Venning, A. 2015. *Countdown to Annihilation: Genocide in Myanmar*. International State Crime Initiative.
Heldt, B. 2007. Peacekeeping Operations and Post-Conflict Transitions to Democracy? 2007 Annual Conference by the Swedish Network of Peace, Conflict and Development Research: "The Democratization Project: Challenges and Opportunities". Uppsala.
Henderson, E. A. 2002. *Democracy and War: The End of an Illusion?* Colorado, US, Lynne Rienner Publishers.
Howard, L. 2019a. Peacekeeping is Not Counterinsurgency. *International Peacekeeping*, 26, 545–548.
Howard, L. M. 2008. *UN Peacekeeping in Civil Wars*. Cambridge University Press.
Howard, L. M. 2019b. Power in Peacekeeping. In: Howard, L. M. (ed.) *Power in Peacekeeping*. Cambridge University Press.
Hunt, S. 2014. The Rise of Rwanda's Women: Rebuilding and Reuniting a Nation. *Foreign Affairs*, 93, 150–156.
Huntington, S. P. 2007. *The Clash of Civilizations and the Remaking of World Order*. Simon & Schuster.
IDEA, U. U. 2010. Democracy, Peace and Security: The role of UN. In: Tommasoli, E. M. (ed.). *Report from the International Round Table on Democracy, Peace and Security: The Role of the UN co-organized by International IDEA, UN Development Programme*. UN Department of Political Affairs and UN Department of Peacekeeping Operations.
IEP. 2016. Global Peace Index. 10th ed. Institute of Economics and Peace.
IEP. 2017. *Global Peace Index*. 11th ed. Institute of Economics and Peace.
IEP 2022. *Global Peace Index 2022*. Institute of Economics and Peace.
Jarstad, A. 2015. *Democratization after Civil War: Timing and Sequencing of Peacebuilding Reforms*. Centre for Research on Peace and Development (CRPD).

Jarstad, A. & Belloni, R. 2012. Introducing Hybrid Peace Governance: Impact and Prospects of Liberal Peacebuilding. *Global Governance*, 18.

Jett, D. C. 1999. *Why Peacekeeping Fails*. St. Martin's Press.

Kim, D. H. 2007. *Nurturing Peace: United Nations Peacebuilding Operations in the Aftermath of Intrastate Conflicts, 1945–2002*. Ph.D., University of Missouri – Saint Louis.

Kosovo, B.I. 2018. *Be in Kosovo* [Online]. Online. Available: http://www.beinkosovo.com/countries-that-have-recognized-kosovo-as-an-independent-state/ [Accessed 05.02.2018].

Kultgen, J. H. & Lenzi, M. 2006. *Problems for Democracy*. Netherlands. Rodopi.

Langer, A. & Brown, G. K. 2016. *Building Sustainable Peace: Timing and Sequencing of Post-Conflict Reconstruction and Peacebuilding*. OUP.

Mansfield, E. & Snyder, J. 1995. Democratization and War. Foreign Affairs Vol. 74, issue 3, p. 79–97.

Marshall, M. G. & Elzinga-Marshall, G. 2015. State Fragility Index. *In*: C.Thakur, A. S. A. R. (ed.). Online.

Marshall, M. G. & Gurr, T. R. 2015. *Polity IV: Center for Systemic Peace and Integrated Network for Social Conflict Research*. Online database. Available at https://www.systemicpeace.org/polityproject.html. Accessed Fev 2017

Mcevoy, J. & O'leary, B. 2013. *Power Sharing in Deeply Divided Places*. University of Pennsylvania Press, Incorporated.

Newman, E. 2014. *Understanding Civil Wars: Continuity and Change in Intrastate Conflict*. Taylor & Francis.

Newman, E. & Rich, R. 2004. *The UN Role in Promoting Democracy: Between Ideals and Reality*. United Nations University Press.

Ozoukou, D. 2014. Building peace or a fragile future? The legacy of conflict in the Cote d'Ivoire. *Insight on Conflict*, p.24/12/2014.

Peou, S. 2004. The UN's modest impact on Cambodia's democracy. *In*: Newman, E & Rich, R. (eds.) *The UN Role in Promoting Democracy: Between Ideals and Reality*. United Nations University Press.

Pickering, J. & Peceny, M. 2006. Forging Democracy at Gunpoint. *International Studies Quarterly*, 50, 539–560.

Pouligny, B. 2000. Promoting Democratic Institutions in Post-Conflict Societies. *International Peacekeeping*, 7, 17–35.

Ross, M. L. 2001. Does Oil Hinder Democracy? *World Politics*, 53, 325–361.

Sieff, K. 2017. The world's most dangerous U.N. mission: The al-Qaeda threat in Mali presents a new challenge to U.N. peacekeepers. *The Washington Post*. February 17, 2017 ed. Washington.

The Economist. 2016. The Philippines under Rodrigo Duterte: Sceptred bile. *The Economist*. The Economist Newspaper Limited.

Themnér, A. & Utas, M. 2016. Governance through brokerage: Informal governance in post-civil war societies. *Civil Wars*, 18, 255–280.

Touval, S. 1994. Why the UN Fails. *Foreign Affairs*, 73.

Ukashi, R. 2008. *UN-reliable: Explaining the failure of the United Nations Interim Force in Lebanon*. University of Manitoba (Canada).

UN-DPKO. 2009. *A New Partnership Agenda. Charting a New Horizon for UN Peacekeeping*. United Nations. New York.

UN-DPKO. 2015. *United Nations Peacekeeping* [Online]. Available: http://www.un.org/en/peacekeeping/about/dpko/ [Accessed 06 Feb 2015].

UN-DPKO. 2016. *A Fact Sheet of Peacekeeping* [Online]. Available: http://www.un.org/en/peacekeeping/about/dpko/ [Accessed 5.12.2016].

UN-DPKO. 2022. *Peacekeeping Fact Sheet*. United Nations.
UN. 1945. *Charter of the United Nations* [Online]. Available: http://www.un.org/en/documents/charter/ [Accessed 28.02.2015].
UN Iraq. 2016. *The United Nations Assistance Mission for Iraq (UNAMI)* [Online]. online: United Nations. Available: http://www.uniraq.org/index.php?option=com_k2&view=item&layout=item&id=945&Itemid=475&lang=en [Accessed].
UN News Centre. 2017. *UN Human Rights Chief Points to 'Textbook Example of Ethnic Cleansing' in Myanmar*. UN News Centre.
UNHCR 2018. *Rohingya Refugee Crisis*. Online.
UNHCR 2022. Global Trends Report. UN High Commission for Refugees.
United Nations 2018. *Declaration of Shared Commitments on Peacekeeping Operations*. UN. New York.
United Nations 2021. Action for Peacekeeping +. *Priorities for 2021–2023*. DPKO, New York.
Wantchekon, L. 2004. The Paradox of Warlord Democracy: A Theoretical Investigation. *American Political Science Review* 80, 98, 17–33.
Watts, S. 2008. *Enforcing Democracy? Assessing the Relationship between Peace Operations and Post-Conflict Democratization*.
Women, U. 2017. *Women in Politics*.
Zakaria, F. 1997. The Rise of Illiberal Democracy. *Foreign Affairs*, 76, 22–43.
Zürcher, C., Manning, C., Evenson, K., Hayman, R., Riese, S. & Roehner, N. 2013. *Costly Democracy : Peacebuilding and Democratization After War*. Stanford University Press.

PART II
Transitions to political, legal, civil, and social orders

5
FROM WAR TO PEACE

When elections and political parties promote democracy?

> Enough of deliberation: politics is about interests and power.
> *Shapiro, 1999*

Metaphorically, how can votes move a country from guns to doves? "Electoral democratization" is subject to several limitations and is far from a cure-all. Establishing or reinstating political order by some form of legitimate authority is paramount in any transition from conflict to peace (Reilly, 2008; William Maley et al., 2003). A convergence of international norms and local expectations makes the electoral process a mechanism for generating internal legitimacy for peace agreements. To explain "how democracies die," Levitsky and Ziblatt (2018) claim that "the tragic paradox of the electoral route to authoritarianism is that democracy's assassins use the very institutions of democracy – gradually, subtly, and even legally – to kill it." Thus, elections would be a tool for the state to perish in a conflict trap, not leading toward peace. Notably, the legitimacy of elections can be undermined if they are considered an international exit strategy, as opposed to part of a much broader process of transformation (Shaw, 2006).

One of the first challenges is that what works in the short term may incur problems in the long time. Additionally, an appropriate balance between internal and external involvement ("internal and external sovereignty") in the performance of key "democratic" responsibilities needs to be struck (William Maley et al., 2003, p. 8). Elections and political parties can either support the transition to more legitimate governance or lend artificial legitimacy to coercive regimes (Sisk, 2014). Importantly, the political overture for participation very often reverts to such regime perpetuation under the concept of electoral authoritarian (EA) regimes (Donno, 2013). Many former rebel groups have become official political parties. The CNDD-FDD in Burundi, the URNG in Guatemala, the FMNL in El Salvador, the NRA associated with the National Resistance

Movement (NRM) in Uganda, the PDK associated with the KLA in Kosovo, FRETILIN and the CNRT in Timor-Leste, as well as the M-19 Democratic Alliance (AD/M-19), Humane Colombia, and the Commons (Comunes) in Colombia are examples. It is unclear whether former freedom fighters in armed groups transformed into formal political parties helped build a new, peaceful, and democratic order or whether they paved the way for a continuation of the conflict. It seems that between the choices of peacebuilding and democratization, democracy is less likely to prevail when victorious guerrilla fighters become "democratic" rulers. Moreover, although widely seen as an integral part of the process of war termination, international (dis)engagement and nation-building, the electoral process can be fragile at best and corrupt at worst and is not in itself a recipe for positive change. Only a small handful of countries, including Qatar and Saudi Arabia, have no form of national-level vote, but yet some form of election takes place at local levels (Emma Graham-Harrison, 2014). Almost everywhere in the world, some kind of election process takes place, being internal to the political party,[1] local or national. This might be empty, fraudulent, or at least partially compromised. Elections are not uncommonly used to give the appearance of democracy without elites facing the threat of a loss of power.

Thus, when are elections turning points for peace in the wake of war (Sisk, 2014)? When and how can elections advance stability in peace processes or, in contrast, exacerbate armed conflicts? The focus of this chapter is on understanding the tensions and contradictions in post-conflict political scenarios and the challenges facing interim governments based on the assumption that elections and the transformation of warring groups into political parties result in opposing driving forces as per the equation: [*elections and political parties = peace versus democracy*]. First, the discussion is concentrated on post-conflict elections as a *condicio sine qua non* toward peace or warlords' democracies. Second, elections are tested as a variable of analysis with the Philosophical–Actors–Tactical (P–A–T) set of 14 dilemmas of peacebuilding and democratization in the aftermath of civil war. Third, democracy requires a multiparty system. Thus, an analysis is also given of the same proposed set of dilemmas in relation to the demilitarization of warring groups and their transformation into democratic political parties. For a better understanding, Figures 1.7 and 1.8 in Chapter 1 represent an aide-mémoire of the 14 dilemmas and their corresponding trade-offs.

5.1 Elections: from the battlefield of war to the ballot box battlefield

A majority of contemporary peace agreements include postwar elections as a mean of conflict management. Although elections remain a contributing factor to democratization, there is some general disillusionment about their usefulness (Alsadi, 2007; Dirmoser, 2005; Gauchet, 2004). This is partly because most war-torn societies lack the political climate, social and economic stability, institutional infrastructure, and even political will to mount successful elections

(Kumar, 1998). By searching for ideal conditions under which to contribute to both goals, wrong choices in the electoral processes may promote democratization but undermine peace, or prioritize peacebuilding but fail in democratization. Beyond being free and fair, democracy-building requires critical choices over the sequencing of elections, the electoral system formula (e.g., proportional representation, closed list), the nature of elections (e.g., for a legislature, constituent assembly, or both), and other critical election-related issues, such as the application of citizenship laws and even the redesign of electoral zones within the devastated or contested territory (Bjornlund, 2004).

Nonetheless, topics such as elections often become a source of increasing tension and renewed violence due to a combination of factors such as (1) lack of coordination; (2) information asymmetries; (3) reinforcement of societal divisions; and (4) mixed feelings of fear, uncertainty, and expectations for the future from the voters. Moreover, a profound security dilemma affects both voters and candidates, whereby competing ethnic, religious, and political actors create social polarization. Thus, for example, spoilers may use violence to disrupt the transition process or overthrow the election result as their power is threatened by democratic elections. They may also intimidate people from going to the polls or simply prevent some actors from participating in the election campaign. This was the case of Colombia's 2022 presidential elections where only 58 percent of voters participated. Despite the 2016 peace accord with the FARC, activity by the National Liberation Army (ELN) leftist guerrilla group, the successors of previously disbanded right-wing paramilitary groups, so-called dissident FARC members, and criminal gangs have continued to impair the ability of citizens in some areas to participate freely in the political process. From the Peace Accord Signature until March 2022, 1.327 social leaders and former guerrilla members reinserted were assassinated (Behar, 2022). Moreover, the assassination of over 50 social leaders, trade unionists, environmentalists, and other community representatives in 2022, as well as death threats to the presidential candidates, are evidence of the security dilemma.[2]

Success in relation to war termination does not necessarily translate into successful democratization (Zirulnick, 2013; Bermeo, 2003; Burnell, 2006). To minimize the risk of transition, postwar elections in Namibia in 1989, El Salvador in 1994, or Mozambique in 1994 played a vital role by being inclusive (Issacharoff, 2015). By contrast, Liberia embodies the impasse: the 1997 flawed elections created more problems than they solved. In 2005, following Liberia's second civil war, elections marked the end of the transition and Ellen Johnson-Sirleaf came to power as Africa's first democratically elected female head of state. Elections in Afghanistan have not led to an end to hostilities. They inversely have intensified the conflict by electing Western-supported marionettes that ultimately culminated in the takeover of the Taliban in 2022.

Delaying elections can also prove fundamental in developing suitable democratic structures and enabling the legitimization of their results, as in the cases of Timor-Leste and Kosovo. Still, they may also provoke substantial turmoil, as in

Burundi (2015), RDC (2015), and Haiti (2016). Furthermore, technical success may not be sufficient. In 1993, the UN-administered polls in Cambodia, but in spite of providing technical expertise, the "losing" party returned to power as a "winner" via coercive maneuvers not long after the peace process broke down (Reilly, 2008; Doyle and Sambanis, 2006). Elections in Angola (1992) and Sierra Leone (1996, its first multiparty election since 1977) led to a resumption of warfare due partly to the threats these polls represented to incumbent elites. Similarly, attempts to foster peace and stability in Rwanda by promoting political liberalization, the prospect of elections, and ethnic power-sharing ultimately failed, in the worst possible way, leading to the 1993 genocide. In Bosnia, postwar elections essentially placed in power nondemocratic elites who had been leaders in the preceding conflict. In Ethiopia (1994 and 2000), elections were sabotaged so that they provided a tool to legitimize the victory of the winning parties to the conflict. Uganda is also an archetypal case where elections are alleged as not free and fair. In power since 1986, the ex-rebel Yoweri Museveni retains his authority with pseudo-elections held in 1996, 2001, 2006, 2011, 2016, and 2021. The "king of Uganda" (Meyerfeld, 2016) managed to maintain his grip on power for over three decades by encouraging a personality cult, employing patronage, compromising independent institutions, and sidelining opponents.[3] This was in spite of numerous accusations by international observers who reported on the "lack of transparency and independence of the Electoral Commission, and an atmosphere of intimidation of the voters as well as the candidates." The media and social media were also repressed, and the main opponents, Kizza Besigye and Bobbi Wine, were arbitrarily imprisoned.

Elections can also be a façade for a so-called warlord or druglord democracy (Wantchekon, 2004, Themnér, 2017). Sudan is a quintessential case. The Second Sudanese civil war (1983–2005) and the war in Darfur led to Sudan being categorized as an authoritarian and fragile state (IEP, 2017; FFP, 2017; Freedom House, 2022). In 1989, Colonel Omar Al-Bashir led a bloodless military coup. In 1993, Al-Bashir appointed himself "president" and took control of both the executive and the legislative powers of the Revolutionary Command Council. Sudan converted to a single-party state in which only members of the National Congress Party (NCP) were part of the new Parliament and government. In the 1996 general elections, Al-Bashir was the only "legal" candidate. Despite being subject to an international arrest warrant, Al-Bashir was a candidate in the 2010 Sudanese presidential election, with multiple political parties participating for the first time in 24 years.[4] However, as the International Crisis Group (2010) reported, his gerrymandered electoral districts enabled him to win the election with 68 percent of the votes. Intimidation was also reported from voters, and the main opposition candidate, Yasir Arman (SPLM), withdrew from the race days before the poll. Additionally, the electoral vote tabulation process was reported by the Carter Center (10 May 2010) as "highly chaotic, non-transparent and vulnerable to electoral manipulation." President Omar Al-Bashir and the ruling National

Congress Party (NCP) had all the substantive and effective political power until been overthrown in 2019 by military commanders and prodemocracy protest movement. The transitional government was meant to share power until national elections could be held, but a new military coup took place in 2021. Intercommunal ethnic violence, especially in the Darfur region, increased throughout the year. UN agencies reported hundreds of people were killed, and nearly 500,000 people were newly displaced as a result of such violence. Displacement levels in Darfur in 2021 were eight times higher than those in the previous year (Freedom House, 2022).

Both cases illustrate the dilemma between peace and democracy where political violence far removed them from being defined as "liberal democracies" (Reilly, 2008). All the above suggests further assessment of how elections and political parties may put democracy and peacebuilding processes in jeopardy, which is discussed next.

5.2 Elections in dangerous place: more dilemmas than solutions

When and how can elections advance stability in peace processes or, alternatively, exacerbate armed conflicts? Should elections be held early even if they risk extremists legitimately winning power? Or should they be postponed until the society is less polarized? (Hoglund, 2008, p. 91). To answer these questions requires analyzing the temporal, security, sequencing, resource, and financial dilemmas as these are directly linked to the ballot. Elections are often held within a year or two of the start of a UN mission or a ceasefire, as they require a certain level of security as well as a basic level of infrastructure in place. This is often followed by a rapid handover to the newly elected local authorities and an exit strategy for a more rapid departure of international troops and personnel. "Premature elections" can be counterproductive: in general, the early application of elections immediately following a conflict increases the likelihood that the contest will become a de facto competition between the former warring armies masquerading as political parties. By contrast, an extended process of consultation and local-level peacebuilding may offer better prospects for a peaceful transition in postwar societies. Whereas Chapter 3 focuses on violence and the democratization process, the following discussion is concerned with dilemmas specifically related to elections and the transformation process of warring political enemies into political parties.

Paris (2004) and other authors have defended the postponement of elections after a ceasefire, often for a two-year period. They argue that before holding elections, priority should be given to the development of moderate political parties and a judicial mechanism to regulate election-related disputes to identify conditions for holding free and fair elections. However, by such postponement, opportunities to support the closure of the war may be missed irreversibly (Jarstad and Sisk, 2008). Moreover, as per the security dilemma, without stable institutional grounding, the process of democratization may be stalled or overturned by threats and intimidation from actors seeking to disrupt the transition. For example, by not accepting the election results or preventing election campaigns or voters from going to the polls.

Besides deciding on the best time for peaceful elections, another sequencing dilemma arises: should the legitimization of authority start from the bottom up or the top down? The advantage of holding national elections before local ones is that it facilitates voter registration and the introduction of the civic education required for electoral and party politics in new democracies. Furthermore, national elections generate incentives for the formation of central, rather than regional, political parties and a formal national authority to deal with the international actors (Linz and Stepan, 1996). In contrast, it is argued that to test whether transitional elections are suitable from a bottom-up democracy-building perspective, it is preferable to conduct municipal or local elections before national ones. The bottom-up approach would allow the real interests and concerns that provoked the conflict to be addressed step by step before national elections are held. Theoretically, gradualism would provide more structural momentum for stability (Mross, 2018). Timor-Leste and Kosovo had delayed elections, and the process started from municipal polls, allowing a gradual process toward democratization. Alternatively, a third approach is to hold national and local elections simultaneously, which has been suggested as beneficial for developing a strong and integrated political party system (Diamond and Platter, 1999).

Additionally, as per the resource quandary, simultaneous elections are more cost-effective. Roads, human resources, transport, electricity, paper, and many other resources are invariably needed for elections to take place. This also leads to a financial dilemma in terms of balancing the present with the future: democracy is a long-term process, but when no national tax system or other national revenue is effectively in place, international funds to implement the peacekeeping mission are limited and work against the clock. This explains why elections are usually held as early as possible in peacekeeping operations settings. Due to financial pressures, many missions have the incentive to withdraw their presence as soon as there are some home-grown institutions, such as representative legislatures and multiethnic peace and security forces that create both the shell of a state and a legitimate political body for the international community to deal with. Therefore, when and how to hold elections interlinks temporal, security, sequencing, resource, and financial dilemmas (Figure 5.1).

Resolving a design dilemma is critical to effectively transitioning from conflict to democratic peace. How should the post-conflict electoral system be set up? First, elections can be strategically designed and calculated to attain power-sharing among groups to discourage zero-sum or winner-take-all outcomes. In most cases, electoral results are decided before the election by defining the rules of the game. Typically, this represents creating a democratic façade that merely enables the return to the old patriarchal system or warlords. In the same vein that Mansfield and Snyder (2005) argue that ballots may facilitate more bullets, Reilly

(2008) reminds us that the post-Dayton elections held in 1996, 1998, 2000, and 2002 were an illustration of Bosnia's voters from different ethnic communities persistently reelecting hardline nationalist leaders, despite overt attempts by the international community to encourage moderate pro-Western winners as an alternative. O'Donnell and Schmitter (1986) claim that transitions from authoritarian rule to uncertain democracies are often the outcome of a division within the authoritarian regime between hard-liners or soft-liners and between radicals and moderates within the opposition.

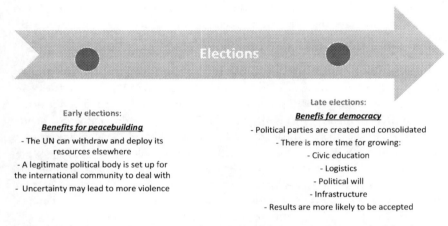

FIGURE 5.1 Elections: hard choices between good for peacebuilding or bad for democratization. Source: Author

Second, the objectives of the referendums are different, related to either independence or self-determination as well as being through a single or phased and gradual series of consultations. Therefore, the goal will determine the game's rules, which leads to the design dilemma: usually, choices are among a plural-majority, a semi-proportional, or a proportional representation (PR) system. Plural-majority systems vary between first-past-the-post, run-off, blocks, and alternative vote systems. By contrast, proportional representation systems characteristically use larger, multi-member districts, and deliver proportional outcomes. Proportional systems are also diverse and may vary between "open" and "closed" versions of a party list PR, "mixed-member" and "single transferable" voting systems. Over the past decade, many new democracies have opted for a semi-proportional system involving the single non-transferable vote as it offers a "hybrid" approach. This contains a mixture of plurality and proportional models so that part of the Parliament is elected via PR, and another share from local districts. UN-administered elections generally prefer the party list PR and this has been frequently used in Mozambique (1994), Liberia (1997), Bosnia (1996, 1998, 2000, 2002), Kosovo (2001), Sierra Leone (2002), Rwanda (2003), and Iraq (2005). The main reason for national PR systems is logistical because it allows for a uniform national ballot as well as the same division of electoral districts. Moreover, in comparison to other methods, it simplifies the different phases of the process (voter registration, vote counting, and the calculation of results).

Obviously, the design of an electoral system is one of the most important political decisions for any country and will also affect every aspect of the political system: the development of the party system, the linkages between citizens and their leaders, political accountability, representation, and responsiveness by electoral choice. It must be emphasized that this takes place in a context where there is probably no new constitution or electoral law in place. Favoring such a system may favor a political party or candidate and, therefore, jeopardize the credibility of the elections. Some systems can also have the effect of fragmenting the legislature and marginalizing minority groups. Encouraging ethnic polarization among the electorate is undemocratic as it should motivate equity and inclusiveness. Moreover, this can lead to violence and jeopardize the peace process (Fjelde and Hoglund, 2014). To illustrate this, the 2005 Afghan parliamentary elections featured over 5,800 candidates – in Kabul alone the ballot paper displayed over 400 names – resulting in a fractionalized and incoherent Parliament that is likely to remain highly divided and whose members will be unable to coordinate around pressing policy challenges. The choice for a single non-transferable vote (SNTV) advantaged smaller parties. Competition within the party brings to the surface personal characteristics that render improbable the development of a party system in the short term. The proportional system seems to preserve civil war organizations by transforming them into political parties while first-past-the-post may lead to corruption and voter violence.

Third, researchers and electoral system designers should be reminded that electoral formulae, with details such as quota denominators and numerical series, are more than inconsequential mathematical minutiae of technicalities. In any evaluation of the merits of the plethora of competing types of electoral systems, the arrangement of proportionality is very common. Defining the mathematical mechanisms governing the transformation of votes into seats has deep political consequences, particularly in post-conflict scenarios, as variants of proportional representation formulae affect how votes are distributed within the legislature. Proportionality, disproportionality, and electoral systems are interlinked (Gallagher, 1991). Therefore, they will affect the dynamics of politics and the different factions' recognition of the representative regime. Exact proportionality is impossible because absolute divisions often produce a fractionated number of seats. Different methods of proportional representation (PR) will produce different results. Rather than distributing seats in a legislature among the parties competing for election, the proportional distribution of seats among federal states is the mathematical equivalent of putting states in the place of parties and the population in the place of votes. However, PR systems aim to allocate seats to parties in proportion to the number of votes received. Several methods of PR are available and can be broadly classified into two types: the largest remainder (LR) methods (Hare, Droop, and the Imperiali) and the highest average (HA) methods (D'Hondt, Sainte-Laguë, equal proportions, modified Sainte-Laguë,

Hungarian Sainte-Laguë, Adams, Danish, Imperiali HA). The D'Hondt method (also known as Jefferson's method and the Bader-Ofer method) is the most commonly used in post-civil war countries with UN intervention, such as Cambodia, Croatia, Guatemala, Kosovo, Serbia, and Timor-Leste.

Two sources of disproportionality are also common. This involves awarding both the largest and the smallest parties more than their proportional share of seats. These two types of disproportionalities have distinctly different political rationales and consequences. The D'Hondt method is widespread and tends to favor large parties and coalitions over scattered small parties. It discourages party fragmentation. The Sainte-Laguë method aims, as far as possible, to achieve equal representation and tends to favor small parties (Benoit, 2000). Gallagher (1991) argues that because PR systems embody different conceptions of what proportionality means and of what minimizing disproportionality entails, these systems should not be seen to be inherently more proportional in their consequences than others. Once again, the danger is that political choices may take over technical designs. In post-civil war conditions, a PR system is not usually chosen according to more neutral and abstract criteria of "fairness" or "efficiency," but according to the relationship between elites and the warring groups (a vertical dilemma) who often have international influence. This has the advantage of minimizing disproportionality and conforming to the decision-takers interests.

Another challenge is related to the role and responsibilities of the institutional bodies in charge of running the elections, intensifying systemic and design dilemmas. Such organizations may take different shapes. They can be an independent, non-partisan, and specific body of state administration. They may form part of a government portfolio such as the Ministry of Interior Affairs. They may occur within government agencies such as the public records office, the tax department, or even the postal service. Fourth, they may involve the creation of a new body before each electoral event (ad hoc institution). Lastly, they may also be formed under the United Nations (as in Cambodia in 1993 or Timor-Leste in 2001). The first three alternatives take place under the umbrella of the design along with the electoral system choice. However, very often there is no infrastructure, technical expertise, or even legitimate institutions that can be run by national actors. If an international body such as the UN runs the elections, there might be technical success and credibility, but there is also the danger of a lack of local ownership. This creates a dependency relationship on outsiders, which is precisely what one does not want to occur in the embryonic phase of the democratic era. For all the above cases, operations, rules, and institutions will have to be designed. However, irrespective of how robust or flexible the Electoral Management Bodies (EMBs) are, they will highly impact the legitimacy, credibility, security, and efficiency of the voting. Furthermore, the diverse interests of outsiders must not be underestimated. A classic case often referred to is that of Bosnia in 1996. In addition to the pressure of starting the development of a national political process, the stress for "instant elections" was largely provoked by the Clinton administration to show progress in the Balkans in time for midterm elections in the United States, rather than for advancing peace and democracy in Bosnia.

Moreover, democracy requires a "certainty of uncertainty" to invoke trustworthiness from all players and to be sustainable in the long term (Reilly, 2008, p. 165). The existential dilemma is what makes adversaries willing to play by the rules of the democratic game. Even if they might lose in the short term, they may still be winners later. Mechanisms are needed that distribute state power among former armed adversaries in a manner that prevents any group from becoming dominant. That way, no single entity will use the power of the state to promote its interests while threatening the security of others, such as in a winner-take-all election model. From this perspective, power-sharing increases the likelihood that adversaries will remain committed to peace. In postwar societies, the uncertainty of elections has a higher probability of resulting in itself a source of violence, posing a significant threat to incumbent elites, which can make them wary of committing to the game at all (Hartzell and Hoddie, 2015). Although the content of a peace agreement may be contrary to the design of a democratic system, without power-sharing agreements, actors may not respect election results due to security fears of being outside the political arena. Following this existential dilemma are the related fears that: (1) a rival is likely to become stronger following an election that places the rival's hands on the levers of state power; and (2) the rival may then use that authority to weaken or otherwise target those who lose elections.

Vertical and horizontal dilemmas are also evident regarding elections. After a civil war, democratization may set off a protracted and inconclusive political struggle followed by a deliberate choice by political leaders to accept the existence of "diversity in unity" (Wantchekon, 2004). To that end, crucial aspects of democratic procedures must be institutionalized. Therefore, the question arises: who can play this democratic game? Can the victims or perpetrators vote and be voted? The democratic system implies inclusion and equality. However, in post-conflict scenarios, including "everyone" might be unfair and lead to the continuation of war. The inclusion of IDPs, refugees, and ex-combatants in the electoral process is a recurring dilemma in postwar elections. As refugees, people have left the territory to be safe outside it. With massive flows of refugees as in Sudan, DRC, Iraq, Colombia, and Rwanda, if they cannot vote, this might exclude a great proportion of the population. The "Syrian migration crisis" is a contemporary example. The exclusion of an estimated 5.5 million refugees and 6.1 million internally displaced (UNOCHA, 2016; OCHA, 2017) people can be unfair and undemocratic.

Democracy is "for, by and from the people"; however, there is no democracy without defining the "demos." Even though most who have stayed are old, injured, infirm, or just unable to leave, many who have remained might support the perpetrators in gaining or remaining in power, which only benefits a minority. Nevertheless, their automatic inclusion is logistically unviable and might also be an oversimplification of the problems that come with war migration flows and citizenship. Moreover, the trade-off between inclusion and exclusion is parallel to that of efficacy and legitimacy, which intertwines the population, the elites, and the warring groups. Furthermore, moral dilemmas also permeate electoral management at all stages. For example, suppose the same people who committed atrocities become part of the new political order and government. In that case, the morality and legitimacy of the new institutions may be seriously questioned, such as in Colombia and Kosovo. Finally, the corruption that fosters opposition to impartiality and liability is a recurrent problem stemming from the transparency dilemma in post-civil war elections.

To illustrate this, the 2016 post-crisis elections in Haiti represent a violent deadlock of temporal, systemic, design, transparent, horizontal, and vertical dilemmas. Since 1986, during the 30 years of Duvalier's dictatorship and particularly since the 2010 earthquake that resulted in 220,000 dead and 1.5 million IDPs, Haiti has experienced a chronic crisis cycle that delayed the legislative and local elections for three years. Elections were usually extremely violent with recurrent attacks from the army, known as "tontons macoutes," siding with Duvalier's regime. The 2015 presidential elections had 54 candidates for a majoritarian voting system. Most were members of previous political party arrangements or political amateurs, and only a few presented a government plan (Globo, 2015). The second round was postponed in December 2015 after allegations of fraud in the first round, and this generated great disturbances from 2016 to 2017. Despite the motto in the flag "L'union fait la force" ('Unity makes strength"), the need for national unity is key for the country's development. However, according to Haitian economist, Kesner Pharel, "in Haiti, no one likes to lose. All 53 loser candidates will say that there was fraud. They unite to destroy' (Globo, 2015). The Temporary Electoral Council (CEP), the body responsible for administering the elections, confirmed that violent incidents a few months prior to the legislative round impeded voters from going to the polls in one-quarter of the voting centers. Moreover, the herculean electoral effort cost money: this unconcluded electoral process cost US$100 million, predominantly donated by the international community and more is needed to prepare the new polls (Globo, 2016). Besides a lack of transparency, the absence of human and infrastructure resources, finances, and security has also contributed to the problem. As a consequence, the developments since 2020 have only worsened the situation, the country being classified from "partly free" to "not free" by Freedom House (Freedom House, 2022). The year 2021 was marked by protests and political disputes over the expiration of President Jovenel Moïse's term in office, his plans to hold a referendum on constitutional reforms, and the continued postponement of overdue elections. His assassination exacerbated the crisis with the lack of a sitting Parliament, as the mandate of most lawmakers had expired. In the midst of an ongoing breakdown in the electoral system and other state institutions, and the corrosive effects of organized crime and violence on civic life, another earthquake in August 2021, deadly attacks on journalists, restriction of the freedom of press, and the COVID-19 pandemic all contributed to the worsening breakdowns of the Haitian electoral and constitutional impasses. Rampant corruption and violence by armed criminal groups undermine basic services and contribute to physical insecurity for the population without proper political representation. The judiciary and law enforcement agencies lack the resources, independence, and integrity to uphold due process and the rule of law. Antigovernment protests often result in excessive use of force by police. Therefore, Haiti illustrates the complexities and interconnectivity of temporal, systemic, design, transparent, horizontal, and vertical dilemmas in disrupted states.

Several choices must be made that go beyond mere electoral management. In a nutshell, institutional design is paramount as we have identified its intricacies. Maley et al. (2003) elucidated that when analyzing the transition from civil strife to civil society, the breakdown of trust leads to unworkable political communities and disunified political elites. Among the alternatives for addressing these problems include the provision of neutral security, the re-socialization of antagonists and the design of institutions to mute the effects of political conflict. Thus, institutional design should not be overlooked or rushed, and it benefits from expert input. A range of abstract features mark institutions that are likely to be effective. Still, issues such as the nature of political authority, the distributive capacity of the state, and the nature of military power will need to be addressed, as well as how new institutions should be legitimated. Either building "liberal" or "illiberal democracies," the "institutional architects" need to address questions such as whether power should be apportioned or alternated, and how offices should be structured and their occupants chosen. Therefore, an "effective institutional design does not offer magic solutions to complex problems, but reduces the risk and costs of political conflict" (Maley, 2012). When the design of elections leads to a political battlefield, it is a lost opportunity to transition from a disruptive setting toward a stable or workable state.

Elections can advance stability in peace processes or exacerbate armed conflicts if the dilemmas regarding when and how they occur do not find their equilibrium between peace and democracy-building. And it goes without saying that elections play a central role in peacekeeping and democratization. Hence, beyond the central dilemma, postwar elections also permeate systemic, vertical, horizontal, operational, temporal, financial, transparency, security, resource, existential, sequencing, design, and moral dilemmas as shown in the trade-offs in Figure 5.2. Obviously, free and fair elections are important but they are not everything. In the aftermath of conflict, domestic political institutions are weak or non-existent, voters are suspicious, and elites' will to hold on power is visceral. After the war, peacebuilding and democratization require a demilitarized political system with multiparty political views. We discuss this next.

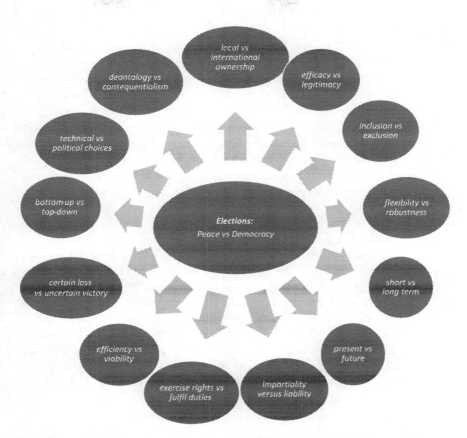

FIGURE 5.2 Elections at the center of peace and democracy-building dilemmas. Source: Author

5.3 Demilitarization of politics and democratization of warlords: victorious guerrilla fighters turned democratic rulers

Contemporary disarmament, demobilization, and reintegration (DDR) programs entail a shift in the nature of politics and anti-politics (CERI, 2004). Political parties are also considered a sine qua non condition in contemporary democracies for the expression and manifestation of political pluralism and the organization of the modern democratic polity. Although liberation movements are tantamount to transitions to democracy, opening up political processes does not necessarily lead to democratization (Ottaway, 1991; Ottaway, 1997). Democratization requires a priori demilitarizing of the political spectrum of governance and power. Thus, it embodies the demobilization of warlords in a way that these elements act following the new democratic system. As Romain Fathi and Bart Ziino (2019) suggested, it is not simply about laying down the weapons and putting on a political party logo t-shirt instead of a camouflaged uniform. It is not about demobilizing "men" but about demobilization of the mind. Either way, failures regarding demobilization leave open the prospect of a resumption in fighting.

In a liberal democracy, political parties are the intermediary link between the people and the state and are expected to perform along two main axes. First, as per the "representative mandate," political parties aim at channeling the interests and preferences of the people into policy proposals. Second, as per the "delegative mandate," they also perform a variety of procedural or institutional functions to organize the political system of the state (Gunther and Diamond, 2001). The successful implementation of peace agreements in civil wars should prioritize the demobilization of soldiers and the demilitarization of politics by transforming former warring armies into peaceful political parties. Without such a transition, "civil wars cannot be concluded, and important normative goals such as the creation and consolidation of democracy and the protection of human rights have little chance of success" (Stedman et al., 2002, p. 668).

The peace agreement between the government of Sierra Leone and the Revolutionary United Front (RUF) of Sierra Leone (Jackson, 1999; Sierra Leone, 1999) offers provisions for the DDR to transform the rebel group into a political party with an "absolute and free pardon and reprieve" for crimes and human rights abuses conducted during the armed struggle. Similar amnesty is present in the 2016 Peace Agreement in Colombia. It includes the transformation of the FARC into a political party Fuerza Alternativa Revolucionária del Común and prophesied the intention of Rodrigo Londoño (also known as Timochenko or Timoleon Jimenez[3]) to run for the presidency in 2018 (Colombia and FARC, 2016). In addition, under the agreement, the FARCs were guaranteed ten seats in the Colombian Congress in the 2018 and 2022 elections. In an atmosphere of distrust, the population were concerned that this would give the newly created party an unfair advantage. As the peace deal was backed by Cuba and Venezuela, there was also fear of radical left-wing policies, as FARC follows a Marxist ideology inspired by the Cuban Revolution.

Giving legitimate power to rebels in national politics can be perilous. Nevertheless, suppose former warring parties have a stake in the postwar political order and believe they have a credible chance of organizational survival and political influence via peaceful means. In that case, it is expected that they will remain involved in implementing the peace deal. Therefore, there are fewer temptations to return to arms. Nevertheless, this issue remains under-examined, mainly because it is addressed very differently by scholars working on peace, war, and conflict resolution studies than by those working on democracy and political science. Thus, the metamorphic process of "changing rebels' stripes" into white-collar executive suits in postwar politics faces multiple dilemmas (Soderberg Kovacs, 2008).

5.3.1 Literature review: transforming warring armies into political parties

Africa, the continent with the largest number of civil wars and the most UN peacekeeping operations since 1989, includes prototypical counter-examples of hybrid democracies, failed states, and mixed results for peace after war. In Uganda, President Yoweri Museveni and his National Resistance Movement (NRM) invented a form of "no party democracy" in the 1980s. Parties, while allowed to exist, were banned from political activity. The multiparty referendum in 2005 demonstrated that this strategy had no future. A total of 95 percent of the Ugandan population affirmed that they wanted to open up the political space to allow different organizations to compete for political power. Although it is hard to imagine a full democracy without a multiparty system that allows competitiveness for power, it is difficult to assert that multiparty systems in African post-conflict countries such as Sierra Leone, Mali, and Liberia are more democratic than a two-party system (such as in Cape Verde and Seychelles),[6] or even dominant party (Uganda, Sudan, Angola, DRC) or single-party systems (Eritrea). On a continent historically tending to subvert or distort democratic rules and practices, only in the early 1990s did a resurgence of multiparty processes increasingly gain ground. The oldest parties originated in 1945 when some small groups of African elites organized to express their political demands for reforming the colonial system, gaining access to colonial governments, and influencing colonial policy. It was only with the independence of African states that parties began to proliferate, but they soon proved to be poorly rooted. With the spillover of civil wars, most African countries became one-party states or dictatorial military regimes. In the space of a few years, authoritarian forms of government came to prevail almost everywhere on the continent. Multiparty politics was only retained in Botswana, Gambia, and Mauritius, while it was introduced in Senegal and Zimbabwe under the auspices of dominant and effectively unchangeable parties.

The track records of the African liberation movements – both regarding their internal practices during the wars of liberation as well as their lack of democratic virtues and respect for the protection of human rights once in power – are far from positive. In Namibia, SWAPO consolidated its dominant position and expanded control over the state apparatus. Its legitimacy was based on being the representative of the majority of the people. Namibia's first decade of independence witnessed a constant consolidation of political power and control by the former liberation movement. Nevertheless, its political culture revealed some disturbing deterioration a decade later. The Namibian case was guided by the goal of achieving a more or less democratically legitimate transition toward independence, but not the firm entrenchment of democracy (Newman and Rich, 2004). Nonetheless, it remains a relatively successful case, as analyzed in Chapter 4.

The debate on what kind of democracy best suits Africa does not find a consensual answer (Utas, 2012; Linebarger and Salehyan, 2012; Bourne, 2012;

Carbone, 2007; Randall and Svasand, 2002). With the emergence of an African version of the global "third wave" of democratization processes in the early 1990s, all sub-Saharan countries shifted from army- or single-party-dominated regimes to "officially" democratic systems. Despite being the youngest continent by population, with a median age of 19.5 years between 2000 and 2020,[7] "mother Africa" is predominantly led by the oldest so-called fathers of the nation. These leaders led independence or liberation struggles by promising "democracy, security, the consolidation of national unity, the elimination of corruption and misuse of power and redressing inequality." Nevertheless, they delivered precisely the opposite by refusing to allow the democratic alternation of power. Africa's six longest presidencies stretch between 29 and 38 years in power. It comprises Teodoro Obiang Nguema of Equatorial Guinea; President Pierre Nkurunziza of Burundi; Zimbabwean president Robert Mugabe, President Paul Kagame of Rwanda,[8] and Yoweri Kaguta Museveni (Kiwuwa, 2015). Since its independence in 1962, Uganda has been marked by violent conflicts, including an eight-year-long military dictatorship led by Idi Amin and a protracted six-year guerrilla war that led to the Museveni coup in 1986. As explained in section 5.1, he is the longest elected president in power. Similarly, Eduardo dos Santos, who died in 2022, ruled Angola for 38 years in power. He stepped down in 2017 due to illness and endorsed João Lourenço as a successor. Since the latter is from the same MPLA party, doing so is basically changing six of one for a half dozen of the other.

Not surprisingly, genuine concerns about the depth of "democratic" change have been raised (Carbone, 2007). Socioeconomic structural restrictions such as widespread and extreme poverty, low literacy levels, state weaknesses or failures, established political practices (notably, authoritarian rule and corruption), and the lack of political reforms in these countries are among the issues of concern. Moreover, long-term rulers rarely enable transitions to postwar democratic development. Nonetheless, 2015 African databases, such as the Afrobarometer (2016) and Freedom House (2017), indicate that reforms have eventually occurred and have brought about a significant quantitative return of multiparty states in Africa despite these qualitative severe flaws. However, with the progress of authoritarian rule worldwide, the African reforms have also followed setbacks.

Notwithstanding how a civil war ends and the specificities of the post-conflict context, academic and policy literature on peace studies and post-civil war democratization highlight that both access to power and reform of the warring organizations are decisive in leading to peace (Mason and Fett, 1996; Toft, 2010; Paris, 2004; Stedman et al., 2002; Stein, 1994). Beyond "non-competitive" and "competitive party systems," the literature needs to address the relationship between the demilitarization of politics with political party formation in more detail. Before applying the proposed model of dilemmas that infringe the transformations of rebels into multiple political party groups contributing to peacemaking and democratization, five mutually non-exclusive post-conflict scenarios for former rebels can be identified (Table 5.1).

TABLE 5.1 Post-conflict scenarios for former rebels

Case	Post-conflict scenarios identified
1	former rebels belong to the post-conflict (local or central) government
2	former rebels constitute a political party
3	former rebels are allowed – or manage – to remain an armed militia
4	most of the rebels are demobilized and do not constitute a political party
5	former rebels join or form another rebel movement after the civil war has ended to reignite a new war

This study demystifies two popular misconceptions. First, it is understandable that victories may involve the complete subjugation of the enemy. However, and surprisingly, allowing a transformation of formerly defeated fighters into a political party might help stabilize a post-conflict context. Kreutz (2010) finds some relative success within each scenario. Impressively, the practice of integrating former rebels into the government, after their military defeat, has led to at least five years of peace in 73 percent of the cases studied from 1946 to 2012, although the percentage decreases as the timeframe become longer. Second, it is believed that when civil wars end by military victories, this dissuades subsequent conflicts (Toft, 2010). However, other research argues that new rebellions are more frequent after a military victory compared to after peace agreements: one in five conflicts resumes within ten years (Kreutz, 2010). In the case of negotiated settlements, demobilizing former rebels and allowing them to form a political party helps to ensure that the peace will hold. Ozoukou (2014) and Walter (2004) agree that providing opportunities for former combatants to discuss with local authorities across the various communities contributes toward peace as it establishes formal channels where the opposition can express their grievances legally or at least non-violently. Nevertheless, this implies the development of the basic political freedoms of association and protest, and, most of all, well-functioning institutions that are essential for democracy but not in place yet.

Moreover, as per the fifth scenario, post-conflict stability is also threatened by the emergence of new rebel groups. Conflict management suggests conflict resolution as well as prevention. Importantly, when preparing for the post-conflict society, mediators and peacemakers must consider more than just the insurgent sides. The emergence of new rebel groups indicates the need for international actors in post-conflict peacebuilding to pay great attention to conflict prevention. Even though formerly belligerent elites may be keen to surrender or sign settlements protecting their personal access to power or resources, there is no guarantee of their former fighters' loyalty (Kreutz, 2010). In the case of the third scenario, when all or some of the troops are allowed to remain as militias, other threats to post-conflict stability exist. The former rebels might remain armed as local security forces, turn into criminal gangs or become private security agents for political actors. As addressed in Chapter 3 on democracy and violence, it seems obvious that preserving violent organizations increases the likelihood of conflict recurrence or escalation, subsequently impeding the democratization and peacebuilding processes. Thus, keeping armed militias might have influenced the fact that in half of the cases following peace agreements, conflict recurs within five years (Kreutz, 2015; Derouen and Jenna Lea, 2009). Moreover, it also seems logical that the risk is much higher when troops and either politicians or the regime remain interconnected as in the first and second scenarios.

Once again, no single policy can guarantee post-conflict stability. The conversion of formerly armed groups into political parties has been recognized by the literature as crucial for the success of various peace processes in the last decades. However, as per the central dilemma, this has proven problematic in several instances. The following section examines this issue in more detail by applying the Philosophical–Actions–Tactics set of dilemmas.

5.3.2 Dilemmas of transforming warring armies into political parties

First, an existential dilemma must be addressed in transforming warring groups into political parties. Warlords will accept demobilization and a compromise for peace only if their inclusion in power-sharing is more attractive than remaining in a state of belligerency. Hence, the first paradox: the more successful former rebels and guerrilla movements were in terms of the liberation struggle, the more difficult they experience the transition into being a political competitor among many in a multiparty democracy (Ottaway, 1991; Manning, 2007). Very often the new parties remain true to their wartime ideology and political platform while trying to adjust to the new political and economic actualities. They find it challenging to take into consideration the opinions and wishes of their former members and loyal devotees. But to survive in the democratic "war of politics," they need to attract as many supporters as possible.

Importantly, Clausewitz was not an enthusiast of democracy and did not write about civil war (Armitage, 2017). However, his aphorism well represents the demilitarization of politics and the problem of the democratization of warlords: "war is the continuation of politics by other means." However, in war to democracy transitions, the transformation of insurgent groups into legitimate political parties can be seen as linked with Michel Foucault' inversion of Clausewitz's maxim. In this sense, "politics (power) becomes the continuation of war by other means" is the apposite (Vanhoutte, 2015; Foucault, 2003, p. 165). Many post-civil war parties and their respective leaders found it difficult to adjust to the accountability and transparency of democratic politics. They remain essentially reliant on personality-driven and clientele-driven mechanisms of internal control and continue to behave as the epitomes of the nationalist and/or populist politics of the liberation struggle.

Thus, these new parties, formed by old players in the conflict, while ostensibly adjusting to the new reality, often neglect to distinguish the interests of the party from those of the nation (Gunther and Diamond, 2001; Marshall and Ishiyama,

2016; Soderberg Kovacs, 2008; Manning, 2008). For example, in Mozambique, the leading political party has attempted to use the party's symbol as the state's emblem. The national flag is designed based on the Mozambican Liberation Front (FRELIMO) colors and includes the image of an AK-47 with a bayonet attached to the barrel. It is the only national flag in the world to feature such a modern rifle. It conveys the mixed message of sovereignty as a permanent stage of war. In 2005, a competition was held to design a new flag for Mozambique. A design was selected with the removal of the image of a Kalashnikov assault rifle. Unsurprisingly, the FRELIMO-led Parliament rejected it and the flag remains the same to this day. Likewise, in the 2016 Ugandan presidential elections, Museveni's campaign slogan was "My country, my president" as if, after 30 years in power,[9] both were the same (Meyerfeld, 2016). Many other cases of political party and state symbiosis can be found, as in Angola (MPLA) and Timor-Leste (FRETILIN). This can be interpreted as "a dangerous precedent bespeaking an authoritarian tendency to conflate the ruling party with the state itself" (Smith, 2004, p. 153) or a threat to democracy itself (Gauchet, 2004). The militant, hierarchical, sectarian, and internally undemocratic natures of many of these warring groups work against the development of peaceful, democratic, transparent, and inclusive policies. On an existential basis, organized groups, warlords, and politicians will accept peace and democratization only on terms under which their investments and privileges are not severely threatened. By the same analogy, according to a Clausewitzian viewpoint of politics, Mearsheimer and Evera (1995) were right: there are times when peace means war.

Second, the decision on who should participate in politics is related to the horizontal dilemma and its correlated trade-offs of inclusion and exclusion. A question encapsulates this dilemma: could ISIL, Al-Qaeda, FARC, the Taliban, or the Tamil Tigers be transformed into legitimate political parties to run for elections in a postwar scenario in Syria, Iraq, Colombia, Afghanistan, or Sri Lanka, respectively? Including an all-encompassing range of the society in the peace agreement legitimizes the peace process. However, the inclusion of warring groups in government rewards violence and, thus, jeopardizes democratization (Hoglund and Zartman, 2006; Stedman, 2000). Moreover, in the aftermath of war, it could be argued that only democratic movements should be allowed to develop into political parties and compete for power. However, excluding rebel groups also opens the room for new actors, and this shift jeopardizes peacebuilding, with a greater probability of a return to violent tactics (Stedman et al., 2002; Manning, 2007). For the sake of peace, the inclusion of some warring parties may offer a motivation for additional groups to use violence to attain equivalent political status. Furthermore, inclusion may not necessarily eliminate violence, as some groups pursue a twofold stratagem of politics and violence (Soderberg Kovacs, 2008; Snyder, 2000; Sindre, 2014). Yet the political process of inclusion often happens at the expense of new political parties. Due to the lack of viable alternatives, this might be inevitable for ending the armed conflict. Nonetheless, there is a significant probability that this might result in reopening the political cleavages that were engendered during wartime alignments. As happened in the 2003 peace agreement in Liberia, a strategy for solving this puzzle is using transitional arrangements. This means establishing a transitional government that includes the warring parties, but for a predetermined and limited period. Nevertheless, once in power, that alternative can be hazardous.

Kosovo also represents how warfare and politics are interrelated in the transition from soldiers to politicians. Ramush Haradinaj was a former commander of the Kosovo Liberation Army (UCK/KLA). Following the dissolution of Yugoslavia, and the KLA's demilitarization after NATO's entry into Kosovo in 1999, the KLA was transformed into the Kosovo Protection Corps (KPC) with Haradinaj appointed as deputy commander. In 2000, he founded the Alliance for the Future of Kosovo (AAK) and became prime minister for 2004–2005, despite having been indicted by the International Criminal Tribunal for the Former Yugoslavia (ICTY), for war crimes and crimes against humanity against Serbs, Romani, and Albanians during the Kosovo War. Although he was acquitted of all charges in 2008 and 2012, he was rearrested in 2015 and 2017, by Slovenian and French police, respectively, following Serbia's international warrants for war crimes. Similarly, former president Hashim Thaçi was a former commander of the KLA, responsible for securing finance and armaments and for training recruits in Albania. After his participation in the Rambouillet negotiations as the leader of the Kosovar Albanian team, in 2000 he founded the Democratic Party of Kosovo (PDK), which won a vast majority in 2007 elections. He declared independence and became the first prime minister in 2008. He was reelected as prime minister in 2014, and President of Kosovo won reelection in 2016 until his forced resignation in 2020 to face a war crimes tribunal with accusations of several crimes against humanity. On the one hand, while the KLA was officially disbanded at the end of the armed conflict in Kosovo in 1999, the new Kosovo Protection Corps was composed primarily of former KLA fighters. On the other hand, the PDK was formed largely from the political leadership of the KLA. A near monopoly of power allowed the Democratic Party of Kosovo to seize control of the machinery of government. Literally, warlords entered politics as peacemakers or democrats. Thus, the horizontal dilemma is at the epicenter of the demilitarization of politics when victorious guerrilla fighters enter the scene as democratic rulers. With the resignation, the political representation changed. In the 2021 snap parliamentary elections, Vetëvendosje (Self-Determination) won 58 seats against 25 for PDK.[10]

Third, it is debatable if it is morally justifiable to include those who committed atrocities to represent the people's voice in political policies and to uphold the rule of law. The 2003 transitional government in the DRC is made up of "former" armed groups with a continued reliance on violence to pursue their economic and political interests. This might not seem morally reasonable for the embryonic democratization process. However, despite such moral quandaries, reality has shown that, even if it is not appropriate or fair, this is necessary and sometimes beneficial to end the war through peaceful means (Collier and Sambanis, 2002; Licklider, 1993; McEvoy and O'Leary, 2013; Stein, 1994; Stedman et al., 2002). Paradoxically, as claimed by Kovacs (2008, p. 135), the efforts to promote both peace and democratization in war-shattered societies through the transformation of armed groups into peaceful parties "might undermine precisely those values that it sought to encourage."

Fourth, when transforming former rebel groups into political parties, the vertical dilemma is identified by the trade-off between popular legitimacy and governance efficacy. Beyond the horizontal and moral dilemmas, if the warring groups are included and transformed into legal political actors, they will strengthen their power based on their popular legitimacy as the victor in their fight. But although rebel factions could be conceivably legitimate, they are not necessarily efficient. Three examples can illustrate this dichotomy. The Democratic Party of Kosovo, originally the Kosovo Liberation Army, enjoyed popular legitimacy but had to make significant adjustments to its collective incentive strategies and identity to compete in postwar politics as new party competitors emerged in the system. Through pressure, the party has adapted more quickly to electoral politics and has managed to find an equilibrium between legitimacy and efficacy. In contrast, despite its comparatively successful electoral results in El Salvador, the former communist guerrilla group, the Farabundo Martí National Liberation Front (FMLN), has struggled with internal ideological and party governance divergences. Some prefer an overture toward pluralistic policies and increased intra-party democracy, while others want strict adherence to a vertical decision-making structure. The challenge was to retain party unity as internal factionalism impacted its capacity to govern. Moreover, the Guatemalan National Revolutionary Unity (URNG) had its general legitimacy and efficacy open to question due to the lack of ideological identity, political clarity, and governance program that seemed lost in its transition to a political party, particularly among the base of its leftist supporters. Hence, in post-conflict situations, failed governance and illegitimate actors also undermine the long-term prospects for a durable peace. Additionally, there is a considerable shift in the relationship between the former rebels and the population. In the emerging new "democratic and peaceful" context, they are supposed to represent the same people they once threatened, extorted, and illegally expatriated.

The vertical relationship concerning political parties and the population is contingent, to a large degree, on whether the insurgent group wins government power in the postwar elections or if it exists as an opposition party. In this regard, the opposition is usually crucial to democracy, but this might not necessarily be obvious in fragile states. In Timor-Leste, the cooperation between FRETILIN and the CNRT between 2015 and 2017 led to a rapprochement equivalent to an informal power-sharing agreement. Although this was positive for state-building, the country was without an effective opposition to the CNRT majority government. The victory of Francisco "Lu Olo" Guterres as president (2017 to 2022) reaffirmed the supremacy of FRETILIN as a former rebel group transformed into a political party. Moreover, in spite of the strategic calculation of nominating Rui Maria de Araujo (FRETILIN) as prime minister (2015–2017), this did not signal a shift toward a younger generation. The so-called 75 generation of militants who fought for independence remained hegemonic in political decision making. Mari Alkatiri, a former prime minister (2002–2006), was reappointed as the new prime minister in 2017 as FRETILIN won the elections. Nevertheless, the political crisis and dissolution of the parliament in December 2017, due to a political deadlock caused by the breakdown of the alliance between CNRT and FRETILIN, also showed that Timor-Leste politics remains largely personality driven. It is fought as if the political parties were still part of the armed resistance wing. The calling of an early election in May 2018 triggered questions about the principles of consensus politics and political inclusion, which leaders always pledge themselves to in the spirit of democracy. New elections seemed necessary to solve the impasse democratically in Timor-Leste by settling the power struggle between political parties and coalitions. To add to the same mélange of old rebel figures in the process of "making of democrats" (Manning, 2008), the constitutional crisis ended with the nomination of former president Taur Matan Ruak (2012–2017) and former military commander as prime minister in June 2018. Despite concerns of violence, no major incidents occurred. The country underwent a peaceful transfer of power and increased its index rankings of democracy/freedom and positive peace (Freedom House, 2018, IEP, 2018). In any case, the old contest of the 75 generation was back to business as usual with the figures of Xanana Gusmão and Ramos Horta[11] (CNRT), Taur Matan Ruak (PLP), and Mari Alkatiri (FRETILIN). Thus, post-conflict politics in Timor-Leste remains driven by former freedom fighters in a typical example of the "democratization of warlords" and their armies through their transformation into political parties.

Fifth, a temporal dilemma can similarly be predicted. In the long run, the lack of democratic progress might also impair prospects for sustainable peace as democracy in these circumstances can be impracticable and of no use to social stability or peace. In the short term, the process of demilitarization can be superficial, fragile, and insubstantial. The shortcomings of the democratic system can thus fuel new grievances if the peace accord and the political order do not bring the significant peace dividends expected. States that fail to move beyond the initial buildup of democratic institutions remain autocratic or neopatrimonial in nature. If so, there are serious implications for the recurrence of war as states of this kind are more prone to armed conflict than democratic and autocratic states (Hegre et al., 2001; Reynal-Querol, 2005). In the 1997 postwar elections in Liberia, the National Patriotic Front of Liberia (NPFL) was converted into the NPP and paved the way to electorally legitimize former warlord Charles Taylor to the presidency. After his swearing-in, Taylor declared that he would not comply with the Abuja peace accords, including the reconstruction of the national army, and he began to oppress the political opposition in the country. Therefore, instead of marking the end of seven years of brutal civil war, these early elections took place without a consolidated and well-structured political system. Consequently, it led to political and security deterioration that ultimately climaxed in a new civil war from 2000 to 2003, when Liberians United for Reconciliation and Democracy (LURD) forced Taylor to leave the country. Thus, the lack of a strong and pluralistic political party system and the short period to convert warlords into legal actors positively contributed to the return of a warrior to power behind the façade of a political party and a weak peace agreement (Themnér, 2017). Additionally, suppose the alternative of establishing a transitional government with the inclusion of the warring parties for a predetermined and limited period is followed to solve the horizontal dilemma. In that case, a new impasse takes over, this time a temporal one, as it is unknown whether this limited period will produce the required results of transition.

Sixth, once a design impasse is identified in postwar politics, investing in changes to the internal authority structures is necessary. For a new internal institutional structural design to be formulated and implemented, decisions must be made, weighing up technical and political choices that will determine members' new responsibilities and roles. Once again, the point must be made that political parties in new post-civil war democracies are different from those in the usual democratic milieu and they should be analyzed accordingly. On the eve of independence from colonial rule, many African liberation movements were declared political parties, without any adequate institutional structure being in place. This lack of sufficient institutionalization is one of the greatest problems facing party systems in new democracies due to its uncertain levels of legitimacy, weak social roots, poor organization, limited geographical spread, and scarce prospects for structured intra-party interactions (Gandhi and Vreeland, 2004; Randall and Svasand, 2002; Stedman et al., 2002; Zürcher et al., 2013). In several cases, such as Uganda, Guatemala, Timor-Leste, and Angola, the traditional leaders of the NRA, URNG, FRETILIN, and MPLA refused to leave their parties. In these instances, the parties' capacity for internal democratization was limited, with a lack of tolerance for internal adjustment or for opening up to new leadership.

For stronger legitimacy and efficacy, the transformation of fighting forces into legal political actors requires technical institutionalization and reorganization. Also, political choices need to be made that assist intra-party interactions and legitimate leadership (Vinegard, 1998). Likewise, it is necessary to abandon excluding ideologies such as ethnonationalism and establish a more democratic encompassing system and its supportive structures. Additionally, the theoretical technicalities of political science are rarely decipherable in postwar scenarios. Typically the typology is built on three criteria (formal organization, programmatic commitments, tolerant pluralist versus proto-hegemonic strategy) in parallel with the 15 "species" of political parties (elite-based parties, traditional local notable parties, clientele-based parties), mass-based parties (socialist: class-based or mass parties and Leninist parties; nationalist: pluralist-nationalist parties and ultranationalist parties; religious: denominational parties and fundamentalist parties), ethnically based parties (ethnic-based parties and Congress parties), electoral parties (personality-based parties, catch-all parties, and programmatic parties), and, finally, movement parties (left-libertarian parties and post-industrial extreme right parties) (Carbone, 2007). Once again, the metamorphosis of insurgency groups into official political actors is a strategic choice that takes advantage of the hybrid conditions set up by a "democratic disorder" or an "undemocratic order" after civil war.

Seventh, the sequencing dilemma is also part of this complex process as it is debatable if the new internal institutional structural reform should start from the bottom up or the top down. It is possible that by initially transforming low-ranking soldiers into political actors, the moral and vertical dilemma could be minimized and there could be space for the development of new leadership and capacity-building. However, it is unlikely that former warlords would want to give up their leadership role. To start from the bottom up requires more time which is counterproductive to the timely "rush" toward democratization through elections. Another important aspect of the sequencing dilemma in multi-warring groups requires deciding which spoiler group would initially be transformed into a political party.

Ninth and tenth, the whole transformation process costs money and time. Efforts to demilitarize politics are also expensive components of peacebuilding and lead to financial and resource dilemmas. Trade-offs between the present and the future, as well as between efficiency and viability are interlinked. Once transformed into legal political parties, the warlords often lack both financial and human resources, as well as poor organizational foundations. The newly created parties have a generally limited representative role and only rarely a constructive protagonist role in developing policy platforms. The parties have to rethink their internal structure with new institutional designs and ways to finance themselves as they can no longer continue to expropriate and extort the fruits of the citizens' labor or control the extraction of raw materials in the areas under their military control (Wantchekon, 2004). Invariably, a national tax system is still not in place in the immediate aftermath of civil war. Thus, the financial dilemma goes hand in hand with the resource dilemma.

Furthermore, if the new system of political parties is not well established, opportunities for corruption inevitably arise due to poor mechanisms of checks and balances. Consequently, two other dilemmas are ignited as transparency and operability are based on the trade-offs between impartiality and liability and the flexibility and robustness of laws and procedures, respectively. Moreover, the lack of trust that exists between the belligerents themselves and between the locals and armed groups must be overcome. Consequently, the security dilemma will limit the individual's choice between exercising their rights (e.g., political party affiliation) or fulfilling their duties (e.g., voting). Various scenarios may ensue: (1) former rebels may belong to the post-conflict (local or central) government; (2) former rebels may constitute a political party; (3) former rebels may be allowed – or managed – to remain an armed militia; and (4) former rebels may join or form another rebel movement after the civil war has ended to reignite a new war. In all of these, a lack of security may, therefore, exist on the streets.

Suspicions must be eliminated at the local level. However, building trust effectively goes beyond the creation (or invention) of institutions or the establishment (or imposition) of national policies.

Last but not least, the systemic dilemma concerns the trade-offs between international and domestic ownership. Who has the right to determine that formerly warring groups are to be considered when transforming themselves into legal political parties (Soderberg Kovacs, 2008)? In many internationally supervised peace processes, such a transformation of former rebels into political parties has emerged as a commonly recognized tool for conflict resolution and democratization. The continued commitment of rebels to the peace process has frequently depended on the international actors' provision of resources. For instance, a UN trust fund with US$17 million was raised to help RENAMO to transform itself into a political party in Mozambique (Vines, 1996; Soderberg Kovacs, 2008). In addition to providing financial assistance, donors have also frequently contributed with technical assistance and training for such armed groups to build their capacity to select candidates, organize election campaigns, and monitor election outcomes. Notably, large amounts of financial resources create suspicions about their origins, expenditures, destinations, and ethical procedures. Assistance to these new parties has in some instances also continued in the post-election period. In some cases, as with the RUF in Sierra Leone and the Khmer Rouge in Cambodia, the international legitimization of armed groups has been aborted or reversed during the implementation process due to the rebels' inability or unwillingness to comply with the terms of the agreement. The considerable influence of international players over the dynamics and outcomes of these processes of rebel conversion raises concerns over ownership and whether the choices always comply with the perceptions and opinions of the domestic audience whose political future is at risk.

Importantly, as Shapiro (1999) suggests, "enough of deliberation: politics is about interests and power". It is imperative to keep in mind that the transformation from peace to war can happen back to front: some legitimate official political parties can transform into warring groups (Berti and Gutierrez, 2016). From politicians to soldiers, violence and politics go hand in hand as some groups pursue a dual strategy of aggression and politics. One example is Hamas, which is commonly categorized as a terrorist organization by the United States, despite having obtained democratic legitimacy through the 2006 legislative elections and the control of Gaza over Fatah in 2007. It is worthwhile to mention that the struggle for power between Fatah and Hamas, the two main Palestinian political parties, is also referred to as the Palestinian Civil War.

Therefore, as affirmed by Jarstad and Sisk (2008), "democratic institutions do not always produce peaceful democrats." Notwithstanding their essential role, postwar elections and the transformation of armed groups into political parties often foment tensions and become a lightning rod for popular discontent and extremist sentiments (Soderberg Kovacs, 2008; Gillies, 2011).

5.4 Summary of the chapter

This chapter contributes to the book questions by applying the P–A–T set of 14 dilemmas of peacebuilding and democratization by focusing on two main issues: elections and the demobilization of warring groups by transforming them into political parties. It is not obvious when elections and political parties promote democracy. First, although democratization is noticeably not all about the ballot, elections are a pivotal issue and are widely seen as an integral part of the processes of war termination, international (dis)engagement, and nation-building. Elections in the wake of war are turning points for peace when this is a mechanism for generating internal legitimacy for peace agreements. However, success concerning war termination does not necessarily mark "success" relative to democratization. Furthermore, elections can also be a façade for a so-called warlord democracy or electoral dictatorship. As shown by the interconnectivity and dynamics of the 14 dilemmas, the establishment or reinstatement of political order by some form of legitimate authority is paramount in any transition from conflict to peace. Therefore, a more realistic and less ideological appraisal of elections is required. Elections can advance stability in peace processes or exacerbate armed conflicts depending on timing, sequencing, design, and resource considerations. As part of a postwar peace deal, elections cannot be postponed for more than a few years. However, if elections are held too soon after the war, they can be a dangerous tool for legitimizing extremist parties without the proper development of the political party system. Independent electoral commissions are preferable, as well as sequences taking a bottom-up approach from local to national elections.

Second, under different circumstances, political parties can help in building a new, peaceful, and democratic order or pave the way for a continuation of the conflict. Beyond the positive and negative effects, the transformation of military groups into political parties is often necessary for ending the war through a negotiated settlement as their motivation increases significantly when granted a legitimate political role. However, exchanging uniforms for suits is not sufficient for turning "spoilers" into democratic players. Even though the conversion of ex-armed groups into political parties has been recognized as crucial for the success of various peace processes in the last few decades, their inclusion has also been proven problematic for the democratization process. The belligerent, hierarchical, ideological, and internally undemocratic nature of many rebel groups works against the development of pacific, democratic, transparent, and inclusive policies. Besides the limitations of political parties in new democracies that emerge from authoritarian rule and those that take place after a civil war, both in theory and in practice, such parties remain an indispensable institutional component of representative democracy, the expression of pluralism, and political participation. Whether this manifest as the democratization of warlords via elections or as the demilitarization of politics, war seems to be the continuation of politics and vice versa.

After the war, democratization is not only related to elections and the transformation of rebel groups into political parties. It also requires a new constitution to enforce peace and uphold the rule of law. On the one hand, constitutionalism can be decisive for peace. On the other hand, it can also face several dilemmas concerning the choices of democracy. Similarly, it is more probable that warring parties will sign a peace deal if they are assured a share in the upcoming rule regime. Therefore, constitutionalism and power-sharing mechanisms will be analyzed, based on the same P–A–T set of dilemmas, in the next chapter as an alternative to persuading adversaries to remain committed to the peace and democracy-building processes.

Notes

1 For example, within the China's Communist Party.
2 Among violence, poverty, and population frustration, the COVID-19 pandemic also impacted the willingness to go to the polls.
3 "How can I leave my banana plantation that I have planted and that now starts to have fruits?" declared Museveni in early January 2016. Corruption and nepotism are high in Museveni's regime: his wife is the vice president and a minister in his government, his brother is the chief of the Army and his son commands the Special Forces (Meyerfeld, B. 2016. Yoweri Museveni, roi d'Ouganda. *Le Monde*, 18.02.2016 at 17h39).
4 Despite the international arrest warrant, Al-Bashir was still participating in international forums, including the United Nations General Assembly.
5 His actions were alleged among the bloodiest and deadliest carried out by the FARC. Among the acts attributed to the FARC group led by Timochenko: kidnapping of a government minister, the bombing of a social club, and the murder of a governor. See BBC 2016. Timochenko, the guerrilla leader who talks peace. *BBC*, 24 November 2016. The 2018 presidential elections were run between Gustavo Petro and Ivan Duque, who won.
6 In Africa, only Cape Verde and Seychelles are listed as two-party systems. Neither has had a civil war and therefore, no UN peacekeeping intervention has been experienced.
7 See Statista 2020. Data also in accordance with Worldometers and the World Bank. www.statista.com/statistics/1226158/median-age-of-the-population-of-africa/ Accessed 20/12/2021.
8 To put this into context, more than 80 percent of Angolans, Zimbabweans, and Ugandans were not born when Dos Santos, Mugabe, and Museveni, respectively, took power. Additionally, Gabon's Omar Bongo had been president for 41 years when he died in office at the age of 73 in 2011. Hastings Banda, Malawi's self-proclaimed president for life, was in his late 90s when he was ousted from office in 1994. Zimbabwe's Robert Mugabe was 94, making him the oldest leader in the world until he was deposed in November 2017. DAVID E KIWUWA. 2015. Africa is young. Why are its leaders so old? *The conversation. Africa review*, 29 October 2015.
9 Museveni took power in 1986. According to Worldeconomics, Uganda's median age is 16.7. In this sense, for the most part of the population, the president and the state are equivalent.
10 In the 2021 snap parliamentary elections, Vetëvendosje won 58 seats, the LDK won 15 seats, PDK won 25 seats, and the Alliance for the Future of Kosovo (AAK) took 8 seats. The Serb List won 10 seats; other minority parties filled the remaining 10 seats. The election was considered "transparent and competitive" by local and international

observers, and it did not feature any significant irregularities. In 2021, voter turnout increased to 48.78 percent from 44.6 percent in the 2019 elections. As a parliamentary republic, the Assembly voted to elect Albin Kurti as prime minister and Vjosa Osmani as president (IFES 2021).

11 Ran as an independent in the previous elections.

References

Afrobarometer. 2016. *Afrobarometer*. Online database. Available at http://www.afrobarometer.org/. Accessed 06/07/2017

Alsadi, W. 2007. *La democracia en America Latina, un barco a la deriva*. Fondo de Cultura Economica. 1ed. Buenos Aires, Argentina.

Armitage, D. 2017. *Civil Wars: A History in Ideas*. Penguin Canada.

BBC. 2016. Timochenko, the Guerrilla Leader Who Talks Peace. *BBC*, 24 November 2016.

Behar, O. 2022. La elección de Petro es un paso hacia la paz en Colombia. Pero no llegará fácilmente. *The Washington post*, July 6, 2022 at 12:55 p.m. EDT.

Benoit, K. 2000. Which Electoral Formula Is the Most Proportional? A New Look with New Evidence. *Political Analysis*, 8, 381–388.

Bermeo, N. 2003. What the Democratization Literature Says-or Doesn't Say-About Postwar Democratization. *Global Governance*, 9, 159–77.

Berti, B. & Gutierrez, B. 2016 Rebel to Political and Back? Hamas as a Security Provider in Gaza: Between Rebellion, Politics and Governance. *Democratization*, 23.

Bjornlund, E. 2004. *Beyond Free and Fair: Monitoring Elections and Building Democracy*. Johns Hopkins University Press, US.

Bourne, R. 2012. *Catastrophe: What Went Wrong in Zimbabwe?* Zed Books, London, UK.

Burnell, P. 2006. *Promoting Democracy Backwards*. Fundación para las Relaciones Internacionales y el Diálogo Exterior (FRIDE). Nov 2006.

Carbone, G. M. 2007. Political Parties and Party Systems in Africa: Themes and Research Perspectives. *World Political Science Review*, 3.

Center, C. May 10, 2010. *Reports Widespread Irregularities n Sudan's Vote Tabulation and Strongly Urges Steps to Increase Transparency*.

CERI. 2004. *The Politics and Anti-Politics of Contemporary Disarmament, Demobilization and Reintegration Programs*. Science-Politique.

Collier, P. & Sambanis, N. 2002. Understanding Civil War: A New Agenda. *The Journal of Conflict Resolution*, 46, 3–12.

Colombia, G. O. & FARC. 2016. Acuerdo Final para la terminacion del conflito y la construccion de una paz estable y duradera. *Peace Agreement*. Colombia: http://www.acuerdodepaz.gov.co/acuerdos/acuerdo-final.

Derouen, K. R. J. & Jenna Lea, A. P. W. 2009. The Duration of Civil War Peace Agreements. *Conflict Management and Peace Science*, 26, 367–387.

Diamond, L. & Platter, M. F. 1999. Toward Democratic Consolidation. *In The Global Resurgence of Democracy*. Johns Hopkins University Press.

Dirmoser, D. I. 2005. Democracia sin demócratas. Sobre la crisis de la democracia en América Latina. *Pensamiento Propio*. N. 21, Enero-Junio 2005, 9–42.

Donno, D. 2013. Elections and Democratization in Authoritarian Regimes. *American Journal of Political Science*, 57, 703–716.

Doyle, M. W. & Sambanis, N. 2006. *Making War and Building Peace: United Nations Peace Operations*. Princeton University Press.

Emma Graham-Harrison, A. S. A. P. A. 2014. 2014: A Good Year for Democracy? *The Guardian*.
FFP. 2017. *Fragile State Index*. The Fund for Peace.
Fjelde, H. & Hoglund, K. 2014. Electoral Institutions and Electoral Violence in Sub-Saharan Africa. *B.J.Pol.S.*, 46, 297–320.
Foucault, M. 2003. *Society Must Be Defended*. Picador.
Freedom House. 2017. *Freedom in the World 2017: Populists and Autocrats: The Dual Threat to Global Democracy*. Freedom House.
Freedom House. 2018. *Freedom in the World 2018: Democracy in Crisis*. Freedom House.
Freedom House. 2022. *Freedom of the World 2022: The Global Expansion of Autoritarian Rule*. Freedom House.
Gallagher, M. 1991. Proportionality, Disproportionality and Electoral Systems. *Electoral Studies*, 10.
Gandhi, J. & Vreeland, J. 2004. Political Institutions and Civil War: Unpacking Anocracy. 32.
Gauchet, M. 2004. *La democracia contra si misma*.
Gillies, D. 2011. *Elections in Dangerous Places: Democracy and the Paradoxes of Peacebuilding*. McGill-Queen's University Press.
Globo, O. 2015. Eleição para presidente no Haiti no domingo terá 54 candidatos. *O Globo*, 23/10/2015 12h10 – Atualizado em 23/10/2015 13h54.
Globo, O. 2016. Haiti chega a acordo para governo de transição após suspensão de eleição. *O Globo*, 06/02/2016 at 18h44.
Gunther, R. & Diamond, L. 2001. *Political Parties and Democracy*. Johns Hopkins University Press.
Hartzell, C. & Hoddie, M. 2015. The art of the possible: Power Sharing and Post-Civil War Democracy. *World Politics*, 67, 37–71.
Hegre, H., Ellingsen, T., Gates, S. & Gleditsch, N. P. 2001. Toward a Democratic Civil Peace? Democracy, Political Change, and Civil War, 1816–1992. *American Political Science Review*, 95.
Hoglund, K. 2008. Violence in War-to-Democracy Transtitions. *In*: JARSTAD, A. K. A. T. D. S. (ed.) *From War to Democracy: Dilemmas of Peacebuilding*. Cambridge University Press.
Hoglund, K. & Zartman, I. W. 2006. Violence by the State: Official Spoilers and their Allies. *In*: Darby, J. (ed.) *In Violence and Reconstruction*. University of Notre Dame Press.
IEP. 2017. *Global Peace Index*. 11th ed. Institute of Economics and Peace.
IEP. 2018. *Global Peace Index*. Institute of Economics and Peace.
International Crisis Group. 2010. Rigged Elections in Darfur and the Consequences of a Probable NCP Victory in Sudan. *In: Policy Briefing*. International Crisis Group.
Issacharoff, S. 2015. The Democratic Risk to Democratic Transitions. *Constitutional Court Review*, Vol. V, 1–31 Juta Company, South Africa.
Jackson, J. 1999. A Tale of Two Countries. Sierra Leone Vs. Kosovo: Why Isn't America Paying More Attention to the War in Africa? *Newsweek*, 7 June 1999.
Jarstad, A. K. & Sisk, T. D. 2008. *From War to Democracy: Dilemmas of Peacebuilding*. Cambridge University Press.
Kiwuwa, D. E. 2015. Africa is Young. Why are its Leaders so Old? *The Conversation. Africa Review*, October 29, 2015.
Kreutz, J. 2010. How and When Armed Conflicts End: Introducing the UCDP Conflict Termination Dataset. *Journal of Peace Research*, 47, 243–250.
Kreutz, J. 2015. Civil War Outcomes and a Durable Peace: Setting the Record Straight. *DIE*, 17/2015.

Kumar, K. 1998. Postconflict Elections and International Assistance. *In*: Krishna, K. & Boulder, C. (ed.) *Postconflict Elections, Democratization, and International Assistance.* Lynne Rienner Publishers.
Levitsky, S. & Ziblatt, D. 2018. *How Democracies Die.* Crown.
Licklider, R. 1993. *Stopping the Killing: How Civil Wars End.*
Linebarger, C. & Salehyan, I. 2012. *Elections and Social Conflict in Africa, 1990–2009* [Online]. San Diego, CA. Available: https://ssrn.com/abstract=2182694 [Accessed].
Linz, J. J. & Stepan, A. C. 1996. Toward Consolidated Democracies. *Journal of Democracy*, 7, 14–33.
Maley, W. 2012. Introduction: Peace Operations and their Evaluation. *Journal of International Peacekeeping*, 16, 199–207.
Manning, C. 2007. Party-Building on the Heels of War: El Salvador, Bosnia, Kosovo and Mozambique. *Democratization*, 14, 253–272.
Manning, C. 2008. *The Making of Democrats: Postconflict electoral politics in Bosnia.* Palgrave Macmillan.
Mansfield, E. D. & Snyder, J. 2005. When Ballots Bring on Bullets Democratic Deceptions II: 3 Edition. *International Herald Tribune*, p.Newspaper Article.
Marshall, M. C. & Ishiyama, J. 2016. Does Political Inclusion of Rebel Parties Promote Peace after Civil Conflict? *Democratisation*, 23.
Mason, T. D. & Fett, P. J. 1996. How Civil Wars End: A Rational Choice Approach. *Journal of Conflict Resolution*, 40, 546–568.
Mcevoy, J. & O'leary, B. 2013. *Power Sharing in Deeply Divided Places.* University of Pennsylvania Press, Incorporated.
Mearsheimer, J. J. & Evera, S. V. 1995. When Peace Means War. *The New Republic*, 213, 16–21.
Meyerfeld, B. 2016. Yoweri Museveni, roi d'Ouganda. *Le Monde*, 18.02.2016 at 17h39.
Mross, K. 2018. First Peace, then Democracy? Evaluating Strategies of International Support at Critical Junctures after Civil War. *International Peacekeeping*, 26, 190–215.
Newman, E. & Rich, R. 2004. *The UN Role in Promoting Democracy: Between Ideals and Reality.* United Nations University Press.
O'donnell, G. & Schmitter, P. 1986. *Transitions from Authoritarian Rule:Tentative Conclusions about Uncertain Democracies.* John Hopkins University Press.
OCHA. 2017. *Humanitarian Need Overview: Syrian Arab Republic.* November 2017 ed.
Ottaway, M. 1991. Liberation Movements and Transition to Democracy: The Case of the ANC. *Journal of Modern African Studies*, 29, 61–82.
Ottaway, M. 1997. From Political Opening to Democratization? *In*: Ottaway, M. (ed.) *Democracy in Africa. The Hard Road Ahead.* Lynne Rienner Publishers.
Ozoukou, D. 2014. Building Peace or a Fragile Future? The Legacy of Conflict in the Cote d'Ivoire. *Insight on Conflict*, 24/12/2014.
Paris, R. 2004. *At War's End: Building Peace after Civil Conflict.* Cambridge University Press.
Randall, V. & Svasand, L. 2002. Political Parties and Democratic Consolidation in Africa. *Democratization*, 9, 30–52.
Reilly, B. 2008. Post-War Elections: Uncertain Turining Points of Transition. *In*: A. K. Jarstad & T. D. Sisk (eds.) *From War to Democracy: Dilemmas of Peacebuilding.* Cambridge University Press.
Reynal-Querol, M. 2005. Does Democracy Preempt Civil Wars? *European Journal of Political Economy*, 21, 445–465.
Shapiro, I. 1999. Enough of Deliberation: Politics is About Interests and Power. *In*: Macedo, S. (ed.) *Deliberative Politics: Essays on Democracy and Disagreement.* Oxford University Press.

Shaw, S. E. 2006. *Building Peace and Democracy or Organizing Exit: Elections and United Nations Peace Operations*. Dalhousie University (Canada).
Sierra Leone. 1999. *Peace Agreement between the Government of Sierra Leone and the Revolutionary United Front of Sierra Leone*. Government of Sierra Leone.
Sindre, G. M. 2014. Rebels and Aid in the Context of Peacebuilding and Humanitarian Disaster: A Comparison of the Free Aceh Movement (GAM) and the Tamil Tigers (LTTE). *Forum for Development Studies*, 41.
Sisk, T. 2014. Elections in the Wake of War: Turning Points for Peace? *Conciliation Resources*. Legitimacy and Peace Processes: from Coercion to Consent.
Snyder, J. 2000. *From Voting to Violence: Democratization and Nationalist Conflict*.
Soderberg Kovacs, M. 2008. When rebels change their stripes: Armed insurgents. In: JARSTAD, A. K. A. T. D. S. (ed.) *From War to Democracy: Dilemmas of Peacebuilding*. Cambridge University Press.
Stedman, S. J. 2000. Spoiler Problems in Peace Processes. In: Druckman, P. S. A. D. (ed.) *International Conflict Resolution After the Cold War*. National Academy Press.
Stedman, S. J., Rothchild, D. & Cousens, E. M. 2002. *Ending Civil Wars: The Implementation of Peace Agreements*. Lynne Rienner Publishers, Inc.
Stein, C. M. 1994. Stopping the Killing: How Civil Wars End (Book). *Contemporary Sociology*, 23, 387–388.
Themnér, A. E. 2017. *Warlord Democrats in Africa: Ex-Military Leaders and Electoral Politics*.
Toft, M. D. 2010. Ending Civil Wars: A Case for Rebel Victory? *International Security*, 34, 7–36.
UNOCHA. 2016. *Global Humanitarian Overview 2016*.
Utas, M. 2012. *African Conflicts and Informal Power: Big Men and Networks*. Zed Books.
Vanhoutte, K. K. P. 2015. "Oh God! What a Lovely War". Giorgio Agamben's Clausewitzian Theory of Total/Global (Civil) War. *Russian Sociological Review*, 14, 28–44.
Vinegard, A. 1998. From Guerrillas to Politicians: The Transition of the Guatemalan Revolutionary Movement in Historical and Comparative Perspective. In: Sieder, R. (ed.) *In Guatemala after the Peace Accords*. Institute of Latin American Studies.
Vines, A. 1996. *Renamo: From Terrorism to Democracy in Mozambique?* James Currey.
Walter, B. F. 2004. Does Conflict Beget Conflict? Explaining Recurring Civil War. *Journal of Peace Research*, 41, 371–388.
Wantchekon, I. 2004. The Paradox of Warlord Democracy: A Theoretical Investigation. *American Political Science Review*, 80, 98, 17–33.
William, M., Sampford, C. & Thakur, R. 2003. *From Civil Strife to Civil Society: Civil and Military Responsibilities in Disrupted States*. United Nations University Press.
Zirulnick, A. 2013. From Moscow to Cairo, a War on Democracy Promotion. *The Christian Science Monitor*, p.Newspaper Article.
Zürcher, C., Manning, C., Evenson, K., Hayman, R., Riese, S. & Roehner, N. 2013. *Costly Democracy: Peacebuilding and Democratization After War*. Stanford University Press.

6
WHEN THE PEN FAILS, THE SWORD RULES

Constitution building and power-sharing for divided societies

> I am the State, the State is Me
> *Louis XIV*

How to move from the "rule of the gun" toward the "rule of power"? Politics is, inter alia, about interests and power (Shapiro, 1999), and, thus, it is at the epicenter of where war, democracy, and peace intersect. After war, the main priority is establishing a political order as "democracy cannot be cultivated in the absence of natural rights or under a state of anarchy" (Wantchekon, 2004, p. 25). A new social contract must be built between the warring groups themselves as well as between the politicized warring groups and the population. Constitutionalism can be decisive to peace. Nevertheless, it also faces numerous dilemmas vis-à-vis the choices of developing democracy. As a Haitian saying goes, "the constitution is paper, a bayonet is iron" (Leininger, 2006). Success in stopping violence after a civil war and establishing the political space and normative law for enduring peace involves a balance of sticks and carrots. If a peace deal guarantees a share of power in the forthcoming government, it is more probable that warring parties will endorse it to preserve their own existence (which presents an existential dilemma). Power-sharing helps to establish what is crucial in the aftermath of civil war: a political order and collaboration between warring factions and elites. Therefore, it assists in providing an alternative to the vertical dilemma. Considering that in divided societies some form of power equilibrium is necessary for operational democratization, power-sharing might be the key that enchains peace and democracy postwar through a new constitution.

When do constitution building and power-sharing assist democracy in prevailing? Despite a large body of literature on constitution building and power-sharing by legal and political sciences specialists, there is room for a greater focus on war-divided societies (Noel, 2005a; Levitt, 2007; Kastner, 2015; McCulloch

DOI: 10.4324/9781003279976-9

and McGarry, 2017). This chapter analyzes constitutional design through the democratic principles of checks and balances, division, and balance of power. It follows the same methodology of peacebuilding dilemmas used in previous chapters regarding elections, demobilization of conflicting armed groups and transformation of dissidents into political parties. Second, the critical characteristics of power-sharing models and consociational democracy, as tools to attract adversaries to remain committed to the peace and democracy-building processes, are analyzed in some depth. Furthermore, semi-presidentialism and coherence between the constitution and the rule of law are also explored as alternatives to minimize the so-called tyranny of the majority. Moreover, Timor-Leste, Uganda, the Democratic Republic of Congo (DRC), Ethiopia, Iraq, South Sudan, Sierra Leone, Philippines, Cyprus, Burundi, Bosnia and Herzegovina, Kosovo, and Djibouti are presented as case studies to illustrate the analysis of the risks of constitutional reform and power-sharing arrangements toward positive peace, but perhaps negative democracy.

6.1 Conceptualization of sharing power and constitutionalism: division, competition, and institutional arrangements

After the war, a new constitution is usually written "for the people" and set in place to be obeyed "by the people." One initial problem is the issue of "which people" write the constitution and how the Constitutional Assembly, whichever form this may take, will be established and legitimized. Written or unwritten, a constitution is simultaneously a legal, political, and social instrument. As a supreme or higher set of laws, its provisions provide a framework under which all regulations, legislation, institutions, and procedures operate, thereby setting out a predictable legal landscape for political rule. It articulates the rights of citizens that institutions, procedures, or legislation must not infringe on and that the state must strive to ensure. Politically, it establishes, distributes, and limits governmental power and provides mechanisms for deliberating and deciding on public policy. Socially, it may reflect a shared identity or civic vision of the state, expressing commonly held values or foundational principles (IDEA, 2017).

There is a strong relationship between deliberative politics and liberal constitutional arrangements to accommodate various interests and power (Shapiro, 1999). Constitutions usually disperse power horizontally while distributing it vertically. The horizontal axis is typically related to how the constitution distributes power among multiple actors and institutions, such as between a president and a prime minister, civilian and military authorities, secular and religious institutions, or between the "party-political" institutions and the independent institutions such as an electoral commission or public service commission. This dispersal of powers can create a system of checks and balances that ensures no single actor or body accumulates a potentially dangerous concentration of power. Conversely, power is also commonly distributed vertically between national or central and sub-national authorities. This creates a dilemma of centralization versus decentralization. On the one hand, centralization allows room for unity, integration, and identity. Decentralization, on the other hand, provides recognition and empowerment to regions and marginalized or minority groups. However, this might cause inefficiencies, duplication of effort, additional expense, or the loss of technical expertise and resources available only at a national level. The balance between decentralization and centralization has to be considered according to the history, traditions, social and political landscape, economic resources, and development needs of each country (Noel, 2005b; McEvoy and O'Leary, 2013; IDEA, 2017). Irrespective of the distinction between horizontal and vertical forms of power distribution and dispersal, it is important to delineate four concepts: power-sharing, power division, the separation of power, and competition for power (Wolff, 2007; Roeder and Rothchild, 2005). Despite the significance of highlighting these distinctions, it is fundamental to keep in mind that a "normal" power dynamic in "peaceful scenarios" does not generally apply to states emerging from a civil war (Kastner, 2015; Levitt, 2007).

Monopolies of power are identified in military autocracies, monarchies, theocracies, tyrannies, despotisms, or one-party dictatorships. "Democracy" may also cohabit with monopolistic domination, if a ruling class or elite lies behind the façade of the electoral competition for power. However, the monopolization of power directly opposes power-sharing. Although it is common to delegate some power to maintain the monopoly, to delegate is not synonymous with sharing. Power-sharing arrangements mean that former enemies govern jointly, advocating for a coordinated policymaking system with autonomy in the group or territory (Jarstad, 2008). In principle, no one likes to "share" power. Nevertheless, "politics is the art of the possible," as stated by Otto von Bismarck (Hartzell and Hoddie, 2015). Power-sharing is more than acknowledging that "what cannot be won on the battlefield is best allocated through a shared forum and a shared executive" (McEvoy and O'Leary, 2013). Therefore, it does not seek a social contract among unified people as Rousseau's proposal. Instead, power-sharing suggests minimal civility among divided communities within a "consociational form" (Lijphart, 1993) or among territorial governments within a "federalist form." Lebanon is an example of power-sharing that keeps the peace but provokes a democratic political paralysis and population segregation. The 1989 Taif Agreement putting in place sectarian power-sharing ended Lebanon's civil war and reinforced a system of coexistence. But it also wrecked its economy and led to widespread protests and cyclical political crises, such as in 2006, 2016, 2019, and 2021 (Ditel, 2022; COAR, 2021; Khatib and Wallace, 2021; Bahout, 2016).

Additionally, it is also important to distinguish power-sharing institutions (PSI) from power-sharing arrangements (PSA). PSIs usually divide power in the political, military, and economic arenas. PSAs bring former belligerents into joint governments and guarantee them proportional representation in the executive, the legislature, the army, and/or the management of the country's wealth and education. In the political arena, a PSA may include elements such as a proportional representation of all parties in the cabinet and legislature, decision making by consensus and mutual group vetoes on contentious issues, the proportional allocation of funds and positions, and the protection of minority groups' rights (Papagianni, 2007). Despite the extensive literature on democratization and checks and balances, power-sharing specific to post-conflict situations remains limited to studies in political science and related disciplines, such as conflict resolution and peace studies (Jarstad and Sisk, 2008; Hartzell and Hoddie, 2015). The most prominent works of power-sharing in deeply divided places after war have been compiled by McEvoy and O'Leary (2013), O'Flynn and Russell (2005), and Roeder and Rothchild (2005).

Inversely, power division suggests a partition of power among the governmental organs of the common state. The most important issues that divide ethnic groups must be decided by a government common to all. An excess of autonomy can create more conflict, a polarized society, and a parallel state within the state structure (Wolff, 2007). Moreover, the separation of power refers to the mechanisms of checks and balances that are often seen as the basic principles of democracy. According to Montesquieu, the separation of power mitigates the centralization of power, whether by a tyranny, monarchy, or oligarchy. In its purest form, it divides the state into at least three main branches with a specific mandate: the legislature, the executive, and the judiciary. The separation of powers between the branches of government and a range of specialized agencies is expected to create multiple and changing majorities. This means that ethnic minorities can form part of political majorities on some issues and be political minorities on others. As a mechanism of checks and balances, policy and order are expected to emerge from the clash of ambitious power holders scattered across multiple institutions.

Finally, the competition for power is a sine qua non principle of democratic government: a political system enshrined in a constitution is one in which politicians compete for authoritative positions for limited terms, in free and fair elections by the citizens, and hold office within constitutional norms that guarantee accountability both via the ballot box and via recourse to the judiciary. Elections for executive and legislative positions are intended to prevent the nefarious monopolization of power. Conversely, judicial and administrative positions are typically distributed meritocratically according to transparent and reviewable procedures. Similarly, when distinguishing among power-sharing, power division, the separation of power, and competition for power, it is important to differentiate between "power to" and "power over." "Power to" is tilted toward a "positive-sum" game because power is operationalized in a joint, collaborative, or cooperative manner, even if the benefits are asymmetrical. By contrast, "power over" is referred to as domination and a "zero-sum relationship" (McEvoy and O'Leary, 2013). Now that those concepts and definitions are set, the following section proceeds with identifying and analyzing the possible dilemmas between keeping the peace and building democracy.

6.1.1 Constitutional reform and dual power-sharing: the alternative of semi-presidentialism as cohabitation of power

O'Flynn and Russell (2005 p. ix) argue that one of the new challenges for divided societies is recognizing that power-sharing incorporated in "constitutional designs adopted at times of crisis are means to survival." Compared to homogeneous societies or well-established democracies, deeply divided societies pose severe difficulties for peace and democratic governance. Therefore, apparently divergent interests and demands can only be accommodated by power-sharing mechanisms. Thus, constitutionalism can be the key to peaceful power-sharing if it can provide room for equilibrium between the competing interests that originally triggered the civil war. In line with Lipjhart (2004), a constitutional design is required for divided societies instead of time and again repeating the tendency to copy the basic constitutional rules of the former era or choosing deliberatively among a wide assortment of constitutional models without pronounced alternatives for its respective pros and cons elements.

To make constitutionalism work, the system must be well designed to block tyrannies and protect some core rights of citizens from potential violations. As the newest nation of the millennium, Timor-Leste provides an extraordinary opportunity for dealing with the dilemmas facing the design of a new constitution in the fog of conflict. The constitution that would serve as the governing blueprint of the state faced temporal, design, resource, operational, financial, vertical, and systemic dilemmas under the United Nations Transitional Administration in East Timor (UNTAET) rule. The Constitutional Assembly had the task of drafting a constitution within 90 days that would make "the Democratic Republic of Timor-Leste a democratic state, sovereign and independent, based upon the rule of law, the dignity of the human person and the will of the people" (Timor-Leste, 2002). FRETILIN had the majority with two-thirds of the seats of the Constitutional Assembly and wanted to push for a constitutional text drafted in Mozambique by Mari Alkatiri and his supporters during the resistance period. Considering the likelihood of Xanana Gusmão becoming the first president, FRETILIN needed to guarantee that the executive powers would stay where they had major control; in the Constitutional Assembly, which would become the National Parliament. Additionally, besides the trauma experienced under Indonesia's invasion under Suharto and bearing in mind Gusmão's personality, there was a concern that with a powerful executive presidency the country could experience a return to despotic rule (Kingsbury, 2009). As Gusmão was planning for a new constitution to be approved after 2002 with more presidential powers, there was a concern, particularly within UNTAET, that his theme of "national unity" would lead to grievances within the population due to the recent self-independence process. Moreover, competing delegitimized parties could have led to the creation of a functional one-party state under Gusmão's tutelage (CNRT). However, mirroring Portugal as the first colonizer, Timor-Leste came up with an alternative to prevent the abuse of power, while providing room for some stability, flexibility and power-sharing: semi-presidentialism.

In post-authoritarian countries, semi-presidentialism has the potential to make a transition to a democratic future by offering a middle ground between constitutionally "pure" presidential and "pure" parliamentary systems of government. This reduces the risk that a single and powerful leader would be able to dominate the political process indefinitely and centralize power (Stacey and Choudhry, 2014). Semi-presidentialism has become the "newest" mechanism for the separation of powers. Around 50 countries across the European, Asian, and African continents, including changes that have arisen from the Arab Spring opted for this system (Choudhry and Stacey, 2014). Moreover, with the exception of Brazil and Angola, all six other Lusophone countries have adopted a form of semi-presidentialism, including Guinea-Bissau and Mozambique (Amorim Neto and Costa Lobo, 2010). Importantly, as we have seen in Chapter 5 on the transformation of political parties, political conditions in democracies emerging from authoritarianism may not be suitable for a parliamentary government, as party structures are often weak or have little experience. Consequently, a democracy can result in the danger of a fractured and divided parliament, incapable of passing legislation or agreeing on a prime minister and government, as seen with Timor-Leste's 2017 political crisis. Therefore, a dual executive structure might be especially attractive to new or transitioning democracies. It provides room for the separation of powers and a balance of competing powers, which might be essential for political reconciliation and, consequently, stability and peace.

Beyond ceremonial or executive roles, this dual executive gives the opportunity for a "cohabitation of power," as it allows different leaders with different ideologies to rule while having different time mandates and powers simultaneously. As no opposition leaders want to lose ground (the existential dilemma), this also creates a system of checks and balances for dealing with the hostile political speeches expected in day-to-day political activity. Although it is not a cure-all, in new democratic states, a constitutional design with a semi-presidential system of power-sharing offers an option for reconciling deep identity divisions. Under such a system, while the presidency is not an exclusive position of executive power, it nevertheless has sufficient veto powers to provide executive leadership in cases where the legislature might be incapable of supporting a prime minister or government.

Lastly, different designs are possible. For example, in Timor-Leste, as a semi-presidential system, two separate elections are held to elect the president and the members of a unicameral Parliament. The president can only serve twice in a lifetime. In the Republic of Congo, since 2015 referendum, the country has become semi-presidential with two independent elections. However, removing mandate limitations has allowed President Denis Sassou Nguesso[1] to secure power for over uninterrupted 40 years. Rwanda reflects the Belgian system. The 2003 constitution granted broad powers to the president, who has the authority to appoint the prime minister and dissolve the bicameral Parliament. To end the Second Civil War in the DRC in 2002, two founding documents emerged: the Transition Constitution and the Global and Inclusive Agreement, both of which describe and determine the makeup and organization of the Congolese institutions until new provisions of the new constitution were approved by referendum would take effect. Under the Global and All-Inclusive Agreement, there was to be one president and four vice presidents, respectively, representing the government, the Rally for Congolese Democracy party, the MLC party, and civil society. The position of those vice presidents expired after the 2006 elections. After three years (2003–2006) in the interregnum between two constitutions, the Democratic Republic of the Congo is now under the regime of the Constitution of the Third Republic. The constitution, adopted by referendum in 2005, and promulgated by President Joseph Kabila in 2006, establishes a decentralized semi-presidential republic. Although Kabila's term would finish in 2011, he postponed the elections to overstay in power. After all, "if you don't have presidential elections, the sitting president is legitimately in power indefinitely." In the DRC, National Assembly elections were held concurrently with the presidential vote. The president appoints the prime minister upon the majority in the Parliament as well as the members of the government (DRC, 2011). New constitutional amendments in 2011 led to a paralysis in the political system by the manipulation of the electoral process by political elites. Nevertheless, it allowed Félix Tshisekedi to gain the presidency in 2019. It is worthwhile noting that although the figure of the four vice presidents does not exist anymore, Kabila holds a lifetime Senate appointment as a former president. Some skeptics of the semi-presidential system have described it as "conflictogenic" and "dictatogenic" because it might ensure frictions, and a reduction of pace in government life, should the president and the prime minister be from different sides of the political arena. That was the case in Timor-Leste and the Republic of Congo (Brazaville) and consolidated states such as France.

By contrast, Kosovo opted for parliamentary republic model where one general election is held. The Assembly will then elect the prime minister for a four-year term by a simple majority (61 votes) of the 120-member Assembly. And then, the Assembly will also elect the president for a five-year term by a two-thirds majority or simple majority if, after two rounds, no candidate has received a two-thirds majority. In 2021, the Assembly elected Vjosa Osmani with a majority of 71 votes in the third round. In reverse, in Iraq, after national elections, the Council of Representatives (CoR) chooses the largely ceremonial president, who, in turn appoints a prime minister nominated by the largest bloc in the Parliament. The prime minister, who holds most executive power and forms the government, serves up to two four-year terms. Lastly, Ethiopia provides a more commonly seen structure: the president is the head of state and is indirectly elected to a six-year term by both chambers of Parliament. The prime minister is the head of government, and is selected just by the largest party in Parliament after elections. Either semi-presidentialist or a parliamentary republic, all those constitutional designs architectures of who-elects-whom and how are not accidental and play a crucial role in keeping the peace while offering room for political navigation.

6.1.2 Risks of constitutional reform: balance and alternation of power in democracy- building

Not all constitutions with power-sharing systems are successful in alleviating conflict (which is the central dilemma). The abuse of political power may still be constitutionally possible. Constitutionalism should offer the option for sufficient foresight to circumvent situations where peace and democracy might be at risk and, importantly, avoid a political vacuum. However, a constitution may also be undemocratic and authoritarian if one can consider that the abuse of political power is constitutionally conceivable. For example, the constitution may assign the authority to the plenitude of the executive power to a person, faction, or party for a limited time. Moreover, emergency powers retained by a dominant executive representation (a faction, party, or national, religious, or ethnic group) might include the provision of "war powers" involving the suspension of basic rights and fundamental freedoms.

A constitution can also maintain unequal and undemocratic structures in divided societies by, for example, excluding the plurality of beliefs, traditions, and social relations through the establishment of eligibility for citizenship based upon just one religion, one language, one ethnicity, or even one gender. In the case of Myanmar, the 2010 Constitutional Reform movement toward a "discipline-flourishing democracy" was strategically planned by the military junta to prohibit Aung San Suu Kyi from running for president of the country. Additionally, the danger exists that courts staffed and controlled by the same party as the executive may not act as guardians of individuals' rights or collective minorities. If so, the so-called rule of law, an important characteristic of a democratic system and of sustainable peace, repeatedly becomes the rule of the dominant majority or faction in power. Therefore, it represents a return to the "rule of the gun." If so, as suggested by Levitt (2007) when analyzing power-sharing models in Africa, it would mean an "illegal peace." In any case, the 2021 coup d'état is evidence that not all constitutions are successful in alleviating conflict. Importantly, by neglecting the separation of power, the balance of power loses its equilibrium and instead heads in the direction of the "rule of power." Moreover, an "interim constitution" also challenges guaranteeing the rule of law and state sovereignty among instability.

Another problem occurs when the changes in the constitution eliminates the principle of the alternation of power. The argument is often based on the idea of stability through continuity. By allowing the head of state and/or government to be reelected *ad aeternum* or through periodic constitutional amendments, the basic democratic principle of the alternation of power is undermined, and, consequently, it might undercut the PSA and lead to the authoritarianism of a warlord in power. Djibuti.[2] Uganda,[3] Rwanda,[4] Burundi,[5] Burkina Faso, and DRC[6] are examples of the latter. Interestingly, the reverse can also happen: there can be a movement from democracy to authoritarianism, as was the case of the "Bolivarian Axis" (Cuba-Venezuela-Bolivia-Ecuador) and its "social revolution" through the obstruction of the principle of alternation of power (O'Donnell and Schmitter, 1986).[7] Thus, the principle of periodic elections may become redundant if there is no political space for opposition nor free and fair elections.

Moreover, there are cases of political vacuums not foreseen by the constitution, such as where a presidential term has finished, yet no elections have been held or their results recognized, while outbreaks of violence have caused destruction and social rupture. This was the case in Haiti in 2016, prompting the need for a peace accord between the executive and the Parliament, which was mediated by the Organization of American States (OAS) to establish a transitional government toward a "peaceful democratic" transition of power.

Despite being an essential mechanism of power-sharing and a key to peace and democracy in the aftermath of conflict, the risk of democratic transitions is directly embodied by constitutionalism. Some cases, like South Africa, opted for an interim constitution that meant the transition from apartheid to democracy was nearly a constitutional continuation. This meant that the rule of law and state sovereignty remained untouched during the transition as a vital condition for stability within the country (Issacharoff, 2015). On the contrary, CAR's constitutional referendum (December 2015) and presidential elections (February 2016) summarize the complexity of constitutionalism as a transitional tool for democratic peace after violent outbreak in 2013.[8] Efforts to undermine the constitutional referendum demonstrated that some actors remain determined to derail the political process to obstruct their country from moving towards a constitutional order, therefore, benefitting from the lack of a democratic rule of law (Al Jazeera, 2015).

During war, the constitution invariably becomes a "useless" document that no longer serves the triadic enterprise of "for the people, to the people and by the people." Despite the lack of legal normativity, there is a struggle over how to implement and enforce the new set of rules of the social contract after war (Kastner, 2015). Additionally, the Constitutional Assembly must be impartial and its process reliable. The constitution must set out publicly accountable mechanisms and transparent procedures, including those measures dividing public authority among multiple offices and institutions (to avoid the transparency dilemma). In the absence of constitutional provisions, violence limits the exercise of people's rights and duties (provoking a security dilemma). Nevertheless, temporal dilemmas are inevitable. Constitutional designs are adopted at times of crisis; therefore, they are frequently put in place within the short term. However, Constitutions are intrinsically intended to last long term. How early or late the constitution is implemented impacts on the efficiency, viability, and durability of its parameters for democracy, the rule of law and political stability. As per the operational dilemma, the constitution must be robust to be fully enforceable but also flexible with regard to interpretation. Additionally, coherence is the key to balance. Once one decision is made on a specific issue, it should be reapplied on future occasions to avoid making the constitution an irrelevant tool for stability and the rule of law. Thus, clear statements and procedures for amendments must be established. For example, a system is needed to set out the process for amendments to the duration of the mandate or political system, whether parliamentarian or presidentialism, or amendments to specific legislation. Nonetheless, other paragraphs regarding territoriality, national unity, the military's role, and the state's defense might be unchangeable clauses. Other examples of issues that, if not flexible or robust, might limit democracy and stability are: (i) the format of the federation or of the state; (ii) direct, secret universal, and periodic voting; (iii) the separation of powers; and (iv) individual rights and guarantees.

Formally or informally, constitution building seems necessary for democracy-building and long-term sustainable peace. In addition, some scholars would suggest that it is the only option for democratic governance in the shadows of war (Pospieszna and Schneider, 2013). However, the main problem with constitutionalism seems to be how to make it work. In divided societies and in the aftermath of conflict, constitutionalism can be a smokescreen masking the absence of successful power-sharing, the lack of an effective rule of law, and the paucity of the protection of individual and human rights. In fact, modern power-sharing is conceived by some enthusiasts as a necessary supplement to constitutionalism and that each mutually reinforces the other (Mukherjee, 2006). The division of powers and competition for power are essential but not enough to calm deeply divided places. They may instead encourage the tyranny of the majority, oppression of national, ethnic, and religious communities and cause conflict itself in the long run. Thus, power-sharing requires not only the sharing of power, the division of power, but the competition for power as well. Therefore, it offers some prospect of reducing "politicides" (killing those deemed political opponents), and "democides" (killing of populations as the ultimate form of exclusion and governments being the major perpetrator), both of which are found in civil wars. In the transition toward democracy and peace, provisions for power-sharing are the ideal although rarely achieved.

6.2 Consociational democracy and power-sharing: alternatives for shared rule, self-rule, and the "tyranny of the majority"

As evident in the classic writings of James Madison, Alexis de Tocqueville, and John Stuart Mill, the question of the potential danger of the "tyranny of the majority" and threats to the individual's property and liberty has been a central concern within the democratic narrative. Nevertheless, democracy, particularly in post-conflict and divided societies, can also be a "tyranny of the minority" if the law or public policy is dictated in the interests of a faction or ethnic group. In this regard, Lijphart (1968)'s theory of consociational democracy is an institutionalized alternative form of democratic conflict management for divided societies to avoid the tyranny of the majority. A consociational democracy is based on power-sharing and human rights. As mentioned in the previous chapter, majoritarian electoral systems may be inept for solving ethnic cleavages as political parties representing ethnic minorities have no chance of ever forming a majority. Therefore, Lijphart (1993), holds that in some instances, majoritarian rule is not only undemocratic but also dangerous and risks resulting in civil strife. Reynal-Querol (2005) defends this assertion, stating that the principle of maximum inclusion is more democratic than that of the majority rule.

Do consociational democracy and its power-sharing mechanisms better enable the transition to peace and democracy? For Lipjhart (2004, p. 99), despite criticisms, "power-sharing has proven to be the *only* democratic model that appears to have much chance of being adopted in divided societies." According to Norris (2008), PSIs work because states with institutions consistent with power-sharing tend to perform better in terms of democracy. These have positive connotations as in "coalition" or "cooperative" government and "consensual" and "inclusive" decision making (McEvoy and O'Leary, 2013).

The great challenge of a post-civil war democracy is how institutions will play both the Hobbesian role of securing the protection of ordinary citizens against illegal expropriation and tyranny as well as the role of ensuring a peaceful power-sharing between the factions. Where genocide, ethnic expulsion, or coercive assimilation have taken place, or seem inevitable, "power sharing is often recommended" McEvoy and O'Leary (2013). As per the existential dilemma, warring factions need to persuade each other and the citizens that they are ready to share supremacy through the alternation of power. In addition to the existential dilemma and the requirement of legitimacy for survival in power, they also need to persuade citizens that political lawlessness and violence will be eliminated if elected. Nevertheless, in the long term, power-sharing can become a source of instability and ineffective governance by an incompetent government. Hence, it would contribute to violent conflict and jeopardize democratization and peacebuilding processes.

In the past two decades, all negotiated settlements ending civil wars have included some form of PSAs (Jarstad, 2008; Mukherjee, 2006; Hartzell and Hoddie, 2003; Adams, 2010). Peace agreements in countries such as Burundi's 2001 Agreement, the DRC's 2003 Sun City Agreement, Liberia's 2003 Accra Agreement, Sudan's 2005 Comprehensive Peace Agreement, Nepal's 2006 Peace Agreement, and that in Colombia in 2016 have stipulated the inclusion of warring parties in government. Mukherjee (2006) appropriately asks why political power-sharing agreements lead to enduring peaceful resolution for some civil wars, but not others. Political power-sharing agreements were offered in 61 of 111 civil wars (54.9 percent) fought between 1944 and 1999. In 55.7 percent of cases, political power-sharing agreements did successfully foster peace. However, for 44.3 percent, the arrangement collapsed shortly after the first 24 months and led to the recurrence of war. Therefore, the effectiveness of political power-sharing agreements in promoting peace varies substantially. Most interestingly, in 39 percent of the successful cases, peace endured from 67 to 94 months only.

6.2.1 Power-sharing arrangements and five case studies: good or bad for democracy and peacebuilding?

Power-sharing divides opinions. Some defend it as a mechanism central to democratic values. Others believe it is incompatible with peacebuilding because it exacerbates tension between inclusion and exclusion (the horizontal dilemma) and the competitive nature of democratic systems (McEvoy and O'Leary, 2013). On the one hand, supporters of power-sharing argue that political power-sharing emphasizes proportionality in the distribution of the central state's authority while guaranteeing a degree of representation for collectives within governing institutions based on their group affiliation. They argue that power-sharing is a valuable tool for winning over all parties. As a result, it entices them to be more willing to sign peace agreements and commit to joint state institutions and a standard political process that would consequently promote mutual trust and reduce grievances. Hence, after war, some form of power-sharing is usually required. Competing parties cannot trust that the other side will uphold agreements entered into for forming democratic governance after a winner take all election that can make the losing side extremely vulnerable (Papagianni, 2007; Jarstad, 2008, p. 107). With some combination of the principles of parity, proportionality, and autonomy, political power-sharing safeguards both "shared rule" and "self-rule" among the relevant proxies. Therefore, consociational democracy seems to be the key to democratization in the aftermath of conflict. Jarstad (2008, p. 123) affirms that "power sharing could ideally work as a catalyst for peaceful cooperation among contending parties after a peace deal is signed." Moreover, consociationalism is expected to depoliticize ethnicity and allow the development of a shared national identity and moderation.

On the other hand, opponents like McCulloch and McGarry (2017) claim that PSAs are ineffective and inefficient in producing peace and stability as they obstruct other peacebuilding values, such as gender equality. Although skeptics of power-sharing agree that it is an important political strategy for managing protracted conflicts by facilitating the democratic accommodation of difference, they present the following five arguments for their disbelief. First, as a mechanism to end the war, some power-sharing agreements allocate and guarantee positions in government to elites and warlords who obviously would only be interested in stopping the violence if they continue controlling power "in democratic and peaceful times" (the existential dilemma). Including warring groups in government can facilitate peace as everyone can mutually rule through sharing power. However, such shortcuts through reserved seats are undemocratic as this breaks the fundamental right of people to choose their representatives through voting and making them accountable (posing a moral dilemma). Hence, elections become a redundant exercise. In other words, consociationalists are criticized for focusing too much on the setup of institutions and not enough on transitional arrangement issues that go beyond such institutions. By sharing power, some groups might, at the same time, effectively block other political movements from power by controlling economic resources and the media to mobilize political support (O'Flynn and Russell, 2005). Even if the government eventually opens the political space, opposition groups may lag behind due to their lack of resources. This asymmetric ignition of parties within a democratization process can affect, in the long run, the prospects of a multiparty democracy (which is a temporal dilemma).

Second, power-sharing measures represent an institutional barrier to democracy because former warring parties have strong incentives to garner political support from their constituent groups, resulting in a trade-off between efficacy and legitimacy for the peace process (the vertical dilemma). Consequently, wartime divisions are transferred into postwar political structures, which prevent democracy from taking root. Since power-sharing positions are often given based on the group's capacity for violence, this sends the message that violence will be rewarded. Thus, if the peace agreement is poorly designed, power-sharing can incite violence. For example, the Sudan 2005 power-sharing accord only included warring parties in the executive branch of government. Such an arrangement lacked any form of democratic legitimacy, and the only access to political power for those excluded was to return to the battle lines.

Third, some peace agreements might distribute state power among contending groups based on their relative power on the battlefield. If so, power-sharing measures may promote exclusion instead of inclusion (the horizontal dilemma) as they prevent fragile or *non*-warring parties from openly and fully participating in government. There is an inherent risk involved when incorporating actors, such as rebels or elites, who do not adhere to the democratic principles of nonviolence nor respect human rights.

Fourth, power-sharing hinders democracy by institutionalizing ethnic differences and making governance and decision making more difficult. It focuses on diverging identities, instead of integrating them. The very act of forming a multiethnic coalition generates or exacerbates intra-ethnic competition. Furthermore, rights are delegated to communities, leading to the over-representation of some and the under-representation of others. Power-sharing relies on cooperation between rivals, which is inherently unstable, and assumes that each group is cohesive and has strong leadership. However, both characteristics are rare in the aftermath of civil war. For Horowitz (1985), consociationalism can lead to the edification of ethnic divisions since grand coalitions are unlikely to happen due to the dynamics of intra-ethnic competition.

And fifth, when power-sharing is promoted by outsiders, there may be further problems of democratic ownership (the systemic dilemma). In sum, democracy and peace can be mutually excluded in a PSA if it is not well designed (as portrayed by the central and the design dilemmas). Hence, critics emphasize that power-sharing freezes the power balances of wartime, preventing the evolution of the political process, and closing the door to new entrants to the political scene (Jarstad, 2008; Hartzell and Hoddie, 2015; Papagianni, 2007; Curtis, 2012). Critics of power-sharing refer to arrangements as "leaderless," and "stalemated," with "deadlocked," or "blocked" decision making (McEvoy and O'Leary, 2013). Cyprus and Lebanon are two examples. Thus, power-sharing largely results from the institutional legacy and the outcome of war.

Five cases illustrate the imbroglio of power-sharing as a conflict resolution tool: Cambodia, Bosnia and Herzegovina, Djibouti, South Sudan, and Cyprus. First, the 1991 Paris Agreement provided former Khmer Rouge members with a legitimate political party in a postwar democratic system based on a power-sharing mechanism. In 1994, the Khmer Rouge withdrew from the peace process. Consequently, the Cambodian National Assembly criminalized the group, and an authoritarian regime (re)ascended a few years later. It is worth remembering that the Khmer Rouge killed 1.7 million people between 1975 and 1979; a fifth of the Cambodian population at the time (End Genocide, 2015).

Second, the Dayton Peace Agreement for Bosnia and Herzegovina effectively reached its objective of ending the 1992–1995 war. Nonetheless, the peacebuilding and democratization processes were inhibited by the power-sharing measures. The peace agreement foresaw a joint government with political representatives from the three main ethnic groups. While for the sake of efficacy, power-sharing measures overrode normal procedures for accountability and democratic legitimacy, the tripartite structure did not work. The international community had to impose laws and remove several politicians from office, which impacted the ownership of the two processes. The political system did not provide *stimuli* to form cross-ethnic and moderate political parties. International players suggested constitutional changes regarding the tripartite presidency and decentralization of the two entities, the Bosniak-Croat Federation and Republika Srpska, and other revisions intended to assist an integrated, centralized, non-ethnic parliamentary democracy with a single president. However, these changes altered the balance of power. Serbian leaders wanted to maintain Republika Srpska, and many Croats believed that they should also have their own autonomous area. The Parliament voted against constitutional changes in April 2006, and the case continues to raise questions about the sustainability of the state of Bosnia and Herzegovina.

Third, the Djibouti war represents a positive example of African peacemaking without external intervention and a peaceful transition after civil war despite being an authoritarian regime.[9] The United Council for Democracy (UMD), led by the Issas ethnicity, and the Front for a Restoration of Unity and Democracy (FRUD), led by the Afars, transformed themselves into political parties and incorporated members of the military fronts as civil servants and part of the regular army. Despite the fact that President Guelleh has been in power since 1999, when he succeeded his uncle, the only other president since independence in 1977, UMD and FRUD continue to share power in Djibouti's administration.

Fourth, violence and political power have long had an intimate relationship in southern Sudan, where rebels fought a 22-year struggle against Sudanese government forces and allied militias before signing the 2005 Comprehensive Peace Agreement (CPA). South Sudan became independent from Sudan in July 2011. But in December 2013, Salva Kiir, the South Sudanese president, and Riek

Machar, his vice president, entered into an open conflict, leading to a cycle of violence estimated to have killed 400,000 people in five years. In 2018, a revitalized peace deal was signed where the two main opposing factions agreed to form a unity government and share responsibility for the armed forces. But the 2018 peace process became a motor for violence in South Sudan as only one part of the peace agreement has been carried out: a reconfiguration of the country's governance structures. International actors have claimed that there has been a marked reduction in political violence since the signing of the second peace agreement and the formation of a power-sharing government two years later. But analysts, conflict monitoring groups, and local residents say the peace agreement has, in fact, caused a significant escalation in violence. In February 2020, establishing a transitional government of national unity (TGoNU),[10] with Riek Machar returning as vice president alongside his rival, President Salva Kiir, raised hopes for a sustainable end to the conflict. But commanders and politicians compete for power in a transitional government by fighting wars in the peripheries. After the unity government's formation, the Transitional National Legislative Assembly was finally inaugurated in August 2021, and violence resumed with the military coup in October 2021.[11] Additionally, political elites have used disarmament campaigns to disempower groups associated with their rivals, putatively under the guise of disarming civilians – a goal the international community supports – while changes to the way local government positions are rewarded have led to a crisis of political legitimacy in much of the country. It is argued that "the peace agreement has created a series of zero-sum struggles for power, in which local politicians are accountable only to the capital and not to the communities they are supposed to represent. Often, these communities become pawns in political games" (Craze, 2022). Further violence risks deepening a humanitarian crisis that has already left more than eight million South Sudanese in need of assistance and over 4.5 million people either internally displaced or living as refugees. The number of people displaced by conflict in South Sudan has cumulatively increased every year since the signing of the peace agreement in 2018, with 144,238 people displaced in 2019, 172,447 in 2020, and 223,498 between January and September 2021 alone.[12] It with worthwhile to note that National Salvation Front was a non-signatory to the peace deal. The 2018 peace agreement does not appear to have changed the basic logic of violence. Just as during the period following the signing of the CPA, violence has become the currency in which political power is traded. The peace agreement has caused other problems, too. Prior to the accord, local, state, and county posts were decided by state governors. Instead, all positions are decided by belligerent parties in Juba according to a power-sharing calculus. In sum, "the power-sharing logic of the peace agreement has meant the appointment of commissioners whose roles are to repress local populations rather than represent them" (Craze, 2022). According to Wight (2017) this divergence in goals and outcomes is explained by a failure to properly account for the importance of informal institutional practices, combined with the interference of strategic interests at the national, regional, and global levels.

As a result, introducing more power-sharing in South Sudan has not, on its own, led to better power-sharing.

Finally, the Cyprus conflict can be oversimplified by the Greek Cypriots' (GCs') desire for *enosis* (union with Greece) against the Turkish Cypriots' (TCs') desire for *taksim* (partition) (Doyle and Sambanis, 2006). In the relative absence of significant normative preconditions for settlement, including a lack of shared vision and mutual trust, federalism and consociationalism have been adapted to serve each side's vital security concerns and to increase each side's leverage in a future federal power-sharing arrangement in Cyprus. Thus, all UN attempts to solve the conflict include a bicommunal and bi-zonal federation in Cyprus. However, there is a very low probability that Cyprus will be reunited as a unitary state under a system of majority rule, as that is precisely the outcome that the TC minority fears the most. At the opposite extreme, a "two states" solution is unacceptable to GCs and faces insuperable international opposition. In effect, it would legitimate and make permanent the division of the island, either along the existing boundary line or along a new negotiated line. Consequently, this only leaves the options of a continuation of the longstanding de facto partition or a reunification under a system of power-sharing. The idea that GCs and TCs can be peacefully reunited under some system of consociational power-sharing, with federal or confederal elements, is one that refuses to die (Bahcheli and Noel, 2005). An acceptable system might yet be found if a change in the international context of the issue forced one or both communities to recalculate their long-term interests. Because the situation has been static for decades, the hope of those who favor reunification is based on the belief that the international context of the Cyprus stalemate has been fundamentally changed by the decision of the EU to admit Cyprus as a member, notwithstanding its division. As a result, it could be possible to reconstitute Cyprus as a single state within the EU and to equip it with new European-style PSIs. However, the TCs have calculated the situation differently: being outnumbered by their Greek counterparts by a ratio of four to one, EU membership would diminish their security, either by weakening or even removing Turkey's protective military umbrella or, if a condition of membership forced them to give up their own state, by making them subject to GC political domination. Although to date, no one has been able to create a power-sharing formula that is minimally acceptable to both sides, this remains the best chance for a successful solution. At a minimum, for a bicommunal and consociational federation to work in practice, political elites must be willing and able to bargain with one another in good faith.

6.2.2 Additional power-sharing arrangements: peaceful alternatives but not so democratic

To analyze in-depth if power-sharing helps make the transition to peace and democracy possible, the other forms of PSAs will be examined, respectively, military, territorial, economic, and cultural. For Hartzell and Hoddie (2015), military power-sharing seeks to distribute authority within the coercive apparatus of the state and involves sidestepping, establishing equilibrium among the opponents. However, this may obstruct the disarmament, demobilization and reintegration (DDR) process by allowing both sides to remain armed. Regarding the paradox of a warlord democracy, Wantchekon (2004) has reminded us that popular arbitration or democracy can only generate cooperation among elites when these parties are disarmed to avoid altering electoral outcomes by force. The mechanisms of military power-sharing consist of integrating the adversaries' armed forces into a unified state security force, either by a proportional formula that reflects the relative size of the armed factions or by providing a strict balance in troop numbers. While generally less appreciated, though just as important, the following separation of power provisions are also essential: the separation of civilians from military power, nomination from appointment, police powers to arrest and interrogate from the judicial power to prosecute, as well as federal governments from state governments or local governments from central governments.

Burundi is an illustrative case of power-sharing elements seen as crucial to peace after a 1995–2003 civil war, which killed more than 300,000 people. Since 2004, the Constitution of Burundi stipulates political power-sharing, with 60 percent of the Deputies from the Hutu ethnic group and 40 percent from the Tutsi ethnic group. Three seats are co-opted to members of the Twa ethnic group. Additional seats may be appointed by the Independent National Electoral Commission to ensure a balance of ethnic representation. Moreover, each ethnic group has its vice presidents to assist the president, as well as staffing the cabinet at the same ratio of 60/40 percent (Jarstad, 2008; Hartzell and Hoddie, 2015). At the military center, the state's security forces consist of an equal number of Hutus and Tutsis. Alternatively, military power-sharing can be established by proportional representation in the administrative and executive functions of the state's security forces by nomination to key leadership positions. Moreover, nation-building should look to build identity and the institutions of the new peaceful state. While power-sharing military positions might freeze the equilibrium between the forces in conflict, cooperation and dialogue still need to be fostered so that former belligerents become accustomed to working together in the PSIs and thus resolving their differences through institutionalized state channels. The argument is that this will build a stronger, more inclusive democracy and peace. However, merely training Hutus and Tutsis to march side by side and wear the same uniform does not suffice to build a state with a genuine "Burundian army" identity. At first glance, Burundi represents a successfully negotiated transition to peaceful governance through power-sharing and a justification for regional and international peacebuilders' involvement. Yet, as analyzed in Chapter 4, Burundi is non-democratic despite its new constitution in 2005 and amendment in 2018. In political and economic crisis since 2015, democratic gains made after the 12-year civil war have been undone by a shift toward authoritarian politics and violent repression against anyone perceived to oppose the ruling party, the National Council for the Defense of Democracy–Forces for the Defense of Democracy (CNDD-FDD). Notably, the Burundian experience illustrates international peacebuilding contradictions: in spite of international rhetoric with an emphasis on liberal governance and inclusive participation, Burundian elites reinterpreted this as an opportunity for stabilization and control. Paradoxically, international, regional, and local actors have produced governance arrangements that may have contributed to an "order" in Burundi that is no longer based on ethnicity competition but where violence, coercion, and militarism remain central (Curtis, 2012).

Territorial power-sharing seeks to distribute political influence among local governments. Under the justification of decentralization for good governance, there is a danger of creating territories that are uncontrollable by the central government by offering them a degree of autonomy. For example, as part of an effort to end the Sudanese civil war, the Addis Ababa Accords of 1972 provided southern Sudan with a degree of regional autonomy from the national government. However, this only lasted for ten years, after which the Second Sudanese civil war erupted. The Sudanese territorial power-sharing was not enough to restore peace, let alone democracy, and it resulted in the South Sudan referendum for independence in 2011. Additionally, as the case of the 2014 Peace Agreement in South Sudan illustrates, granting autonomy to a rebellious region might increase the danger that the relationship with the government will turn violent again.

Economic power-sharing attempts to address the question of access to and control of economic resources. When a minority ethnic group loses an election, it loses not only the administrative power in office but also the means for protecting its survival by not being able to access the state's resources (Haysom and Kane, 2009). Peace agreements might also design elements regarding the distribution of wealth, income, or control of natural resources or production facilities along a group basis based on proportionality. In the case of the 1999 Lomé Peace Agreement for Sierra Leone, economic power-sharing was established by creating a Commission for the Management of Strategic Resources and appointing rebel leader Foday Sankoh as its chairman. In that case, it is arguable that these "wealth sharing formulae" reinforced the "political sharing formulae" through some amalgamation of parity, proportionality, and autonomy.

The cultural aspects of power-sharing must also be anticipated. The goal of power-sharing not only involves the arrangement of political institutions to prevent a monopoly, whether permanent or temporary, of the executive, legislative, judicial, bureaucratic, and military powers. Modern power-sharing deliberately avoids the full-scale integration or coercive assimilation of "cultures" within the polity (McEvoy and O'Leary, 2013). Because so many civil wars are based on ethnicity and religious beliefs, policies, and practices of "cultural protectionism" are frequently designed. Altogether, the Philippines-MILF agreement presents an example of complex PSAs. After the Bangsamoro Agreement, the government had exclusive power over 58 areas, including agriculture, industry, labor, tourism, culture, language, education, sports, traditional laws, the environment, and health. The Philippine government has retained power in defense, foreign policy, currency, citizenship, immigration, customs, and common market. Revenues from natural resources such as waters will be shared (Nationalia, 2014).

6.2.3 Power-sharing in Kosovo: consensus, consociational democracy, or no democracy at all?

For Lijphart (1993), in highly polarized and volatile settings, the choice is not between consociational and majoritarian democracy but between consociational democracy and no democracy at all. The ethnic minorities' special status in Kosovo's constitutional regime is an example of how the consociational system of democracy can oppose democratic human rights to reach a stalemate of hard politics. Based on the rationale that ethnic quotas act as incentives for democratic stabilization after conflict and promote the integration of minorities in society, various power-sharing guarantees for ethnic communities have been introduced in Kosovo since 2001 (Doli and Korenica, 2013). As per the horizontal dilemma, "we the people" had to be classified and included through ethnic quotas in both the legislature and the executive and veto powers. Out of the 120 seats of the Assembly of Kosovo, 20 seats are guaranteed for non-majority communities, divided as ten for the Serb national minority; four among Ashkali, Egyptian, and Roma minorities; three for the Bosniak minority; two for the Turkish minority in Kosovo; and one for the Gorani community (Kosovo, 2008, Art. 64). Additionally, two out of five deputy presidents of the Assembly of Kosovo are required to be from minority communities: one from the Serb community and one from other non-majority communities and at least one vice chair of each of the parliamentary committee come from an ethnic community different from the community of the chair (Articles 67 and 77). The greatest deadlock is seen regarding the adoption of laws of vital interest, which require a double majority: the majority of votes of present and voting deputies from majority ethnic communities and a two-thirds majority of votes by the present and voting deputies from minority communities (Article 81). Therefore, as mentioned by Ardian Arifaj, when the Assembly discussed issues like the need for a Kosovar National Army to protect its sovereignty, membership of the European Union, or the demarcation of borders with Montenegro, these were blocked by the Serbs, following orders from Moscow.[13]

In Kosovo, communities also have guaranteed representation on the executive as at least one minister in the government must be from the Serb community and at least one from other minority communities. The same is true, on a proportional basis, for deputy ministerial seats. Besides that, at the local level of municipalities, the post of vice president of the Municipal Assembly for Communities is reserved for a representative in municipalities with at least 10 percent of the population belonging to non-majority communities (Article 62). At least 15 percent of the judges from the Supreme Court and any other court must be from the minority communities (Article 103). Minority communities also have reserved seats in the Kosovo Judicial Council. Additionally, ethnic communities are entitled to equitable representation in employment in public institutions and publicly owned enterprises at all levels (Article 61). Through these means, ethnic quotas have been established and are necessary for the inclusion of these communities in political institutions in Kosovo. However, reserved seats and minority veto powers have had adverse effects on stability, inter-ethnic cooperation, and the integration of communities. As per the temporal dilemma, in the short term, the national and local power-sharing mechanisms represent an incentive for minorities to accept the official institutions and pacify the conflict. In the longer time, these could help make representative institutions more legitimate (avoiding the vertical dilemma). However, this mainly depends on the quality of the representation rather than its mere presence.

Communities currently have legal powers to influence decision making, but being "protected like polar bears" limits the principle of the competition of power, and the inclusion of communities has not yet led to minority integration. According to Puhie Demaku,[14] a former member of the Assembly of Kosovo and president of the Committee on Foreign Affairs, it is believed that veto powers have a negative influence on democratic stability. A further point is that although it is "fair and democratic" that minorities are included through respect for human rights and equality, it is neither "legitimate nor democratic" that minority parties are so strong in Parliament compared to the percentages of their votes. With reserved seats, communities are over-represented as the minority presence in Parliament significantly increases, which causes a significant imbalance between the parliamentary strength of the majority ethnic group and their size in terms of the overall population. Nevertheless, the resentment of the majority (Albanians, who precisely were the minority under Serbian rule) is primarily due to such reserved seats and veto powers (which is a moral dilemma). As a counter-strategy to block approvals, the "Vetevendosje!" political movement used recurrent use of tear gas bombs to cancel sessions in the National Assembly. Additionally, political instability and resentment culminated in the disintegration of the government through a vote of no confidence in 2017.

The constitution of Kosovo provides for a broad degree of self-rule to ethnic minorities through affirmative human rights law standards – both at personal and collective levels (avoiding the vertical dilemma). While PSA at both central and local levels (dealing with the design dilemma) succeeded in including minority representatives in political institutions, they have failed in securing cooperation and mutual understanding. Even though ethnic quotas were needed initially after the conflict as a mechanism of including communities in Kosovo institutions, their negative effects, such as low accountability (illustrating the transparency dilemma), excessive use of the veto, and ethnicization of politics, may jeopardize their positive effects (Lončar, 2015). Moreover, Kosovo's state model was shaped under international supervision (UNMIK), which aimed to establish a state free from mono-ethnicity. It is regarded as both multiethnic and a state of citizens. Hence, contrary to the expectations generated by the power-sharing literature, ethnic quotas and a minority veto may not be a suitable mechanism for reconciliation. As illustrated in Kosovo, long-term democratic stability has decreased. Moreover, guaranteed seats encourage voters to vote for members of their communities, reducing the opportunities for multiethnic cooperation.

Finally, popular support by referendum after a peace deal or democratic model might be necessary to endorse negotiated peace agreements. It becomes more problematic when the arrangement is imposed by international actors as this unlocks the systemic dilemma between local ownership and international "expertise" in domestic affairs. In Kosovo, power-sharing was imposed by UN provisions without a consensus among the formerly warring parties. In contrast, the 1998 Belfast Agreement received the support of both communities of Northern Ireland through a referendum. The fact is that without popular support for the power-sharing arrangement, there is an exponential chance for it to fail. Thus, this delays all the democratization and peacebuilding processes and makes it a challenge like that of Sisyphus.

6.2.4 Summing up power-sharing dilemmas: positive peace and negative democracy

Power-sharing is an "anti-democratic mechanism." It removes the influence of the population as it distributes power among selected actors prior to any potential popular vote and rewards violence by granting positions to warring parties. This lack of larger societal participation and inadequate justice are reasons that both violate the principle of democracy (Jarstad, 2008). Yet power-sharing can affect peace positively by: (1) the inclusion of warring parties; (2) intragroup contestation; (3) international dependence; and (4) the leveling of power relations. On the other hand, power-sharing can affect democratization negatively by: (1) the exclusion of moderate elites; (2) a lack of popular support; (3) external intervention preventing local ownership of the political process; and (4) freezing ethnic division by group representation (Jarstad, 2008). Even though power-sharing itself is not inherently democratic, when successful, it may represent the art of the possible within a minimalist form of democracy (Hartzell and Hoddie, 2015).

Most elements of power-sharing do not require democracy to function, and they are present in non-democratic states like Sudan and former Soviet Union states such as Georgia and Ukraine. Military power-sharing in which government and rebel armies are integrated into a single unit does not require democracy in itself. However, power-sharing provides the assurances necessary to encourage rivals to play by the game's electoral rules and abide by the norms of a pseudo-democratic system (Jung, 2012). By providing a set of shared rules that can serve as the basis for constructing the rule of law, a transition to a consolidated democracy is probable.

The difficulties that post-civil war conditions pose for a transition to democracy are usually underestimated. Yet, it is precisely where these difficulties are the worst, and where the emergence of democracy is least likely, that PSIs seem to be most prone to be considered. As suggested by Pospieszna and Schneider (2013), there appears to be an illusion of "peace through power sharing." It justifies that PSIs should be advocated with great caution. They not only require constitutional design choices, but also because legitimacy is often deemed more important than efficacy in the aftermath of war.

While PSIs such as proportional representation or federalism cannot prevent a war from recurring, PSAs in the form of grand coalitions reduces this risk marginally. The power balance agreed on in a peace deal may be challenged later. Over time, there is a risk that the agreement does not reflect the perceived power relations, and some actors may even challenge it by force. Democratic freedoms must be guaranteed for their potential to change the government's political orientation or their potential to vote for candidates of different ethnic affiliations. Furthermore, PSA reflects power relations at the time of the negotiation. If power shifts change, there is a risk of conflict. For this, a "sunset clause" should be included, as in the cases of South Africa and Sierra Leone (Stedman, 2002; Papagianni, 2007; Jarstad, 2008;). Therefore, as an alternative to unblock the temporal dilemma, PSAs should be transitional. Nevertheless, once in power, a group is unlikely to want to devolve its power. Often parties in conflict demand a permanent share of power and are usually unwilling to agree to "down the road" provisions such as referendums on independence or partition. Thus, during interim periods, efforts should be made to expand political participation beyond the members of the power-sharing governments. Moreover, in other cases, the abolition of power-sharing is itself a source of conflict because the actors demand permanent regulations regarding government positions.

As for the horizontal dilemma, inclusion is preferable to exclusion. As per the design dilemma, an inevitable corollary is that the success of the power-sharing is concomitant to how it defines the PSI and PSA. The principles of parity, proportionality, and autonomy are key as well as proportionality in the separation of power among the legislative, executive, and judicial institutions. Metaphorically, "how the cake will be distributed" will define its sustainability and efficiency. Of course, as expected, political choices will dominate over technical and efficacy options.

The success is in the design of an arrangement that facilitates prevailing moderate parties and new parties to join. One approach is to stipulate a minimum quota and leave some positions in Parliament open to independent actors to ensure that voters have a choice between several candidates on each ballot. Moreover, regarding the sequencing dilemma, the PSI and PSA are usually established in a top-down way instead of a bottom-up approach. Following the resource dilemma, sharing power might be efficient but not necessarily viable when there is a lack of human resources or expertise. For example, some warring parties may have to accept taking control of the economic resources without the human capacity for this, leading the country into further poverty and restricting development, which once again can be a source of popular discontentment and return to civil war. The same rationale applies to political and military PSIs, which leads to a security dilemma. If the PSA fails, it will return to violence and, therefore, restrict individuals' safety and the possibility to exercise their political rights and civil duties. Depending on the proportionality of the design of the PSA or the establishment of the PSI, some public services might be compromised and favor their own supporters. Likewise, public security forces might be dominated by a specific group that ignores, denies, or dismisses the protection of a different political faction or ethnicity, either at the police station or when providing certain documents for daily life or traveling.

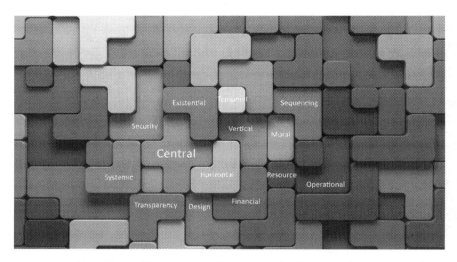

FIGURE 6.1 Transitional dilemmas regarding power-sharing: a puzzle. Source: Author

Furthermore, to maintain their existence in power, warring parties after civil war have to rethink their methods of funding as illegal expropriation, and the extortion of the population will no longer be feasible in the new power-sharing framework. Ethical minorities also have to rethink ways to finance their survival (both of which relate to the financial dilemma). Additionally, PSIs and arrangements are made behind closed doors. Thus, accountability and impartiality are in jeopardy as per the transparency dilemma. Finally, power-sharing will be susceptible to political changes and natural dynamic cleavages due to the art of political arrangement. If not robust enough, it will not be credible and will fail (which is an operational dilemma). In sum, power-sharing institutions and arrangements present elements for positive peace, but they might be negative for democracy.

Notes

1 Sassou Nguesso has held power since 1979, with the exception of a five-year period in the 1990s. In March 2021, he secured a fourth presidential term since returning to power in 1997, winning 88.4 percent of the vote. The election was marked by a

boycott from the opposition Pan-African Union for Social Democracy, intimidation, and an internet shutdown Freedom House 2022. Freedom of the World 2022: The Global Expansion of autoritarian rule.
2 Djibouti is a republic ruled by a powerful président, Ismail Omar Guelleh, who has been in office since 1999 and is not subject to term limits. While Djibouti technically has a multiparty political system, the ruling Union for a Presidential Majority (UMP) uses authoritarian means to maintain its dominant position. The opposition's ability to operate is severely constrained, and journalists and activists who air criticism of Guelleh or the UMP are regularly harassed or arrested. The president, who holds most executive power, serves five-year terms. President Guelleh was elected to a fifth term in April 2021. A core element of the 2014 political agreement – meant to end the opposition's boycott of the legislature following deeply flawed elections in 2013 – was a pledge to reform the Independent National Electoral Commission (CENI), which the opposition has accused of bias. These reforms had not been carried out as of 2021. Other electoral provisions favor the dominant party, for example by awarding at least 80 percent of the seats in each multimember parliamentary district to the party that wins a majority in that district. Ibid.
3 President Yoweri Museveni won reelection (6th mandate) in January with 58.6 percent of the vote while Robert Kyagulanyi Ssentamu – better known as Bobi Wine – won 34.8 percent. The preelectoral and postelectoral periods were marked by repression, with authorities abducting opposition supporters, disrupting internet access, interfering with journalists, and preventing observers from monitoring the contest. In 1986, he was the first of many African rebel leaders (as founder of the Popular Resistance Army (PRA) that then joined the Uganda Freedom Fighters (UFF), to create the National Resistance Army (NRA) with its political wing, the National Resistance Movement (NRM)) to successfully take power by force from an established government claiming to represent a new generation of African rulers: democratic and with no relationship to the corrupt and inept elites of the past. He pledged to rebuild the country, without the petty conflicts of self-interested political parties or the scourge of tribalism, while embedding his project in a vision of pan-Africanism Pham, P., Vinck, P. & Eric Stover, A. M., Marieke Wierda, and Richard Bailey 2007. *When the War Ends: A Population-Based Survey on Attitudes about Peace, Justice, and Social Reconstruction in Northern Uganda*, Harvard Humanitarian Initiative.
4 Amendments passed in 2015 retained a two-term limit for the presidency and shortened terms from seven to five years. However, the changes explicitly stated that incumbent Paul Kagame, who has ruled the country since 1994, was eligible for an additional seven-year term, after which he could run for two of the new five-year terms. This extended Kagame's rule until 2034 and the Rwandan Patriotic Front (RPF). That would represent four decades since he effectively took power. Kagame, an ethnic Tutsi, fought in Yoweri Museveni's rebel army and became a senior Ugandan army officer after Museveni's military victories carried him to the Ugandan presidency. He won elections in 2003 and 2010 and his Rwandan Patriotic Front (RPF) is the ruling party.
5 "Burundi: Peace Sacrificed?," International Crisis Group, Crisis Group Africa Briefing N°111, May 2015, pp. 1–8. Despite the failed coup attempt on May 2015 and the violent popular mobilisation against Nkurunziza's third term, he was elected with a turnout rate under 30%. The May 2018 referendum to alter the Constitution also brought violence and concern of a return to civil war. Burundi adopted a new constitution in 2005 after a series of agreements ended the country's 12-year civil war. The constitution was amended in 2018 through a referendum. Among other provisions, the amended constitution lengthened presidential terms from five years to seven, consolidating the rule of then president Pierre Nkurunziza – who had served three terms – and the CNDD-FDD.
In January 2020, CNDD-FDD insiders selected Évariste Ndayishimiye, a former army general and interior minister, as the party's candidate to succeed Nkurunziza

for that May's election. Ndayishimiye won 71.5 percent of the vote. The president appoints a vice president, who must be approved separately by a two-thirds majority in both houses of Parliament. The 2018 constitutional amendments reintroduced the position of prime minister. In late June 2020, Prosper Bazombanza was named vice president, while former public security minister Alain-Guillaume Bunyoni was named prime minister.

6 "DRC 2016: Why do the elections matter to the world?," Iaccino, L, Patel, R & Buchanan, E 2015, International Business Times _IBT UK, November 28, 2015, 09:00 GMT. In January 2015, violence erupted as the Congolese people demanded that Kabila respect democracy and the constitution by stepping down at the end of his mandate in December 2016. He originally took office after the assassination of his father, President Laurent-Désiré Kabila in 2001. Under Articles 75 and 76 of the Constitution, should the office of president become vacant, the chairman of the Senate would assume the presidency in an acting capacity. Besides that, elections have been postponed until 2018. The DRC has 24 trillion dollars of untapped mineral resources vital to global industries, which is more than the GDP of the United Kingdom and the United States combined. It contains the world's second-largest rainforest teeming with life, an estimated population of 79 million people and the potential to power much of Africa. Six million people have died in the DRC in the deadliest conflict since the Second World War IACCINO, L., PATEL, R. & BUCHANAN, E. 2015. DRC 2016: Why the elections matter to the world. *International Business Times _IBT UK*, November 28, 2015 09:00 GMT.

7 On 22 February 2016, a very contentious and debatable referendum was held in Bolivia to alter Article 68 of the Constitution and allow President Evo Morales to be eligible for the fourth consecutive term in office and to run in the 2019 election and potentially remain in power until 2025. This would represent nearly two decades as Morales took power in 2006 LA Razon, 2016. Resultado oficial: El No gana con una diferencia de 138.357 votos. *La Razón Digital*, 10:11 / 23 de febrero de 2016. Referendums in Ecuador (2008) and Venezuela (2009, 2017) on the elimination of the principle of the alternation of power based on continuity have also resulted in violent outbreaks, as in 2017 in Caracas. These have generated international concern.

8 The new CAR constitution created a Senate and a safeguard for freedom of worship and religious freedoms, barred members of the interim government from standing in legislative and presidential elections as well as limiting the presidency to two consecutive terms. As per the existential dilemma, the mechanism of the alternation of power helps to commit to the democratic process. The landlocked nation was ruled under an interim power-sharing arrangement with a Christian President, Catherine Samba-Panza, and a Muslim Prime Minister, Mahamat Kamoun, amid ongoing violent eruptions between armed groups from both religions. In March 2013, Muslim Seleka rebels overthrew the CAR President, Francois Bozize (Christian), resulting in more than 1 million refugee and thousands of deaths (Al Jazeera. 2015. CAR votes in referendum amid deadly violence. *Al Jazeera*, 13 Dec 2015, UN News Centre 2015. Referendum held in much of Central African Republic despite disruptions – UN peacekeeping chief, UN). Considered the most dangerous UN peacekeeping mission currently in place, MINUSCA deployed an 11,000-strong UN force in 2014. Part of the population has been supportive of the UN initiative and has asked for security due to being intimidated by spoilers who wanted to boycott the referendum. Two million people, representing 95 percent of the electorate, were registered to vote at more than 5,500 stations demonstrating "the strong desire for change," and trust that MINUSCA and the UN system would continue technical, logistical, and security support. Violent spoilers disrupted the process in some areas, including injuring UN peacekeepers. However, part of the population has accused the UN of a lack of impartiality. Although UN peacekeepers came from many contributing nations, mainly France with 2,000 soldiers, a large number were also provided by Chad, a Muslim country.

9 The 2013 elections marked the first time that the opposition had won any seats in the National Assembly.
10 Under the new Transitional Government of National Unity (TGoNU) South Sudan's President Salva Kiir nominated 20 ministers, while SPLM-IO's Riek Machar nominated nine ministers, Sudan Opposition Alliance (SSOA) nominated three ministers, Former Detainees nominated two ministers, and other opposition political parties nominated one minister.
11 In October 2021, General al-Burhan staged a coup, dissolved the TSC and transitional government, and detained Prime Minister Hamdok and several government ministers and advisors. Following the coup, local and regional government officials were removed and replaced, and General al-Burhan reconstituted the Sovereign Council with himself as chair. Although Prime Minister Hamdok was later released, reinstated, and attempted to replace officials appointed by the coup leaders, the military continued to control the government at the end of the year. As of July 2022, the TLC has yet to be formed.
12 Not including economic crisis exacerbated by heavy flooding that has displaced more than 800,000 people since May 2021 as well as COVID-19 pandemic (Craze, J. 2022). How South Sudan's peace process became a motor for violence. *The New Humanitarian*, 3 February 2022.
13 Mr Ardian Arifaj, political advisor to the former president of the Republic of Kosovo, Mr. Hashim Thaçi. Interview held at the President's Office in Pristina, on 20 September 2016.
14 Former Member of the political party "Vetevendosje!" Interview held in Pristina on 20 September 2016. The 2021 parliamentary elections resulted in landslide win for the nationalist party Vetëvendosje, which received nearly 50 percent of the vote – the largest electoral share in Kosovo's history and was able to form a government without relying on the support of the country's largest political parties.

References

Adams, J. 2010. Voting for Policy, Not Parties: How Voters Compensate for Power Sharing. By Orit Kedar. New York: Cambridge University Press, 2009. 240p. $85.00. *Perspectives on Politics*, 8, 1257–1258.
AL Jazeera. 2015. CAR votes in referendum amid deadly violence. *Al Jazeera*, 13 Dec 2015.
Amorim Neto, O. & Costa Lobo, M. 2010. Between Constitutional Diffusion and Local Politics: Semi-Presidentialism in Portuguese-Speaking Countries. In: PAPER, A. A. M. (ed.).
Bahcheli, T. & Noel, S. 2005. Power Sharing for Cyprus Again? European Union Accession. In: Noel, S. J. R. (ed.) *From Power Sharing to Democracy: Post-conflict Institutions in Ethnically Divided Societies*. McGill-Queen's University Press.
Bahout, J. 2016. *The Unraveling of Lebanon's Taif Agreement: Limits of Sect-Based Power Sharing*. Carnegie Endowment for International Peace.
Choudhry, S. & Stacey, R. 2014. *Semi-Presidentialism as Power Sharing: Constitutional reform after the Arab Spring*. IDEA and the Center for Constitutional Transitions at NYU Law.
COAR. 2021. *Conflict Analysis. Lebanon. National Level. Online*. Centre for Operational Analysis and Research.
Craze, J. 2022. How South Sudan's peace process became a motor for violence. *The New Humanitarian*, 3 February 2022.
Curtis, D. 2012. The international peacebuilding paradox: Power sharing and post conflict governance in Burundi. *African Affairs*, Oxford University Press on behalf of Royal African Society, 72–91.

Ditel, C. 2022. Beyond Lebanon's Power-Sharing. *Contemporary Arab Affairs*, 15, 6–18.
Doli, D. & Korenica, F. 2013. The Consociational System of Democracy in Kosovo: Questioning Ethnic Minorities' Special Status in Kosovo's Constitutional Regime. *International Journal of Public Administration*, 36, 601–613.
Doyle, M. W. & Sambanis, N. 2006. *Making War and Building Peace: United Nations Peace Operations*. Princeton University Press.
DRC 2011. *Constitution de la Republique Democratique du Congo*.
End Genocide. 2015. *End Genocide*. Online.
Freedom House. 2022. *Freedom of the World 2022: The Global Expansion of Autoritarian Rule*. Freedom House.
Hartzell, C. & Hoddie, M. 2003. Institutionalizing Peace: Power Sharing and Post-Civil War Conflict Management. *American Journal of Political Science*, 47, 318–332.
Hartzell, C. & Hoddie, M. 2015. The Art of the possible: Power Sharing and Post-Civil War Democracy. *World Politics*, 67, 37–71.
Haysom, N. & Kane, S. 2009. *Negotiating Natural Resources for Peace: Ownership, Control and Wealth-sharing*. Briefing Paper.
Horowitz, D. 1985. *Ethnic Groups in Conflict-Group Comparison and the Sources of Conflict*. ch. 4 and 5. Berkeley, US, University of California Press.
Iaccino, L., Patel, R. & Buchanan, E. 2015. DRC 2016: Why the elections matter to the world. *International Business Times _IBT UK*, November 28, 2015 09:00 GMT.
IDEA. 2017. *Constitution Brief*. February 2017 ed.
Issacharoff, S. 2015. The Democratic Risk to Democratic Transitions. *Constitutional Court Review*, Vol. V, 1–31 Juta Company. South Africa.
Jarstad, A. 2008. Power sharing: Former enemies in joint government. *In*: Jarstad, A. K. & D., S. T. (eds.) *From War to Democracy: Dilemmas of Peacebuilding*. Cambridge University Press.
Jarstad, A. K. & Sisk, T. D. 2008. *From War to Democracy: Dilemmas of Peacebuilding*. Cambridge University Press.
Jung, J. K. 2012. Power-sharing and democracy promotion in post-civil war peacebuilding. *In*: Leininger, J., Grimm, S & Freyburg, T (ed.) *Not All Good Things go Together: Conflicting Objectives in Democracy Promotion*.
Kastner, P. 2015. *Legal Normativity in the Resolution of Internal Armed Conflict*. Cambridge University Press.
Kingsbury, D. 2009. *East Timor: The Price of Liberty*. Palgrave Macmillan.
Kosovo. 2008. *Constitution of the Republic of Kosovo*. Kosovo.
LA Razon. 2016. Resultado oficial: El No gana con una diferencia de 138.357 votos. *La Razón Digital*, 10:11 / 23 de febrero de 2016.
Leininger, J. 2006. Democracy and UN Peacekeeping: Conflict resolution through statebuilding and democracy promotion in Haiti. *In*: A. von Bogdandy & R. Wolfrum (eds.) *Mack Plank Yearbook of United Nations Law*. Volume 10, 465–530. Koninklijke Brill N.V. The Netherlands.
Levitt, J. 2007. Illegal Peace? Power Sharing with Warlords in Africa. *Proceedings of the Annual Meeting (American Society of International Law)*, 101, 152–156
Lijphart, A. 1968. Typologies of Democratic Systems. *Comparative Political Studies*, 1, 3–44.
Lijphart, A. 1993. Consociational Democracy. *In*: Krieger, J. (ed.) *In The Oxford Companion to Politics of the World*. Oxford University Press
Lina, K. & Wallace, J. 2021. *Lebanon's Politics and Politicians*. Chatam House.
Lipjhart, A. 2004. Constitutional Design for Divided Societies. *Journal of Democracy*, 15(2), p.96–109.

Lončar, J. 2015. Power-sharing in Kosovo: Effects of Ethnic Quotas and Minority Veto. *In*: J. Teokarević, B. B. S. Surlić (ed.) *Perspectives of a Multiethnic Society in Kosovo.* Youth Initiative for Human Rights.
Mcculloch, A. & Mcgarry, J. 2017. *Power-Sharing: Empirical and Normative Challenges.* Taylor & Francis.
Mcevoy, J. & O'leary, B. 2013. *Power Sharing in Deeply Divided Places.* University of Pennsylvania Press, Incorporated.
Mukherjee, B. 2006. Why Political Power-Sharing Agreements Lead to Enduring Peaceful Resolution of Some Civil Wars, But Not Others?. *International Studies Quarterly*, 50, 479–504.
Nationalia. 2014. *Philippines Prepare to Grant Amnesty to MILF Guerrillas, Draft Autonomy Law for Bangsamoro.* Nationalia, 29.12.2015.
Noel, S. 2005a. *From Power Sharing to Democracy: Post-Conflict Institutions in Ethnically Divided Societies.* MQUP.
Noel, S. J. R. 2005b. *From Power Sharing to Democracy: Post-conflict Institutions in Ethnically Divided Societies.* McGill-Queen's University Press.
Norris, P. 2008. *Driving Democracy: Do Power-Sharing Institutions Work?* Cambridge University Press.
O'flynn, I. & Russell, D. 2005. *Power Sharing: New Challenges for Divided Societies.* Pluto Press.
O'donnell, G. & Schmitter, P. 1986. *Transitions from Authoritarian Rule:Tentative Conclusions about Uncertain Democracies.* John Hopkins University Press.
Papagianni, K. 2007. *Power-sharing: A Conflict Resolution Tool? AFRICA Mediators'retreat,* Vol, 2, 23–33. Centre For Humanitarian Dialogue. HD Centre, Geneva.
Pham, P., Vinck, P. & Eric Stover, A. M., Wierda, M. & Bailey, R. 2007. *When the War Ends: A Population-Based Survey on Attitudes about Peace, Justice, and Social Reconstruction in Northern Uganda.* Harvard Humanitarian Initiative.
Pospieszna, P. & Schneider, G. 2013. The Illusion of 'Peace Through Power-Sharing': Constitutional Choice in the Shadow of Civil War. *Civil Wars*, 15, 44–70.
Reynal-Querol, M. 2005. Does democracy preempt civil wars? *European Journal of Political Economy*, 21, 445–465.
Roeder, P. G. & Rothchild, D. 2005. *Sustainable Peace: Power and Democracy after Civil Wars.* Cornell University Press.
Shapiro, I. 1999. Enough of Deliberation: Politics is About Interests and Power. *In*: Macedo, S. (ed.) *Deliberative Politics: Essays on Democracy and Disagreement.* Oxford University Press.
Stacey, R. & Choudhry, S. 2014. *Semi-presidential Government in the Post Authoritarian Context.* Center for Constitutional Transitions NYU Law.
Timor-Leste. 2002. *Constituição da Republica Democratica de Timor-Leste. Constitution of the Democratic Republic of East-Timor. Part V_ Chapter.* 1st ed. Timor-Leste: Government of Timor-Leste.
UN News Centre. 2015. *Referendum Held in Much of Central African Republic Despite Disruptions – UN Peacekeeping Chief.* UN.
Wantchekon, L. 2004. The Paradox of Warlord Democracy: A Theoretical Investigation. *American Political Science Review*, 80, 98, 17–33.
Wight, P. 2017. South Sudan and the Four Dimensions of Power-Sharing: Political, Territorial, Military, and Economic. *African Conflict and Peacebuilding Review*, 7, 1.
Wolff, S. 2007. Conflict Resolution Between Power Sharing and Power Dividing, or Beyond? *Political Studies Review*, 5, 377–393.

7
NO JUSTICE, (NO) PEACE?

Democratic injustice or undemocratic justice in the name of human rights and reconciliation

> *Fiat pax fiat justitia.*
> Latin proverb
> Let peace be made, justice be done.

"Justice for peace" is generally a cliched expression describing the idealistic notion that the first would lead to the second. For Aristotle, politics is primarily concerned with the pursuit of justice. However, this chapter argues that in post-conflict contexts, transitional justice seems the pursuit of politics instead of about fulfilling the demands of moral and legal justice (Bachmann and Fatic, 2015). The need for justice often contrasts with the frustration about injustices during the transitional process that might trigger a return to conflict. Contrary to the idea that "without justice, there is no peace," this chapter demonstrates that transitional justice is part of a political hybrid process that displays both democratic injustice and undemocratic justice when incorporating human rights and amnesty. Opposing the common belief that transitional justice contributes to peacebuilding and democracy-building, the chapter argues that transitional justice can be as peaceful and undemocratic as democratic and violent. Under this assumption, transitional justice will be analyzed as an opposing force toward peacebuilding or democratization as per the equation: [*transitional justice: peace versus democracy*]. By juxtaposing the processes of peacebuilding, democracy-building, and state-building, and with the same analytical approach involving the dilemmas of transition from civil war, the chapter will examine cross-cutting elements such as amnesty, human rights, truth and reconciliation commissions, transitional law, and justice sector reform. These issues will accordingly consider the perspectives of *jus in bellum, jus at bellum*, and *jus post bellum*.

The content of this chapter contributes to the field of knowledge in two main ways. First, it advances the literature by identifying challenges usually under-explored.

DOI: 10.4324/9781003279976-10

Second, it advocates that transitional justice is not limited to the "will for justice" as a moral social need. It is an essential element for avoiding the conflict cycle and moving toward sustainable peace and liberal democracy. The Rwandan Gacaca Courts and the justice reform in Timor-Leste will be analyzed in further detail as examples. The chapter concludes that the process of amnesty might be a necessary evil for peace without justice. In contrast, the truth and reconciliation commissions, as well as the war crime ad hoc tribunals, might be pseudo-democratic variables for peace with some justice. The awareness of those dilemmas might be the missing tool to minimize the paradox between the need for transitional justice and the frustration of ongoing injustice during the transitional process.

7.1 Human rights: would amnesty ensure peace and democracy?

In disrupted states, an issue that invariably arises as part of the transition is how the perpetrators of past evils, both civil and military, should be held to account (William Maley et al., 2003). Logically, all sides in a conflict will provide the reasoning that their acts were motivated by justice. Even though amnesties might be legal constitutional prerogatives in many post-conflict environments, it is unclear if their use eases to end civil wars and encourages transition toward a new political and military status quo (Stein, 1994; Stedman et al., 2002). It is often taken for granted that amnesties are needed to bargain with rebels and prevent future fighting and are a motivation to lay down weapons. However, when amnesties have been used to end a conflict, a return to the battlefield has followed (Dancy, 2016). Furthermore, the process of rebel inclusion itself may hamstring the democratization process. This can be due to the constitutional use of amnesty provisions in the peace process or to limiting the possibility of other actors emerging and influencing what they see as a more just postwar political agenda (Pham et al., 2007). Subsequently, the deadlocks between fairness and unfairness lead to an unequivocal question concerning the debate on post-conflict transitional dilemmas: to give or not to give amnesty for a rebel group? Therefore, the use of amnesty, although legal from a legal positivism perspective, might result in several dilemmas between prioritizing the peace process or a democratic ethos, which are discussed below.

The central dilemma is evident when democracy and peace are in a stalemate. Amnesty is a political decision that might provide peace but under undemocratic pillars. Democracy comprises the rule of law, which may not provide "justice for all," but it at least supplies some essential minimal conditions for achieving justice through political rather than military means. An amnesty puts "some people or group" above or outside the law. With no compensation for the victims who survived, an amnesty seems a political, dangerous, and necessary choice for peace, but there is a strong argument that it is unjust. Thus, justice and democracy may also find themselves in opposition to the greater tension between conflict and peace.

In a significant number of peace agreements, from Angola in 1991, the Philippines in 2012, and Colombia in 2016 to Mozambique in 2019, armed groups such as the People's Movement for the Liberation of Angola (MPLA) and the Moro National Liberation Front (MILF) have been granted amnesty for war crimes (Nationalia, 2014; UN peacemaker, 2015). However, analogously to the argument in Chapter 3 that democratization cannot be a license to violence, amnesty cannot serve as a reward to perpetrators. Amnesties directly oppose justice as a demand and supply dynamic: people "demand" justice but the government "grants" amnesties. By suspending the usual procedural requirements and expectations of the state as a neutral arbitrator for justice for all people, and by the government offering an amnesty to those who would generally be punished for breaking the law, an amnesty is inevitably a contravention of justice. Pardons can perhaps help advance a process toward peace. However, they undermine democracy's legitimacy. Especially when the presidential prerogative is overused or misused, the potential to erode public trust is greater. The peace agreement between Colombia and FARC (2016) included amnesty for the rebels. Among other reasons, the peace agreement was rejected in the 2016 referendum because the majority of the voters perceived the amnesty not only as undemocratic, unfair, and unjust to the victims, but also as making the government look soft and powerless. Despite the rejection at the referendum, the peace agreement was still implemented as signed, including the transformation of former criminals into members of a legitimate political party. Thus, in the transitional process from a lawless state to democratic peace and social justice, elements of the rule of law may compete with those of amnesties and human rights (Figure 7.1).

The horizontal dilemma and the trade-off between inclusion and exclusion are at the core of this imbroglio: who should be forgiven? If amnesty should be granted, should it include those who committed gross human rights violations? Who should be included or excluded in the case of many rebel groups in the same violent conflict, such as in Angola, Colombia, and Nicaragua? If one rebel group

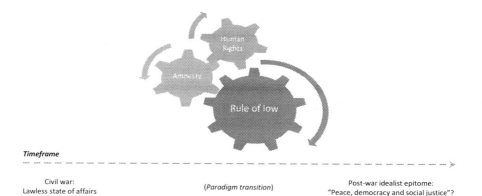

FIGURE 7.1   Contradictory elements of justice. Source: Author

is "included" through an amnesty, how can others be "democratically" excluded? For example, for peace in Mindanao, an amnesty was given by the government of the Philippines only to the MILF. However, the peace agreement might not suffice as other guerrillas did not join it (e.g., the Moro National Liberation Front (MNLF), the Bangsamoro Islamic Freedom Fighters (BIFF, former MILF dissidents themselves) and the Islamist Abu Sayyaf). For those who did not join, the fight continues for the independence of the whole of Mindanao (Nationalia, 2014). Similarly, the 2016 peace agreement in Colombia might not suffice as it gave amnesty to the members of the FARC, while excluding the other rebel groups. Interestingly, there is no amnesty provision for members of the armed forces because the government has not recognized the victims of such violence as "conflict victims." It is not in the military's best interest to require "amnesty," as that means that there is something they otherwise should be held accountable for.

The moral dilemma goes beyond any belief in pardon and mercy. Trying to merely copy the legacy of Nelson Mandela's South African model of forgiveness is unlikely to work as an effective recipe for all civil war transitions. The aphorism of "laissez-faire, laissez-passer" is paradoxically debatable as impunity and injustice should not be rewarded for the sake of peace and stability.

The vertical dilemma poses the trade-off between legitimacy and efficacy. Giving amnesty for war crimes, also implies the recognition of and grant of legitimacy to the rebels as political actors. The relationship between the free and former rebels with the population is shifted as, from now on, they will be equal citizens with the same rights. Hereafter, civil and military mutual responsibilities must be taken into account, reunited, and reinserted under the civil war reconciliation umbrella of efforts and governmental policies. The population's feelings of impunity lead to a security dilemma where the population is concerned by a possible rise in violence and no guarantee of individuals' safety.

The existential security dilemma is crucial when warring groups will lay down arms only if amnesty is given. Here, participation in amnesty might mean protection, but non-participation might result in prosecution. For the sake of their own freedom, they may agree to cease fighting if granted amnesty, especially when the prospects for an outright victory are slim. As long as the rebels act in accordance with the terms of the agreement that provides for their political power share, it might also be unlikely that they will face trial, no matter the magnitude or cruelty of erstwhile human rights abuses. However, if the rebels fail to implement the agreement, despite previous guarantees of amnesty, there is a high probability they will be held responsible for crimes committed during the armed conflict (Ozoukou, 2014; Soderberg Kovacs, 2008, p. 144; Stedman et al., 2002).

The temporal dilemma shows us that when an action is undertaken too soon or too late, it can lead back to the vertical dilemma of efficiency versus legitimacy, as well as impacting upon individual safety and undermining institutional security. Some authors argue that amnesty is more successful if given during war rather than after (Dancy, 2016). Once again, a decision between technical/constitutional/jurisprudential choices and political choices must be made.

But many more questions remain about the viability and desirability of granting amnesty. Should it be granted for all or only a few and, if so, based on what criteria and provisions? Should the severity of crimes that are given an amnesty be defined? Should the pardon be a prerogative of the chief of state, or should it rather be ratified by the Parliament or by a popular referendum? In other words, should a pardon be imposed or gained (top down or bottom up)? Should the pardon agreement be transparent or worked out behind "closed doors"? Consequently, these questions reflect three additional dilemmas: sequencing, design, and transparency. Not surprisingly, the parties directly involved in the civil war and negotiating for a durable peace agreement might have totally divergent views. These views may be worlds apart from the provisions in international law protocols on human rights, about the extent and scope of concession in issues such as what constitutes a war crime, arms control, the death penalty, detention, disappearances, discrimination, exile, freedom of expression, indigenous peoples' rights, refugees and internally displaced persons (IDPs), and sexual abuses as a tool of war and torture.

The operational dilemma contrasts flexibility and robustness. Either the policy is flexible to everyone or it is robust against all perceived perpetrators. No exceptions should exist. But the post-civil war context is a state of exception: a new reality is being built upon foundations of violence, the source of which is not yet sufficiently quelled for the more stable means and routines of political power to hold sway. Nevertheless, the danger persists that the amnesty may be perceived as a political circus for pardoning comrades and punishing adversaries. This inevitably exacerbates the already polarized population and might lead to a return to armed conflict.

Along similar lines, efficiency and viability, as well as present needs and future demands, are in place in the resource and financial dilemmas. While amnesty may seem to be a viable means for reaching a peace agreement that may eventually pave the way for a new democratic era, obstacles such as resource scarcity, including legal experts and institutional legal means, may still occur. One argument is that amnesty is necessary, as it would be operationally impossible to prosecute thousands of cases committed during a war (*jus in bellum*) and after the war (*jus post bellum*). Not only would the scale of human and financial resources required be unattainable, but it would be a great financial burden for new generations if resources for compensation and reparation were to be misused and if the conflict reoccurs in the new future.

Another problem is that the respect for sovereignty and the ownership of the process might also be jeopardized as per the systemic dilemma. The international community would inevitably attempt to influence its agenda by assisting amnesty implementation and monitoring its progression. Besides international organizations such as the UN, OAS, AU, and EU, a plethora of international NGOs, such as Human Rights Watch and Amnesty International, are usually in the field, with overlapping activities. The 1999 is an archetypal example. The UN signed as a witness to the agreement, with an explicit reservation stating that it does not accept immunity for war crimes and crimes against humanity precisely because the amnesty provisions were not applicable to "international crimes of genocide, crimes against humanity, war crimes and other serious violations of international humanitarian law." In May 2000, the RUF ambushed and abducted hundreds of the newly arrived UN peacekeepers, and the peace process broke down. Ironically, the government of Sierra Leone asked the UN for assistance in establishing a court "to try and bring to credible justice" members of the RUF for crimes committed during the conflict. This so-called Special Court soon became a model for an alternative to the ad hoc tribunals created by the UN. The first indictments were issued in March 2003 against the leadership of several parties that had participated in the civil war, including most of the top RUF leaders and commanders (ICTJ, 2006; Bellamy, 2002; William Maley et al., 2003).

While in postwar societies, and from a democratic perspective, amnesty might be a divergent path to the prospects of democratization (Baker, 2001), amnesties alone do not seem sufficient to stop a conflict. They might put peace and democracy at a crossroads. In practice, as a tool for stability, amnesty places peace and conflict resolution *before* justice and human rights, not the reverse. As a preliminary conclusion, amnesty is intertwined with the 14 dilemmas portrayed in this book where choices for peace can limit democracy and vice versa. Notably, the opposite is also the case: undemocratic and unjust choices can undermine human rights. Amnesty is not the result of applying a principle of justice but of political compromise that rewards perpetrators and violence with impunity and may even facilitate a return to violence. Furthermore, if justice matters for liberal democracy, investigation of the truth and human rights abuses are usually considered necessary in the post-civil war agenda of priorities. This will be analyzed next.

7.2 Justice matters: Truth and reconciliation commission and ad hoc tribunals

In theory, peace and justice should not be seen as separate goals. Nevertheless, in practice, they often are. Thus, although amnesties might not work and political compromise is necessary, institutional elements of justice are still essential to advance a democratic culture and establish a legal order. Ideally, institutional mechanisms need to provide victims with a sense of justice and, thus, put an end to a culture of impunity by offering an essential focus for reconstructing the judiciary and the criminal justice system in conformity with the principles of the rule of law (Kritz, 2001). Contrary to the forgiveness rationale of an amnesty placing peace *before* justice, building a stable peace in the post-conflict stage ideally requires, in the long term, an approach that places justice *prior* to peace by stressing the urge to prosecute abuses committed during the war. It is arguable that only by publicly and collectively acknowledging the horror of past human rights violations can a country set up the rule of law and a culture of human rights toward reconciliation. The establishment of truth and reconciliation commissions and war tribunals is an example of attempts to reconcile the two goals: truth commissions are responsible for gathering evidence of abuses committed during a war. In contrast, tribunals are responsible for judging them. Truth commissions and tribunals are dealing with *jus in bellum* even though operating within a *post bellum* scenario. In this section, truth and reconciliation commissions and war crime ad hoc tribunals are analyzed together because they face the same intertwined set of peacebuilding and democratization dilemmas.

Based on the central dilemma, bringing the offenders to justice might oppose efforts to build peace by prioritizing democracy. Furthermore, the moral dilemma is important, as the nature of duty, and the obligation to investigate, punish, and provide justice versus prioritizing the outcomes of the decision may create more violence and injustice. The existential dilemma is also paramount: in order to defend their existence, rebel forces may feel that they might face trial, condemnation, and incarceration, and thus they are inclined to violently oppose the establishment of truth and reconciliation commissions and/or war crime ad hoc tribunals.

Following the vertical dilemma, justice processes must not only be efficacious. They also need to be perceived as legitimate by the domestic population and international players involved. Elites and political parties might often advocate for no truth commission at all or for a model with minimal powers or no operational resources. As per the transparency dilemma, domestic prosecutions and truth commissions' activities are often not impartial. Additionally, if they follow a democratic rationale, they require providing extensive information to the population via radio, newspapers, television, or the internet. However, the media can be as helpful as it can be harmful if the information transmitted limits or influences the investigative procedure.

As per the systemic dilemma, the ownership of restoring justice is crucial and usually falls into international hands instead of local ones. Very often, war tribunals and truth commissions are led by international judges and foreign experts. They might also include a corps of forensic pathologists, such as DNA and ballistic testers, who are required for mass grave exhumations to collect evidence of genocide (Plunkett, 2003, p. 218). This raises the combination of two additional dilemmas: resources and finances. With a vacuum of expert human resources and financial facilities, while local ownership would be more legitimate, in all likelihood it is neither efficient nor viable. Moreover, the search for justice may well create the impression of unfairness. On the one hand, the will to seek the truth and bring closure to the death of beloved ones is understandable. But, on the other hand, truth does not bring back the dead. Thus, it is arguable that instead of expending financial and human resources on the past by excavating tombs and disinterring cadavers, some would argue that it would be more suitable to invest in education and health for the future of the survivors and the next generation.

This leads to an operational dilemma between robustness and rigidity for the following reasons. First, it is not possible to seek "for half the truth" or "partial justice." Truth and reconciliation commissions and war crime ad hoc tribunals must be robust in their endeavors against atrocities despite the need for flexibility due to the extreme circumstances and political interests involved. Second, cross-cultural sensitivities and religious beliefs may also contribute to the flexibility or rigidity required for these investigatory techniques. Third, with a huge amount of cases, it is usually operationally impossible to investigate and judge them all. But this also leads back to the moral dilemma, as justice should not be haphazardly applied.

Furthermore, a temporal dilemma is present in three distinct ways. First, the realization of justice is a long-term process, but people want "justice now." This urgency calls for short-term resolution. A key challenge to overcoming the temporal difficulty is the gathering of evidence and expert and impartial analysis. Second, many truth commissions and tribunals, such as the International Criminal Tribunals for the Former Yugoslavia and for Rwanda and the truth commissions in El Salvador, Sri Lanka, and Timor-Leste, have been ad hoc; therefore, their mandates have lacked institutional longevity. Third, it might not be in the political interests of the current power holder to immediately seek the truth. Developments in international law and war crimes, such as the adoption in 1998 of the Rome Statute for an International Criminal Court, which came into existence in 2002 (ICC, 2015), were attempts to grapple with such quandaries.[1] Similarly, in the same year, the truth commission in Rwanda was converted into a permanent body. Additionally, if the processes take too long, this leads to a security dilemma. A citizen's perspective of (in)security will prevail if the truth is not revealed and if perpetrators are set free rather than subjected to a "fair" trial.

Moreover, by prioritizing political choices over technical ones, these institutions can be designed to be empty shells: having only a limited mandate with no financial or human resources. Therefore, a design dilemma can be identified. For example, the institutions can be punitive or non-punitive, conducted by the military or by civilians, while testimony can be mandatory or voluntary, and the investigators may have the obligation to disclose everything they discover, while others may not be so obligated. Moreover, the members can be exclusively nominated and controlled by the head of state, or through a meritocratic selection process. Consequently, this leads to the horizontal dilemma, which corresponds to the impasse of who should be investigated by the truth commission or condemned by the tribunals. For example, should they only include atrocities committed by military actors and rebels or should they include civilians as well? Likewise, should they only include state actors, or should non-state actors also count? Who should be investigated or prosecuted first? The sequencing dilemma is obvious: from a bottom-up or top-down perspective, the legitimacy of the process and empowerment of the institutions can be compromised entirely if only the leaders or the bottom down hierarchy are accountable for the investigation.

With respect to all the points made above, Rwanda is a quintessential case study enabling us to apply the P–A–T theoretical framework. Almost a million people died in the 1994 genocide, and around 125,000 people who were accused of participating in the genocide were imprisoned (International Crisis Group,

2002; Sarkin, 1998). No non-totalitarian judicial system anywhere in the world, and certainly not in Rwanda in the aftermath of conflict, has been designed to deal with such a large scale of indictments. Likewise, the human, financial, and other resources required to carry through these prosecutions and incarcerations created a great financial burden for the state, significantly affecting its capacity for productive growth. Moreover, in the case of Rwanda, both Hutus and Tutsis must be investigated. If all cases are included, efficiency, time, viability, resources, and transparency are demanded. If it excludes some cases, morality and legitimacy are seen as questionable. On the one hand, both are essential for dealing with the pain and suffering of the victims. On the other hand, such an enormous number of prisoners, a disproportionately small number of prisons, and those with problematic infrastructure conditions result in human rights questions.

The ongoing animosity and retributive violence between the current and former governments and their respective followers is evidence that the power-sharing status quo might not be functioning. Moreover, the Rwandan government is not prepared to channel all responsible parties through the traditional legal system. As per the legitimacy of the vertical dilemma, attempts to do so have led to an escalation in human rights violations, resentment, and distrust of the system among both victims and offenders. As reflected by the security dilemma, even if the system had the capacity, it does not provide victims with a means of telling their stories and voicing their hostilities in a controlled and non-violent manner. As portrayed by the horizontal dilemma, they are not participants in the process and, therefore, their chances of psychological assistance are severely limited.

Accordingly, a properly constituted commission should generate public awareness of what really happened. Additionally, because a large percentage of the Rwandan people are rural, illiterate, and poor, the use of radio broadcasts has been essential for reaching the widest possible audience. This is necessary for countering the extensive propaganda being circulated by the displaced Hutu leadership that denies the genocide and entrenches the belief among the perpetrators that they were only acting in self-defense. According to the existential dilemma, based on a historical revisionism of genocide denial, there is a tendency of the Hutus at the same time to justify their actions based on their own perceived or feared losses of property, prestige, position, security, and self-esteem, which turns perpetrator and victim upside down (International Crisis Group, 2002; Sarkin, 1998). Thus, transparency and existential dilemmas lead to a moral interrogation: genocide negation is a second cruel nightmare for survivors and families of victims in a process where first comes the deed, then the pain, and finally the moral affront of denial. The strategy is to avoid the obvious: punishment. Based on Article 11 of the Universal Declaration of Human Rights, all accused have the right to defence (OHCHR-UN, 1948). Nevertheless, some argue "what genocide?" (Reuchamps, 2008). Therefore, they cannot be convicted of crime of genocide because genocide had not been carried out at all. Moreover, in a manner reminiscent of George Orwell's statement that the man who controls the past controls the future, the government not only exercises control over the reconciliation process, but also the narrative of what and how it should be remembered as it uses the term "genocidaire" explicit to relate to Hutus. For the temporal dilemma, not only is the process long, but also, depending on who is in power and jointly with the existential dilemma, it might not be in their political interest to immediately show the truth. As for sequencing, either by a top-down or bottom-up approach, it must be decided who should be held to account first. The Rwandan government alleged that the process should begin at the local level to bring communities together in moving toward reconciliation and social reinsertion. However, it failed to hold responsible those who are guilty, and no real reconciliation was offered for the survivors as no consensus was reached on "what" they are reconciling on (Hayman, 2009; Dallaire, 2005).

7.3 *Leges inter arma silent*: in the limbo between traditional and legal justice systems

A truth and reconciliation commission or ad hoc tribunals can facilitate a national catharsis (Sarkin, 1998). An alternative is to make use of traditional community-based mechanisms. Transitional justice is a significant issue that encapsulates the conflict between peace and democracy after a civil war as it might enable peace, but this differs from reconciliation. On rebuilding the rule of law, a legal axiom affirms that "amidst the clash of arms, the laws are silent."[2] At the time and place of actual conflict (*locus belli*), the rule of law is on "hold." After the war, a relative lawless situation prevails. This may be due to an absence of law enforcement or because of a conflict between the traditional mores and the legal system. There may be a conflict between a legal system that is rooted in the former rule of the former oppressor and that of the new regime to come. Contrary to what we have identified in the previous sections of this chapter on amnesty, the justice discussed hereafter stands *post bellum* as the creation of a legitimate legal basis is sought for moving to a stable and enduring democracy (William Maley et al., 2003). Examples of transitional justice decisions vary from fundamental choices, such as the kind of penal code to be adopted (Roman or common law), to much more simple issues, such as on which side of the road to drive. Beyond politics, culture and identity are key players as decisions might be associated with the identity of the oppressor or the previous status quo. Transitioning from war to democratic peace requires some hard political and operational choices. Some are related to "when, where, who, and why" (a moral dilemma *for* holding a political trial), others to "what, how, whose, which, how many, and how much" (dilemmas arising *from* the trial itself). This section is exclusively focused on applying the P–A–T set of proposed dilemmas commonly faced in the transition from a traditional system of justice to a justice system.

Traditional justice is not a substitute for legal justice but must work as a prelude to a national truth and reconciliation process (Sarkin, 1998). The former can bring justice, the latter can seek the truth; both are crucial ingredients of a peaceful and democratic future (Reuchamps, 2008, p. 1). Rwanda is a classic example of the dilemmas between the two systems. In 2002, Rwanda's traditional Gacaca courts were revived as a way to process the millions of criminal cases that arose following the 1994 genocide against the Tutsi. The word "Gacaca" refers to "a bed of soft green grass" on which a community and leaders known for their integrity and wisdom gathered to discuss and resolve conflicts. The traditional dispute resolution system dealt with issues within or between families and members of the same community. If the parties were not happy, they could take their case to the chief or even the king. Those who were accused of lesser crimes (participation, profiting through seizing Tutsi property, etc.) were put on trial in Gacaca courts and those accused of organizing and leading the genocide were referred to the International Criminal Tribunal. Gacaca courts and a truth commission are complementary and are similar to nearly all systems of traditional law: they are conditional upon culture and established upon principles of ethics and reverence for ancestral wisdom. According to the National Commission for the Fight against Genocide (NCFG-Rwanda, 2018), over the decade from 2002 to 2012, almost 2 million genocide-related cases were tried through Gacaca courts. Gacaca is arguably the most extensive post-conflict justice system in human history. The courts produced an enormous archive of documents and audiovisual files related to their work and the genocide. Another outcome of this traditional conflict resolution system is that perpetrators cooperated by telling survivors where their deceased relatives' bodies could be found so that these could be exhumed and reburied with dignity. Consequently, genocide memorials have been built all over the country and, in most cases, they are designed to harbor the remains. Thus, the Gacaca courts are credited with laying the foundation for peace, reconciliation, and unity in Rwanda (NCFG-Rwanda, 2018).

Transitional mechanisms of conflict resolution can bring justice and humans rights into effect, nevertheless with several challenges. The body of literature on justice reform tends to agree with three common recommendations on lessons for best practice when using the traditional system after the armed Conflict. First, they should be used as an interim measure. Second, they should be mostly led by national ownership alongside considerable international legal aid expertise, as Plunkett (2003) well expresses below. Third, they should be used at the local level to ease and speed up the resolution of some of the vast number of cases and alleviate the pressure on the courts and prisons.

> The rule of law is like a giant wall tapestry, whose fabric is woven over time from the many threads of different laws and various rules. Armed Conflict may tear the tapestry to shreds. The task for the peacekeeper is to see what can be done to pick up the remnant pieces, (…) so as to help the people to re-weave it themselves back into their *own* rule of law.
>
> *(Plunkett, 2003 p. 212, emphasis added)*

It is fundamental in peace operations that the establishment or restoration of the rule of law must take priority over the constitutional settlement. Two broad models are available to assist the reconstruction of a legal system: enforcement and negotiation (Plunkett, 2003, p. 9). The first model involves establishing a functioning criminal justice system and a criminal justice commission, employing legitimate minimal and lawfully sanctioned coercive measures. These include arrest, prosecution, detention, and trial by war crimes tribunals and transitional UN peace operations courts; techniques of public shaming and office disqualification by peace operation criminal justice commissions; and the rebuilding, resourcing, and training of local judges, police, prosecutors, defenders, and custodial officers. The second model seeks to engage the local population in bringing about fundamental shifts in consciousness, securing voluntary compliance by negotiating with local actors to facilitate community participation. It involves assessment, monitoring, evaluation, education, and the joint rule of law training, to replace the culture of violence with agreed upon management systems. This training is needed at the elite leadership level and the functionary and village level. Two types of work techniques exist: the Rapid Participatory Rule of Law Appraisal, which is designed to assess the real needs of locals so that they can be properly addressed, and the Rule of Law Participatory Assessment, Monitoring, and Evaluation setting of baselines for performance by which the achievements of institutions set up pursuant to the enforcement model can be evaluated (William Maley et al., 2003, p. 9). Although not perfect, it would generally be preferable to use the two models to complement each other.

While the absence of conflict can be possible without democracy, in this case, it can be envisioned that there can be peace with traditional law. As per the central dilemma, if democracy is chosen, it requires another judicial method to keep public order and space for a stable social coexistence. In a country without a functioning tax system, the cost of operating an entire judiciary is usually problematic when compared to maintaining the traditional system with local community leaders. However, it is cheaper than the high cost of maintaining a military structure at war. Provisions for secure salaries for the judges, court staff, prosecutors, defenders, police, and correctional and custodial officers must be provided. In cases of extreme poverty and starvation through war, in line with prisoners' human rights for dignity, criminals may be better housed, fed, and kept safe from violence and weather than war victims in nearby villages. This also provides an incentive to restore the cycle of violence and crime in order to be taken into custody. There is also the danger of widespread perceptions among the population of general unfairness. The traditional system might be cheaper, faster, and perceived as more legitimate by the local community. Where there is sufficient cultural and religious unity, an appeal to traditional cultural and religious beliefs might be more helpful for reintegration and conciliation when inclusive, transparent, and impartial, as it is done publicly by the community leader with all the parties involved. Therefore, it minimizes altogether the temporal, financial, resource, vertical, horizontal, and moral dilemmas. Notably, the traditional system claims to be robust enough to keep the social order and solve disputes but flexible enough to be adjusted and act as a tool for conflict prevention (resolving the operational dilemma). Nevertheless, and despite other political variables in the conflict, if all these prerogatives were accurate, they would have prevented the war from breaking out in the first place.

Furthermore, there are cases, such as Timor-Leste, Angola, and Kosovo, where previous laws and procedures are not unanimously accepted by the disrupted populations and warring factions even though a local legislature or executive government exists. To use the laws of one group over the other will imperil the neutrality of the UN peace operation and the success of a transition to peace as per the existential dilemma, in which the new conditions threaten the existence or power of some parties. If so, restoring the rule of law may fail and result in anarchy. Additionally, a UN peace operation can use existing local laws and local courts to enforce the law only if they reasonably meet international standards not to clash with other premises such as the Universal Declaration of Human Rights. Furthermore, the special legal needs required by peacekeepers to enforce order on a transitional basis invariably fall outside of domestic legislation. As a result, peacekeepers frequently find themselves entering a legal vacuum, legal chaos, or, at the very least, considerable legal ambiguity (Plunkett, 2003, p. 215).

In principle, everyone wants their version of "justice." However, in a post-conflict arena, the selection of judges, the penal code to be used, the language within which the trial is conducted, and the source of payment are basic dilemmas. In many peacekeeping operations, there is a complete absence of a legal culture and a legal profession. Effectively, to sustain the rule of law, law schools and bar associations will also need to be established to educate and nurture a corps of professional legal practitioners. In the absence of local judges, prosecutors, and defenders, these roles are taken by international personnel, who usually come from another legal system and rarely speak the local language. Moreover, the former local judges and clerks may have been raised under autocratic systems, and, therefore, they may have a distorted understanding of the nature of courts in that society. Consequently, this leads to the vertical dilemma of legitimacy versus efficacy. Although international legal experts are legally qualified, albeit in systems that may be alien to the country in which they are now aspiring to bring stability, the local population may not perceive the trials as legitimate. For example, in Timor-Leste, most trials were conducted by international judges drawing upon the Indonesian or Portuguese legal systems. The verdict was usually issued in English or Portuguese to a Timorese person, who might only speak one of the 32 local languages, such as Tetum, Makassai, or Baiqueno, among others.[3] When there is no effective local independent judiciary or police, and where existing officials are unwilling to act or where local officials are themselves the perpetrators of the offenses, the peacekeepers will be required to take on the tasks of the arrests, prosecutions, and trials of serious offenders. To add to the complexity of this legal limbo, peacekeepers must also comply with the UN code of conduct, which is usually ambiguous or vague for diplomatic reasons, although in line with international law. Thus, a systemic dilemma takes over as justice should be done with local ownership and within national parameters and interests.

Additionally, capacity building requires on-the-job training and working alongside special judges, prosecutors, and defenders, who will phase out their roles as the local courts are established, and their capacity is developed. This leads to two kinds of temporal dilemmas. First, it might take too long to develop these professional resources. Second, motivated by the high salaries of the aid development industry, some international experts take over the role and provide insufficiently effective training or no training at all in order to keep their contracts. Consequently, this second issue intersects with the moral impasse as professional ethics are required, particularly in post-conflict and humanitarian zones. Moreover, depending on the national origins of the international experts and the professional backgrounds they bring to the conflict, the procedures may lack impartiality, liability, and neutrality as per the transparency dilemma. Finally, corruption is cross-cutting to all issues and dilemmas addressed in this book on post-civil war reconstruction and reconciliation.

Moreover, the horizontal quandary is related to the inclusion or exclusion of war perpetrators in the new judicial system. As shown in Chapter 5, when a warlord may become a "democratically" elected president, his legitimacy is debatable. Analogously, a perpetrator of genocide who has received an amnesty can become a judge or prosecutor. Similarly, if horizontal inclusion is chosen, vertical legitimacy is jeopardized. Still, regarding the horizontal quandary, it is important to compare the conflicting viewpoints of the leadership elites and bureaucrats with the population's perspectives during war. Preferences concerning the system of rules radically differ between times of war and times of state-building. Bureaucrats may disagree as to whether they stress adherence to the authority of "the state" or to their "group or front" and such a difference undermines the idea of the rule of law having a legitimate source. An effective negotiation model for legal sector reform should directly and continuously include four levels: (1) the great mass of the population; (2) the military commanders, police, and local warlords; (3) the central leadership as the ruling factional elites; and (4) the peacekeepers.

A resource dilemma occurs when human and infrastructure resources are absent, which very often is the case. Police stations, courthouses, and prisons are often the first structures to be burnt to the ground during social conflict. Human rights watchers are caught between two fighting fronts. On the one hand, they require justice and the trials and prosecutions of offenders have to be fair. On the other hand, prison conditions are usually inhumane. So it is often the case that these same "watchers" end up fighting for the human rights of the same criminals who were once denounced as wrongdoers of war crimes and crimes against humanity. Additionally, it is logistically complex to issue warning mandates and to get the suspect, victim, or witness to trial. Courthouses and penitentiaries need reconstruction, maintenance, and the basics for running any state institution. Even electricity or toilets can be problematic, particularly in remote areas where the majority of the crimes were committed. The courts also require adequate administrative support and often the standard of education of the administrators may be very basic.

Timor-Leste, as the first state created in the 21st century, is a case showing how justice matters as well as how difficult it is to make an effective legal transition. From 1999 to 2002, as a UN protectorate, a mix of Indonesian, Portuguese, and international systems were dominant. Consequently, in terms of criminal law, Timor-Leste was subject to four sets of legal codes that at times contradicted and competed with each other. The first was the Portuguese criminal code, which itself requires reform. The second was the Indonesian penal code, which was enforced during 24 years of occupation and, thus, understandably conjured up bad memories for many of the locals despite their familiarity with it. Moreover, the Indonesian code is also very short, limited in scope, and, in many aspects, is open to a variety of interpretations. Its "looseness" also facilitates misreading and this, in turn, enables corruption. Third, there were UN regulations, mostly written by "experts" from industrialized countries, and many of their laws had no relevance to post-civil war situations or local difficulties.[4] Finally, there was Timorese traditional law, which was generally efficient, quick to implement, cost-effective, and legitimate for the community. However, it also had a downside: from the international law perspective, it allows serious crimes not to be treated with strong penalties. For example, a rape of a child could be sorted out with the compensation of a few piglets, chickens, or some community work.

However, Timor-Leste has demonstrated progress in the construction of the justice sector with several institutions in place since 2008, such as a Court of Appeal, four out of 13 district courts, a Public Defender's Office, and an Office of the Prosecutor-General. Civil and criminal codes have been implemented.[5] Of course, Institutions are not created out of tin air. It takes time, resources and political will, regardless of how industrialized or democratically mature the country is. Importantly, they are created in times of peace to mitigate conflict, not during conflict. Still, despite the improvement of institutions since 2002, the country struggles with several challenges. As of 2018, some national institutions were still not in place, despite projections by its constitution (Timor-Leste, 2002). These include the Supreme Court of Justice and other courts of law; a High Administrative, Tax, and Audit Court and other administrative courts of the first instance; and military courts. Moreover, the customary system is very powerful throughout the country. This is due to a number of factors, such as tribal traditions, practices, and rituals, as well as the fact that the Western legal system is not fully accessible nor accepted. All the above exemplify how timing is an important challenge for state, peace, and democracy-building processes (demonstrating the temporal dilemma).

Moreover, physical security for judges, prosecutors, defenders, police, and correctional and custodial officers must be guaranteed as this is essential for the transition undertaken by the peacekeepers. In the early stages and especially after the departure of the peacekeepers, they will be at most risk. If safety, impartiality, and legitimacy are not guaranteed, this interconnects with the transparency, moral, and vertical dilemmas. Particularly in the transitional phase, a proper witness protection program to ensure the safety of informants and their families is crucial to bringing about viable prosecutions. However, this also may require the

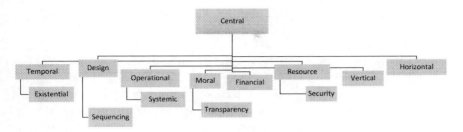

FIGURE 7.2   Dilemmas in transitional justice. Source: Author

permanent relocation of victims and witnesses, which is very costly and not viable due to a lack of resources in the aftermath of conflict. In some instances, this might involve protecting entire villages whose inhabitants witnessed atrocities.

Determining what comes first and how it will be done is vital for sustainable peace and embryonic democracy. Obviously, the arduous task of reestablishing a competent, independent, and fully resourced local judiciary takes time and must be implemented gradually. Therefore, the sequencing and design dilemmas are of fundamental importance in the reform of the judicial sector and its transition from a traditional to a legal structured system. This includes, for example, how offices should be designed. Courts require copies of the existing laws and basic legal materials and texts that are to be interpreted, translated, and applied. Prison custody programs, bail procedures, and alternatives to imprisonment, such as fines, community service, probation, and parole, where appropriate, also need to be implemented to reduce prison populations and public costs and speed up social reinsertion and reconciliation.

Finally, the existential dilemma is also relevant when considering transitional justice. Depending on each side of the conflict, actors will either endorse a structural legal system or prefer to empower the traditional rule with customary and more subjective procedures where they can survive and possibly hold power. Figure 7.2 illustrates the dilemmas identified regarding moving from the legal limbo created by the transition from one justice system to developing another.

7.4 Summary of the chapter

Although justice does matter, the motto of "no justice, no peace" is not necessarily true in transitional times. This chapter argued that in post-conflict contexts, justice is the pursuit of political choices. It contributes to the book's questions by presenting two main arguments. First, post-conflict transitional justice is a hybrid dynamic process: it can be equally as peaceful and undemocratic as it can be democratic and violent. Consequently, the reconciliation process is a mere sideshow if it postpones the transition toward stability and development or reignites the armed conflict. Second, although much has been said about transitional justice, a great deal of analysis fails to move beyond the dominant human rights, legal, or philosophical perspectives and does not sufficiently engage with war and peace studies and the political sciences. Given that postwar justice involves elements of volatility, uncertainty, complexity, and ambiguity (VUCA), negotiation through a set of theoretical dilemmas and their respective trade-offs may be the key to guiding fragile states through the transitional political process of reconciliation after civil wars.

Moreover, this chapter identifies challenges that have usually been overlooked. It also examines cross-cutting issues, such as amnesty, human rights, truth and reconciliation commissions, war crime tribunals, and the role of the international community. Finally, the chapter advocates that transitional justice is not limited to a moral need but is an essential element for avoiding the conflict cycle and moving toward sustainable peace and liberal democracy. The political elites must be seen as willing to help and support the justice system without exclusively promoting their own agendas to not jeopardize the independence of the justice apparatuses and the mechanisms for checks and balances. Furthermore, an amnesty might bring peace without democratic justice. War crime ad hoc tribunals as pseudo-democratic variations for democratic peace might result in some, or almost no, justice. As for the legal limbo in a postwar context, the traditional law might be the antithesis of the new democratic rule of law to be implemented and may place human rights subject to different arguments for the same verdict.

Disarmament and the reintegration of combatants is a problem of fundamental importance in states where the plowshare is an oddity to soldiers – both adult and child – who only know the power of an AK47. Additionally, the reform of a country's security sector is also essential in post-conflict contexts. This subject is addressed in the next chapter in more minutiae, with reference to the transitional dilemmas when the civil war ends.

Notes

1 Up to January 2016, 23 cases in nine situations have been brought before the International Criminal Court. Warrants of arrest have been issued by Pre-Trial Chamber I for Al Bashir (South Sudan), Muammar Mohammed Abu Minyar Gaddafi (Libya) and Laurent Gbagbo and Charles Blé Goudé are in the Court's custody for crimes against humanity (murder, rape, other inhumane acts or – as the alternative – attempted murder and persecution) allegedly committed in the context of post-electoral violence in Côte d'Ivoire between 16 December 2010 and 12 April 2011. Preliminary examinations in a number of situations including Afghanistan, Colombia, Georgia, Guinea, Iraq, Nigeria, Palestine, and Ukraine are in place by the Office of the Prosecutor ICC. 2015. *International Criminal Court* [Online]. Online. Available: www.icc-cpi.int/en_menus/icc/situations%20and%20cases/Pages/situations%20and%20cases.aspx [Accessed 04 jan 2016].
2 Latin proverb: *leges inter arma silent*
3 A real tower of Babel: Timor-Leste has constitutionally two official languages, Tetum and Portuguese. Additionally, 31 local languages are spoken: Tetum-Praça, Baiqueno, Becais, Búnaque, Fataluco, Galóli, Habo, Idalaca, Lovaia, Macalero, Macassai, Mambai, Quémaque, Uaimoa, Naueti, Mediki, Cairui, Tetum-Terik, Dadu'a, Isní, Nanaek, Rahesuk, Raklungu, Resuk, Sa'ane, Makuva, Lolein, Adbae,

Laclae e Tocodede. During the transition time, English and Bahasa Indonesian are accepted by the constitution as working languages. Moreover, Chinese languages such as Mandarin, Cantonese, and Hakka are also spoken by small communities.
4 Some law even mentioned "snow," although Timor-Leste has tropical weather. Its capital Dili is located at 8° 33' S, 125° 34' E.
5 As of 2016, district courts are only available in the districts of Dili, Baucau, Oecussi, and Suai.

References

Bachmann, K. & Fatic, A. 2015. *The UN International Criminal Tribunals: Transition without Justice?: Routledge Research on the United Nations*, Routledge.

Baker, P. 2001. Conflict Resolution versus Democratic Governance: Divergent Paths to Peace? *In*: Hampson, F. O., Crocker, C. A. & Aall, P. (eds.) *Turbulent Peace: The Challenges of Managing International Conflict*. United States Institute of Peace Press.

Bellamy, A. J. 2002. Pragmatic Solidarism and the Dilemmas of Humanitarian Intervention. *Millennium - Journal of International Studies*, 31, 473–497.

Colombia, G. O. & FARC. 2016. *Acuerdo Final para la terminacion del conflito y la construccion de una paz estable y duradera*. Peace Agreement. http://www.acuerdodepaz.gov.co/acuerdos/acuerdo-final.

Dallaire, R. 2005. *Shake Hands With The Devil: The Failure of Humanity in Rwanda*.

Dancy, G. 2016. *Are Devil Deals Necessary? Conflict Amnesties and Sustainable Peace*.

Hayman, R. 2009. Going in the 'Right' Direction? Promotion of Democracy in Rwanda Since 1990. *Taiwan Journal of Democracy*, 5, 51–75.

ICC. 2015. International Criminal Court [Online]. Online. Available: https://www.icc-cpi.int/en_menus/icc/situations%20and%20cases/Pages/situations%20and%20cases.aspx [Accessed 04 jan 2016].

ICTJ. 2006. The Special Court for Sierra Leone Under Scrutiny. *In*: Perriello, T. & Wierda, M. (eds.) *Prosecutions Case Studies Series*. International Center for Transitional Justice.

International Crisis Group. 2002. Rwanda at the End of the Transition: A Necessary Political Liberalisation. *International Crisis Group*, Africa Report N°53.

Kritz, N. J. 2001. The Rule of Law in the Post-conflict Phase: Building a Stable Peace. *In*: Hampson, F. O., Crocker, C. A. & Aall, P. (eds.) *Turbulent Peace. The Challenges of Managing International Conflict*. United States Institute of Peace Press.

NATIONALIA. 2014. *Philippines Prepare to Grant Amnesty to MILF Guerrillas, Draft Autonomy Law for Bangsamoro*. Nationalia, 29.12.2015.

NCFG-RWANDA. 2018. *Gacaca Courts* [Online]. Government of Rwanda. Available: http://gacaca.rw/ [Accessed 01.06.2018].

Ohchr-UN. 1948. *Universal Declaration of Human Rights*.

Ozoukou, D. 2014. Building peace or a fragile future? The legacy of conflict in the Cote d'Ivoire. *Insight on Conflict*, 24/12/2014.

Pham, P., Vinck, P. & Eric Stover, A. M., Wierda, M. & Bailey, R. 2007. *When the War Ends: A Population-Based Survey on Attitudes about Peace, Justice, and Social Reconstruction in Northern Uganda*. Harvard Humanitarian Initiative.

Plunkett, M. 2003. Rebuilding the rule of law. *In*: W. Maley, Sampford, C. & Thakur., R. (eds.) *From Civil Strife to Civil Society: Civil and Military Responsibilities in Disrupted States*. United Nations University Press.

Reuchamps, M. 2008. *What Justice for Rwanda? Gacaca versus Truth Commission? Working Papers in African Studies Series*, 256.

Sarkin, J. 1998. Preconditions and processes for establishing a Truth and Reconciliation Commission in Rwanda - The possible interim role of Gacaca community I courts. *Southern African Legal Information Institute*. University of Cape Down, 223–237.

Soderberg Kovacs, M. 2008. When rebels change their stripes: Armed insurgents. *In*: A. K. Jarstad & T. D. Sisk (eds.) *From War to Democracy: Dilemmas of Peacebuilding*. Cambridge University Press.

Stedman, S. J., Rothchild, D. & Cousens, E. M. 2002. *Ending Civil Wars: The Implementation of Peace Agreements*. Lynne Rienner Publishers, Inc.

Stein, C. M. 1994. Stopping the Killing: How Civil Wars End (Book). *Contemporary Sociology*, 23, 387–388.

TIMOR-LESTE. 2002. Constituição da Republica Democratica de Timor-Leste. *Constitution of the Democratic Republic of East-Timor. Part V_ Chapter.* 1st ed. Timor-Leste: Government of Timor-Leste.

UN Peacemaker. 2015. UN peace agreement database search. *In*: UNITED NATIONS (ed.). http://peacemaker.un.org.

William, M., Charles, S. & Ramesh, T. 2003. *From Civil Strife to Civil Society: Civil and Military Responsibilities in Disrupted States*. United Nations University Press.

8
SILENCING THE GUNS THROUGH DDR AND SSR

The securitization of peace or governance of insecure democracy?

> Si vis pacem, para bellum
> or
> Si vis bellum, para pacem[1]

The maxim "peace first" illustrates that security is the primary objective of armed conflict interventions. In other words, a sustainable peace can usually be achieved only within a secure environment. Nevertheless, peace agreements themselves rarely end violence. Similarly, the ending of civil war does not necessarily mean the end of violence. It is also mistakenly believed that the presence of security guarantees peace when actually the inverse is also true: peace guarantees security (Uri, 2008). Post-conflict reconstruction and security usually involve dealing with fighters in the aftermath of war. Therefore, to keep the peace or maintain democratic governance, the issues of disarmament, demobilization, reintegration (DDR), and security sector reform (SSR) are usually at the center of post-conflict agendas. Although DDR and SSR are frequently imprinted into peace agreements and UN resolutions, they are often poorly implemented (Muggah, 2008). This may be due to a lack of awareness on the part of core stakeholders and mediators as well as strategic decisions made by the warring parties. Moreover, civil-military cooperation in disrupted states tends to be complicated by weaknesses in their mandates or by mandates that are poorly focused (Terry, 2003). Additionally, the literature often establishes a strong nexus between security and development under the concepts of the "securitization of development" or the "development of security" (Muggah, 2008).

Studies on disarming conflicts provide evidence for the idea that peace cannot be won just on the battlefield (Regehr, 2015). By rethinking postwar insecurity under the premise of hybridity explored in this book, it might be possible to better identify the means to move from "interim stabilization" toward

DOI: 10.4324/9781003279976-11

"democratic security promotion" (Willems, 2015; Stahn, 2006). However, some gaps need to be addressed, such as the question of how new state security institutions should be legitimized by the national elites, the grassroots, and the international community. The process of preventing the continuation or further outbreak of civil war involves distinguishing between the "just enough" approach for securing peace and acceptance of an insecure democracy (Alden et al., 2011). Therefore, in this chapter, security sector reform is postulated as the contrasting force for achieving democratic peace after armed conflict and the transition toward a civil order, as per the equation: [*security sector reform = peace versus democracy*].

The focus of this chapter is the central dilemma originating from the efforts of building peace and democracy through DDR and SSR. First, a review of what we know about state-building and security promotion is given. Second, the problem raised in trusting the enemy is analyzed by identifying the main dilemmas of DDR and SSR. Finally, case studies of Central African Republic (CAR) and Timor-Leste's experiences regarding their security sector reform close the gap between theory and practice.

8.1 What do we know about DDR and SSR?

What do disarmament, demobilization, and reintegration, as well as security sector reform, really mean? And what are their main challenges in the post-conflict phase? The aim of UN DDR programs is to remove "the immediate threat to a fragile peace posed by groups of armed, uncontrolled and unemployed ex-combatants" (United Nations, 2010). They are usually implemented under short timeframes, from one to three years, during the "emergency phase" of a transition. Minimalist experts argue that it should be conceived as a short-term tool focused on security and stability. Maximalist experts defend it as a potential bridge to longer-term development. In contrast, SSR policymakers and practitioners focus on three main tasks for a sustainable "reform." The first is to restore order by neutralizing and delegitimizing so-called illegal, non-statutory armed groups (militias, gangs, community defense groups, etc.). The second task involves reestablishing formal state security forces to maintain public order within the rule of law, presuming the existence of a formal state. The third task involves restoring or establishing state institutions that oversee and monitor these security forces ensure compliance with formal rules and international norms. That involves an extensive state-building effort to include executive actors such as the interior and defense ministries, parliamentary bodies, the judicial system, and civil society. This is convoluted in contexts where the democratic political control of armed and other security forces has not yet been institutionalized (von Dyck, 2016). Thus, conceptually, some sources consider DDR as a subcomponent of the larger SSR agenda, while others view them as "two separate but related activities." Regardless of which concept, and in response to an increased demand for better DDR–SSR synergies, this section analyzes DDR and SSR together because they face similar dilemmas between peace and democracy in civil war contexts.

Very significantly, sustainable peace and development depend on people's perception of safety and trust in the state's ability to secure a social contract. One of the most critical and complex challenges confronting a post-conflict society is the creation of faith in state institutions through credibility and legitimacy. So far, it is clear that state-building is crucial for peace and democracy-building as new state institutions must be created and well designed to avoid the pitfalls of violence. Respect for the rule of law may face extraordinary obstacles. Post-conflict societies require establishing consistent and transparent principles of state institutions and people willing to respect the state's exercising of a monopoly on the legitimate use of force. Such outcomes do not flow naturally and require considerable effort. This is especially the case in territories where state institutions have been oppressive.

Nevertheless, building trust in the Leviathan requires not only transparent and operational institutions, but also a transformation in the perception of citizens so that they are better placed to see institutional improvements. The informal mechanisms that often emerge in times of conflict also complicate factors further, as they can create economic and political incentives that militate against respect for the rule of law (Chesterman, 2004, p. 154). However, if a society is accustomed to decades of brutality, it is exceedingly hard to discontinue a culture of violence. As Plunkett highlighted, "the military and police kill as the primary means to keep order, and the ruling elite kills as the principal means of political process" (Plunkett, 2003, p. 211). Militarized domestic institutions characterize this status quo. It is relevant to note Auerswald (2000) concept of a "disarmed democracy"; the behavior of democracies in inter-state conflict is shaped as much by domestic political calculations as by geopolitical circumstances. Variations in the structure of a democracy's institutions of governance make some types of democracies more likely to use force than others. Although there is significant variation among parliamentary, presidential, and semi-presidential democracies, the ability to signal its intentions, as well as the likelihood to engage in armed conflict is associated with how politically militarized domestic institutions are. The strategies developed in DDR and SSR attempt to create "order, stability, and peace" after war by empowering the state and are built upon responsible democratic governance, whose primary responsibility is to provide security as part of its social contract with the people within it. However, postwar politics tend to put public security at peril. As the case of Iraq and the subsequent formation of ISIL[2] show, the failure of DDR and SSR can jeopardize peace, state-building, and democracy-building.

In this sense, DDR and SSR both support ex-combatants becoming active participants in the peacebuilding process through a threefold strategy. First, by stopping the shooting and removing the weapons from the hands of combatants; second, by inducing the combatants out of old military structures; third, by reinserting combatants socially and economically into society. This last task is usually slow and onerous. It is estimated that from 2000 to 2005, over one million ex-combatants (also called "beneficiaries" by the literature) participated in some aspect of DDR promoted by UN and non-UN actors (UNWG, 2006). That leads to two further challenges: cost and transparency. It is not easy to gather final official figures or disaggregated data out of many hidden costs. Yet, to have at least a horizon of understanding, it is estimated the annual budget worldwide for those processes surpassed US$2 billion in 2007 (Muggah, 2008, p. 7). DRC estimated US$100 million for a third attempt to demobilize its militias in 2014, which again failed (Humanitarian, 2014). The DDR process in Colombia was initially estimated at US$2.3 billion (Colombia, 2016). The simple fact that actual financial figures are neither readily available nor accurate is a strategic political choice by those directly involved in the DDR/SSR processes. It also excludes the people from it by limiting means of accountability. This lack of transparency leads to a very common scenario of dissatisfaction. On the one hand, ex-combatants complain that they have not received "enough" for handing over their weapons and they do have the proper means to be reinserted or reintegrated. On the other hand, the general population claims: "where did all this money go?"

There are two generations of DDR and SSR efforts. Prior to the 1980s, the first generation was shaped by the geopolitical imperatives of the Cold War and focused on designing "right size" armed forces as an interim stabilization measure. The arrangements included the civilian service corps (Kosovo, South Africa), military integration (Angola, DRC), transitional security forces (Iraq-Sunni Awakening Councils), dialogue and sensitization (Rwanda, northern Uganda), and transitional autonomy (Cambodia, Mindanao [the Philippines]). The second generation is focused on gaining a broader understanding of security through sound good democratic governance. With the increase in liberation movements and with the legacy of "new wars," the demand for peacekeeping operations has also increased. As a result, there was a need to establish mechanisms to secure peace and allow democracy and development to follow. With the discourse on peace and security growing, the UN Security Council (UNSC) sanctioned a second-generation DDR operation. The first was in Namibia (1989–1990) to dismantle South African and South West African People's Organization (SWAPO) forces as well as ethnic and paramilitary units. Similar initiatives followed in Africa, Central America, and Asia, such as in Angola, El Salvador, and Cambodia, respectively. Second-generation arrangements vary and might include community security mechanisms for violence reduction (Haiti, North Macedonia), youth and gang programs (El Salvador, Guatemala), "weapons for development" (Bosnia, Mali), "weapons lotteries" (Mozambique, Congo), and urban and health population programs (Colombia). Additionally, SSR takes on different dynamics depending on whether it happens pre-crisis, during the conflict, or in post "internal" or post "cross-border" conflict contexts. As the African continent has the largest number of peacekeeping operations, it also has the vast majority of DDR/SSR operations (UN-DPKO, 2010).

In the fog of modern war, constructing systems of the rule of law under civilian authority is habitually puzzling. SSR must provide room for trust-building, information sharing, and security-enhancing activities. Despite the growing literature on this aspect, from Uganda to Bosnia-Herzegovina, there is little evidence demonstrating which models work, which do not, and whether DDR and SSR are effective in contributing to civilians' security or in promoting broader development objectives. Part of the reason is the absence of disaggregated longitudinal baseline data with which to render any statistically valid analysis (Muggah, 2008, p. 15). In some cases, as in the DRC and Haiti, collective violence had resumed soon after, or even prior to, when the DDR came to an end. Nevertheless, three main recommendations can be found in the literature that best encapsulates the efforts of DDR and SSR: (1) not to be overlooked; (2) not to be rushed toward a baseless short-term foundation; and (3) to be cognizant of dependency on international support while not jeopardizing the national ownership perspective. Table 8.1 summarizes the concepts, typologies and common challenges faced in the DDR and SSR process (Muggah, 2008; UN-DPKO, 2012; UN-DPKO, 2010).

Nevertheless, in contemporary SSR debates, security promotion efforts face strong criticisms. First, weapons and ammunition collection, although fundamental, do not suffice to promote genuine stability or security in societies wracked by war. The more weapons are collected, the more they can be smuggled, either internally from corrupt state members and power holding elites, or externally by states interested in fueling the conflict. Although DDR and SSR are necessary, progress is also required on the political and economic fronts.

Second, the gap between the expectations about those activities and their effectiveness is based on the claim that they are often too narrowly focused, inflexible, and technocratic. DDR and SSR are often implemented with additional activities such as international arms control, economic embargoes, and amnesties (see Chapter 7). Nevertheless, some argue that they are divorced from the political, social, and economic contexts in which such activities are inevitably embedded. DDR and SSR should not only focus on the repatriation of ex-combatants, but also on the so-called vulnerable groups, such as child and female soldiers and HIV/AIDS-affected combatants. The international community has begun to support a multidisciplinary viewpoint of security, taking into account the overlapping of other post-conflict priorities, including the development of a new legal system, economic development and job creation, health and rehabilitation for war victims and perpetrators, as well as the strengthening of government institutions. Thus, a new concept emerges in this field: reintegration, reconciliation, and rehabilitation (3Rs). It is an integrated alternative for effectiveness to be jointly implemented with DDR and broadly associated with governance, state consolidation, and economic recovery. In the southern Philippines and Aceh, DDR was associated with national safety net and food security initiatives and urban and rural housing renewal schemes. Similarly, second-generation programs in the Republic of Congo, Mozambique, Sierra Leone, Sudan, and Haiti

TABLE 8.1 Definitions, common challenges, and typologies of DDR and SSR processes

	DDR			SSR
	Disarmament	Demobilization	Reintegration	
Definition	Related to the collection, documentation, control, and disposal of small arms, ammunition, explosives, and light and heavy weapons from combatants and often from the civilian population	Related to the formal and controlled discharge of active combatants from armed forces and groups, including a phase of "reinsertion" that provides short-term assistance to ex-combatants	Related to the process by which ex-combatants acquire civilian status and gain sustainable employment and income. It is a political, social, and economic process with an open time-frame, primarily taking place in communities at the local level	Related to the process to ensure the development of effective, efficient, affordable, and accountable security institutions after war, as in the police and military
Challenge	• Ongoing armed conflict • Lack of political will for disarmament • Real numbers of weapons not easily obtained and verified • Initial commitment to disarming may be low • High number of weapons circulating in the community • Lack of legal framework governing weapons ownership • The proliferation of militias and fluctuating numbers of their members, thus difficulty in defining who is a militia member, which greatly challenges the generation and management of lists and baselines	• Often a poor understanding of the types of groups and organizations that are being demobilized (militias, clans, ethnic groups), as well as of their needs and agendas	• Reintegration is a much longer process than disarmament and demobilization • Lack of national economic recovery; creating alternative livelihoods and/or jobs is exceptionally difficult in post-conflict or conflict settings, with severely challenged economies • Big challenge to reintegrate child soldiers, who are usually also orphans	• Postwar instability • Lack of political will and trust as former enemies will work together to secure the country • Lack of understanding of the different roles of the police and the army • Lack of resources, training, and equipment • Lack of a legal framework governing the new institutions • Difficulty of coordination among domestic and international actors

Contexts	Context's focus and examples	
Pre-crisis	Focus on downsizing, "right size force"	CAR, Djibouti
During conflict	Limited demobilization and reintegration combined with amnesty	Côte d'Ivoire, Mindanao
Post "cross-border" conflict	DDR only	Ethiopia, Eritrea, Iraq
Post "internal" conflict	DDR +3Rs (reintegration, reconciliation and rehabilitation)	Timor-Leste, Kosovo, Angola

Source: Author. Inspired by UN-DPKO, 2012, Muggah, 2008.

also included comprehensive maximalist approaches at some point. Additionally, the case of the Tamil Tigers in Sri Lanka shows that reintegration was the key element toward peace. Nonetheless, the result was debatable, with low levels of reconciliation and rehabilitation, and, thus, it was significantly compromised in terms of democracy.

Third, beyond the need for a maximalist approach to DDR, there is often a lack of clear benchmarks for "success." While, in theory, demobilization seems obvious via stockpiling arms (characteristic of a minimalist approach), in practice, the link with reintegration is much more difficult (a maximalist approach). The social engineering – rehousing, resettling, and integrating former soldiers and their families into areas that may be hostile to them – is ambitious to the extreme (Colleta and Muggah, 2009).

Finally, there is the usual coordination problem as too many actors, either domestic or external, want to control the agenda. In the context of wider UN reforms, an ongoing debate also exists over how best to coordinate the DDR architecture among disparate security and development agencies and whether they can practicably deliver. There is no substitute for the political commitment from national leadership or warring parties willing to disarm and demobilize. Thus, it is advocated that in a peacekeeping environment, a successful DDR program depends significantly on the ability of the UN system to integrate (plan, manage, and implement) a coherent and effective DDR strategy among the different international agencies operating within the nation. The UN Integrated Disarmament, Demobilization, and Reintegration Standards (IDDRS) try to solve these issues, but cases such as South Sudan and Haiti appear to have disintegrated. Part of the reason is that it is still required to communicate the goals and parameters through political cleavages and distinct mandates, bureaucracies, or organizations (UNWG, 2006). By the same token, there are concerns that generic approaches cannot adequately account for the heterogeneous and differentiated motivations of armed groups. Thus, a case-by-case perspective should take precedence for enhanced effectiveness.

Despite the contraventions to point to completely successful cases, and in line with UNSC Resolution 2141 (2014), four basic necessary tenets or characteristics are fundamental to an SSR approach. First, it must be recognized that SSR is political in nature, both in the host nation and by the donor(s) state (s). Thus, a successful SSR approach must tackle the politics as well as the technical and holistic aspects of reform. Second, it must balance effectiveness and accountability. The ultimate aim is to improve human security, not just that of the state. Third, national ownership of SSR must consist of the structural involvement of the entire nation and not just a declaration of political buy-in. Finally, it must be sustainable in the long term and beyond the support of donors (ISSAT, 2015). The omission of one of these tenets tends to diminish the case for successful SSR, such as in the several attempts in DRC. A number of cases show the risks of abandoning reform efforts prematurely (either from donor assistance reduction or attention deficit or from host nation rejection), such as Iraq, Macedonia,

South Africa, and Nigeria. A few cases illustrate the tentative progress of reform, including Burundi, Kenya, Liberia, Sierra Leone, and Zimbabwe (ISSAT, 2015; Meharg et al., 2012).

8.2 Trusting the enemy: dilemmas of post-conflict securitization and governance

Even though silencing the guns and demobilizing fighters would seem vital to security, it is even more helpful to systematically understand how insecurity countermeasures can undermine peace and democracy. Beyond the challenges of peace agreements and demilitarization, what are the main dilemmas of post-conflict security promotion? SSR can assume multiple forms as governments emerging from war demobilize and reintegrate former combatants either into newly reconstituted security structures or into civilian livelihoods. However, security services are often heavily politicized and are confronted with major capacity gaps that can frustrate integration. Similarly, the absorptive capacities for civilian reintegration are usually limited as economic and social development are not yet self-sustaining. Importantly, these difficulties are not exclusive to postwar or fragile states. Consolidated states might also face generally similar dilemmas when cleaning up corruption or renewing their national institutions, such as the police forces in New York, Los Angeles, Rio de Janeiro, or Sydney in the 1990s and 2000s.

As with the archetypal "prisoner's dilemma" of game theory, DDR and SSR are both rooted in an existential dilemma due to suspicion and distrust among parties. The prisoner's dilemma is a paradox in which acting in one's own self-interest seems more rationally desirable, but it often leads to a worse result if the parties have to cooperate with each other in the decision-making process. In postwar settings, a key challenge for demobilization is the mistrust between parties and their incentives to bluff their true intentions until they are the stronger party after demobilization. Nevertheless, for democracy to take root, actors mobilized for war must abandon military methods and engage in the unfamiliar operations of negotiation and compromise, which makes them vulnerable. Subsequently, after a long period of war and human rights abuses, the demobilization of former fighters as well as many civilians in the conflict zone is problematic. The lack of mutual trust is the Achilles' heel: the absence of confidence between the belligerent groups, as well as with the locals, must be solved. If not, it is unlikely that any political strategies to demobilize former fighters will be able to create post-conflict stability effectively. Beyond creating institutions or national policies, building trust effectively requires the elimination of suspicions and fears at the local level as well as at the decision-making level. Alternatives are dialogue and sensitization programs, as in the cases of the Rwandan *Ingando* process and the *Labora* farm experiment in northern Uganda (Colleta and Muggah, 2009; Themnér, 2011). Colombia also included *Programas de sensibilización*, whose results are yet to be seen. Additionally, part of the second-generation approach toward postwar reintegration is the use of sport to advance "peace and development" by breaking the ice and promoting trust, rehabilitation, and reconciliation, as in the case of Sierra Leone (Dyck, 2011). Yet, if only one side demobilizes, not only will the other side(s) take advantage of the situation, but also new rebel groups will be formed by veterans of the demobilized faction(s) of the last war, or these will become mercenaries fighting in other conflicts in the region. The origins of ISIL are an example of that. Additionally, these leaders also have to convince their followers that they should demobilize and be prepared to make concessions (Jarstad and Sisk, 2008).

Vertical quandaries rise based on the trade-offs of legitimacy and efficacy. Different security actors (both state and non-state) will dispute such matters as whose security interests are promoted, which actions providing security are legitimate, and who is considered a legitimate security actor. Likewise, as mentioned in earlier chapters, in the case of transforming rebels into political parties, can the new institutions be legitimate if the same people who have committed atrocities become part of the new security forces that are meant to protect civilians, the state, and the "national interests"? Any institution in the security sector is intrinsically a peacemaker, as its role is to guarantee safety and social compliance with the rule of law. Hence, the dilemma arises: is it possible for the very same people who were previously belligerents to be entrusted with securing the peace? Examples such as the new national police force of Nicaragua, the Compas (Sandinista National Liberation Front [FSLN]), and the Contras (Democratic Revolutionary Alliance and Nicaraguan Democratic Force), who had to work toward a new era after the Sandinista regime helped us answer that question. As suggested by Hoglund (2008), the inclusion of former members of repressive regimes or rebel groups within the police and military creates serious problems of legitimacy for the new security forces. Many groups from the original armed struggle have been forced to make critical trade-offs between keeping their legitimacy in the eyes of their wartime constituencies and their need to make appeals to a broader constituency, which includes former enemies. Among several lessons learnt from failed DDR/SSR programs in DRC, is the technical understanding that despite the need for reconciliation, "no army in the world can entertain undisciplined soldiers" (Humanitarian, 2014). In the past, the DRC has allowed the reintegration of individuals in the FARDC whose alleged involvement in the commission of atrocities had been extensively documented, just to see the continuation in the commission of serious crimes. The permanent impunity has allowed renewed cycles of violence. To keep the political will, the option of military reintegration cannot be dismissed but must be slowly phased out as other alternatives emerge.

Importantly, reforms required for the new era of democratic peace are jeopardized by the high probability that former belligerents keep to their wartime tactics, modus operandi, and mentality. If so, this results in "no reform." These issues are challenging to overcome. In many cases, there have been general amnesty provisions for former combatants in exchange for laying down their guns and committing to the peace process. As demonstrated in the previous chapter, this has been considered a necessary "pact with the devil" for ending the war (Dancy, 2016, p. 7). However, from a democratic point of view, such exemptions from the rule of law and principles of human rights risk facilitating a culture of impunity.

Furthermore, in terms of remobilizing civil society, the establishment of a forum for reconciliation and community-building must be combined with efforts to strengthen individual confidence in fair and just state institutions. The war itself further polarizes civil society, leaving a bitter legacy of resentment and mistrust, greed, and grievances (Collier and Hoeffler, 2004). The presence of divided communities suspicious of each other's intentions hinders human rights protection and the development of the rule of law. In the case of inter-ethnic crimes, a member of one group is unlikely to report another member of the same group to the police. Consequently, this obstructs police work that relies heavily on the community and complicates cross-ethnic human rights advocacy (Belloni, 2008). However, former combatants have experience and know-how, which saves time and money in building the capacity of a new force. Consequently, while it is argued that an outcome of no reform due to the simple transition of the former combatants into security roles is more efficient, others argue that the establishment of a new institution requires completely new members and new mindsets if legitimacy is to be achieved (Willems, 2015; Colleta and Muggah, 2009). A third position defends a mixture in which old experienced members work together with new officers as an interim measure (UN-DPKO, 2012; ICG, 2013).

The vertical dilemma can also help us understand why some ex-combatants reengage in organized violence, while others do not. This is not purely a reflection of poor DDR and SSR processes. Cases such as the Republic of Congo (ex-Cobras, Cocoyes, and Ninjas) and Sierra Leone (ex-Armed Forces Revolutionary Council, Civil Defense Force, and Revolutionary United Front), show that former fighters have access to elites through second-tier individuals, such as former middle-level commanders who can act as intermediaries between the two. Thus, beyond the state and non-state actors, the remobilizer's perspective must be incorporated to convince ex-combatants to abandon arms and to generate selective incentives and social networks to grow feelings of affinity. Therefore, it is not only the elite and grassroots levels, but the crucial middle level as well that must be incorporated (Themnér, 2011).

As represented by the horizontal quandary of inclusion and exclusion, it is critical that all actors work closely and in tight coordination, which, in itself, may become the main obstacle. Policing a democracy is vastly more arduous than policing a totalitarian state since the rights of citizens must be properly recognized and "the voices of the people heard." It is important for these groups to be provided with positive and constructive activity. They must be integrated into the peace process from the peace negotiations to peacekeeping itself and all that follows from peacebuilding activities. Once included, the former combatants can become strongly connected with civil society.

As per the transparency dilemma, joint planning, coordination, and capacity development require impartiality and accountability. However, the recruitment process may also generate fears that the newly trained police will immediately fall into the patterns of the old police or army. Usually, the criteria for recruitment to the police and armed forces are highly politicized as every faction will claim its share of opportunity or overstate its training capabilities. Moreover, the ceremonies of weapon destruction are usually conducted for accountability not only to the population, but also mostly to the donors as well. Beyond the need to display the effectiveness of the UN, national institutions, and civil society, these formalities of weapon destruction also offer a symbolic message of deterrence and commitment to peace, such as in Rwanda, Liberia, and Sierra Leone.

Moral dilemmas arise when corruption and patrimonial relationships take precedence over citizenship rights, consequently jeopardizing institutional legitimacy as well as impartiality, effectivity, and accountability. Such moral impasses are also present when former child soldiers are included, as in the cases of Sierra Leone and Liberia. Additionally, as DDR involves compensation, financially "rewarding" bad behavior creates a moral dilemma and fosters a sense of injustice.

Moreover, the unemployment of the "demobilized" combatants may also spawn violence. Thus, within the nexus of rehabilitation and reconciliation, it is essential to provide former soldiers with work if a government wants to prevent a spiral of violence. In the DRC, poor demobilization facilitated new recruitment by other rebel groups. Thus, many rebel fighters have been through demobilization programs, only to be re-recruited by rebel groups. The combination of no alternative economic livelihood, the frustration and uncertainty engendered by long waiting, pressure to rejoin by former leaders, and continuing insecurity in their home areas leads to mobilization and integration into new groups (Humanitarian, 2014). However, job creation is no easy matter. When many people are competing for only a few positions, reserving jobs for former soldiers can create discontent among those who remain unable to get a job through merit. Inevitably, this leads to embitterment by those who observe how their own credentials and experience are discounted while former wrongdoers are favored. Despite this issue, it is generally understood that in order to secure peace and transform "warriors into workers," the reintegration of the "demobilized" remains a necessary evil, especially for those seeking democratic justice (Colletta, 1995).

The security dilemma is of high concern. A security vacuum cannot be left unresolved. Disarmament exercises may not reestablish security and may become the source of further insecurity (Collier, 1999). A dilemma arises when the size of the security sector is reduced at the same time as new threats surface. A substantial threat in countries emerging from war is the frequency of increase in violent crime, including armed robbery and looting, car hijackings, and domestic violence. Several factors explain the rise in violent crime in countries such as Guatemala, El Salvador, Afghanistan, Syria, and Iraq. Among these is the lack of effective institutions to deal with crime, widespread poverty, and easy access to arms. Profitable economic activities that have funded violent campaigns of guerrillas or rebels during the conflict are commonly turned into networks of organized crime. Restrepo and Muggah (2008 p.30) have explored whether DDR interventions contribute to reductions in homicides, such as with the Colombian paramilitaries. After the demobilization of more than 30,000 members of the United Self-Defense Forces of Colombia (AUC) between 2003 and 2006, their research revealed a 13 percent reduction in homicide rates compared to non-participating areas. While the process saved the lives of between 1,400 and 2,800 people in the first two years, there are considerable national variations. In some regions, rates of homicides rose, and various forms of increased criminality (such as armed hold-ups) substituted homicides in others, making no positive cause-effect relationship with the DDR process. Since the implementation of the 2016 peace agreement, a high rate of homicide per capita is still present, and there is no evidence that the DDR process contributed to more individual security. Instead, according to the United Nations Verification Mission (Colombia, 2022), 80 percent of these crimes were committed by criminal organizations, including the Clan del Golfo, FARC-EP dissident groups, and ELN. Since the agreement, the Office of the High Commissioner for Human Rights (OHCHR) has also registered an increase in killings of human rights defenders and forced displacement and confinement.

With the above-cited examples, not only does the security nexus remain unclear, but also its sustainability in the long term is questionable. Conventional approaches to disarmament have too often been undermined by insufficient attention to vital questions about states or societies. In Haiti and Sudan, DDR itself was not endorsed by the various armed groups, nor were the programs themselves equipped to address the heterogeneity of these same actors. In Somalia, chaotic disarmament left deactivated groups at the mercy of those still armed. In Cambodia, the failure to disarm the armed factions left the existing power equation in place in Phnom Penh despite the 1993 vote of the Cambodian people (William Maley et al., 2003).

Often soldiers and rebels might remain partially organized within their existing command structure and can potentially assume a spoiler function, as in Angola where ex-combatants triggered insecurity when they returned to communities, escalating levels of banditry and sexual assault (William Maley et al., 2003). The public security gap generated by the absence of an effective and legitimate police force has led to situations where the military has been called in to cooperate in dealing with crime in a joint task force. Nevertheless, the police and the army have different mandates. Confusion among the population during this transition time can lead to disastrous incidents, such as the 2008 crisis in Timor-Leste. It has also been suggested that because of the experience of war, there is a higher tolerance for the use of violence more generally (Fjelde et al., 2012; Hoglund, 2008).

8.2.1 Good timing for DDR/SSR: cost, sequencing, ownership, and other dilemmas

As per the temporal dilemma, which balances short- and long-term perspectives, timing is particularly challenging. Dealing with the security problems that arise when ex-combatants try to adjust to everyday life, helps enable longer-term political and peace processes. In Liberia, the 2003 peace agreement proposed that the new army would not include any elements from the old military apparatus. With this proposal, a high degree of legitimacy was obtained. However, it took more time compared to the alternative of retaining the old institution under a new name. None of these are short-term processes. Nevertheless, they remain a high priority. The failure to take action against violence aggravates instability. But measures need to be cautiously undertaken as acting too quickly can create new grievances and increase the risk of escalating violence (Hoglund, 2008).

Beyond time and the willpower of political elites, human capacity-building and financial resources are necessary. Interventions often approach capacity development with a simplistic economic bias that treats beneficiaries as a homogeneous unit responding rationally to monetary incentives. Depending on the relative geopolitical importance of the country and the generosity of donors, the efficiency of the implementing agencies, and the recipient state's capacity and local purchasing power, the average expenditure for disarming, demobilizing and reintegrating a single ex-combatant in 2007 amounted to some US$1,250 per capita, but in some cases, such as Colombia, it was over US$9,000. In 2002, the DDR budget in Angola alone was US$270 million (Muggah, 2008, p. 7). Thus, financial and resource dilemmas must be jointly tackled as the state may not have a tax system that suffices to finance the process. It may also lack local know-how for its implementation. For example, funds and resources used to reform the police can be channelled to boost the military budget, which can be a way to circumvent military spending as stipulated in the peace agreement. Moreover, some argue that to move toward peace, investment in health and education is more important for future generations than weapons.

In line with systemic and temporal impasses, UN agencies should develop long-term reintegration or development opportunities that complement and reinforce the overall DDR and SSR processes and be mindful not to jeopardize the national ownership of such important reforms. The US policy in Iraq is a counter-illustration to this. After the 2003 invasion, the US- led military coalition chose to dismantle the Iraqi army and create a new one, which was, inevitably, ill-trained, ill-equipped, and lacking in experience. The US military policy of rearming and retraining a defunct apparatus was difficult enough, but all this was being attempted during an anti-government and anti-U.S. insurgency that was gathering strength, which meant that the war had not really concluded. As this insurgency gathered momentum, the coalition was forced to train thousands of new soldiers in a hurry. Thus, leaving new troops and untested leadership unprepared to face a standing army marshalled by ISIL, including veterans of the original Sunni pro-Saddam Iraqi army that had been disbanded eight years previously. The US plan of improving the capacity of the armed forces in unstable regions, notably in the Great Lakes (to counter the violence extremist of Al-Shabaab in Somalia, Boko Haram in Nigeria, and Al-Qaeda in the Islamic Maghreb) has shown risk to be double counterproductive: either by escalating violence back in the region, as well increasing the risk of terrorist activities against US targets (Larsdotter, 2015). Thus, not only is the timing important, but also the systemic quandary shows that external actors should back up the government for its security sector reform and not take over the army restructuring.

Usually, the financial and resource dilemmas are temporally solved by international donors such as the UN or regional organizations such as OEA and AU. The UN policy accepts that once a conflict has come to an end, it is essential that reform of a country's security sector takes place. Consequently, DDR has become an integral part of post-conflict peace consolidation, featuring prominently in the mandates of peacekeeping operations over the last 20 years as in the MONUSCO, UNOCI, and MINUSTAH. Consequently, as per the systemic dilemma, a quandary emerges regarding the ownership of the processes. It is believed that the processes should be led by national authorities, and the reform should be undertaken without discrimination and with full respect for human rights and the rule of law. Nevertheless, as in the case of Afghanistan, conventional approaches to DDR tend to neglect the many ways in which discrete activities are interpreted by local actors. Additionally, externally imposed interventions tend to ignore locally existing security arrangements such as the interests of commanders, the rank and file, and their layered relationships within communities.

Moreover, the UN considers that security sectors usually include structures, institutions, and personnel responsible for the management, provision, and oversight of security. These could consist of defense, law enforcement, corrections, intelligence services, and institutions responsible for border management, customs, and civil emergencies, as well as human rights training for protecting the political liberties that are fundamental in a functioning democracy. In some cases, elements of the judicial sector responsible for cases of alleged criminal conduct and the misuse of force are included. The security sector should also include management and oversight bodies and, in some instances, may involve informal or traditional security providers. In the field, international experts take over responsibilities such as facilitating national dialogues, developing national security policies, strategies and plans, strengthening oversight, managing and coordinating capacity, articulating security sector legislation, mobilizing resources for SSR and DDR-related projects, harmonizing international support for SSR education, training and institutional building, and monitoring and evaluating the programs and results of defense sector reform. In some cases, the peacekeepers stand mainly as a buffer between belligerents and take on policing activities to uphold basic civilian security, such as the arrest, prosecution, and trial of serious offenders. This requires a robust mission mandate. However, there is always the danger that allowing excessive and liberal use of force policies, either by local security institutions or by international police, may undermine democratization. Importantly and little discussed in the academic literature are the problems caused by the privatization of intelligence services or the control of foreign countries over something essentially of national interest (Chesterman, 2008).

Finally, there is the problem of former enemies working jointly to protect the civilians they used to kill. Trusting the enemy encompasses three more dilemmas: operational, design, and sequencing. While there is no single design model for DDR and SSR, it is generally accepted that the security sector includes defense, law enforcement, corrections, intelligence services, and institutions responsible for border protection. But for implementation to take place, many details must be previously agreed on regarding the power-sharing arrangements (PSA), as analyzed in depth in Chapter 6. A particular framework strategy is needed to address irregular armed groups (UN-DPKO, 2010). It should also be decided whether or not command structures should be destroyed, weakened, or left intact. It seems rational that reintegration only happens after demobilization.

As for the sequencing dilemma, DDR does not emerge spontaneously "from below," but is part of a broader means of securing the legitimate control of force "from above." Regardless of who enforces the intervention (elite power holders or internationals), UN best practice policies usually advocate a gradual operational approach, particularly when the takeover results in the exit of the UN mission. Timor-Leste is an example of a gradual handover of the UN police mandate to the PNTL in 2012. Finally, competing priorities issued from above generate the potential to undermine more localized community-based initiatives from below, such as the investment in livelihood alternatives, community support, and the strengthening of municipal and national capacities to absorb demobilized ex-combatants.

8.2.2 A note on the privatization of peace: more problems than solutions?

Notably, the so-called privatization of peace is at the center of many debates by policymakers and researchers. The use of private military and security companies (PMSCs) as a possible solution to peacekeeping challenges is controversial. A principal reason given for their increased use since the 1990s has been UN member states' unwillingness or inability to respond to a burgeoning number of crises. A further rationale is that these companies offer solutions to the political, financial, and institutional constraints faced by the UN and other bodies. Whereas the UN is slow, expensive, and militarily inefficient, private firms claim they will be able to deploy better equipped and experienced personnel in a timely and cheaper manner. Importantly, when there are casualties in the field, the deployment of private firms takes the pressure off the politicians by circumventing domestic discontent and off the government as it will not be held accountable for private company "losses" (Bellamy et al., 2010, p. 333).

Nevertheless, "the world may not be ready to privatize peace" as it creates more challenges than it solves (Annan, 1998). Private military companies might be contracted for logistics and training services. Their use as soldiers does not comply with the principles of peacekeeping: private contractors are non-combatants under international humanitarian law. However, this makes it extremely difficult to hold states and international organizations accountable for their unlawful acts, particularly sexual abuses and war crimes. While PMSC's may strengthen the UN's Rapid Reaction Force for better UN international policing, their use in international peacekeeping inevitably undermines the moral legitimacy to which the UN aspires (Cameron, 2017).

Overall, a successful transition needs an integrated approach. Not only should the SSR be conducted simultaneously with the disarmament processes, but also it should take place in parallel with the reform of the judicial system. It is debatable whether elections can be held deprived of demobilization without posing a serious threat to stability. Based on policy drawn from UN lessons learned, a successful SSR should be included at a sector-wide level (national and local spheres of decision making) as well as at the component level (different institutions that are integrated into the security sector). Moreover, cross-cutting issues such as professional integrity, gender, and human rights, should also be involved (UN-DPKO, 2012). As an alternative to minimize the effects of the dilemmas between peace and democracy, Figure 8.1 illustrates an integrated approach scheme that might enable and facilitate the move from a combatant-centric approach toward a broader perspective promoting good governance.

8.3 A case study on the security sector of Central African Republic: worse than a failure

SSR/DDR in Central African Republic (CAR) has compiled a history of failures: "worse than a failed state, CAR has an anatomy of a ghost state" (ICG, 2007).[3] Thus, the Central African Republican deserves comprehensive scrutiny as the country has been at a turning point in its stabilization process since the electoral crisis of December 2020. Nine years after a coup that plunged the country into chaos in 2013 and led to the dissolution of the Central African Armed Forces (FACA, or Forces Armées Centrafricaines), the military has reestablished its presence. However, unclear recruitment procedures, multiple chains of command, lack of training, and poor budget management could undermine soldiers' loyalty to the state and push them to rise up or join a new rebellion (ICG, 2022). Ethnic polarization in the rank and file and nepotism on the part of heads of state in Bangui have long hindered the creation of an army capable of securing the country. Successive governments have nonetheless undertaken several reforms since the mutinies of the 1990s. President Ange-Félix Patassé (1993–2003) downsized the number of FACA troops from 4,000 to 3,000 and reduced to 40 percent the proportion of Yakoma among them – the latter being the ethnic group of his predecessor, André Kolingba (1986–1993).

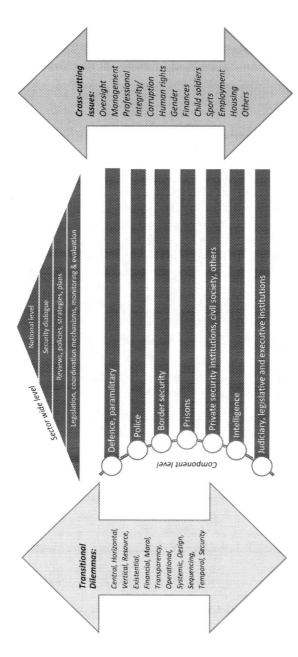

FIGURE 8.1 Dilemmas for DDR/SSR: an integrated approach. Source: Author. Inspired from UN-DPKO (2012, p. 17)

Under President François Bozizé (2003–2013), troop numbers rose to 7,000, with Gbaya soldiers (Bozizé's community of origin and a third of the population) predominating. In March 2013, the Séléka, a Muslim-majority rebel coalition from the Northeast, seized power, plunging the country into its worst security crisis in recent history (ICG, 2013). The FACA disbanded, and many soldiers joined the predominantly Christian anti-balaka self-defense militias. At the same time, the UN placed the Central African Republic under embargo, preventing the supply, sale, or transfer of arms and military equipment to the country (ICG, 2022).

In 2017, after a turbulent transition and a return to constitutional order, the Central African Republic adopted a National Defense Plan with the support of MINUSCA. The FACA was to be restructured into a garrison army and soldiers assigned to permanent bases with their families. In line with the strategic priorities of defending the country's territorial integrity and protecting the population, the National Defense Plan also involved increasing troop numbers to 9,800. New recruitment processes were to include background checks and a training program supported by the European Union Training Mission (EUTM). In 2018, after the Central African government submitted a request for an exception to the embargo, the UN Sanctions Committee authorized not only the delivery of armaments from Moscow, but also the deployment of Russian instructors to train FACA troops and accompany them in the hinterland. Despite an easing of the arms embargo and gradual redeployments in several towns, however, the army's presence in the hinterland remained weak until 2020. The situation changed dramatically in December 2020, when the Coalition of Patriots for Change (CPC) threatened to seize the capital, Bangui. A new rebel movement comprising both ex-Séléka and anti-balaka elements and led by François Bozizé, the CPC saw the presidential and legislative elections in progress at the time as illegitimate. The FACA and Russian and Rwandan allied forces sent at President Faustin Archange Touadéra's request then launched a counteroffensive. Between January and March 2021, their military operations significantly reduced armed groups' control over the surrounding area. Some defeated rebel fighters chose exile in Chad, alongside Bozizé, or in neighboring Sudan. Others turned to banditry. While the counteroffensive helped rapidly redeploy troops to the country's main urban centers, it did so at a high price in human lives, and Central African authorities have yet to take appropriate measures to sanction those responsible for major human rights violations. These operations also led the government away from the National Defense Plan's initial objectives. The European Union suspended the training support program in December 2021 following interference by the Russian private security Wagner group in the FACA command. The training provided by Russian instructors since 2018 initially lasted three months but was reduced in 2021 to a few weeks to speed up deployments and without any mention of human rights and international humanitarian law (ICG, 2022).

The CAR army seems once again to fall into politicization. The number of new troops has dramatically surpassed the Plan's projected increase. Former rebels are directly integrated without any legal recruitment procedure, security checking, or quality training. Those recruitments are a response to the December 2020 rebellion. In addition, to improve their social position, some young people are seemingly ready to pay officers between US$77 to US$154 to get onto recruitment lists. Thus, random recruitment procedures could compromise some minority groups' inclusion and the population's trust in the army.

Moreover, the Central African state does not have the financial resources necessary to maintain its current personnel. The 2022 Finance Law cut the defence budget by 21 percent, totalling just over US$37 million (CAR Finances, 2022). The math figures do not make sense. This lack of funding for defense is visible on two levels. First, the government can no longer allocate deployment bonuses to encourage new recruits to stay in the hinterland. In addition, soldiers deployed in the provinces whose salary is transferred to a bank account in the capital officially receive a cash bonus of around US$49 per month, to cover on-the-ground expenses. In practice, however, officers often retain a portion of these bonuses before they reach the lower-ranking recipients. To make up for this shortage of funds, soldiers prey on the local population. The army's rackets – illegal taxation at city gates, extortion, and robberies – have rapidly replaced those of armed groups in state-controlled areas. Furthermore, the lack of resources has led to the militarization of the country's capital. Due to salary payment problems, many FACA members choose to stay in Bangui. The militarization of the capital generates significant risks in a country where tensions are mounting around President Touadéra's succession, especially within the ruling party, and certain actors could easily mobilize poorly paid and disgruntled personnel. Additionally, since mid-2021, the FACA have frequently recruited local militias, mostly former anti-balaka fighters, whom they pay to help track and attack rebels hiding in the bush. This system generates an additional financial burden while resources are already lacking for soldiers in the regular army. Nicknamed the "Black Russians," these militiamen recently demonstrated in Bambari, in the country's center, to demand payment of their fees. In addition, they are held responsible for several massacres of civilians, especially among the Fulani in the country's center and east.

The official budget does not indicate how the state remunerates Wagner's Russian mercenaries deployed in the country. Political interests explain this neglect of the budget law. No official information leads to no accountability, which seems convenient to both the CAR and the Russian governments. Since their deployment in December 2020 to support the army's counteroffensive, Russian forces have de facto assumed command of the FACA on the battlefield. Troopers are discontented with how Wagner mercenaries humiliate and physically abuse Central African officers and soldiers. Therefore, there is a deterioration in the relations with the "Russian bilateral forces," as the Central African authorities refer to them. In addition, to limit cases of sexual and gender-based violence, most female FACA members were ordered to return to the capital at the end of 2021. Without a firm response from Central African chiefs of staff, a growing concern among officers could cause soldiers to rise up or join the rebels, once again. Lastly, the size of the troops and their gender or ethnic composition are unknown (ICG, 2022). To say the least, DDR/SSR in Central African Republic failed to implement the urgent need for transition and has an anatomy of a ghost (ICG, 2007; ICG, 2013).

8.4 A case study on the security sector of Timor-Leste: a partial or no reform?

The experience of Timor-Leste regarding SSR might well be considered as representing a security sector no-reform. The independence process was composed of three axes: the military, the political, and the clandestine resistance. In the same way that the political front was transformed into the political party FRETILIN, the guerrilla army was transformed into the national army in an evidently convenient fusion as if the political party' interests and those of the nation were synonymous. Having been established for over 25 years, since August 1975, FALINTIL was the guerrilla army of the FRETILIN national liberation movement. In February 2001, the armed branch of the revolutionary group was transformed into the national army of the new state: FALINTIL became the F-FDTL.

After becoming the official military force of the independent state of Timor-Leste, the constitution created a new role to protect Timor-Leste from external threats. As seen in Chapter 6, the constitution has a fundamental role in establishing the foundation of peace, democracy, and development. Therefore, constitutional architects foresaw the need to limit the army powers to guarantee "national independence, territorial integrity and the freedom and security of the populations against any aggression or external threat, in respect for the constitutional order." Moreover, according to Article146 §3, the F-FDTL "shall be non-partisan and shall owe obedience to the competent organs of sovereignty in accordance with the constitution and the laws, and shall not intervene in political matters" (Timor-Leste, 2002). Besides this change of name and roles, this did not represent a change of mindset. Even the national coat of arms consists of the colors of the 1975 generation struggle. Although this case may indicate a lack of reform, and despite the 2006 crisis and common criticisms of the political turmoil in 2008 and 2018, the country has shown evidence of relative security and transfer of power with no widescale internal or external violent outbreak. Table 8.2 presents a case study of SSR in Timor-Leste using the proposed framework of dilemmas.

8.5 Summary of the chapter

If peace comes first, silencing the guns is crucial. The security sector reform and disarmament, demobilization, and reintegration processes are at the center of peacebuilding, state-building, and democracy-building after intra-state armed conflict. Nevertheless, they face important dilemmas between a "just enough approach" to securing peace by disarming the conflict or democratically

250 Transitions to political, legal, civil and social orders

TABLE 8.2 Case study: SSR in Timor-Leste

Dilemmas	Trade-offs	Testing the P–A–T set of transitional dilemmas with the army of Timor-Leste
Central	Peace vs. Democracy	The 2006 and 2008 crises are evidence that DDR and SSR are crucial to state-building to prevent the peacebuilding and democratization processes from failing.
Existential	Certain Loss vs. Uncertain Victory	To secure power in the democratic regime, FRETILIN transformed its military wing into the F-FDTL, the national military force of the independent new state.
Financial	Present vs. Future	The F-FDTL annual budget is US$27 million (Min of Finance of Timor Leste, 2017). Although this represents 1.5 percent of the total, combined with US $47 million attributable to the police (PNTL), it represents 6 percent of the total annual budget. A further US$105 million goes to compensation benefits for the veterans (7.5 percent). These amounts might understandably raise concerns as they represent a heavy burden on Timor-Leste's economy. It is arguable that these funds could be invested better in roads, schools or hospitals. However, to solve the 2008 crisis, the government offered to provide financial compensation to the "petitioners" who wished to return to civilian life. That, in turn, created financial pressure on the national budget with some seeing it as a necessary cost for maintaining "internal" security.
Vertical	Efficacy vs. Legitimacy	On one hand, members of the FALINTIL are viewed by the population to have high legitimacy as they are the heroes who fought for the nation's independence. Therefore, they would also be deemed more efficient as they already have considerable experience. On the other hand, they might not be perceived as legitimate by other parts of the population and international actors as they have a guerrilla warfare modus operandi. Although they are seen as a subversive influence on a nation-state, the democratic principle dictates that opportunities should be given to everyone meeting the requirements. Moreover, the F-FDTL has suffered from serious morale and disciplinary problems, arising from FALINTIL's transition from a guerrilla organization to a regular military institution, which has impacted its efficacy and legitimacy. Consequently, a large number of soldiers have been disciplined or dismissed. The Timor-Leste government was aware of these problems before the 2006 crisis but did not rectify the factors contributing to low morale due to other political priorities at the early stages of the democratization process. Beyond legitimacy, the professionalization of the troops has resulted in a transformation of its identity from a popular national army to one with a more elitist orientation in the eyes of the population.
Horizontal	Inclusion vs. Exclusion	The political elites chose a mixed model of how to join the F-FDTL. Regarding the bottom level, the 1st Battalion was established out of 650 members selected from 1,736 former FALINTIL applicants, most members being from the country's eastern provinces. This is important in understanding the 2006 crisis in terms of an East–West ethnic and territorial axis in the eastern half of the island. Nevertheless, the 2nd Battalion consisted mainly of new personnel under 21 who had not participated in the independence struggle. Due to the force's prestige and relatively high pay in comparison to the few jobs available the local economy, there were 7,000 applications for the first 267 positions in the battalion (Grenfell, 2015). Among other criteria, the inclusion of old and new members requires them not having criminal records, which in many postwar contexts might be a challenge.

(Continued)

TABLE 8.2 (Continued)

Dilemmas	Trade-offs	Testing the P–A–T set of transitional dilemmas with the army of Timor-Leste
		Regarding the highest level, the commander of the F-FDTL from 2002 to 2011 was Taur Matan Ruak (José Maria de Vasconcelos), who also commanded the military (FALINTIL) during the resistance. Although a former FRETILIN member, he ran as an independent and became President from 2012 to 2017 and, later on, a member of the Parliament through the People's Liberation Party (PLP) leading him to the role of prime minister. Here again, in post-conflict scenarios, democratization makes room for "warlords" or "national heroes" to move from the battlefield of conflict to the highest rank of politics. The horizontal dilemma shows more relevance when there are more rebel groups to be included or excluded from the transition, such as in Nicaragua and DRC. However, this is still an important factor in the case of Timor-Leste. Thus, regarding the structure of the F-FDTL corps, Timor-Leste shows elements of hybrid reform: At the bottom level, it was a partial reform, but at the commander's level, it was a no reform.
Moral	Cause vs. Consequence	Some might defend the narrative of "martyrs of the fatherland" (referred as "Mártires da Pátria" in Portuguese) and therefore, the recognition of the veterans by including them into the military. Others assert that "guerrilla fighters" should not be rewarded. Together with the horizontal dilemma, a key flaw in this process was that FALINTIL's high command was allowed to select candidates for the military from FALINTIL members without external oversight. As a result, the selection was conducted based on applicants' political allegiance, not their capacity. That again leads to a no reform feature.
Sequencing	Bottom-up vs. Top-down	The F-FDTL gradually assumed responsibility for the country's security from the UN peacekeeping force. The process was top down as it was mainly driven by international forces and local political leadership. However, it was also bottom up as the less disrupted regions were gradually handed over first and the more important one, Dili, last.
Operational	Flexibility vs. Robustness	Although small, the guerrilla tactics operationally employed by FALINTIL are still foremost in the mindset of the new army. Its current doctrine is focused on low-intensity infantry combat tactics as well as counter-insurgency tasks. In times of transition, a certain flexibility is required due to the shortage of personnel, equipment, and know-how. However, a robust military structure is crucial for national security issues.
Transparency	Impartiality vs. Accountability	The transformation process to the F-FDTL was closed to the public and did not involve all parties. Three main issues derive from this lack of transparency. First, it might be argued that as the institution was founded based on FRETILIN's military wing, it does not act impartially regarding the defence of the "national" interests. However, they might be liable precisely because they fought for the nation. Second, the acquisition process for much of the equipment is unclear, such as how the Chinese built 43-metre Type-62 class patrol boats, two fast patrol boats from the Indonesian company PT Pal, two small Albatroz-class patrol boats from the Portuguese Navy or even a new HQ palace estimated at US$7 million and "donated" by China came about. Third, the veteran issue was not conducted transparently nor with accountability, which has led to disenfranchisement and frustration among various groups. Ultimately, this situation became politicized by these groups forwarding their own interests.

(Continued)

TABLE 8.2 (Continued)

Dilemmas	Trade-offs	Testing the P–A–T set of transitional dilemmas with the army of Timor-Leste
Resource	Efficiency vs. Viability	Although all the F-FDTL's personnel were initially FALINTIL veterans, this has not translated into more efficiency. As the force's composition has changed over time and few soldiers from the insurgency remain due to the narrow age requirement, the expansion and equipment of the force have not been viable yet. This lack of resources deeply impacted the efficiency of the F-FDTL, which resulted in serious morale and disciplinary problems leading to the 2006 crisis which in turn jeopardized the viability of the institution. In May 2009, the F-FDTL accepted its first intake of recruits since the 2006 crisis. While the regional diversity of the 579 new recruits was generally much greater than that of the pre-crisis intakes, 60.3 percent of officer candidates were from the country's eastern districts. Despite growing efforts, the F-FDTL still faces shortages of qualified staff and poor conditions of service due to limited resources.
Security	Exercise rights vs. Fulfil duties	As part of the transition, a security limbo is created and might impact the population's perspective regarding their safety. Despite the existence of compulsory military service, some may refuse it based on a variety of reasons, including distrust of ruling authorities, human rights arguments or psychological trauma.
Temporal	Short term vs. Long term	Existing studies place a priority on security to enable peace, democracy, and development. Despite all the efforts to rapidly transform FALINTIL into the F-FDTL, with massive training support from the international community, building a professional army capable of defending the nation is a thorough process. It is important to understand that, in terms of its identity, in Timor-Leste's case, the process of forming a national force started in 1975, not 2002.
Design	Technical vs. Political Choices	During the 1999-2002 transition period under UNTAET administration, three options among political and technical choices were on the table: (1) FALINTIL's preference for a relatively large and heavily armed military of 3,000–5,000 personnel, (2) a force of 1,500 regulars and 1,500 conscripts and (3) a force of 1,500 regulars and 15,000 volunteer reservists. Considering the country's security needs, economic situation, and the basis of national defense planning, the last option was recommended by the countries that were contributing peacekeeping forces. However, as indicated by the systemic dilemma, the international community's agenda may be different from the local one. Some national authorities preferred to establish a single smaller paramilitary force instead of a large police force and FALANTIL's preferred large army. One argument was based on the fact that the country does not face any external threats. Besides initial clashes and ongoing tensions with Indonesia during the referendum, Timor-Leste has been able to build stable and peaceful relations within the region, such as with Singapore, Malaysia, and Thailand as well as Indonesia. Thus, the government's limited resources would be better spent on, for example, strengthening the PNTL instead of developing two large forces, one for police and the other for the military. As political choices take over decisions about technicalities, the political leadership argued that although the country does not face an external threat, it was necessary to maintain a military capacity to deter future aggression, especially considering its geostrategic position, its deeper sea level for undetectable submarine passages in the Indian Ocean, the territorial enclave of Oecussi, and remaining border delimitation issues with Indonesia and Australia. The establishment of the F-FDTL was also seen as a political means of integrating the dominant FRETILIN party members into the new country's military decision-makers.

(Continued)

TABLE 8.2 (Continued)

Dilemmas	Trade-offs	Testing the P–A–T set of transitional dilemmas with the army of Timor-Leste
		Finally, the F-FDTL was established in February 2001, comprising two small infantry battalions, a small naval component, and several supporting units. Many design choices also had to be decided. Among them were the institutional mandate which soon showed evidence of wrong choices made with an almost total state collapse in 2006: the F-FDTL's secondary role was to establish internal security, which overlapped with that of the PNTL. As a consequence of the crisis, part of the forces had to be dismissed, and the F-FDTL had to undergo another reform process under UNMIT. The F-FDTL's role has been broadened with new responsibility such as crisis management, supporting the suppression of civil disorder, responding to humanitarian crises and facilitating cooperation between different parts of the government. Other technical and political choices faced multiple challenges such as how to protect maritime and air space, or who would perform the duties of a "federal police" within a unitary state of 13 districts. As for mainstream gender issues, technical choices prevailed: despite a conservative social structure, FDTL places men and women on an equal basis of eligibility.
Systemic	Local vs. International Ownership	UNTAET, serving as the executive and legislative, made key decisions between 1999 and 2002, in consultation with the National Council. In 2004 the commander of the F-FDTL formed a team of international contractors, to develop a long-term strategic vision document for the military. The resulting Force 2020 document was made public in 2007 with the equivalent status to a defence white paper, as it sets out an aspirational vision for the development of the F-FDTL by 2020. Besides proposing the expansion of manpower, it also sets longer-term goals such as establishing an air component and purchasing modern weapons, such as anti-armor weapons, armored personnel carriers, and missile boats, by 2020. Despite criticism from the UN, donors, and the Australian government, Force 2020 was really a plan influenced by outsiders via private contractors instead of high-ranking national officials. It has been adopted, and its adoption was based on the justification that it will transform the F-FDTL into a professional force capable of defending Timor-Leste's sovereignty and contributing to the nation's stability. The 2006 crisis left the F-FDTL "in ruins": its strength fell to half from January to September 2006 and the proportion of western Timorese in the military fell from 65 percent to 28 percent. Consequently, as the F-FDTL started a rebuilding process, it required 1,500 police and military liaison personnel under an UNMIT mandate to reestablish democratic order. With this heavy presence of international forces in the territory, following an international agenda, tension arose between the need for international expertise and the local will to take ownership of its own country. The presence of an Australian-led International Stabilization Force (ISF) also contributed to this ownership dilemma. It is also argued that part of the crisis was due to the failure of UNTAET to establish adequate foundations for the Timor-Leste's security sector by developing legislative and planning documents, administrative support arrangements and mechanisms for the democratic control of the military. However, this kind of argument is typically related to blaming others instead of taking ownership of its own problems.

(Continued)

TABLE 8.2 (Continued)

Dilemmas	Trade-offs	Testing the P–A–T set of transitional dilemmas with the army of Timor-Leste
		Growing cooperation between the F-FDTL and other nations' military forces helped to professionalize Timor-Leste's armed forces and keep them from being a spoiler on peace and stability issues. In May 2008, Timor-Leste signed a military cooperation agreement with a consortium of seven other Portuguese-speaking countries, with Brazil and Portugal agreeing to assist with the military training of F-FDTL personnel and aid from military advisors from Australia, New Zealand, Malaysia, and the United States.
		Some parts of the SSR seem to work better than others. The F-FDTL's small naval component, mainly equipped by the United States and trained by Australia, have not shown major disruptions. Last but not least, the country has shown awareness of international agreements and has ratified the Nuclear Non-Proliferation Treaty, Biological and Toxin Weapons Convention and Chemical Weapons Convention in 2003.

governing *in*security. An effective transition to democratic peace must account for the ways in which former fighters are inserted into a state-building project and must move away from the myth of "once a soldier, always a soldier." Nonetheless, postwar politics might place public security at risk.

Failing those two processes will jointly jeopardize peace and democracy, and, consequently, socioeconomic development after conflict. Thus, by rethinking postwar insecurity, this chapter contributes to the book by addressing the lacunas in the literature through the identification of common DDR and SSR dilemmas that oppose the achievement of the dual goals of peace and democracy in fragile states. Additionally, to close the gap between theory and practice, two case studies were presented. First, CAR's reform is a failure. Second, Timor-Leste is a "non-reform" through the common practice of transforming a guerrilla resistance group into the national army at the initial stage and then a gradual reform through time.

Institutional development in a post-conflict environment and in many young democracies is a long process involving generations. How the security sector responds to several future challenges will dictate the viability of the democratic order. Thus, the security transition reflects a hybrid reality as different security actors, both state and non-state, put peace and democracy at a crossroads, diametrically opposed to each other. The key to success in this geopolitical space is to find the optimum balance of dynamic security provisions. To be effective, DDR/SSR must transcend from a minimalist emphasis on "interim stabilization" toward maximalist aims of "democratic security promotion" associated with enhanced development and fundamental changes in governance. In a nutshell, security matters and effectiveness depend more and more on cooperation and coordination. Additionally, it is recommended to move away from the combatant-centric approach that has dominated the literature and to include the intermediary level of command as this level holds together meaningful relationships among elites, senior commanders, and the local community.

The construction of comprehensive peace agreements aims to reconcile several different and sometimes competing goals. Democratic principles such as freedom of speech, fairness, and transparency are great tools playing out in the media as a method to influence and control the masses. However, they can also be incorporated into a violent, obstructionist, and unfair political apparatus. This issue is taken up in the next chapter in more detail, where the Philosophical–Actors–Tactical set of proposed transitional dilemmas is used to review the role of the media and the consequences of its manipulation when civil wars end.

Notes

1 Latin adage translated as "If you want peace, prepare for war." If reversed, "Si vis bellum, para pacem" means "If you want war, prepare for peace." In order words, a leader who is planning a war should prepare for elements for peace bargain, domestically as well as externally.
2 "ISIS was born out of the U.S. invasion of Iraq in 2003. When U.S. administrators, under Paul Bremer, decided to 'de-Baathify' the Iraqi civil and military services, hundreds of thousands of Sunnis formerly loyal to Saddam Hussein were left without a job. Al Qaeda chose to capitalize on their anger and established al Qaeda in Iraq (AQI) to wage an insurgency against U.S. troops in Iraq and subsequently expand to Syria and Libya" (Cassis, T. 2015. A brief history of ISIS. *The Week*, PACK, J., Smith, R. & Mezran, K. 2017. The Origins and Evolution of ISIS in Libya. *In:* East, R. H. C. F. T. M. (ed.) June 2017 ed. Washington,DC: Atlantic Council of the United States.) The Arab Socialist Ba'ath Party was a political party that espoused Ba'athism, which is an ideology that calls for the unification of the Arab world into a single state.
3 "La République centrafricaine est pire qu'un État failli: elle est quasiment devenue un État fantôme." Republique Centre Afrique: Anatomie d' un état fantôme. International Crisis Group, 2007, p. 1

References

Alden, C., Thakur, M. & Arnold, M. 2011. *Militias and the Challenges of Post-Conflict Peace: Silencing the Guns*. Zed Books.
Annan, K. 1998. Secretary-General Statements and Messages. *In:* LECTURE, S. R. O. I. I. T. A. D. F. (ed.) 26 June 1998.
Auerswald, D. P. 2000. *Disarmed Democracies: Domestic Institutions and the Use of Force*. University of Michigan Press.
Bellamy, A. J., Williams, P. D. & Griffin, S. 2010. *Understanding Peacekeeping*.
Belloni, R. 2008. Civil Society in War-to-Democracy Transitions. *In:* Jarstad, A. K. & Sisk, T. D. (eds.) *From War to Democracy: Dilemmas of Peacebuilding*. Cambridge University Press.
Cameron, L. 2017. *The Privatization of Peacekeeping: Exploring Limits and Responsibility under International Law*. Cambridge University Press.
Car Finances, M. O. 2022. Loi de finances 21 015 Budget d'etat.
Cassis, T. 2015. A Brief History of ISIS. *The Week*.

Chesterman, S. 2004. *You, the People: The United Nations, Transitional Administration, and State-building*. Oxford University Press.
Chesterman, S. 2008. 'We Can't Spy ... If We Can't Buy!': The Privatization of Intelligence and the Limits of Outsourcing 'Inherently Governmental Functions'. *The European Journal of International Law*, 19.
Colleta, N. J. & Muggah, R. 2009. *Rethinking Post-War Insecurity: From Interim Stabilization to Second Generation Security Promotion*. The Journal of Humanitarian Assistance. Feinstein International Center at Tufts University.
Colletta, N. 1995. *From Warriors to Workers: The World Bank's Role in Post-Conflict Reconstruction*. Leaders, no. 204.
Collier, P. 1999. On the Economic Consequences of Civil War. *Oxford Economic Papers*, 51, 168–183.
Collier, P. & Hoeffler, A. 2004. *Greed and Grievance in Civil War*, Working Paper.
COLOMBIA, G. O. 2016. Controladoria General [Online]. Available: https://www.contraloria.gov.co/ [Accessed].
COLOMBIA, U. 2022. Report of the Secretary General. *In*: 2022, M. T. J. (ed.) *S/2022/513*. United Nations.
Dancy, G. 2016. *Are Devil Deals Necessary?* Conflict Amnesties and Sustainable Peace.
Dyck, C. 2011. Football and Post-War Reintegration: Exploring the Role of Sport in DDR processes in Sierra Leone. *Third World Quarterly*, 32, 395–415.
Fjelde, H., Höglund, K., Samhällsvetenskapliga, F., Institutionen för Freds- Och, K., Humanistisk-Samhällsvetenskapliga, V. & UPPSALA, U. 2012. *Building Peace, Creating Conflict?: Conflictual Dimensions of Local and International Peacebuilding*. Nordic Academic Press.
Grenfell, D. 2015. Rethinking Governance and Security in Timor-Leste. *In*: Sue Ingram, L. K., Mcwilliam, A. (ed.) *A New Era? Timor-Leste after the UN*. ANU Press.
Hoglund, K. 2008. Violence in war-to-democracy transtitions. *In*: JARSTAD, A. K. A. T. D. S. (ed.) *From War to Democracy: Dilemmas of Peacebuilding*. Cambridge University Press.
Humanitarian, T. N. 2014. *DDR in eastern DRC - Try, Try Again*. The New Humanitarian (IRIN OCHA).
ICG. 2007. *Republique Centre Afrique: Anatomie d' un etat fantome*. International Crisis Group.
ICG. 2013. République centrafricaine : Les urgences de la transition. In: *Rapport Afrique N°203 | 11 juin 2013*. International Crisis Grouo.
ICG. 2022. *Centrafrique: Éviter une nouvelle désintégration de l'armée*. International Crisis Group. 10 May 2022 ed. Enrica Picco.
Issat, D. 2015. *The Case for SSR as a Conflict Prevention Measure [Online]*. Geneva Centre For Security Sector Governance (DCAF).
The International Security Sector Advisory Team (ISSAT). Available: https://issat.dcaf.ch/Share/Blogs/ISSAT-Blog/The-Case-for-SSR-as-a-Conflict-Prevention-Measure [Accessed].
Jarstad, A. K. & Sisk, T. D. 2008. *From War to Democracy: Dilemmas of Peacebuilding*. Cambridge University Press.
Larsdotter, K. 2015. Security Assistance in Africa: The Case for Less. *Parameters* 45, 2.
Meharg, S., Arnusch, A. & Merrill, S. 2012. *Security Sector Reform: A Case Study Approach to Transition and Capacity Building*. Lulu.com.
Min of Finance of TIMOR LESTE. 2017. Annual State Budget. *In*: FINANCES, Dili: Goverment of Timor-Leste.

Muggah, R. 2008. *Security and Post-Conflict Reconstruction: Dealing with Fighters in the Aftermath of War*. Taylor & Francis.

Pack, J., Smith, R. & Mezran, K. 2017. The Origins and Evolution of ISIS in Libya. Rafik Hariri Center For the Middle East June 2017 The Atlantic Council of the United States.

Plunkett, M. 2003. Rebuilding the Rule of Law. *In*: W. Maley, Sampford, C. & Thakur, R. (eds.) *From Civil Strife to Civil Society: Civil and Military Responsibilities in Disrupted States*. United Nations University Press.

Regehr, E. 2015. *Disarming Conflict: Why Peace Cannot be Won on the Battlefield*. Between the Lines.

Restrepo, J. & Muggah, R. 2008. Colombia's Quiet Demobilization: A Security Dividend? *In*: Muggah, R. (ed.) *Security and Post-Conflict Reconstruction: Dealing with Fighters in the Aftermath of War*. Routledge.

Stahn, C. 2006. 'Jus ad bellum', 'jus in bello' ... 'jus post bellum'? – Rethinking the Conception of the Law of Armed Force. *European Journal of International Law*, 17, 921–943.

Terry, F. 2003. Reconstituting Whose Social Order? NGOs in Disrupted States. *In*: W. Maley, Sampford, C. & Thakur, R. (eds.) *From Civil Strife to Civil Society: Civil and Military Responsibilities in Disrupted States*. United Nations University Press.

Themnér, A. 2011. *Violence in Post-Conflict Societies: Remarginalization, Remobilizers and Relationships*. Taylor & Francis.

TIMOR-LESTE. 2002. Constituição da Republica Democratica de Timor-Leste. *In*: *Constitution of the Democratic Republic of East-Timor*. Part V_ Chapter 1st ed. Government of Timor-Leste.

UN-DPKO. 2010. Second Generation Disarmament, Demobilization and Reintegration (DDR) Practices in Peace Operations: A Contribution to the New Horizon Discussion on Challenges and Opportunities for UN Peacekeeping. *In*: Operations, U. N. D. O. P., Institutions, O. O. R. O. L. A. S. & Disarmament, D. A. R. S. (eds.).

UN-DPKO. 2012. *The United Nations SSR Perspective*. *In*: United Nations, Department of Peacekeeping Operations, Office of Rule of Law and Security Institutions & Perspective, S. S. R. U. (eds.). United Nations.

United Nations. 2010. *Second Generation DDR*.

UNSCR 2151. 2014. The Maintenance of International Peace and Security: Security Sector Reform: Challenges and Opportunities. *In*: Nations, U. (ed.) *Resolution 2151*. Adopted by the Security Council at its 7161st meeting, on 28 April 2014 ed. United Nations.

UNWG. 2006. *Integrated Disarmament, Demobilization and Reintegration Standards (IDDRS)*.

Uri, S. 2008. *Peace First: A New Model to End War*. Berrett-Koehler Publishers.

Von Dyck, C. 2016. *DDR and SSR in War-to-Peace Transition*. Ubiquity Press.

Willems, R. C. 2015. *Security and Hybridity after Armed Conflict: The Dynamics of Security Provision in Post-Civil War States*. Taylor & Francis.

William, M., Charles, S. & Ramesh, T. 2003. *From Civil Strife to Civil Society: Civil and Military Responsibilities in Disrupted States*. United Nations University Press.

9

FROM WAR TO PEACE

Voters but not yet citizens

> Put peace above politics... As important as it is, humanitarian action can never be a substitute for political solutions.
> *Secretary-General Ban Ki-Moon*[1]

In the transition toward social order, civil society and the media play a crucial role. Importantly, for democracy to work, some rights can be counter to the interest of the public. Thus, for the greater good of all, some rights of the few might be suppressed. In this chapter, a set of dilemmas are analyzed specifically to the politicization and "incivility" of civil society and the challenges toward a peace media reform. With more than 100 million refugees worldwide (UNHCR, 2022), civil society is the buffer that fulfills the urgent needs left by failed states and ineffective international organizations. In fact, as a former UN secretary-general stated, "civil wars are 'civil' only in the sense that civilians – that is, non-combatants – have become the main victims" (Annan, 1998). Moreover, the gender-based perspective of civil society in the postwar transition is fundamental: during war, 80 percent of victims are women and children (Rehn and Sirleaf, 2002). Some would argue that there would need to be a "global civil society" as its challenges have to be understood in the context of globalization. In other words, the concept of civil society is no longer confined to the borders of the territorial state (Kaldor, 2001; Kaldor, 2003). Recent global movements are evidence of that, such as #climatestrike, #metoo, #blacklivesmatter, and #standforUkraine. Yet, the problem of how to move from civil strife to civil society in disrupted states remains colossal (William Maley et al., 2003).

As opposed to the public and private sectors, civil society represents the organized "people's voice" that will participate in the constitution of the new democratic political realm. Over the past two decades, the distrust of the state's

DOI: 10.4324/9781003279976-12

willingness or capacity to respond to the population's needs have resulted in the ascendancy of the role of civil society (Kaldor, 2003). In war-torn countries, civil society is invariably absent, weak, or divided. Nonetheless, without civic participation, peace is unlikely to be self-reinforcing and sustainable (Belloni, 2008, p. 198). In a vacuum of state institutions, the influence of the population represents a political apparatus of power that might exacerbate competition and disruption rather than coordination and cooperation. It is also questionable how democratic civil society may be, considering the remarkable amount of political power groups within civil society may hold without anyone directly electing or appointing them. Thus, with so many divergent interests, civil society can be an instrument for, as well as an obstacle to, the transition toward social order as per the equation: [*People= Peace versus democracy*].

Additionally, the media can be a powerful instrument that can oppose or assist democracy and peacebuilding. Some argue that in times of peace and even in the most consolidated states, real and cyberspace media may contribute to a "mediocracy," a hidden "fourth pillar of power" after the executive, legislative, and judiciary branches of government (Carroll, 2010; Eko, 2012; Le, 2010). Notwithstanding the recommendations of best practice policies, it may be difficult to develop a "peace media" platform that is well disposed to democracy and dedicated to fostering peace. Thus, this chapter presents an analysis of the risks that civil society and media reform entail for efforts at democratization, state-building, and peacebuilding.

9.1 Civil society: the people's voice on human rights and the parallel state

Civil society refers to the agglomeration of non-government organizations (NGOs) and institutions, local or international, that manifest common interests and the will of citizens or global concerns (UN, 2009). In the aftermath of civil war and the process of peacebuilding, non-state actors, such as NGOs and international non-government organizations (INGOs), are vital despite their diversity of interests and values. INGOs are less bureaucratic when compared with country-to-country international organizations, and they are mainly free from the sovereign constraints of states, albeit they must operate within the domestic national legislation of the host countries. Many of their workers are volunteers. Examples of INGOs include Red Cross organizations; church-related agencies, such as Caritas; organizations of medical and educational community volunteers; as well as worldwide corporations, such as Save the Children, Oxfam, and Amnesty International.

Through mutual respect, dialogue, compromise, and economic and social integration, it is believed that civil society plays an important role in creating a political culture of social solidarity, stimulating political participation, generating cross-cutting cleavages, disseminating information to citizens, producing social conditions for economic reforms, and supporting the demobilization of former combatants as well as the process of the postwar return home of refugees and displaced persons. It also offers an additional mechanism of checks and balances by monitoring the exercise of state power and promoting social justice from the bottom up (Autesserre, 2014; Terry, 2003). Even though the literature repeatedly acknowledges the importance of the "people's voice" as agents and recipients of peace and democracy from the micro level, in practice, democratization and its processes are operationalized under a "top-down" approach. On the one hand, civil society can nurture trust and reciprocity and can foster tolerance and diversity, thus becoming a tool for "bonding social capital" (Putnam, 1993). On the other hand, the problem is that with different ethnic, racial, religious, and political associations, there is no "community" to bond with after the war.

When states fail to avoid crises and protect their citizens, volunteers are important actors in peacekeeping that fill the gap in addressing the constantly evolving challenges that occur within failing states. The concept of "good governance" moves away from the idea that governance is only the responsibility of the state toward the idea of the joint obligation of citizens and the state through a "vibrant civil society." Some authors argue that "civil society does what formal state actors are not doing" (Greig, 2015). For example, where there is no formal and functioning state, groups and organizations can patrol neighborhoods in the absence of operational police. Moreover, even where the state still maintains some capacity to deliver services to its citizens, civil society can still complement the work of domestic institutions by helping to improve economic and political performance, control crime and corruption, provide opportunities to former combatants to demobilize after war, and support the process of refugees and displaced persons returning to their homes after war's end. Thus, one argument is that a vibrant civil society is essential for a more democratic and prosperous society and is generally a necessary agent for achieving the Sustainable Development Goals (SDGs) (UN, 2018).

Another argument is that civil society may bring more chaos. Instead of contributing to reducing the gap between the state and the people, civil society may also create and constitute a kind of parallel state precisely when efforts are being made to build stability and state unity. Thus, by seeking their own interests, NGOs and INGOs end up eroding the already fragile state and state-building efforts (Schwartz, 2008). During times of transition, despite the perception of having lost "everything," there is a rise in opportunities for mobilization "to do something somehow for someone" (Gurr, 2000; Pereira Watts 2017). This ideal vision must be weighed against the frequent reality of a fragmented, factionalized, and occasionally xenophobic civil society. Even in consolidated democracies, civil society is a vague and general concept, which can be filled with different contents (Belloni, 2008). Thus, by comprising a complex network of intergovernmental and non-governmental organizations, and individual volunteers, civil society resembles a "non-system" (Beigbeder, 1991).

Additionally, civil society is not a panacea for improving coordination among its own agencies to resolve humanitarian action problems and cooperation with the government and international organizations. These problems are more fundamental and deeply rooted, arising from the paradox that politicized humanitarian action has the potential to prolong the conflict and thus the suffering of its victims (Van Oudenaren, 2017). Moreover, some NGOs/INGOs have sought to maintain strict and complete neutrality, while others have responded with overtly political commitments. Considering the complexity of emergencies, the diversity of humanitarian actors' agendas and objectives can sometimes be byzantine. Humanitarian crises have political causes. A government can easily avoid the responsibility of their unwillingness or ineptitude to protect its people and benefit from calamity by creating a narrative of purely humanitarian needs. If so, the participation of NGOs/INGOS may be seen as necessary, when, in fact, they may simultaneously be contributors to a vicious relation of doing good while generating more chaos. Haiti, Somalia, and Darfur are examples of it.

Operationally, civil society is on the frontline, an interface between the main agents and reaching the unreachable and most needed in a timely manner. However, "peace warriors" have a different motivation and mindset than soldiers or freedom fighters. Consequently, they may overestimate their power and mystify their workers as "good souls, quite naïve, yet very brave." This is the hero syndrome of the "doers" that picture themselves as warriors without weapons (Junod, 1951), who may forget that it might be necessary to make pacts with the "devil" in violent situations, such as in Rwanda and Somalia (Dallaire, 2005; Walch, 2016). Political feuds and fake NGOs often coexist alongside these peace warriors, who discover that their rhetoric often becomes politicized. Consequently, feelings of frustration and futility soon develop among the refugees in conflict and disaster zones (Pereira Watts, 2016). Nevertheless, they can also be tagged as part of the conflict, by creating more harm and disorder, often driven by financial motivations for their own personal endeavors. Fraud, greed, corruption, and apathy permeate the industry in response not only to disasters, but also to political agendas and economic opportunities (Schwartz, 2008). Furthermore, good intentions are not enough. There is an appealing motto of "have fun and save the world" that attracts rogue volunteers as "international humanitarian tourists," as it gives them the opportunity to explore adventurous places that they probably would not otherwise (Borland and Adams, 2013). Yet, due to their lack of expertise on the ground, their participation might be counter-effective or redundant despite good intentions and necessity.

At the international level, there is an intersection between collective responsibility, community, and human security that has moved the Westphalian state-centered political humanitarian principle toward the responsibility to protect (R2P) principle. Thus, beyond not doing any harm and needing to respect humanitarian principles and moral values, the role of civil society can only be safeguarded if the principles of responsibility to protect are as germane as the responsibilities required while protecting (RwP) (Pereira Watts, 2016; Pereira Watts 2017). Although legal and political conundrums might differ, criticisms about the lack of transparency, effectiveness, and accountability of civil society persist. After all, the multibillion-dollar humanitarian industry is shaped by covert interests, lack of accountability, and ineffective coordination. However, as valid as these criticisms are, civil society remains a problematic yet unavoidable element in the peacebuilding and democratization stratagem. Therefore, a further analysis regarding the role of civil society in post-conflict places is necessary, as follows.

9.1.1 Dilemmas on how to go from civil strife to civil society in disrupted states: politicized and "uncivil" agents

Among the dilemmas confronting civil society in times of transition is the one between inclusion and exclusion (horizontal). To make peace agreements and democracy work, it is incumbent to include the third sector. Nevertheless, rarely do its representatives have a seat at the negotiating table, such as the Chad Peace Agreement (Welle, 2022). One of the reasons is also etymological and operational: contrary to the private and public sectors, whose definition is clear, "*non-government organizations*" are defined[2] by what they are *not*. This vagueness is symptomatic of their disparate activities, which makes their legitimate insertion difficult, being the "(civil) society" pillar.

The vertical and operational dilemmas are explicit trade-offs between legitimacy and efficacy, and between flexibility and robustness, respectively. The horizontal trade-off may enhance legitimacy, but civil society's inclusion may make the decision-making process less efficient (posing a vertical dilemma). Arguably, an alternative for overcoming the bumpy start of the democratization process is to include a broad range of actors in peace negotiations and the future government, as in the peace accords in the DRC in 2002 and Liberia in 2003 (Belloni, 2008). Nevertheless, having too many actors and too much flexibility paralyzes the process of consensus-building and cooperation, which is also part of robust democratization. The involvement of civil society representatives has both positive and negative consequences, making the decision whether such representatives should be included a difficult one. While the horizontal dilemma raises the issue of whether civil society should be integrated, the vertical dilemma concerns the legitimacy and efficacy of those segments and interests of society that should be represented. In other words, if NGOs are to be included, which ones? How many? The latest Chad Peace Agreement (Welle, 2022) was signed between the military government and 42 rebels groups. Despite the fact that the largest rebel group – the Front for Change and Concord in Chad (FACT) – refused the deal, there are already too many parts. Including the people's voice sounds democratic, but it would fail in achieving a peace treaty.

Legitimacy is also related to the background of the organization. Very often, prominent politicians can create their own NGO to benefit from political connections in obtaining funding and influence as well as maintaining a profitable alternative in times out of the political mandate. As well as political parties' and elites' misuse, false NGOs can also be created by governments to promote misleading propaganda. It is not rare to find the influence of family ties blurring the separation between government elites and civil society.

The legitimacy quandary is also present in the significant discrepancy between organizations working in the bigger cities and the larger number of smaller civic groups that struggle for visibility and funding (Lucuta, 2014). Additionally, the sheer number of NGOs can be a nightmare for establishing dialogue and implementing policies in a coordinated and cooperative way. In Haiti, for example, it was estimated that there were over 10,000 NGOs after the 2010 earthquake that resulted in 250,000 dead, 1.5 million homeless, and tons of collapsed construction debris (Pereira Watts, 2011). The lack of organization and coordination blurs the line between legitimacy and efficacy, resulting in redundant or overlapping efforts and the misuse of scarce resources. Paradoxically, if a civil society becomes too efficient, a parallel state takes over and makes the effort of nation- or state-building redundant.

Furthermore, moral, existential, and security dilemmas are also pertinent. Civil society's activity is political, even if not necessarily party affiliated (Pereira Watts, 2017). In conflict-ridden areas, polarized interests make a civil society resemble a politicized society. As McEvoy and O'Leary (2013) astutely note: "in a deeply divided place there may be more than one 'civil society,' and their relations may be far from civil." Obviously, there exists a wide spectrum of organizations diversified along ethnic, religious, and national lines. But during times of transition, while some people organize themselves around democratic and liberal values, others resort to violent and/or illegal actions. Hence, the latter being perceived as far from "civil." A "good" civil society should not only be juxtaposed against "bad" states or parallel actors of a weak state, but also against a "bad" civil society (Paris, 2004). Such "uncivil" organizations as mafia-like groups and paramilitary gangs are tools of political parties with the means to enhance segregation and community polarization. In most conflict regions, the main threats to stability and obstacles to peacebuilding and democratization are not the conflict per se, but criminality following the security dilemma. Such criminal groups may see state-building as a threat to their interests and actively oppose it by violent and intimidating "participation" within civil society. Divided communities suspicious of each other's intentions can impede human rights protection and the development of the rule of law, and, in some cases, they can foster corrupt and patrimonial relationships as the alternative to citizenship rights (Themnér and Utas, 2016). The influence of uncivil and even xenophobic practices by civil society becomes robust in fragile or pseudo-states. Ethnic, national, and religious organizations may also uphold exclusivist values and norms that are incompatible with democratic practices. Thus, when civil society organizations are not civic, multiethnic, and multi-religious, they can create a significant obstacle to achieving a sustainable democratic peace instead of constituting a tool for a positive transition from armed conflict (Belloni, 2008).

Additionally, there is the ethical problem of inevitable selectiveness: how to triage the neediest victims? The principles of civil society intertwine with the four pillars of humanitarian aid: *humanity + impartiality + neutrality + independence*. Assistance ultimately should be directed to an individual in need, and not on the basis of gender, race, ethnicity, ideology, or faith, even though there may be collective problems that may well be identified through these classifiers. Nevertheless, the "right" to receive and a "duty" to provide assistance beyond borders is far from straightforward. For example, should NGOs provide relief assistance with discretion, neutrality, and impartiality, or should they publicly denounce human rights violations at the risk of being expelled and thus not providing assistance at all? On many occasions, such as in Sierra Leone, Liberia, and Cambodia, it has been proved that humanitarian relief, such as food and medication, has been delivered together with illegal weapons that would fuel the conflict. Thus, under the umbrella of morality, the four principles of civil society and humanitarian aid might oppose necessity and efficiency.

The demand for aid rarely matches the supply. Therefore, hard choices and constant triage must be made when saving friends or enemies (Moore, 1998; Moore, 2013; Damrosch, 2000). Beyond the unprecedented number of refugees and internally displaced persons (IDPs), the world faces the largest humanitarian crisis since the end of World War II, with more than 45 million people in 43 countries, including Afghanistan, Yemen, South Sudan, Somalia, and Ethiopia, facing starvation and famine (OCHA, 2022). Adding to the complexity, in the "modern" era, other global issues such as climate change; population growth; volatile financial and commodities markets; epidemics, including Ebola and COVID-19; and water scarcity all contribute to the enormity of this problem. The Global Report on Food Crises estimates up to 282 million people faces food insecurity in 2021 (FAO, 2022). This can directly affect the return to violence in certain places already disrupted by internal conflict. The basis of selective decisions is not only sometimes morally puzzling, but may also involve conflicting expectations regarding the international response and the extent of the so-called selectivity gap (Pereira Watts 2017). Notably, the principles of consistency and coherence are critical for a legitimate political order. But they are also important for compliance with rules, as coherence is considered a key factor in explaining why laws compel. When demand for aid is so high, inconsistency and hard choices are inevitable between saving friends or enemies.

As for independence, even though most NGOs receive a significant amount of money from states, they do not necessarily result in governmental policy control as they are officially autonomous bodies. However, whether from governments or private donors, NGOs and INGOs face the dilemma of tackling emergencies and running sustainable aid projects while maintaining independence from their founders' interests. In practice, civil society is not a unitary actor; therefore, independence, impartiality, or neutrality are rarely found together. Paradoxically, politics creates a micro dynamic of cooperation and competition within civil society. In conflict zones, humanitarian aid relief requires negotiation with rebel groups to access the "unreachable": the neediest and more isolated victims. Beyond breaching moral principles concerning the responsibility to protect and moral structures involved in the act of protecting (R2P & RwP), this encompasses problems of corruption and the divergence of aid that fuel the black market and enmeshes humanitarian actors as part of what sustains the conflict (Walch, 2016). CAR, DRC, and Somalia are three examples.

Temporal, resource, financial, security, and systemic dilemmas are also intertwined. People's needs are urgent, but relief does not come at the same speed. Therefore, building a vibrant civil society highlights the importance of a long-term perspective as it also involves the development of appropriate political frameworks, such as the consolidation of the rule of law and security (William Maley, 2003). Human resources are often deadlocked between efficiency and viability in an anarchic and disordered conjuncture. Moreover, overstretched NGOs and INGOs usually struggle with funding and their efforts are often concentrated more on fundraising than program design and implementation. With high poverty and unemployment rates, civil organizations cannot self-fund and governments struggle without an efficient tax system. However, the temporal impasse is also related to so-called short-termism versus projectism: with insufficient funds and capable human resources, NGOs must work on short-term projects instead of long-term development.

Private business also plays a fundamental role in the humanitarian industry in the move from relief to development. Private companies usually have the budget and mechanisms to create jobs, infrastructure, and opportunities that emerge after the crisis. Additionally, the systemic quandary is correlated to the circumstance that international assistance may be indispensable for guaranteeing the survival and subsequent development of local civil society groups. The international community faces several dilemmas when promoting "local ownership" and "capacity-building." Peacekeeping, with its complex web of interests, challenges, competing objectives, and actors, owes as much to civil society as the leading agents in affecting positive change to the otherwise unchangeable. However, peacebuilding operations also attempt to support local NGOs as this makes donors look good and helps to overcome the ownership trade-off by building the local capacity in moving toward a goal of self-rule. Consequently, donors or international organizations may become part of the problem as aid also creates a parallel market and helps to undermine governmental capacity instead of fostering cooperation and the pooling of resources.

Peacekeeping can also epitomize a design dilemma with a shift from a bottom-up to a top-down rationale by inducing the prioritization of activities according to the donor's agenda and its international funding instead of the more indispensable necessities on the ground. This also leads to an additional "territorial dilemma," which is not included in the P–A–T set of transitional dilemmas proposed by this book. In a globalized world, how "local" or "national" should the movements promoted by civil society be? Many civil society organizations are international institutions claiming to work globally for local issues. They can be theoretically well designed with specialized human resources and financial capital. But, by being external actors, they rarely reflect local civil society's needs despite hiring local staff (Belloni, 2008). If needs are not tackled, security concerns increase. And continuity is required from the emergency to the development projects. It is usually easier to start, hard to maintain, and strategically challenging to end an aid project. Additionally, continuity and coherence depend on funds, design, and human resources.

Furthermore, a transparency dilemma is also evident from two perspectives. First, the successful conclusion of peace negotiations may require a high degree of confidentiality, precluding, or complicating any opening into the political process for new actors other than the main warring parties. This need for confidentiality can lead to closed negotiations for a peace agreement, often outside the country. This increases the possibility that its terms will respond to the demands of the participants and their immediate constituencies, including the military and the political and economic elites, which can jeopardize the process's popular support and legitimacy. Second, as with the decision about which NGO to support, the monitoring and evaluation process, activities and outcomes, as well as funding transfers, may lack transparency. Most expenditure is for salaries and office support (rent, computers, chairs, electricity, etc.) and, hence, not directed at the primary activity. It is extremely difficult to assess the veracity and accuracy of the "activities reports." For example, concerns and suspicions about corruption have triggered foreign donors to bypass the Haitian government and channel financial and material assistance through NGOs. Subsequently, as some organizations were "cashing-in" and causing more harm than helping or rebuilding, this has made Haiti a "republic of NGOs." Moreover, some NGO and INGO projects have often had more money than the entire Haitian government. Among other consequences, the Haitian government has had little chance to develop the human or institutional capacity to deliver services. Similar circumstances can be found in other cyclical humanitarian aid locations, such as South Sudan, Congo, and Iraq, as well as other fragile states (Pereira Watts, 2016; Brock et al., 2012). When such occurrences take place, the lack of accountability of civil society debilitates the transition from war to peace. It thus is antithetical to the principles of democracy that are supposedly being engendered.

What is the main priority to come out of a plethora of priorities in the aftermath of conflict? The sequencing and design dilemmas are related to which plea has the loudest voice: justice, employment, health, education, stopping violence against women, human rights, water and sanitation, housing, poverty, and agriculture are competing for attention. Simultaneously, a typical top-down or bottom-up impasse occurs when the question arises whether the "development of local capacity" should be focused on large national institutions for the whole country or whether it should be concentrated on local associations in remote places. Additionally, when political ideology and funding decisions are guided by non-multicultural and integrationist values, political or technical choices concerning the establishment and operation of institutions may lead to a clash between peace and democracy by excluding part of the population through tyranny by the majority or by the minority.

Thus, civil society can fall prey to a short-term vision and subordination to a donor's agenda without an inclusive approach, sustainable funds, transparency, and sufficient legitimacy. In extreme cases, civil society can be misused as a tool for corruption and money laundering or become an expression of nationalism and ethnoreligious racism. It may become an organ of criminal organizations' illegal activities, be subject to a political party's whims, or represent the façades of the elite's interests. Therefore, although including the "people" makes sense, time, continuity, cost, selectiveness, and accountability remain critical issues for building peace, democracy, and good governance after the war. It is methodologically complex to determine the effectiveness that is individually and collectively made. Notably, a successful civil society must not overtake or diminish the role of the state. It must contribute toward state-building by serving as the interface between the main agents and preventing failed states from becoming "pseudo-republics of civil society anarchy" (Pereira Watts, 2016).

9.2 Media reform and freedom of speech: (un)peaceful, (not) free and (un)fair

The mass media are a powerful instrument. Freedom of expression and press freedom are considered cornerstones of a democratic society. There are a variety of indexes, such as Freedom House, the Global Peace Index, Polity IV, the Democracy Index, and the Fragile States Index, that provide collected data on these freedoms. These civil liberties are also formulated as a fundamental human right in Article 19 of the Universal Declaration of Human Rights (OHCHR-UN, 1948). Political organizations might misuse these civil rights and publish incitements for revenge through speeches that bring up socio-political differences rather than similarities. During extreme cases of conflict, the media have played an essential part in promoting genocidal violence, as in Rwanda, Bosnia, and Kosovo (Thompson, 2007). Nevertheless, they have also peacefully promoted civic education and electoral information in Timor-Leste's 1999 referendum and subsequent elections. A responsible media apparatus is characterized by being peaceful, neutral, transparent, and impartial. Additionally and in theory, the democratic values of the media are ideally to be "independent, non-partisan and secular" (Diez, 2014). Once again, the hybrid dynamic in post-conflict scenarios differs greatly from "normal" political conjectures. Therefore, so-called media reform is encircled by transitional dilemmas, as follows.

The vertical and horizontal dilemmas are explicit: for the sake of legitimacy, the inclusion of the media in all phases of the peace and democratization processes is desirable. But for the sake of efficacy and security, certain negotiations need to exclude the media. For example, the 2016 negotiations between members of the government of Colombia and members of FARC were secretly held in Havana. Nonetheless, during armed conflict, the media commonly become extremely polarized and may serve as a tool for propaganda for a warring party. Often, they are caught up in making ethnic overtures and mobilizing people for violence using military metaphors with fighting rhetoric. Thus, even if it might be a legitimate tool, the media can be counter-effective for the transition to peace and democracy if misused to influence the processes (Paris, 2004). Moreover, even during democratic times, the media system is invariably owned by elites. The problem is exacerbated in war settings when editors-in-chief are appointed by elites and warlords to give voice to only one party.

Crucial to democratic accountability, a functioning and diverse media should provide accurate and truthful information to the citizens and critical scrutiny of political issues. However, as per the transparency dilemma, that is usually not the case. Balance is another debatable issue that overlaps with impartiality and accountability as well as with efficiency and legitimacy (posed by the vertical dilemma). Too much attention is given, particularly by Western media, to what might make headlines, such as events in Syria, Iraq, and Afghanistan, and little attention is given to "less hot places," such as Ukraine, Abkhazia, or Burundi. Consequently, not only does this create a moral quandary about selectiveness, but it also engenders "news fatigue" and some mistrust in their corporate reputation about how truthful the information is (Carroll, 2010). Moreover, although the media can put much pressure on many actors to respond, this pressure can lead to policy failures. On this, the conflict in Syria is a cautionary tale (Doucet, 2018).

As depicted in the resource and operational dilemmas, there is a lack of adequate human resources training in journalism or media technology in countries emerging from war. Accessibility is another issue. Most disrupted states have a precolonial legacy of the oral tradition, an alienated managerial class, and dominant systems based on political patronage (Bourgault, 1995). With an average of 80 percent of the territorial infrastructure destroyed by the end of the conflict and high rates of poverty and illiteracy, the radio might be more suitable than television and newspapers, where more technology and investment are invariably needed (Collier, 1999). However, although the radio might be more cost-efficient in terms of mass access, it can limit democratization as only one information channel centralizes the distribution of news (Nyamnjoh, 2005). This situation also involves a financial quandary. Setting up the media industry should be a private matter, but this is rarely the case in the aftermath of conflict. As the tax system might not yet be in place, there may be no funds to finance media reform, among many other urgent priorities. Without funds and human capability, there is room for corruption, which leads back to the transparency and vertical dilemmas of impartiality and legitimacy (Frère and Marthoz, 2007).

As part of the transition, media reform is usually part of the agenda for democratization, with a "media advisor officer" under the political or civil affairs department of UN missions. A transition usually consists of efforts to create new laws guaranteeing freedom of expression and restructuring the media infrastructure, including forming some independent media agencies and widening the range of media outlets and ownership (Hoglund, 2008). Media reform seems secondary and is slow to progress among so many priorities in building peace, democracy, and socioeconomic development. Promoting codes of conduct and licensing systems and interrupting the transmission or dissemination of hate media appear to be techniques for developing a more effective and "democratic" media after a war, as was implemented in Kosovo (Paris, 2004, p. 198). Therefore, media reform also taps into the systemic, sequencing, and design dilemmas by confronting the role of local and international ownership, by opposing technical and political choices, and by favoring a top-down instead of a bottom-up approach through laying down legal parameters and enforcement processes.

Simple questions such as which language should be used can be yet another example of competition and conflict. Therefore, the horizontal trade-off of inclusion and exclusion is once again active. For example, Timor-Leste is an extraordinary Babel Tower with two official languages in the constitution, two extra "working languages" during the transitional period, and another 31 local languages (2002). The dissemination of new laws or even the establishment of an educational curriculum added complexity to the already turbulent postwar transition with 1 million inhabitants at the time. Within the conceptual political platform of "unity in diversity," the issue of the "us" and the "other" obstructs the transition toward democracy. The cases of Afghanistan, Georgia, Chad, Ethiopia, and Guinea-Bissau are examples of it (Woolman and Fleisch, 2014). Ideally, information about elections, legal provisions, and governance policies should include everyone. However, it is unlikely that it will be inclusive of all the linguistic ethnicities. How can citizens be aware of new laws if the media does not equally transmit to its diverse population? Thus, the media also may contribute to the persecution or marginalization of minorities through lack of transparency, ethnic favoritism, emotive tactics in election campaigns or political declarations, hate speech and other measures to inflame an ethnic majority against minorities, or vice versa. Consequently, this also engenders a general perception of insecurity among the population.

Media reform takes time. If done too soon or too late, it will negatively impact upon democratization and peacebuilding processes. Furthermore, the moral dilemma permeates all the previously presented dilemmas, with anti-corruption measures, fairness, and freedom of the press and actors being prerequisites. On the one hand, the power of influence and time is immense and can be a tool for peacebuilding. On the other hand, it can be an effective instrument to reinforce hostilities and block the implementation of human rights. Moreover, another aspect is the abilities of the state and the international community to influence a responsible media as well as the potential risk of government-financed (non-commercial) media to be used for propaganda as well as the possibility to implement laws for balanced reporting.

Finally, recent media forms like the internet and social media have created new means by which to impact democratization. Examples include the role of Facebook during the Arab Spring and the organization of many political movements in Ukraine, Thailand, Hong Kong, and around the world. The so-called netocracy, a symbiosis of the internet and democracy, shows its colossal power to influence millions of people in seconds. Some governments, like those in China and Russia, recognize this power and control access to the internet and social media within their territory, such as on issues on the South China Sea, Tibet, and the Crimea. "Voter-generated content," for instance, videos on YouTube have been identified as a drift toward "videocracy." As examples, the election of Silvio Berlusconi as Italy's prime minister in 1994 was seen by many as a "media coup d'état." The overthrow of Nicolae Ceauşescu in Romania in 1989 was mooted as the "first revolution on live television."

9.3 Summary of the chapter

Differing from previous chapters focused on the political, legal, and civil orders, this chapter contributes to the book's issues by focusing on the transition to the social order. Democracy requires a thriving civil society and an independent media. However, within the hybrid postwar context, their inclusion may also be an obstacle to a peaceful social order. Civil society may play an important role by helping to fulfill the needs that fragile states and other institutions cannot provide. Nevertheless, certain kinds of civil organizations erode the power of formal institutions by creating a parallel state. The politicization of this sector of society may impact negatively on the efficiency and legitimacy of government. Where there is a Pandora's box of agents and political elites, there is no such thing as true independence, especially in a multibillion-dollar industry shaped by covert interests, a lack of accountability, and ineffective coordination. Further, although freedom of expression and the press are considered cornerstones of a democratic society, mediocracy can corrode the political apparatus if political parties and elite power holders misuse their power to foster co-option, control, and disruption rather than coordination and cooperation. Notwithstanding policy recommendations, building a "peace media" platform through a reform that contributes to the transition toward peace and democracy via a public agenda remains complex.

Despite persisting clientelism and corruption, a degree of transparency and political accountability exists and is dependent on time and the maturity of the social capital. Domestic ownership is crucial to (re)building social capital. Active citizen diplomacy must be placed at the center of conflict resolution; not at its receiving end. Through promoting social and political spaces for dialogue instead of ethnic or national segregation, good governance becomes a joint obligation for citizens and the government. The rationale should be inverted: a vibrant civil society and a functional peace media are the effect of a well-functioning democratic state and not its cause. In the aftermath of a civil war, the "people" may be transformed into voters, but they are not yet citizens in terms of their full participation in the political democratic spectrum. Nevertheless, without civic ownership and media reform, the reconstitution of social order in disrupted settings is unlikely to be self-reinforcing and sustainable. Figure 9.1 summarizes a possible arrangement of dilemmas facing the social order.

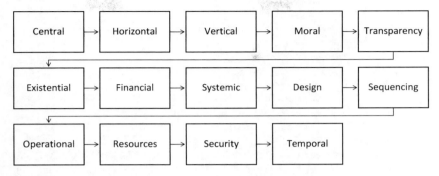

FIGURE 9.1   Dilemmas facing social order. Source: Author

Note

1 News Centre, 2016.
2 This inability of a more precise definition is not exclusive to the English language. No better term has appeared in other languages, such as French, Spanish, Portuguese, German, Russian, and Italian.

References

Annan, K. 1998. Secretary-General Statements and Messages. *In*: SG reflects on intervention in thirty fifth annual Ditchley Foundation Lecture. 26 June 1998.
Autesserre, S. 2014. Going Micro: Emerging and Future Peacekeeping Research. *International Peacekeeping*, 21.
Beigbeder, Y. 1991. *The Role and Statuts of International Humanitarian Volunteers and Organizations: The Right and Duty to Humanitarian Assistance*. Springer Netherlands.
Belloni, R. 2008. Civil Society in War-to-Democracy Transitions. *In*: Jarstad, A. K. & Sisk, T. D. (eds.) *From War to Democracy: Dilemmas of Peacebuilding*. Cambridge University Press.
Borland, K. & Adams, A. 2013. *International Volunteer Tourism: Critical Reflections on Good Works in Central America*. Palgrave Macmillan US.
Bourgault, L. M. 1995. *Mass Media in Sub-Saharan Africa*. Indiana University Press.
Brock, L., Holm, H.-H., Sorensen, G. & ET Stohl, M. 2012. *Fragile States: War and Conflict in the Modern World*. Cambridge, UK, Polity Press.
Carroll, C. 2010. *Corporate Reputation and the News Media: Agenda-setting within Business News Coverage in Developed, Emerging, and Frontier Markets*. Taylor & Francis.
Collier, P. 1999. On the Economic Consequences of Civil War. *Oxford Economic Papers*, 51, 168–183.
Dallaire, R. 2005. *Shake Hands With The Devil: The Failure of Humanity in Rwanda*. Arrow Ltd - Mass Market; 1st edition (1 October 2004).
Damrosch, L. F. 2000. The Inevitability of Selective Response? Principles to Guide Urgent International Action. *In*: C.Thakur, A. S. A. R. (ed.) *In Kosovo and the Challenge of Humanitarian Intervention: Selective Indignation, Collective Action, and International Citizenship*. United Nations University Press.
Diez, F. 2014. *Periodismo Responsable: Periodismo de paz* [Online]. Reconciliacion Colombia. Available: http://www.reconciliacioncolombia.com/blog/2014/08/periodismo-responsable-periodismo-de-paz [Accessed 18 dec 2015].

Doucet, L. 2018. Syria & the CNN Effect: What Role Does the Media Play in Policy-Making? *Daedalus*, 147 Ending Civil Wars: Constraints & Possibilities, 141–157.

Eko, L. S. 2012. *New Media, Old Regimes: Case Studies in Comparative Communication Law and Policy.* Lexington Books.

FAO. 2022. *Global Report on Food Crises.* GRFC.

Frère, M. S. & Marthoz, J. P. 2007. *The Media and Conflicts in Central Africa*, Lynne Reinner Publishers.

Greig, R. 2015. *Refugees, Feuds And Fake NGOs: Volunteers Doing Humanitarian Work International Aid Organizations Aren't.* International Business Times (IBT).

Gurr, T. R. 2000. *Peoples Versus States: Minorities at Risk in the New Century`.* United States Institute of Peace Press.

Hoglund, K. 2008. Violence in War-to-Democracy Transitions. *In*: JARSTAD, A. K. A. T. D. S. (ed.) *From War to Democracy: Dilemmas of Peacebuilding.* Cambridge University Press.

Junod, D. M. 1951. *Warrior Without Weapons.* The MacMillan Company.

Kaldor, M. 2001. A Decade of Humanitarian Intervention: The Role of Global Civil Society. *In*: H. K. Anheier, M. G., and M. Kaldor (ed.) *Global Civil Society.* University Press.

Kaldor, M. 2003. *Global Civil Society: An Answer to War.* Wiley.

Le, E. 2010. *Editorials and the Power of Media: Interweaving of Socio-cultural Identities.* John Benjamins Pub.

Lucuta, G. M. 2014. Peacebuilder Nations in Action. *Insight Conflict*, 12/09/2014.

Mcevoy, J. & O'leary, B. 2013. *Power Sharing in Deeply Divided Places.* University of Pennsylvania Press, Incorporated.

Moore, J. E. 1998. *Hard Choices: Moral Dilemmas in Humanitarian Intervention.* Rowman & Littlefield, Lanham, Oxford, ICRC.

Moore, T. 2013. Saving Friends or Saving Strangers? Critical Humanitarianism and the Geopolitics of International Law. *Review of International Studies*, 39, 925–947.

NEWS CENTRE, U. 2016. 'Put peace above politics,' Ban tells leaders of South Sudan. 25 February 2016 ed.

Nyamnjoh, F. B. 2005. *Africa's Media: Democracy and the Politics of Belonging.* Zed Books.

OCHA. 2022. *Global Humanitarian Overview.* 2022 ed.

Ohchr-UN. 1948. *Universal Declaration of Human Rights.*

Paris, R. 2004. *At War's End: Building Peace after Civil Conflict.* Cambridge University Press.

Pereira Watts, I. 2011. *Haiti: Um aniversário a não ser comemorado em 6 lições (Haiti: 6 reasons to not celebrate one year earthquake' anniversary).* Mundorama.

Pereira Watts, I. 2016. The Role of Independent Volunteers in Humanitarian Crises. *E-International Relations*, Jun 29 2016.

Pereira Watts, I. 2017. Is Humanitarian Aid Politicized? *E-International Relations.* Apr 13 2017 ed.

Putnam, R. 1993. *Making Democracy Work: Civic Traditions in Modern Italy.* Princeton University Press.

Rehn, E. & Sirleaf, E. J. 2002. *Women, War, Peace: The Independent Experts' Assessment on the Impact of Armed Conflict on Women and Women's Role in Peace Building.* UNIFEM.

Schwartz, T. 2008. *Travesty in Haiti: A True Account of Christian Missions, Orphanages, Food Aid, Fraud, and Drug Trafficking.* BookSurge Publishing.

Terry, F. 2003. Reconstituting whose social order? NGOs in disrupted states. *In*: W. Maley, Sampford, C. & Thakur, R. (eds.) *From Civil Strife to Civil Society: Civil and Military Responsibilities in Disrupted States.* United Nations University Press.

Themnér, A. & Utas, M. 2016. Governance Through Brokerage: Informal Governance in Post-civil War Societies. *Civil Wars*, 18, 255–280.
Thompson, A. 2007. *The Media and the Rwanda Genocide*, Pluto Press.
Timor-Leste. 2002. Constituição da Republica Democratica de Timor-Leste. *In: Constitution of the Democratic Republic of East-Timor. Part V_ Chapter.* 1st ed. Government of Timor-Leste.
UN. 2009. *Civil Society [Online]*. Available: http://www.un.org/en/sections/resources-different-audiences/civil-society/ [Accessed 05.08.2015].
UN. 2018. *Sustainable Development Goals (SDGs)*.
UNHCR 2022. *Global Trends Report*. UN High Commission for Refugees.
Van Oudenaren, D. 2017. Politicised humanitarian aid is fuelling South Sudan's civil war. *In*: Irin (ed.).
Walch, C. 2016. *Conflict in the Eye of the Storm: Micro-dynamics of Natural Disasters, Cooperation and Armed Conflict*. Uppsala University.
Welle, D. 2022. *Chad: 'Historic Agreement' No Guarantee for Peace*. Deutsche Welle (DW).
William, M., Charles, S. & Ramesh, T. 2003. *From Civil Strife to Civil Society: Civil and Military Responsibilities in Disrupted States*. United Nations University Press.
Woolman, S. & Fleisch, B. 2014. The Problem of the 'Other' Language. *Constitutional Court Review*, Vol. V. 135–171. Juta Company. South Africa.

PART III

Conclusion and recommendations

FROM HYBRID DEMOCRATIC PEACE TOWARD AN INTEGRATED TRANSITION

Conclusion, limitations, and recommendations

> There is scarcely any peace so unjust,
> but it is preferable, upon the whole, to the justest war
> *Erasmus, 1917 [1521]*

This book focuses on civil wars. It seems that the famous assertion of Charles Tilly that wars make states and states makes war to be true in most of the intrastate war cases analyzed (Sorensen, 2001; Tilly et al., 1985; Kaspersen, 2017). Although Tilly's statement referred to state formation, it corroborates this book's emphasis on state *trans*formation. Nevertheless, the literature is still unable to answer in a convincing ways crucial questions such as why can some war-torn countries make the transition to peace and democracy while others cannot? This transition phase represents the crossroads leading toward real positive change, not merely a pause in the same conflict or an interlude between two wars.

Is democracy a good idea? Yes. But, with conflicting objectives, not all good things come together (Leininger et al., 2012). When the civil war ends, a hybrid system of peace, with both positive and negative aspects, and a political regime that is both democratic and authoritarian coexist. Precisely because it is a transition, undemocratic elements are necessary for securing a minimum of peace. Violence might erupt through democratic foundations. Under this hybrid dynamic, if the post-civil war transition is not effective, this often results in anocracies. However, failed democracies and fragile states have been proved to be most dangerous and turbulent, compared to consolidated democracies and non-democracies. Neither democracy nor peacebuilding is panaceas as the hybrid nature of a post-civil war peace is characterized by tension between autocracy and democracy. For instance, Nepal and Sri Lanka have experienced a significantly low level of violence after their respective armed insurgencies and civil wars. The shift toward illiberal peacebuilding is conducted by domestic actors through national and subnational processes of co-option and repression (Smith et al., 2020). The risks to a democratic transition deserve a deeper understanding of such contradictions to effectively set the foundations for sustainable peace, liberal democracy, and socioeconomic development after war. Thus, by juxtaposing democracy and peacebuilding, this book is based on the interplay of a central dilemma: $[Civil\ war\ transition = peace\ versus\ democracy]$.

This book examines two main questions: what are the dilemmas that oppose the choice for peace or democracy after the civil war? And what role do UN operations play in bringing simultaneously peace and democracy to post-civil war countries? By expanding the understanding of the synergy between peacemaking, democracy-building, and state-building through case analyses of UN peacebuilding operations (1989–2022), the book has advanced the literature by identifying a platform of common dilemmas necessary to build peace, democracy, and a functional state after civil wars (Chapter 1). By combining what democratization studies and security and peace studies usually deal with separately, it proposes an innovative Philosophical–Actors–Tactic (P–A–T) framework of 14 dilemmas: central, existential, design, financial, horizontal, moral, operational, resource, security, sequencing, systemic, temporal, transparency, and vertical dilemmas. It is unrealistic to expect that peace, democracy, and a consolidated state will emerge from the ashes of war all at the same time and at the same levels. The P–A–T framework of dilemmas does not pretend to be a cure-all recipe, nor does it provide a laboratory of solutions to put countries afflicted by civil strife into "the path to Denmark" (Krasner and Eikenberry, 2018; Börzel and Grimm, 2018). Instead, it provides an integrated tool for awareness toward better decision making or room for the least bad option among complex postwar challenges. On the assumption that sequentialist templates are to be avoided, this study identifies emerging evidence of what might work and what does not to minimize the risks in liberal peace transitions. Importantly, it highlights the complexity of a constellation of intertwined factors and emphasizes their dynamism as solving one dilemma leads to another.

This book also analyzes the main challenge of the role of UN interventions in civil wars and its agenda for peace and democracy, legality, and legitimacy (Chapter 2). It explores the problems related to democratization and its relationship with violence in place of peace (Chapter 3). Chapter 4 provides evidence that peacekeeping is good for building peace, democracy, and the state, while simultaneously being bad for all three processes. It offers a new approach to the role of UN peacekeeping missions in building a "peaceful, democratic and strong state." Much of the literature draws conclusions about UN operations in labeling them either as successes or as failures, related either to stopping the fighting or to viewing them on a mandate approach. In this book, most cases of UN interventions between 1989 and 2022 were found to be more verisimilar, showing only partial success. Thus, contrary to those binary outcomes of success or failure, this book proposes quadruple options that consider "moderate levels of peace and moderate levels of democracy." Democracy works well when contradictory features balance each other. Furthermore, the transition from an internal armed conflict requires moving toward political, legal, civil, and social orders. Thus, 12 issues have been analyzed, all of which are commonly found during transition times: elections and political parties; the constitution and power-sharing; amnesty, truth commissions, ad hoc war crime tribunals and transitional justice; DDR and SSR; and media reform and civil society (Chapters 5–9). To further the findings of this book, it is recommended that the transition toward economic order should be analyzed. Such an analysis is not included in this book due to limitations of length.

After the civil war, what comes next? If civil war's modern usage is a tool of politics and statecraft, as Clausewitz's vision asserts, then it seems that politics itself has always been a form of civil war by other and less deadly means (Armitage, 2017). On the other hand, Hannah Arendt argues that politics is society's glue and serves as the means of conflict resolution through compromise, conciliation, negotiation, and consensus. In the aftermath of civil conflict, this conciliation is yet to occur. Post-civil war transition is more about achieving political goals than about fulfilling the demands of morality or humanity amid social trauma and calamities. Indeed, it is as much the art of the possible as Sun Tzu's art of (new) war. As this book addresses it in depth, some aspects of democratization contradict conflict resolution and state-building. Undoubtedly, in the transition from war to democracy, peace might fail when warlords paradoxically become peacemakers and agents of decision-taking, purportedly in the interests of the state as well as the security and well-being of its people. Modern liberal democracy stands at a crisis point (Fukuyama et al., 2015; Freedom House, 2022; EIU, 2021). Nevertheless, the assertion that it is the least worse option available as it is less violence prone remains true. Paradoxically, consensus-based democracy is a problem endemic to democratization. By constantly creating paralysis, it can become a bottleneck for progress toward peace.

Importantly peacebuilding and postwar democratization are simultaneous tasks contingent on the direct influence of the elites. This understanding helps to shed light on why peacebuilding missions often bring some peace, but rarely democracy, to war-torn countries. After civil war, law enforcement institutions must be developed concurrently, such as the creation of an effective police force and a criminal justice system. Similarly, political institutions, for instance, a depoliticized judiciary and an electoral commission, must also be established. Without these institutions, democracy will fail as the promise to obtain security for citizens or political rights for the warring factions will be only fallacies.

According to the methodology used in this book, it is more accurate to say that the UN's ambition to promote democratization via peacebuilding operations in a post-civil war scenario succeeds at a moderate level. Between the two alternatives of peace or democracy, peace should be prioritized over a particular regime type; therefore, peace comes first. Despite the uniqueness of each conflict, it is nevertheless debatable whether the promotion of a "democratically good enough" political regime can or should proliferate everywhere. The fact is that, like it or not, the hybrid democratic peace is often what is only possible in the fog of civil war. To be trapped in the "middle/moderate level" might not mean that the UN peace operation failed. Based on the available evidence, depending on the momentum of a specific conflict, the prioritization of peace at the expense of democracy or vice versa was considered necessary. This supports the main argument presented in this book that pursuing both peace and democracy in the aftermath of civil war may undermine each other. Regardless of the multiple concepts of "peace," it is a never-ending process, which, like democratization, experiences progress and regression akin to a roller coaster dynamic. As there are sometimes "necessary wars," this consequently infers that there is a "necessary peace" (Uri, 2008). If so, the "moderate" or "good enough" approach might be the "necessary step" toward a transformation of the conflict into a different dynamic rather than its resolution.

Despite these conclusions, and as suggested in Chapter 4, a stronger understanding of the meso-level cases of success entails further investigation. Considering the limitations of this book, it is recommended that the analysis be expanded with more variables, such as the level of democracy before the war starts, the GDP per capita, the level of illiteracy, how the war ended, the terrorist threat, natural resources, failed past agreements, whether the country is a former colony or has borders with a Perm-5 country, the geography, the predominant religion, ethnicity or race, the length of the conflict, the number of rebel groups, and the scale of destructiveness.

Beyond encounters for conflict resolution in an effort to create sustainable democratic peace, is prevention the answer to avoid violent conflict? Prevention efforts also lead to several challenges. Despite the increased call for preventive initiatives, it is difficult for policymakers to sell preventive actions to UN member states that will also have to convince their home constituencies to support involvement. Preventive actions are political, not technical, requiring the use of precious political capital for uncertain results whose achievements may be invisible. Therefore, it is difficult to evaluate the success of preventive actions. Moreover, when the UN acts "preventively," it is indeed interfering in the internal affairs of its member states and, therefore, breaching the principle of sovereignty. Although this book does not address in detail mechanisms to prevent violence due to size and scope restrictions, it affirms that structural prevention is essential. Rather than sticks or carrots, the international community should incentivize governments to forge policies and programs at the national or subnational level that inhibit armed violence. It should also encourage participatory governance in the long term. As addressed in Chapter 5, elections and the transformation of rebel groups into political parties well represent Foucault's inversion of Clausewitz's axiom. Thus, "war is the continuation of politics by other means" as well as "Politics (power) becomes the continuation of war by other means" (2003, p. 165). Paradoxically, it also means that when politics is successful, it prevents war.

The transition from hybrid politics to peace requires an integrated approach that is no longer combatant-centric. To better understand the complexity of interests that contributes to minimizing transitional risks, it is recommended to include an intermediary level, such as the elites and middle-rank officials, as well as to give preference to a bottom-up approach of institutional designs and peacebuilding practices. In conclusion, civil wars remain a critical issue in contemporary global affairs, often becoming "global wars." The effectiveness of the United Nations in promoting peace and democracy as well as aiding state-building might be debatable. Nevertheless, the organization was not designed to interfere in civil wars and it remains the international organization with the largest experience in peacebuilding (Guéhenno, 2018). From war to peace, how to bring political stability and democratization it is not an obvious exercise. Undoubtedly, it requires an alignment of interests and factors to avoid falling into the trap of "electoral authoritarian regimes" without conflict resolution. And this is precisely the essential aim of this book: to assist with an integrated approach when peace and democracy are at the crossroads. Hopefully, it can also contribute to making peacekeeping a more robust, more effective, and a comparatively more cost-efficient conflict resolution tool for current conflicts and for avoiding failed transitions and fragile states (Figure 10.1).

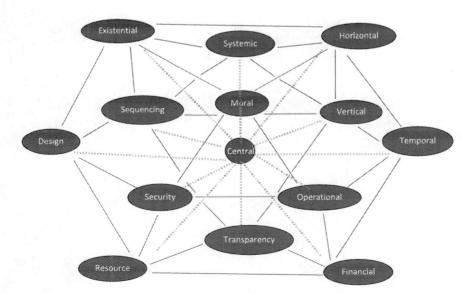

FIGURE 10.1 Tridecagonal structure of hybrid democratic peace transitional dilemmas.
Source: Author

References

Armitage, D. 2017. *Civil Wars: A History in Ideas*. Penguin Canada.
Börzel, T. A. & Grimm, S. 2018. Building Good (Enough) Governance in Postconflict Societies & Areas of Limited Statehood: The European Union & the Western Balkans. *Daedalus*, 147 Ending Civil Wars: Constraints & Possibilities, 116–127.
EIU. 2021. *Democracy Index: The China Challenge*. Economic Intelligence Unit.
Erasmus, D. 1521. Querela Pacis. *Complaint of Peace*. 1917 ed. Open Court.
Foucault, M. 2003. *Society Must Be Defended*. Picador.
Freedom House. 2022. *Freedom of the World 2022: The Global Expansion of Autoritarian Rule*. Freedom House.
Fukuyama, F., Kagan, R., LARRY Diamond, Carothers, T., Plattner, M. F., Schmitter, P. C., Levitsky, S., Way, L. & Rice, C. 2015. *Democracy in Decline?* Johns Hopkins University Press.
Guéhenno, J.-M. 2018. The United Nations & Civil Wars. *Daedalus*, 147, 185–196.
Kaspersen, L., & Strandsbjerg, J. 2017. *Does War Make States? Investigations of Charles Tilly's Historical Sociology*. Cambridge University Press.
Krasner, S. D. & Eikenberry, K. 2018. Conclusion. *Daedalus*, 147 Ending Civil Wars: Constraints & Possibilities, 197–211.
Leininger, J., Grimm, S. & Freyburg, T. 2012. *Do all Good Things Go Together? Conflicting Objectives in Democracy Promotion*. Routledge.
Smith, C. Q., Waldorf, L., Venugopal, R. & Mccarthy, G. 2020. Illiberal Peacebuilding in Asia: A Comparative Overview. *Conflict, Security & Development*, 20, 1–14.
Sorensen, G. 2001. War and State-Making: Why Doesn't it Work in the Third World? *Security Dialogue PRIO*, 32, 341–354.
Tilly, C., Evans, P. B., Rueschemeyer, D. & Skocpol, T. 1985. *War Making and State Making as Organized Crime*. Cambridge University Press.
Uri, S. 2008. *Peace First: A New Model to End War*. Berrett-Koehler Publishers.

APPENDIX

284 Appendix

Table A.1 The state of affairs of democracy and peace in the countries torn by civil wars with UN peace operations

	Country[1]	Acronym	Mission name	Start Date	End Date	Led by	Type of mission[2]	Country part of the Peacebuilding Commission (PBSO) 2005
1	Afghanistan	UNAMA	United Nations Assistance Mission in Afghanistan	Mar-02	Present	DPA	Political	No
2	Angola	UNAVEM I	United Nations Angola Verification Mission I	jan/89[9]	Jun-91	DPKO	Traditional	No
		UNAVEM II	United Nations Angola Verification Mission II	Jun-91	fev/95	DPKO	Traditional	
		UNAVEM III	United Nations Angola Verification Mission III	fev/95	Jun-97	DPKO	Traditional	
		MONUA	United Nations Observer Mission in Angola	jun/97 [10]	fev/99	DPKO	Observation	
3	Bosnia-Herzegovina	UNMIBH	United Nations Mission in Bosnia and Herzegovina	dez/95	dez/02	DPKO	Enforcement	No
4	Burundi	ONUB	United Nations Operation in Burundi	Jun-04	dez/06	DPKO	Multidimensional	Yes
		BINUB	UN Integrated Office in Burundi	Jan-07	dez 2010	DPA	Multidimensional	
		BNUN	UN Office in Burundi	Jan-11	Dec-14	DPA	Multidimensional	
		MENUB	UN Electoral Observation Mission in Burundi	Jan-15	Dec-17	DPA	Multidimensional	
5	Cambodia	UNAMIC	United Nations Advance Mission in Cambodia	out/91[11]	Mar-92	DPKO	Multidimensional	No
		UNTAC	United Nations Transitional Authority in Cambodia	Mar-92	set/93	DPKO	Multidimensional	

6	CAR	MINURCA	United Nations Mission in the Central African Republic	abr/98[12]	fev/00	DPKO	Traditional	yes
		BONUCA	UN Peacebuilding Office in the Central African Republic	Fev/00	Apr-09	DPA	Multidimensional	
		BINUCA	United Nations Integrated Peacebuilding Support Office in the Central African Republic	Apr-09	Abr/14	DPA	Multidimensional	
		MINUSCA	United Nations Multidimensional Integrated Stabilization Mission in the Central African Republic	abr/14[13]	Present	DPKO	Multidimensional	
		MINURCAT	United Nations Mission in the Central African Republic and Chad	set/07	dez/10	DPKO	Multidimensional	
7	Côte-Ivoire	UNOCI	United Nations Operation in Côte d'Ivoire	abr/04	Present	DPKO	Multidimensional	No
8	Croatia	UNPROFOR	United Nations Protection Force	fev/92	Mar-95	DPKO	Enforcement	No
		UNCRO	United Nations Confidence Restoration Operation in Croatia	mai/95	Jan-96	DPKO	Enforcement	
		UNTAES	United Nations Transitional Administration for Eastern Slavonia, Baranja and Western Sirmium	Jan-96	Jan-98	DPKO	Multidimensional	

(*Continued*)

Table A.1 (Continued)

	Country[1]	Acronym	Mission name	Start Date	End Date	Led by	Type of mission[2]	Country part of the Peacebuilding Commission (PBSO) 2005
		UNMOP	United Nations Mission of Observers in Prevlaka	Jan-96	dez/02	DPKO	Multidimensional	
		UNCPSG	UN Civilian Police Support Group	Jan-98	out/98	DPKO	Multidimensional	
9	Cyprus	UNFICYP	United Nations Peacekeeping Force in Cyprus	Mar-64	Present	DPKO	Traditional	No
10	DRC	MONUC	United Nations Organization Mission in the Democratic Republic of the Congo	Nov-99	Jun-16	DPKO	Multidimensional	No
		MONUSCO	United Nations Organization Stabilization Mission in the Democratic Republic of the Congo	Jul-16	Present	DPKO	Multidimensional	
11	El Salvador	ONUSAL	United Nations Observer Mission in El Salvador	Jul-91	abr/95	DPKO	Multidimensional	No
		MINUSAL	United Nations Mission in El Salvador	May-95	Ago/95	DPA	Multidimensional	
12	Georgia	UNOMIG	United Nations Observer Mission in Georgia	ago/93	Jun-09	DPKO	Traditional	No
13	Guinea-Bissau	UNIOGBIS	United Nations Integrated Peacebuilding Office for Guinea Bissau	abr/99	Present	DPKO/DPA	Multidimensional	Yes

14	Haiti	MICIVIH	OAS/UN International Civilian Mission in Haiti	Fev/93	Mar-00	DPA	Multidimensional	No
		UNMIH	United Nations Mission in Haiti	set/93	Jun-96	DPKO	Enforcement	
		UNSMIH	United Nations Support Mission in Haiti	Jul-96	Jul-97	DPKO	Multidimensional	
		UNTMIH	United Nations Transition Mission in Haiti	ago/97	dez/97	DPKO	Multidimensional	
		MIPONUH	United Nations Civilian Police Mission in Haiti	dez/97	Mar-00	DPKO	Enforcement	
		MINUSTAH	United Nations Stabilization Mission in Haiti	jun/04[15]	Oct-17	DPKO	Multidimensional	
		MINUJUSTH	United Nations Mission for Justice Support in Haiti	Oct-17	Present	DPKO	Multidimensional	
15	Iraq	UNAMI	United Nations Assistance Mission in Iraq	Aug-03	Present	DPA/DPKO	Multidimensional	No
16	Kosovo	UNMIK	United Nations Interim Administration Mission in Kosovo	Jun-99	Present	DPKO	Multidimensional	No
17	Liberia	UNOMIL	United Nations Observer Mission in Liberia	set/93	set/97	DPKO	Enforcement	Yes
		UNMIL	United Nations Mission in Liberia	set/03[16]	Present	DPKO	Multidimensional	
18	Libya	UNSMIL	United Nations Support Mission for Libya	Feb-11	present	DPPA	Political	No
20	Mali	MINUSMA	United Nations Multidimensional Integrated Stabilization Mission in Mali	abr/13	Present	DPKO	Multidimensional	No

(*Continued*)

Table A.1 (Continued)

	Country[1]	Acronym	Mission name	Start Date	End Date	Led by	Type of mission[2]	Country part of the Peacebuilding Commission (PBSO) 2005
21	Mozambique	ONUMOZ	United Nations Operation in Mozambique	dez/92	dez/94	DPKO	Multidimensional	No
22	Namibia	UNTAG	United Nations Transition Assistance Group	abr/89	Mar-90	DPKO	Multidimensional	No
23	Nepal	UNMIN	United Nations Mission in Nepal	Jan-07	Jan-11	DPKO	Multidimensional	No
24	Nicaragua	ONUCA	United Nations Observer Group in Central America	Nov-89	Jan-92	DPKO	Traditional	No
19	North Macedonia	UNPREDEP (FYROM)	United Nations Preventive Deployment Force	Mar-95	fev/99	DPKO	Preventive	No
25	Rwanda	UNAMIR	United Nations Assistance Mission for Rwanda	out/93	mar/96[17]	DPKO	Observation	No
26	Sierra Leone	UNOMSIL	United Nations Observer Mission in Sierra Leone	Jul-98	out/99	DPKO	Multidimensional	Yes
		UNAMSIL	United Nations Mission in Sierra Leone	out/99	dez/05	DPKO	Multidimensional	
27	Somalia	UNOSOM I	United Nations Operation in Somalia I	abr/92	Mar-93	DPKO	Traditional	No
		UNOSOM II	United Nations Operation in Somalia II	Mar-93	Mar-95	DPKO	Traditional	
		UNSOM	United Nations Assistance Mission in Somalia	Jun-13	Present	DPA	Multidimensional	
28	South Sudan	UNMISS	United Nations Mission in the Republic of South Sudan	Jul-16	Present	DPKO	Multidimensional	No

29	Sudan	UNMIS	United Nations Mission in the Sudan	Mar-16	Jul-16	DPKO	Multidimensional	No
		UNISFA	United Nations Organization Interim Security Force for Abyei	Jun-16	Present	DPKO	Multidimensional	
		UNAMID	African Union–United Nations Hybrid Operation in Darfur	Jul-16	Present	DPKO	Hybrid	
30	Timor-Leste	UNAMET	UN Mission in East Timor	Jun-99	Oct-99	DPA	Political	No
		UNTAET	United Nations Transitional Administration in East Timor	out/99	mai/02	DPKO	Multidimensional	
		UNMISET	United Nations Mission of Support in East Timor	mai/02	mai/05	DPKO	Multidimensional	
		UNOTIL	UN Office in Timor-Leste	May-05	Aug-06	DPA	Political	
		UNMIT	United Nations Integrated Mission in Timor-Leste	ago/06	dez/12	DPKO	Multidimensional	
31	Western Sahara	MINURSO	United Nations Mission for the Referendum in Western Sahara	abr/91	present	DPKO	Observation	No

UPDATED: Ago 2022

[1] Table organized by alphabetical order of the countries.
[2] Category type set up according to the mandate of each mission. With the exception of Afghanistan, it maintains coherence with the analysis of Fortna (2008b).

Appendix **289**

Table A.1 (Continued)

	Country[1]	Freedom House[2] Classification and scores												
		2006 [3]	2012	2013	2014	2015	2016	2015	2017[4]	2018	2019	2020	2021	2022	Trend arrow
1	Afghanistan	Not Free 5.5, 6.5	Not Free 6,6,6	Not Free 6,6,6	Not Free 6,6,6	Not Free 6,6,6	Not Free 6,6,6	Not Free 6,6	Not Free 24,10,14	Not Free 26,12,14	Not Free 27,13,14	Not Free 27,13,14	Not Free 27,13,14	Not Free 10,1,9	↑
2	Angola [5], [6]	Not Free 5.5, 6, 6	Not Free 6,5	Not Free 6,5	Not Free 5.5, 5, 6	Not Free 6,5	Not Free 6, 6, 6	Not Free 6,5	Not Free 24,10,14	Not Free 26,10,16	Not Free 31,11,20	Not Free 32, 11, 21	Not Free 31, 10, 21	Not Free 30, 10, 20	↑
3	Bosnia-Herzegovina	Partly Free 3.5, 3,4	Partly Free 4,.,3	Partly Free 3,..,3	Partly Free 3,4	Partly Free 4,3,4	Partly Free 4,4,4	Partly Free 4,3	Partly Free 55,21,34	Partly Free 55,21,34	Partly Free 53,19,34	Partly Free 53,21,34	Partly Free 53,21,34	Partly Free 53, 19,34	↑
4	Burundi	–	Not Free 5.5	Not Free 5.5	Not Free 5.5, 5.6	Not Free 5.5, 5.6	Not Free 7, 6, 6.5	Not Free 4, 3	Not Free 14, 4,10	Not Free 18, 4,14	Not Free 14, 3,11	Not Free 13, 3,10	Not Free 14, 4,10	Not Free 14, 4,10	↑
5	Cambodia [7], [8]	Not Free 5.5, 5,6	Not Free 6,5	Not Free 6,5	Not Free 5.5, 5.6	Not Free 6,5	Not Free 6,5, 5,5	Not Free 6, 5	Not Free 31,11,20	Not Free 31,11,20	Not Free 26,6,20	Not Free 25,5,20	Not Free 24,5,19	Not Free 24,5,19	↑
6	CAR [9]	Not Free 7,7	Not Free 5,5	Not Free 5,5	7,7,7	7,7,7	Not Free 7,7,7	Not Free 7,7	Not Free 10,4,6	9,4,5	9,4,5	10,4,6	9,3,6	7, 3,4	↑
7	Côte-Ivoire	–	Not Free 6,6	Partly Free 5.5	Partly Free 4.5, 4,5	Partly Free 5,4	Partly Free 4, 4,4	Partly Free 5,4	Partly Free 51,20,32	Partly Free 4, 4,4	Partly Free 51,19,32	Partly Free 51,19,32	Partly Free 51,19,32	Partly Free 49,19,30	↑
8	Croatia	Free 2,2,2	Free 1,2	Free 1,2	Free 1.5,2,1	Free 1,2	Free 1.5,1,2	Free 1, 2	Free 52,20,32	Free 52,20,32	Free 52,20,32	Free 52,20,32	Free 52,20,32	Free 52, 20,32	↑
9	Cyprus [10]	Not available	Free 1,1,1	Free 1,1,1	Free 1,1,1	Free 1,1,1	Free 1,1,1	Free 1, 1	Free 93,38,56	Free 93,38,55	Free 93,38,55	Free 93,38,55	Free 93,38,55	Free 93,38, 55	↑
10	DRC	Not Free 6,6,6	Not Free 6, 6,6	Not Free 6, 6,6	Not Free 6,6	Not Free 6,6	Not Free 6,5, 7,6	Not Free 6, 6,6	Not Free 19,4,15	Not Free 17,4,13	Not Free 15,13,12	Not Free 18,4,14	Not Free 20,5,15	Not Free 19,4,15	→
11	El Salvador	Partly Free 2.5, 3,2	Partly Free 2,3	Partly Free 2,3	Partly Free 2.5, 3,2	Partly Free 2,3	Partly Free 2.5, 2,3	Partly Free 2, 3	Free 70,34,36	Free 70,34,36	Free 67,32,35	Partly Free 66,32,34	Partly Free 63,30,33	Partly Free 59,26,33	↑
12	Georgia	–	Partly Free 3, 3,3	Partly Free 3,3	Partly Free 3, 3,3	Partly Free 3, 3,3	Partly Free 3, 3,3	Partly Free 3, 3	Partly Free 64,37,27	Partly Free 64,26,38	Partly Free 63,25,38	Partly Free 61,37,27	Partly Free 61,24,37	Partly Free 58,32,26	↑
13	Guinea-Bissau	Partly Free 5,5,5	Partly Free 4,4	Partly Free 6,5,5	Partly Free 5,5,5	Partly Free 5,5,5	Partly Free 5,5,5	Partly Free 5, 5	Partly Free 40,16,24	Partly Free 41,16,25	Partly Free 43,17,23	Partly Free 46,17,29	Partly Free 44,17,27	Partly Free 43,17,23	↑

Appendix **291**

14	Haiti	Partly Free 4.5,5,4	Partly Free 4,5	Partly Free 4,5	Partly Free 5,5,5	Partly Free 5,5,5	Partly Free 5,5,5	Partly Free 5, 5	Partly Free 39,15,24	Partly Free 41,17,24	Partly Free 41,17,24	Partly Free 38,16,22	Not Free 37,15,22	Not Free 33,11,22	↓
15	Iraq	Not available	Not free 5, 6	Not free 6,6,6	Not free 6,6,6	Not free 27,12,15	Not free 6, 6	Not free 31,17,14	Not Free 31,16,15	Not free 32,17,15	Not free 31,17,14	Not free 31,17,14	Not Free 29,16,13	↑
16	Kosovo	Partly Free 4, 4,4	Partly Free 5,4	Partly Free 5,4	Partly Free 4, 4,4	Partly Free 3.5, 3,4	Partly free 4, 4	Partly Free 58,24,38	Partly Free 52,24,38	Partly Free 54,34,30	Partly Free 56,25,31	Partly Free 54,23,31	Partly Free 56,25,31	↑
17	Liberia [13]	Partly Free 3.5, 4,3	Partly Free 3,4	Partly Free 3,4	Partly Free 3.5, 4,3	Partly Free 3.5, 3,4	Partly Free 3, 4	Partly Free 62,28,34	Partly Free 62,27,35	Partly Free 60,27,33	Partly Free 62,27,35	Partly Free 60,27,33	Partly Free 60,27,33	→
18	Libya	Not Free 6,6	Not Free 7,6	Partly Free 4,5	Partly Free 6,6	Partly Free 6,6	Not Free 6,6	Not free 13,3,10	Not free 9,1,8	Not free 9,1,8	Not free 9,1,8	Not free 9,1,8	Not free 9,1,8	↑
20	Mali	Partly Free 3, 3,3	Not free 7,5	Not free 7,5	Partly Free 3.5, 3,4	Partly Free 5,4	Partly Free 5,4	Not Free 45,17,28	Not Free 44,17,27	Not free 44,18,26	Not free 32,8,24	Not free 33,9,24,	Not free 32,8,24	→
21	Mozambique	Partly Free 2.5, 3,2	Partly Free 4,3	Free 4,3	Free 2, 2,2	Free 2, 2,2	Partly Free 4,3	Partly Free 53,20,33	Partly Free 52,20,32	Partly Free 43,14,29	Partly Free 51,19,32	Partly Free 43,14,29	Partly Free 43,14,29	↓
22	Namibia	Not available	Partly Free 2,2	Partly Free 2,2	Partly Free 3.5, 4,3	Partly Free 3.5, 3,4	Free 3, 4	Free 77,30,47	Free 77,30,47	Free 75,29,46	Free 77,31,43	Free 77,31,43	Free 77,31,43	←
23	Nepal	Partly Free 3, 3,3	Partly Free 4,4	Partly Free 4,4	Partly Free 3.5, 3,4	Partly Free 4.5, 5,4	Partly Free 4, 4	Partly Free 52,24,32	Partly Free 55,25,30	Partly Free 57,25,32	Partly Free 54,25,39	Partly Free 56,25,31	Partly Free 57,25,32	↑
24	Nicaragua	Not Free 5.5, 5, 6	Partly Free 5,4	Partly Free 5,4	Not Free 6, 6, 6	Not Free 6, 6, 6	Not Free 4,3	Not Free 47,12,36	Not Free 44,12,32	Not Free 44,12,32	Not Free 32,10,22	Not Free 30,10,20	Not Free 23,5,18	↑
19	North Macedonia [11]	—	Partly Free 3,3	Partly Free 3,3	Partly Free 4.5, 4,5	Partly Free 67,28,39	Partly Free 2,2	Partly Free 57,21,36	Partly Free 67,28,39	Partly Free 58,21,37	Partly Free 59,28,37	Partly Free 66,27,39	Partly Free 67,28,39	↑
25	Rwanda	Partly Free 3, 3,3	Not Free 6,6	Not Free 6,6	Not Free 6,5	Not Free 6,6	Not Free 6, 6	Not Free 24,8,16	Not Free 23,8,15	Not Free 23,9,14	Not Free 22,8,14	Not Free 21,8,13	Not Free 22,8,14	→
26	Sierra Leone	Not Free 7, 7, 7	Partly Free 2,3	Partly Free 2,3	Partly Free 3, 3	Partly Free 3, 3	Partly Free 3, 3	Partly Free 65,28,38	Partly Free 65,28,38	Partly Free 66,28,38	Partly Free 65,28,37	Partly Free 65,28,37	Partly Free 65,28,37	←

(*Continued*)

Table A.1 (Continued)

	Country[1]	Freedom House[2] Classification and scores											
		2006 [3]	2012	2013	2014	2015	2016	2017[4]	2018	2019	2020	2021	2022	Trend arrow
27	Somalia	–	Not Free 7,7	Not Free 7,7	Not Free 6,5, 6,7	Not Free 7,7	Not Free 6,5, 7, 6	Not Free 5,0, 5	Not Free 7,1, 6	Not Free 7,1, 6	Not Free 7,1, 6	Not Free 7,1, 6	Not Free 7,1, 6	↑
28	South Sudan	–	Not Free 6, 5	Not Free 6, 5	Not Free 7,7, 7	Not Free 7, 6	Not Free 1,–3,4	Not Free 4,–2,6	Not Free 2,–2,4	Not Free 2,–2,4	Not Free 2,–2,4	Not Free 2,–2,4	Not Free [12] 1,–3,4	↑
29	Sudan	–	Not Free 7,7	Not Free 7,7	Not Free 10,0,10	Not Free 7,7	Not Free 10,0,10	Not Free 6,2, 4	Not Free 8,4, 4	Not Free 7,3,14	Not Free 12,2,10	Not Free 17,2,15	Not Free 10,0,10	←
30	Timor-Leste	Partly Free 3, 3	Partly Free 3, 4	Partly Free 3, 4	Partly Free 3, 3	Partly Free 3, 3	Partly Free 3, 3	Free 65,29,36	Free 72,33,39	Free 69,32,37	Free 71,33,39	Free 72,33,39	Free 72,33,39	←
31	Western Sahara	Not Free 6,5, 6, 7	Not Free 7,7, 7	Not Free 7,7, 7	Not Free 7,7, 7	Not Free 7,7, 7	Not Free 7,7, 7	Not Free 4,–3,7	Not Free 4,–3,7	Not Free 4,–3,7	Not Free 4,–3,7	Not Free 4,–3,7	Not Free 4,–3,7	↑

UPDATED: Dec 2022

[1] Table organized by alphabetical order of the countries.
[2] It respectively includes the rating of Freedom Rating, Civil Liberties and Political Rights 1 = best, 7 = worst. For methodology description, please refer to http://freedomhouse.org/report/freedom-world.
[3] The first Freedom House report was published in 1999 with reference to 1998.
[4] Prior to the 2017 edition, Freedom in the World assigned a country or territory two ratings— one for political rights and one for civil liberties—based on its total scores for the political rights and civil liberties questions. The ratings are still included in the raw data available for download https://freedomhouse.org/reports/freedom-world/freedom-world-research-methodology Accessed 01/07/2022

Each rating of 1 to 7, with 1 representing the greatest degree of freedom and 7 the smallest degree of freedom, corresponded to a specific range of total scores. The average of the ratings determined the status of Free, Partly Free, or Not Free. While the underlying formula for converting scores into status remains identical, starting in the 2020 edition Freedom in the World no longer presented the 1–7 ratings as a separate element of its findings.

[5] For methodological coherence, analysis considers from the starting of the UN mission, therefore, from the first operation in 1989.
[6] For information, the results from the Freedom House if we consider the last mission would be similarly "not free": 1999 Not Free 6, 6, 6; 2002 Not Free 5,5, 5, 6; 2007 Not Free 5,5, and 2012 Not free 5,5,5, 6.
[7] For methodological coherence, analysis considers from the starting of the UN mission, therefore, from the first operation in 1991. In the case of Cambodia, there was only 4 months difference between the start of the first and the second mission.
[8] For methodological coherence, analysis considers from the starting of the UN mission, therefore, from the first operation in 1998.

[9] It is important to notice there is a 14 years lapsus between MINURCA and MINUSCA. For information, the results from the Freedom House if we consider the last mission would be similarly "not free": 2016 7, 7, 7. Clear deterioration.
[10] In the case of Cyprus, a retrospective analysis of the last -15, -10, -5 and -2 years is possible. Freedom house results are: 2015 Free 1,1,1; 2012 Free 1,1,1; 2007 Free 1,1,1; and 2002 Free 1,1,1.
[11] For information, results from Freedom House would be similar if we consider from the year of termination: 1998 Not Free 6, 6.5, 7; 2003 Not Free 6, 6.5, 7; 2008 Not Free 5.5, 5, 6 and 2013 Not Free 5.5, 5, 6.
[12] Deterioration compare to 2011, year of its independence.
[13] "The Libyan Civil War is related to 2011. Clear unresolved issues directly evolved into the Second Lybian Civil war since 2014 until the date. Therefore, for this data base, the priod of both wars are combined."

Table A.1 (Continued)

	Country[1]	Polity IV Trend Classification	Democracy Index EIU Classification and score 2006	2012	2013	2014	2015
1	Afghanistan	Authoritarian	Authoritarian 3.06	Authoritarian 2.48	Authoritarian 2.48	Authoritarian 2.77	Authoritarian 2.77
2	Angola	Authoritarian	Authoritarian 2.41	Authoritarian 3.35	Authoritarian 3.35	Authoritarian 3.35	Authoritarian 3.35
3	Bosnia-Herzegovina	Susceptible to collapse	Hybrid 5.78	Hybrid 5.11	Hybrid 5.02	Hybrid 4.78	Hybrid 4.83
4	Burundi	Authoritarian	Authoritarian 4.51	Authoritarian 3.60	Authoritarian 3.41	Authoritarian 3.33	Authoritarian 3.33
5	Cambodia	Weak Democracy	Authoritarian 2.62	Authoritarian 3.00	Authoritarian 4.60	Authoritarian 4.96	Authoritarian 4.93
6	CAR	State Failure	Authoritarian 1.99	Authoritarian 1.49	Authoritarian 1.61	Authoritarian 1.49	Authoritarian 1.57
7	Côte-Ivoire	Weak Democracy	Authoritarian 3.38	Authoritarian 3.25	Authoritarian 3.25	Authoritarian 3.53	Authoritarian 3.31
8	Croatia	Democracy	Flawed democracy 7.04	Flawed democracy 6.93	Flawed democracy 6.93	Flawed democracy 6.93	Flawed democracy 6.93
9	Cyprus	Democratic	Flawed democracy 7.60	Flawed democracy 7.29	Flawed democracy 7.29	Flawed democracy 7.40	Flawed democracy 7.53
10	DRC	Authoritarian	Authoritarian 2.76	Authoritarian 1.92	Authoritarian 1.83	Authoritarian 1.75	Authoritarian 2.11
11	El Salvador	Democracy	Hybrid 6.64	Hybrid 6.47	Hybrid 6.56	Hybrid 6.64	Hybrid 6.64
12	Georgia	Democracy	Hybrid 4.90	Hybrid 5.82	Hybrid 5.82	Hybrid 5.82	Hybrid 5.88
13	Guinea-Bissau	Authoritarian	Authoritarian 2.00	Authoritarian 1.43	Authoritarian 1.26	Authoritarian 1.93	Authoritarian 1.93
14	Haiti	State Failure	Authoritarian 4.19	Authoritarian 3.96	Authoritarian 3.94	Authoritarian 3.82	Authoritarian 4.02
15	Iraq	State Failure	Hybrid 4.01	Hybrid 4.10	Hybrid 4.10	Hybrid 4.23	Hybrid 4.08
16	Kosovo	Democracy	Not available	Not available	Not available	Not available	Not available
17	Liberia	Democracy	Hybrid 4.95	Hybrid 4.95	Hybrid 4.95	Hybrid 4.95	Hybrid 5.31
18	Libya	State Failure	Authoritarian 1.84	Hybrid 5.15	Hybrid 4.82	Authoritarian 3.80	Authoritarian 2.25
20	Mali	Weak Democracy	Hybrid 5.99	Hybrid 5.12	Hybrid 5.90	Hybrid 5.79	Hybrid 5.70
21	Mozambique	Democratic	Hybrid 5.28	Hybrid 4.88	Hybrid 4.77	Hybrid 4.66	Hybrid 4.60
22	Namibia	Democratic	Flawed Democracy 6.54	Flawed Democracy 6.24	Flawed Democracy 6.24	Flawed Democracy 6.24	Flawed Democracy 6.31
23	Nepal	Democratic	Authoritarian 3.42	Hybrid 4.16	Hybrid 4.77	Hybrid 5.32	Hybrid 4.86
24	Nicaragua	Authoritarian	Authoritarian 5.68	Authoritarian 5.46	Authoritarian 5.56	Authoritarian 5.32	Authoritarian 5.26
19	North Macedonia	Weak Democracy	Flawed Democracy 6.33	Flawed Democracy 6.16	Flawed Democracy 6.16	Flawed Democracy 6.25	Flawed Democracy 6.02
25	Rwanda	Authoritarian	Authoritarian 3.82	Authoritarian 3.26	Authoritarian 3.38	Authoritarian 3.25	Authoritarian 3.07
26	Sierra Leone	Weak Democracy	Authoritarian 3.57	Hybrid 4.71	Hybrid 4.64	Hybrid 4.56	Hybrid 4.55
27	Somalia	State Failure	Non available	Non available	Non available	Non available	Non available
28	South Sudan	Weak Authoritarian	Not available	Not available	Not available	Not available	Not available
29	Sudan	Authoritarian	Authoritarian 2.90	Authoritarian 2.38	Authoritarian 2.54	Authoritarian 2.54	Authoritarian 2.70
30	Timor-Leste	Democracy 6.41	Democracy 7.24	Democracy 7.16	Democracy 7.24	Democracy 7.24	Democracy 7.24
31	Western Sahara	Failed state [19]	Not available	Not available	Not available	Not available	Not available

UPDATED: Dec 2022
[1] Table organized by alphabetical order of the countries.

Appendix   295

2016	2017	2018	2019	2020	2021	2022
Authoritarian 2.55	Authoritarian 2.55	Authoritarian 2.97	Authoritarian 2.85	Authoritarian 2.85	Authoritarian 0.32	Authoritarian 0.32
Authoritarian 3.40	Authoritarian 3.62	Authoritarian 3.62	Authoritarian 3.72	Authoritarian 3.66	Authoritarian 3.37	Authoritarian 3.96
Hybrid 4.87	Hybrid 4.87	Hybrid 4.98	Hybrid 4.86	Hybrid 4.84	Hybrid 5.04	Hybrid 5.00
Authoritarian 2.40	Authoritarian 2.33	Authoritarian 2.33	Authoritarian 2.15	Authoritarian 2.14	Authoritarian 2.13	Authoritarian 2.13
Authoritarian 4.27	Authoritarian 3.63	Authoritarian 3.59	Authoritarian 3.53	Authoritarian 3.10	Authoritarian 2.90	Authoritarian 3.18
Authoritarian 1.61	Authoritarian 1.52	Authoritarian 1.52	Authoritarian 1.32	Authoritarian 1.32	Authoritarian 1.43	Authoritarian 1.43
Authoritarian 3.81	Authoritarian 3.93	Hybrid 4.15	Hybrid 4.11	Hybrid 4.11	Hybrid 4.22	Hybrid 4.22
Flawed democracy 6.75	Flawed democracy 6.63	Flawed democracy 6.57	Flawed democracy 6.57	Flawed democracy 6.50	Flawed democracy 6.50	Flawed democracy 6.50
Flawed democracy 7.65	Flawed democracy 7.59	Flawed democracy 7.59	Flawed democracy 7.59	Flawed democracy 7.56	Flawed democracy 7.43	Flawed democracy 7.38
Authoritarian 1.93	Authoritarian 1.61	Authoritarian 1.49	Authoritarian 1.13	Authoritarian 1.13	Authoritarian 1.40	Authoritarian 1.48
Hybrid 6.64	Hybrid 6.43	Hybrid 5.96	Hybrid 6.15	Hybrid 5.90	Hybrid 5.72	Hybrid 5.06
Hybrid 5.93	Hybrid 5.93	Hybrid 5.50	Hybrid 5.42	Hybrid 5.31	Hybrid 5.12	Hybrid 5.20
Authoritarian 1.98	Authoritarian 1.98	Authoritarian 1.98	Authoritarian 2.63	Authoritarian 2.63	Authoritarian 2.75	Authoritarian 2.56
Authoritarian 4.02	Authoritarian 4.03	Authoritarian 4.91	Authoritarian 4.57	Authoritarian 4.22	Authoritarian 3.48	Authoritarian 2.81
Hybrid 4.08	Hybrid 4.09	Hybrid 4.06	Hybrid 3.74	Hybrid 3.62	Hybrid 3.51	Hybrid 3.33
Not available	Not available	Not available	Not available	Not available	Not available	Not available
Hybrid 5.31	Hybrid 5.23	Hybrid 5.35	Hybrid 5.45	Hybrid 5.32	Hybrid 5.43	Hybrid 5.43
Authoritarian 2.25	Authoritarian 2.32	Authoritarian 2.19	Authoritarian 2.02	Authoritarian 1.95	Authoritarian 1.95	Authoritarian 2.06
Hybrid 5.70	Hybrid 5.64	Hybrid 5.41	Hybrid 4.92	Authoritarian 3.93	Authoritarian 3.48	Authoritarian 3.23
Hybrid 4.02	Hybrid 4.02	Authoritarian 3.85	Authoritarian 3.65	Authoritarian 3.51	Authoritarian 3.51	Authoritarian 3.51
Flawed Democracy 6.31	Flawed Democracy 6.31	Flawed Democracy 6.25	Flawed Democracy 6.43	Flawed Democracy 6.52	Flawed Democracy 6.52	Flawed Democracy 6.52
Hybrid 5.18	Hybrid 5.18	Hybrid 5.28	Hybrid 4.66	Hybrid 5.22	Hybrid 4.41	Hybrid 4.49
Authoritarian 4.81	Authoritarian 4.66	Authoritarian 3.63	Authoritarian 3.55	Authoritarian 3.60	Authoritarian 2.69	Authoritarian 2.50
Flawed Democracy 5.23	Flawed Democracy 5.57	Flawed Democracy 5.87	Flawed Democracy 5.97	Flawed Democracy 5.89	Flawed Democracy 6.03	Flawed Democracy 6.010
Authoritarian 3.07	Authoritarian 3.19	Authoritarian 3.35	Authoritarian 3.16	Authoritarian 3.10	Authoritarian 3.10	Authoritarian 3.10
Hybrid 4.55	Hybrid 4.66	Hybrid 4.66	Hybrid 4.86	Hybrid 4.86	Hybrid 4.97	Hybrid 5.03
Non available	Non available	Non available	Non available	Non available	Non available	Non available
Not available	Not available	Not available	Not available	Not available	Not available	Not available
Authoritarian 2.15	Authoritarian 2.15	Authoritarian 2.37	Authoritarian 2.37	Authoritarian 2.37	Authoritarian 2.54	Authoritarian 2.47
Democracy 7.19	Democracy 7.19	Democracy 7.19	Democracy 6.41	Democracy 7.06	Democracy 7.06	Democracy 7.06
Not available	Not available	Not available	Not available	Not available	Not available	Not available

Appendix

Table A.1 (Continued)

	Country[1]	Fragile State Index (FFP) (score 0-120)					
		2012	2013	2014	2015	2016	2017
1	Afghanistan	High alert 106	High alert 106.7	High alert 107.9	High alert 107.9	High alert 107.9	High alert 107.9
2	Angola	High warning 85.1	High warning 87.1	High warning 87.4	High warning 87.9	High warning 90.5	High warning 91.1
3	Bosnia-Herzegovina	High warning 77.9	High warning 76.5	High warning 77.4	High warning 77.4	High warning 74.3	High warning 73
4	Burundi	Alert 97.5	Alert 97.6	Alert 98	Alert 98.1	Very high alert 100.7	Alert 98.9
5	Cambodia	High warning 88.7	High warning 88	High warning 87.9	High warning 87.4	High warning 87.9	High warning 85.7
6	CAR	Very high alert 103.8	Very high alert 105.3	Very high alert 110.6	Very high alert 111.9	Very high alert 112.1	Very high alert 112.6
7	Côte-Ivoire	Very high Alert 103.6	Very high Alert 103.5	Alert 101	Alert 100.1	Alert 97.9	Alert 96.5
8	Croatia	Less Stable 56.3	Less Stable 54.1	Less Stable 52.9	Less Stable 51	Less Stable 52.4	Less Stable 50.6
9	Cyprus	low Warning 66.8	low Warning 67	low Warning 67.9	low Warning 66.2	low Warning 64	low Warning 62.6
10	DRC	Very high alert 111.2	Very high alert 111.9	alert 90.8	Very high alert 109.7	Very high alert 110	Very high alert 110
11	El Salvador	Elevated warning 74.4	Elevated warning 73.2	Elevated warning 72	Elevated warning 71.4	Elevated warning 72.5	Elevated warning 73.1
12	Georgia	Elevated warning 84.8	Elevated warning 84.2	Elevated warning 79.3	Elevated warning 79.2	Elevated warning 78.9	Elevated warning 78.9
13	Guinea-Bissau	Alert 99.2	Alert 101.1	Alert 99.9	Alert 100.6	Alert 99.8	Alert 99.5
14	Haiti	High alert 104.9	High alert 105.8	High alert 104.3	High alert 104.5	High alert 105.1	High alert 105.3
15	Iraq	High alert 104.3	High alert 103.9	High alert 104.5	High alert 104.4	High alert 104.7	High alert 105.4
16	Kosovo	Not available	Not available	Not available	Not available	Not available	Not available
17	Liberia	Alert 93.3	Alert 95.1	Alert 97.3	Alert 95.5	Alert 95.5	Alert 93.8
18	Libya	High warning 84.9	High warning 84.5	Alert 95.3	Alert 87.8	Alert 96.4	Alert 96.3
20	Mali	warning 77.9	High warning 89.3	High warning 86.9	High warning 92.9	High warning 87.8	Alert 95.2
21	Mozambique	high warning 82.4	high warning 82.8	high warning 85.9	high warning 86.9	high warning 87.8	high warning 89
22	Namibia	Elevated warning 71	Elevated warning 70.4	Elevated warning 71.5	Elevated warning 70.8	Elevated warning 71.1	Elevated warning 70.4
23	Nepal	High warning 93	High warning 91.8	High warning 91	high warning 90.5	high warning 91.2	high warning 91

Appendix

					State fragility score (0-25)	Index fragility
2018	2019	2020	2021	2022	2014	2017 [2]
High alert 106.3	High alert 1075	High alert 102.9	High alert 102.1	High alert 105.9	Extreme fragility 25	Extreme fragility 21
High warning 89.4	High warning 87.8	High warning 87.3	High warning 89	High warning 88.1	Very high fragility 16	Very high fragility 17
High warning 71.3	High warning 71.3	High warning 70.2	High warning 70.9	High warning 73	Low fragility 4	Low fragility 4
Alert 97.4	Alert 98.2	Alert 97.9	Alert 97.1	Alert 95.4	Extreme fragility 21	Extreme fragility 21
High warning 84	High warning 82.5	High warning 80.3	High warning 80.6	High warning 80.5	Medium fragility 11	Medium fragility 11
Very high alert 111.1	Very high alert 108.9	High warning 107.5	High warning 107	High warning 108.1	Extreme fragility 24	Extreme fragility 23
Alert 94.6	Alert 92.1	Alert 89.7	Alert 90.7	Alert 89.6	Very high fragility 16	Very high fragility 17
More Stable 48.7	Less Stable 51	More Stable 46.1	Less Stable 49.8	More Stable 49.3	No fragility 2	No fragility 2
Warning 60.3	low Warning 57.8	Warning 56.1	Warning 57.4	Warning 56.9	No fragility 3	No fragility 3
Very high alert 110.7	Very high alert 110.2	Very high alert 92.1	Very high alert 108.4	Very high alert 107.3	Extreme fragility 23	Extreme fragility 24
Elevated warning 71.2	Elevated warning 71.2	Elevated warning 68.9	Elevated warning 71.6	Elevated warning 70.8	Low fragility 4	Low fragility 4
Elevated warning 76.5	Elevated warning 72	Elevated warning 72.6	Elevated warning 71.2	Elevated warning 71.8	Low fragility 6	Low fragility 6
Alert 98.1	Alert 95.5	Alert 92.9	Alert 91.3	Alert 91.3	High fragility 17	High fragility 17
High alert 102	High alert 99.3	High alert 97.7	High alert 97.5	High alert 99.7	High fragility 16	High fragility 14
High alert 102.2	High alert 99.1	alert 95.9	alert 96.2	High alert 93.8	Very high fragility 18	Very high fragility 18
Not available	Not available	Not available	Not available	Not available	Low fragility 7	Low fragility 7
Alert 92.6	Alert 90.2	Alert 90	Alert 89.5	Alert 88.2	High fragility 13	High fragility 13
Alert 94.6	Alert 92.2	Alert 95.2	Alert 92.2	Alert 94.3	High fragility 13	High fragility 13
Alert 92.9	Alert 94.5	Alert 96	Alert 96.6	Alert 98.6	Medium fragility 11	Medium fragility 11
high warning 86.9	high warning 88.7	Alert 91.7	Alert 93.4	Alert 94.3	Low fragility 5	Low fragility 5
High warning 68.8	High warning 66.4	High warning 65.1	Low warning 64.3	Low warning 62.9	High fragility 12	High fragility 11
Elevated warning 87.9	Elevated warning 84.7	Elevated warning 82.6	Elevated warning 82.2	Elevated warning 80.6	Medium fragility 8	Medium fragility 8

Table A.1 (Continued)

Country[1]	Fragile State Index (FFP) (score 0-120)					
	2012	2013	2014	2015	2016	2017
24 Nicaragua	Elevated warning 79.6	Elevated warning 79.2	Elevated warning 78.4	Elevated warning 79	Elevated warning 79	Elevated warning 79.2
19 North Macedonia	Low warning 69.1	Low warning 68	Low warning 66.4	Low warning 66.1	Low warning 67	Low warning 69.1
25 Rwanda	High warning 89.3	High warning 89.3	Alert 90.5	Alert 90.2	Alert 91.3	Alert 90.8
26 Sierra Leone	Alert 90.4	Alert 91.2	High Warning 89.1	High Warning 91.9	High Warning 91	High Warning 89.3
27 Somalia	Very High Alert 114.9	Very High Alert 113.9	Very High Alert 112.6	Very High Alert 114	Very High Alert 114	Very High Alert 113.2
28 South Sudan	Very High Alert 108.4	Very High Alert 110.6	Very High Alert 112.9	Very High Alert 114.5	Very High Alert 113.8	Very High Alert 113.9
29 Sudan	Very High Alert 109.4	Very High Alert 111	Very High Alert 110.1	Very High Alert 110.8	Very High Alert 111.5	Very High Alert 111
30 Timor-Leste	Alert 92.7	Alert 91.5	Alert 90.6	Alert 90.5	Alert 90.8	Alert 91
31 Western Sahara	Not available	Not available	Not available	Not available	Not available	Not available

UPDATED: Dec 2022

[1] Table organized by alphabetical order of the countries.
[2] Most updated State Fragility Index 2017 report. Data related to 2016. Important to note that the previous report is of 2014 and 2011.

					State fragility Index fragility score (0-25)	
2018	2019	2020	2021	2022	2014	2017 [2]
High warning 75.3	High warning 78.1	High warning 77.1	High warning 77.1	High warning 77.7	Very high fragility 16	Very high fragility 16
Low warning 64.8	Low warning 64.6	Low warning 62.1	Low warning 64.5	Low warning 62.6	Very high fragility 16	Very high fragility 16
High warning 89.3	High warning 87.5	High warning 86	High warning 85	High warning 83.7	Very high fragility 14	Very high fragility 13
High Warning 89.1	High Warning 86.8	High Warning 84.4	High warning 83.4	High warning 82.4	Extreme high fragility 20	Extreme high fragility 20
Very High Alert 113.4	Very High Alert 112.3	Very High Alert 110.9	Very High Alert 110.9	Very High Alert 110.5	Extreme high fragility 22	Extreme high fragility 22
Very High Alert 113.4	Very High Alert 112.8	Very High Alert 110.8	Very High Alert 109.4	Very High Alert 108.4	Extreme high fragility 22	Extreme high fragility 22
Very High Alert 108.7	Very high alert 108	High warning 104.8	High warning 105.2	High warning 107.1	Extreme high fragility 22	Extreme high fragility 22
Alert 90.5	Elevated Warning 85.5	Elevated Warning 82.7	Elevated Warning 80.9	Elevated Warning 79.3	Low fragility 7	Low fragility 7
Not available	Not available	Not available	Not available	Not available	Not available	Not available

Table A.1 (Continued)

	Country[1]	Global Peace Index [2] Rank classified over 163 countries					
		2008	2012	2013	2014	2015	2016
1	Afghanistan	Very low 158	Very low 161	Very low 162	Very low 161	Very low 161	Very low 160
2	Angola	Medium 119	Medium 119	Medium 101	Medium 100	Medium 75	Medium 98
3	Bosnia-Herzegovina	Medium 71	Medium 53	Medium 49	Medium 41	Medium 50	Medium 60
4	Burundi	142 Low	122 Low	Low 126	Low 122	Low 133	Low 138
5	Cambodia	Medium 104	Medium 107	Medium 108	Medium 109	Medium 95	Medium 104
6	CAR	Very low 151	Very low 154	Very low 157	Very low 158	Very low 159	Very low 157
7	Côte-Ivoire	Medium 133	Medium 128	Medium 146	Medium 131	Medium 121	Medium 118
8	Croatia	High 47	High 26	High 28	High 26	High 25	High 26
9	Cyprus	High 43	Medium 66	Medium 64	Medium 73	Medium 64	Medium 71
10	DRC	Low 148	very low 157	very low 153	very low 153	very low 154	very low 152
11	El Salvador	Medium 105	Medium 114	Medium 107	Medium 105	Medium 118	Medium 111
12	Georgia	Low 153	Low 143	Low 136	Low 111	Medium 89	Medium 85
13	Guinea-Bissau	Low 135	Low 128	Low 124	Low 136	Low 110	Medium 116
14	Haiti	Medium 116	Medium 78	Medium 72	Medium 93	Medium 95	Medium 81
15	Iraq	Very low 161	Very low 158	Very low 158	Very low 156	Very low 158	Very low 161
16	Kosovo	Not available	Not available	Not available	Not available	Not available	Not available
17	Liberia	Medium 95	Medium 71	Medium 61	Medium 59	Medium 70	Medium 66
18	Libya	Medium 84	Very Low 141	Very Low 148	Very Low 142	Very Low 151	Very Low 151
20	Mali	High 38	Low 126	Very Low 138	Very Low 145	Very Low 145	Very Low 145
21	Mozambique	Medium 72	Medium 57	Medium 67	Medium 78	Medium 79	Medium 83
22	Namibia	Medium 76	high 70	high 65	high 65	high 68	high 60
23	Nepal	Medium 74	Medium 82	Medium 83	Medium 76	Medium 60	Medium 69
24	Nicaragua	High 60	high 62	high 65	high 64	high 75	high 64
19	North Macedonia	high 61	high 62	high 68	high 67	high 65	Medium 97
25	Rwanda	High 50	Medium 81	Medium 109	Medium 121	Medium 123	Medium 109
26	Sierra Leone	High 50	High 60	High 55	High 56	High 51	High 48
27	Somalia	Very low 160	Very low 162	Very low 160	Very low 159	Very low 157	162 Very low
28	South Sudan	Non Independent	Very low 127	Very low 149	Very low 155	Very low 160	Very low 160
29	Sudan	Very low 158	Very low 159	Very low 159	Very low 160	Very low 156	Very low 156
30	Timor-Leste	Medium 75	High 40	High 42	High 50	High 55	High 55
31	Western Sahara	Not available	Not available	Not available	Not available	Not available	Not available

UPDATED: Dec 2022

[1] Table organized by alphabetical order of the countries.
[2] For methodology details, refer to www.visionofhumanity.com.

2017	2018	2019	2020	2021	2022	Trending
Very low 162	Very low 162	Very low 163	Very low 163	Very low 163	Very low 163	→
Medium 75	Medium 100	Medium 79	Medium 85	Medium 92	Medium 78	→
Medium 63	Medium 84	Medium 62	Medium 65	Medium 57	Medium 58	→
Low 142 Medium 70	Low 141 Medium 89	Low 135 Medium 75	Low 131 High 63	Low 129 High 68	Low 131 High 62	→ ↑
Very low 158	Very low 155	Very low 158	Very low 156	Very low 154	Very low 155	→
Medium 120	Medium 121	Medium 109	Medium 107	Medium 108	Medium 108	→
High 26 Medium 68 very low 151	High 31 Medium 64 very low 153	High 23 Medium 64 very low 157	High 21 Medium 64 very low 157	High 14 High 65 very low 157	High 15 High 67 very low 158	→ ↑ →
Medium 113	Medium 115	Medium 113	Medium 114	Medium 114	Medium 114	→
Medium 93 Medium 114 Medium 81 Very low 163	Medium 94 Medium 122 Medium 83 Very low 161	Medium 89 Medium 105 Medium 94 Very low 160	Medium 82 Medium 100 Medium 106 Very low 162	Medium 86 Medium 101 Medium 99 Very low 159	Medium 95 Medium 110 Medium 115 Very low 157	↑ ↑ → →
Not available	Not available	Not available	Not available	Not available	Not available	→
Medium 86 Very Low 159	**Medium 82** Very Low 157	**Medium 57** Very Low 156	**Medium 60** Very Low 155	**Medium 76** Very Low 156	**Medium 75** Very Low 151	→ ↓
Very Low 143	Very Low 144	Very Low 144	Very Low 143	Very Low 149	Very Low 150	→
Medium 104 high 57 Medium 88 high 71 Medium 97	Medium 104 high 55 Medium 74 high 61 Medium 77	Medium 107 high 57 Medium 81 high 61 high 56	Medium 108 high 55 Medium 72 Medium 122 High 47	Medium 111 high 59 Medium 80 Medium 129 High 37	Medium 122 Medium 68 Medium 73 Medium 124 High 36	→ ↓ → → ↓
Medium 102	Medium 121	Medium 86	Medium 84	Medium 81	Medium 72	↓
High 42 Very low 156	High 37 Very low 160	High 54 Very low 154	High 58 Very low 158	High 52 Very low 158	High 50 Very low 156	→ →
Very low 160	Very low 155	Very low 161	Very low 160	Very low 160	Very low 159	→
very low 155	very low 153	Very low 150	Very low 152	Very low 152	Very low 154	→
High 48 Not available	High 48 Not available	High 52 Not available	High 47 Not available	High 54 Not available	High 54 Not available	↑ -

Table A.2 Democracy and Peace in countries torn by civil wars without UN intervention

	Country[1]	Conflict Start Date	Conflict End Date	Freedom House					
				2 years	5 years	10 years	15 years	2012	2013
1	Algeria	Dec-92	Feb-02	Not available	Not available	Not free 5.5,5,6	Not free 5.5,5,6	Not free 6,5	Not free 6,5
2	Djibouti	Nov-91	dez-94	Not available	Not available	Partly Free 4.5, 5,4	Partly Free 5, 5,5	Not free 6,5	Not free 6,5
3	Colombia	May-64	Nov-16	Partly Free 65,29,36	Partly Free 64,29,35	Not available	Not available	Partly Free 3,4	Partly Free 3,4
4	Ethiopia	Nov-20	present	Not available	Not available	Not available	Not available	Not Free 6,6	Not Free 6,6
5	Myanmar	Aug-88	present	Not available	Not available	Not free 7,7,7	Not free 5.5,5,6	Not available	Not available
6	Nigeria	Feb-09	present	Partly Free 4, 4,4	Partly Free 4.5, 5,4	Not available	Not available	Partly Free 4,4	Partly Free 4,4
7	Peru	May-82	Dec-96	Not available	Not available	Not available	Not available	Free 2,3	Free 2,3
8	Philippines [2]	Mar-69	Mar-14	Not available	Not available	Not available	Not available	Partly Free 3, 3,3	Partly Free 3, 3,3
9	Sri Lanka	Jul-83	May-09	Not available	Not available	Not available	Partly Free 3.5, 4,3	Partly Free 5, 4	Partly Free 5, 4
10	Syria	Mar-11	present	Not free 7,7,7	Not free 7,7,7	Not available	Not available	Not free 7,7,7	Not free 7,7,7
11	Yemen	Jun-04	Feb-15	Partly Free 5, 5,5	Not free 5.5,5,6	Not free 6,6,6	Not available	Not free 6,6,6	Not free 6,6,6

No data on Ukraine was included as the book was written prior to the conflict.

[1] The Libyan Civil War is related to 2011. Clear unresolved issues directly evolved into the Second Lybian Civil war since 2014 until the date. Therefore, for this data base, the priod of both wars are combined.

[2] For better comparative analysis considering the duration of the "Moro conflict" and violence breakdowns, the Freedom House provides the following results: 2000 (Free, 2,5,3,2); 2005 (partly free, 3,3,3); 2010 (partly free, 3,3,3).

2014	2015	2016	2017	2018	2019	2020	2021	2022	Trend arrow
Not free 5,5, 5,6	Not free 6,5,5	Not free 5,5,6,5	Not free 35,11, 24	Not free 35,10, 25	Not free 34,10,24	Not free 34,10, 24	Not free 32,10,22	Not free 32,10,22	→
Not free 5,5, 5,6	Not free 6,5,5	Not free 5,5,6,5	Not free 26,7,19	Not free 26,7,19	Not free 26,7,19	Not free 24,5,19	Not free 24,5,19	Not free 24,5,19	↓
Partly Free 3,4	Partly Free 3,4	Partly Free 64, 29,35	Partly Free 64,29, 35	Partly Free 65,29, 36	Partly Free 64,29,35	Partly Free 66,29, 37	Partly Free 64,29,35	Partly Free 64,29,35	→
Not Free 6,6	Not Free 6,6	Not Free 7,6,15	Not Free 12,4,8	Not Free 12,4,8	Not Free 24,10,14	Not Free 23,12, 11	Not Free 22,9,13	Not Free 23,12,11	→
Not free 6,6,6	Not free 6,6,6	Partly Free 5, 5,5	Partly free 32,42, 18	Partly free 31,13, 18	Partly free 30,13,17	Not free 30,14, 16	Not free 28,13,15	Not free 9,0,9	↓
Partly Free 4,5, 5,4	Partly Free 4,5, 5,4	Partly Free 4, 3,5	Partly Free 50,25, 25	Partly Free 50,25, 25	Partly Free 50,25,25	Partly Free 43,20, 23	Partly Free 45,21,24	Partly Free 43,20,23	→
Free 2,5, 3,2	Free 2,3	Free 2,5,3,2	Free 72,31, 41	Free 72,30, 42	Free 72,30,42	Free 72,31, 42	Free 71,29,42	Free 72,30,42	→
Partly Free 3, 3,3	Partly Free 3, 3,3	Partly Free 3, 3,3	Partly Free 63,27, 33	Partly Free 62,27, 35	Partly Free 61,26,35	Partly Free 59,25, 34	Partly Free 55,25,30	Partly Free 55,20,30	→
Partly Free 5, 5,5	Partly Free 5, 5,5	Partly Free 3,5, 3,4	Partly Free 56,24, 32	Partly Free 55,24, 31	Partly Free 55,23,32	Partly Free 56,24, 32	Partly Free 56,23,33	Partly Free 55,23,32	→
Not free 7, 7,7	Not free 7,7,7	Not free 7,7,7	Not free -1,-3, 2	Not free 1,-3,3	Not free 0,-3,4	Not free 0,-3,3	Not free 1,-3,4	Not free 1,-3,4	→
Not free 6, 6,6	Not free 6,6,6	Not free 6,5,7,6	Not free 14,2, 12	Not free 13,1, 12	Not free 11,1,10	Not free 11,1, 10	Not free 11,1,10	Not free 9,1,8	↓

Table A.2 (Continued)

	Country	Polity IV Trend 2017	Global Democracy Index (EIU) Classification and score			
			2012	2013	2014	2015
1	Algeria	Weak Democracy	Authoritarian 3.83	Authoritarian 3.83	Authoritarian 3.53	Authoritarian 3.95
2	Djibouti	Weak Democracy	Authoritarian 2.74	Authoritarian 2.96	Authoritarian 2.99	Authoritarian 2.90
3	Colombia	Democracy	Free 6.63	Free 6.55	Free 6.55	Free 6.62
4	Ethiopia	Autocracy	Authoritarian 3.72	Authoritarian 3.83	Authoritarian 3.72	Authoritarian 3.83
5	Myanmar	Weak Democracy	Authoritarian 2.35	Authoritarian 2.76	Authoritarian 3.05	Hybrid 4.15
6	Nigeria	Democracy	Authoritarian 3.77	Authoritarian 3.77	Authoritarian 3.76	Hybrid 4.62
7	Peru	Democracy	Flawed Democracy 6.47	Flawed Democracy 6.54	Flawed Democracy 6.54	Flawed Democracy 6.58
8	Philippines	Democracy	Flawed democracy 6.30	Flawed democracy 6.41	Flawed democracy 6.77	Flawed democracy 6.84
9	Sri Lanka	Democracy	Flawed democracy 5.75	Flawed democracy 5.69	Flawed democracy 5.69	Flawed democracy 6.42
10	Syria	State Failure	Authoritarian 1.63	Authoritarian 1.86	Authoritarian 1.74	Authoritarian 1.43
11	Yemen	State Failure	Authoritarian 3.12	Authoritarian 3.79	Authoritarian 2.79	Authoritarian 2.24

2016	2017 [3]	2018	2019	2020	2021	2022
Authoritarian 3.83	Authoritarian 3.56	Authoritarian 3.5	Hybrid 4.01	Authoritarian 3.77	Authoritarian 3.77	Authoritarian 3.66
Authoritarian 2.83	Authoritarian 2.76	Authoritarian 2.87	Authoritarian 2.77	Authoritarian 2.71	Authoritarian 2.74	Authoritarian 2.74
Free 6.67	Free 6.67	Free 6.96	Free 7.13	Free 7.04	Free 6.48	Free 6.72
Authoritarian 3.6	Hybrid 4.42	Authoritarian 3.35	Authoritarian 3.44	Authoritarian 3.38	Authoritarian 3.3	Authoritarian 3.17
Hybrid 4.20	Authoritarian 3.83	Authoritarian 3.83	Authoritarian 3.55	Authoritarian 3.04	Authoritarian 1.02	Authoritarian 0.74
Hybrid 4.50	Hybrid 4.44	Hybrid 4.44	Hybrid 4.12	Hybrid 4.1	Hybrid 4.11	Hybrid 4.23
Flawed Democracy 6.65	Flawed Democracy 6.49	Flawed Democracy 6.6	Flawed Democracy 6.6	Flawed Democracy 6.53	Flawed Democracy 6.09	Flawed Democracy 5.92
Flawed democracy 6.94	Flawed democracy 6.71	Flawed democracy 6.71	Flawed democracy 6.64	Flawed democracy 6.56	Flawed democracy 6.62	Flawed democracy 6.73
Flawed democracy 6.48	Flawed democracy 6.48	Flawed democracy 6.19	Flawed democracy 6.27	Flawed democracy 6.14	Flawed democracy 6.14	Flawed democracy 6.47
Authoritarian 1.43	Authoritarian 1.43	Authoritarian 1.43	Authoritarian 1.43	Authoritarian 1.43	Authoritarian 1.43	Authoritarian 1.43
Authoritarian 2.07	Authoritarian 2.07	Authoritarian 1.95	Authoritarian 1.95	Authoritarian 1.95	Authoritarian 1.95	Authoritarian 1.95

Table A.2 (Continued)

	Country[	Fragile State Index (FFP) (score 0-120)					
		2012	2013	2014	2015	2016	2017
1	Algeria	high warning 78.1	high warning 78.7	high warning 78.8	high warning 79.6	high warning 78.3	high warning 76.8
2	Djibouti	Very high warning 83.8	Very high warning 85.5	Very high warning 87.1	Very high warning 88.1	Very high warning 89.7	Very high warning 88.9
3	Colombia	Very high warning 84.4	Very high warning 83.8	Very high warning 83.1	Very high warning 82.5	Very high warning 80.2	Very high warning 78.9
4	Ethiopia	High alert 97.9	High alert 98.9	High alert 97.9	High alert 97.5	High alert 97.2	Very High alert 101.1
5	Myanmar	Alert 96.2	Alert 94.6	Alert 94.3	Alert 94.7	Alert 96.3	Alert 95.7
6	Nigeria	High alert 101.1	High alert 100.7	High alert 102.4	High alert 103.5	High alert 101.6	High alert 103.5
7	Peru	Warning 73.5	Warning 72.3	Warning 71.9	Warning 71.9	Warning 72	Warning 71.9
8	Philippines [2]	High warning 83.2	High warning 82.8	High warning 85.3	High warning 86.3	High warning 84.7	High warning 84.4
9	Sri Lanka	Alert 92.2	Alert 92.9	Alert 92.6	Alert 907	high warning 87.7	high warning 86.6
10	Syria	Alert 94.5	Alert 97.4	High alert 101.6	High alert 107.9	High alert 110.8	High alert 110.6
11	Yemen	High alert 104.8	High alert 107	High alert 105.4	High alert 108.1	High alert 111.5	High alert 111.1

[1] Most updated State Fragility Index 2017 report. Data related to 2016. Important to note that the previous report is of 2014. There is no report published in 2016.

					State fragility Index and fragility score (0-25) [1]	
2018	2019	2020	2021	2022	2014	2017 [4]
high warning 75.8	high warning 75.4	high warning 74.6	high warning 73.6	high warning 72.2	High fragility 12	High fragility 11
Very high warning 87.1	Very high warning 85.1	Very high warning 82.7	Very high warning 82.4	Very high warning 81.3	High fragility 13	High fragility 12
Very high warning 76.6	Very high warning 75.7	Very high warning 76.6	Very high warning 76.6	Very high warning 78.4	High fragility 10	High fragility 10
High alert 99.6	High alert 94.2	High alert 94.6	High alert 99	High alert 99.3	Very high fragility 19	Very high fragility 19
Alert 96.1	Alert 94.3	Alert 94	Alert 93.8	High Alert 100	Very high fragility 18	Very high fragility 19
Alert 99.9	Alert 98.5	Alert 97.3	Alert 98	Alert 97.2	Very high fragility 18	Very high fragility 18
Warning 70.1	Warning 68.2	low Warning 67.6	Warning 71.4	low Warning 69.8	Low fragility 6	Low fragility 6
High warning 85.5	High warning 83.1	High warning 85.5	High warning 81	High warning 80.5	High fragility 12	High fragility 12
high warning 84.9	high warning 84	high warning 81.8	high warning 80.5	warning 79.3	Medium fragility 11	Medium fragility 11
High alert 111.4	High alert 111.5	High alert 110.7	High alert 110.7	High alert 108.4	Very high fragility 16	Very high fragility 15
High alert 112.7	High alert 113.5	High alert 112.4	High alert 111.7	High alert 111.7	Extreme high fragility 21	Extreme high fragility 21

Table A.2 (Continued)

	Country	Global Peace Index Over 163 countries												Trending over the last decade
		2008	2012	2013	2014	2015	2016	2017	2018	2019	2020	2021	2022	
1	Algeria	Medium 130	Medium 135	Medium 133	Medium 127	Medium 127	Medium 118	Medium 117	Medium 109	Medium 119	Medium 120	Medium 119	Medium 109	←
2	Djibouti	Medium 70	Medium 65	Medium 76	Medium 75	Medium 102	Medium 91	Medium 109	Medium 107	Medium 103	Medium 110	Medium 104	Medium 113	→
3	Colombia	Low 151	Low 152	Low 150	Low 148	Low 147	Low 145	Low 145	Low 146	Low 145	Low 142	Low 146	Low 144	↑
4	Ethiopia	Low 138	Low 148	Low 141	Low 132	Low 129	Medium 129	Low 131	Low 134	Low 133	Low 134	Low 140	Low 149	→
5	Myanmar	Low 139	Medium 117	Medium 125	Medium 120	Medium 128	Medium 127	Medium 107	Medium 104	Medium 124	Medium 126	Low 132	Low 139	→
6	Nigeria	Low 147	Low 147	Low 151	Low 151	Low 150	Low 149	Low 148	Low 149	Low 149	Low 147	Low 145	Low 143	→
7	Peru	Medium 94	Medium 94	Medium 94	Medium 92	Medium 93	Medium 102	Medium 94	Medium 71	Medium 83	Medium 87	Medium 88	Medium 101	↑
8	Philippines [2]	Low 140	Low 134	Low 128	Low 136	Low 137	Low 136	Low 136	Low 138	Low 133	Low 132	Low 129	Medium 125	↑
9	Sri Lanka	Low 146	Low 146	Medium 118	Medium 108	Medium 106	Medium 115	high 61	Medium 80	Medium 76	Medium 82	Medium 103	Medium 90	←
10	Syria	Medium 113	Very low 151	Very low 156	Very low 162	Very low 161	Very low 162	Very low 162	Very low 163	Very Low 162	Very Low 161	Very Low 161	Very Low 161	→
11	Yemen	Low 131	Low 149	Low 147	Low 149	Low 149	Low 149	Very low 157	Very low 159	Very low 159	Very Low 159	Very Low 162	Very Low 162	→

INDEX

Action for Peace (A4P/A4P) 27, 137
Afghanistan 1, 3, 15, 27, 50, 56, 73, 117, 121, 130, 169, 240, 264, 268, 269
Agenda for Peace 27, 118, 278
Al Qaeda 22, 95, 128, 169, 243
amnesty xii, 25, 35, 51, 58, 63, 103, 164, 210, 211, 279
Angola xviii, 1, 13, 20, 27, 30, 50, 101, 121, 123, 135, 165, 168, 169, 173, 187, 212, 222, 232, 235, 242
anocracies 5, 6, 9, 11, 30, 91, 119
Arab spring 6, 15, 77, 121, 187, 269

Belarus 20, 96
Boko Haram 22, 128
Bosnia-Herzegovina xix, 27, 61, 117, 122, 123, 132, 233
bottom-up approach 28, 81, 132, 156, 176, 203, 219, 269, 281
Brahimi report 27, 118
Burkina Faso 1, 17, 190
Burundi xx, 27, 92, 106, 117, 123, 151, 154, 166, 183, 198, 199, 205, 237, 268

Cambodia 27, 30, 44, 117, 121, 123, 136, 154, 159, 175, 183, 195, 232, 241, 264
Central African Republic (CAR) xx, 63, 117, 140, 141, 206, 230, 235, 245, 247, 249, 254, 265
Chad 1, 13, 20, 128, 139, 140, 206, 247, 262, 269

checks and balances xii, 5, 25, 30, 35, 55, 63, 70, 134, 174, 183, 185, 187
civil society xii, 7, 10, 12, 25, 30, 36, 49, 63, 132, 140, 162, 188, 230, 239, 240, 246, 258, 260, 264, 267, 270
consolidated democracies 6, 18, 25, 29, 91, 260, 277
contingent sovereignty 24, 34, 68, 74, 77, 83
correlates of war (COW) 31
Côte d'Ivoire xx, 13, 27, 61, 104, 107, 117, 121, 122, 129, 135, 235
cyber wars 18
Cyprus 28, 81, 117, 121, 183, 197

delegative democracy 24
Department of Peacekeeping Operations (DPKO) 5, 14, 31, 106, 116, 118, 119
Department of Political and Peacebuilding Affairs (DPPA) 32, 118, 122, 125
dilemmas, definition 29
disarmament, demobilization, and reintegration (DDR) 36, 53, 63, 101, 109, 136, 163, 198, 229–231, 234, 237, 240, 242, 245, 247, 249, 254
DRC 4, 13, 17, 27, 48, 75, 92, 100, 117, 121, 123, 130, 133, 135, 160, 165, 174, 183, 188, 190, 192, 233, 238, 240, 251, 265

El Salvador 27, 77, 95, 117, 121, 123, 151, 171, 232, 240

election dispute resolution (EDR) 105, 106
Election Violence Education and Resolution (EVER) 105
electoral democracy 24, 70, 107
electoral management bodies (EMB) 103, 105, 159
electoral violence 90, 91, 93–96, 102, 103, 109
Ethiopia 2, 14, 17, 93, 94, 96, 98–100, 124, 128, 183, 188, 235, 264, 269

failed states xiii, 3, 9, 11, 16, 18, 71–73, 77, 82, 83, 122, 165, 258, 267
FARC 95, 125, 153, 164, 212, 241, 267
fragile democracies 3, 6, 16, 58, 91

Gacaca Courts 211, 220
Georgia 20, 27, 82, 117, 121, 123, 202, 269
global civil wars xiii, 12
gradualism 23, 156
Guinea 1, 17, 119, 166
Guinea-Bissau xvi, 27, 72, 117, 119, 122, 123, 187, 269

Haiti 17, 20, 25, 56, 57, 61, 74, 77, 82, 92, 105, 108, 117, 121, 123, 154, 161, 162, 190, 232, 236, 241, 261, 266
High-Level Independent Panel on Peace Operations (HIPPO) xvi, 118
Holy Trinity 34, 80
human rights xii, 1, 3, 5, 10, 14, 29, 34, 35, 71, 83, 90, 95, 96, 99, 100, 104, 106, 107, 110, 115, 117, 120, 127, 164, 194, 200, 210, 212, 214, 215, 221, 237, 239, 243, 246, 264, 266, 269
hybrid peace 6, 10, 47, 49, 51, 57, 59, 61, 64, 65, 71
hybrid regime 20, 35, 71, 119, 121, 123, 124, 128, 136, 138

Iraq 13, 15, 17, 20, 27, 49, 72, 73, 117, 119, 121, 127, 133, 141, 157, 160, 169, 183, 188, 232, 236, 240, 242, 266, 268
ISIS/ISIL 22, 49, 127, 169, 238, 242

Kenya 4, 94, 101, 103, 108, 237
Kosovo 4, 21, 27, 37, 50, 52, 71, 73, 81, 108, 117, 121, 122, 130, 134, 153, 156, 157, 159, 161, 171, 188, 200, 201

Lebanon 20, 48, 49, 122, 184, 195
Liberia 27, 48, 50, 96, 101, 117, 119, 121–123, 135, 153, 165, 170, 172, 192, 237, 240, 262, 264
Libya 6, 12, 27, 50, 72, 73, 117, 141

Mali 117, 121, 133, 137, 165, 232
media reform xii, 25, 36, 59, 63, 117, 258, 259, 267–270, 279
Montenegro 21, 108, 200
Mozambique 31, 117, 121–123, 132, 140, 153, 157, 169, 175, 186, 187, 212, 232
Myanmar xvi, 1, 13, 17, 20, 92, 124, 125, 127, 128, 189

negative peace 6, 31
Nicaragua 6, 13, 21, 27, 77, 117, 121, 123, 212, 238
Niger 1, 19, 96, 128
Nigeria 2, 17, 94, 101, 104, 106, 128, 237, 243
North Macedonia (former Macedonia) 21, 27, 117, 121, 123, 133, 232

peace agreement 4, 7, 28, 51, 52, 59, 79, 90, 95, 125, 160, 164, 169, 173, 192, 195, 196, 212, 214, 241
peace media 107, 258, 259, 270
peacemaking 4, 11, 31, 79, 118, 166, 195, 278
political violence 91–93, 95, 96, 100, 102, 104, 107–109, 114, 123, 155, 196
positive peace 6, 31, 125, 172, 183, 202, 204
power sharing 154, 160, 168, 182, 185–187, 189, 191, 194
power-sharing agreement 160, 171, 192
power-sharing arrangement (PSAs) 183, 184, 193, 197, 202
power-sharing institutions (PSIs) 35, 184, 203, 204
prisoner's dilemma 237
privatization of peace 101, 224
proportional representation system (PR) 24, 103, 157, 158

reconciliation 187, 202, 210, 211, 213, 215, 216, 219, 225, 226, 233, 236, 238, 240
representative democracy 24, 176
responsibility to protect (R2P) 7, 34, 69, 72, 74–76, 79, 82, 83, 261, 265
responsibility while protecting (RwP) 34, 69, 75, 83, 261, 265
Rwanda 15, 20, 27, 58, 61, 83, 92, 117, 121, 122, 137, 154, 157, 160, 166, 187, 190, 217, 219, 220, 240, 261, 267

Security Sector Reform (SSR) 109, 229–232, 234, 236–238, 241, 245, 246, 254

selectivity gap 78, 79, 264
sequentialism 23, 48, 64
Serbia 21, 81, 159
Sierra Leone 13, 15, 18, 20, 27, 100, 117, 119, 121, 123, 135, 154, 157, 164, 165, 175, 183, 199, 203, 204, 233, 238, 240, 264
Somalia 13, 18, 27, 57, 63, 91, 93, 95, 117, 121, 123, 241, 243
South Sudan 12, 13, 17, 27, 50, 56, 58, 107, 117, 141, 183, 195–197
spoiler 174, 241, 254
Sri Lanka 2, 54, 124, 126, 236, 277
statebuilding 13, 110, 231, 259, 277
Sudan 1, 8, 12, 13, 27, 50, 56, 58, 92, 107, 117, 121, 154
Syria 1, 12, 16–18, 27, 49, 122, 124, 125, 191, 240, 268

Tamil Tigers 54, 126, 169, 236
terrorism 13, 17, 18, 58, 73, 92, 94, 95, 98, 118, 126, 133

Timor-Leste 4, 13, 27, 52, 61, 78, 86, 93, 100, 117, 121, 129, 152, 159, 169, 171, 186, 187, 222, 241, 249, 254
top-down approach 48, 81, 260
transitional justice xii, 63, 116, 126, 210, 219, 225, 279
transitional violence 34, 63, 97, 109
transitology 23
truth commissions and ad hoc war crime tribunals xii, 25, 63, 74, 216, 217

Uganda 23, 74, 92, 99, 152, 154, 165, 166, 173, 183, 190, 203, 205, 232, 237

volatility-uncertainty-complexity-ambiguity (VUCA) 48, 50, 59, 64, 226

Western Sahara 27, 117, 121, 122
Westphalia peace 72

Yemen 2, 8, 16, 17, 20, 71, 124, 125, 264

Zimbabwe 96, 165, 237

Printed in the United States
by Baker & Taylor Publisher Services